D1544615

To Dous –
A fellow "Mega" think...

MEGAPOLITAN AMERICA

MEGAPOLITAN AMERICA

A New Vision for Understanding America's Metropolitan Geography

Arthur C. Nelson, FAICP, and Robert E. Lang

American Planning Association
Planners Press

Making Great Communities Happen

Chicago | Washington, D.C.

Copyright © 2011 by the American Planning Association
205 N. Michigan Ave., Suite 1200, Chicago, IL 60601-5927
1030 15th St., NW, Suite 750W, Washington, DC 20005-1503
www.planning.org/plannerspress

ISBN: 978-1-932364-97-2
Library of Congress Control Number 2011913073

Design and typesetting by Scribe, Inc. (www.scribenet.com)
Printed in the United States of America

CONTENTS

LIST OF FIGURES

LIST OF TABLES

FOREWORD

THINKING MEGA

Armando Carbonell

The authors Nelson and Lang, known to friends and colleagues as Chris and Rob, are indeed friends and colleagues of mine and of the Lincoln Institute of Land Policy, whose mission they have helped to advance in many ways on different occasions, not least in their authorship of this first complete and systematic analysis of the American megapolitan system. *Megapolitan America* is a valuable resource for planning and public policy, but it is also part of a new—or, at least, renewed—way of thinking about regions and urban systems. The concise intellectual history provided in the first chapter situates the megapolitan construct within a family of ideas that has attracted increasing attention from academics and policy makers in recent years as they attempt to remake urban and regional planning theory and practice for a country that must respond to new economic, social, and environmental challenges as it continues to grow and change. I am grateful for the authors' generous acknowledgment of the contributions of Bob Yaro and myself to this budding field of megaregional planning, and I will use this foreword to reflect on the field's recent history and development.

In the spring of 2004, Bob Yaro, Jonathan Barnett, and I taught a graduate planning studio at the University of Pennsylvania boldly titled "Plan for America," aiming in one semester to do no less than create a plan for the United States (later wisely amended to "a framework for national planning") out to the year 2050. Based on current trends, the Penn studio projected significant regional differences in the distribution of population growth and economic activity through mid-century as the U.S. population reached 420 million: intense growth in the Sun Belt and coasts and continued depopulation of the Great Plains, Mississippi Delta, and Appalachia. The resulting trend-based growth pattern was characterized by high levels of land consumption and consequent environmental impact, as well as increasing inequality between "hot" and "cold" regional economies.

In response to this scenario, and in the absence of a national spatial planning system, we went in search of a means to effectively plan at scales above the metropolitan area or state for large-scale infrastructure, natural systems (which we called ecostructure), and economic development. In seeking a planning mechanism that was attuned to the differences among regions but that could still form the basis of a coherent national system, we eventually arrived at the megaregion, which made its first appearance in a map sketched by the Penn students during a mid-semester London workshop with Sir Peter Hall and guest faculty gathered from around Europe. For us, the megaregion was a means to an end: a synthesis of planning concepts that could address the technical and political challenges of creating a national system through a bottom-up regional process.

The result of the mapping exercise was a notional partitioning of the United States based on networks of linked metropolitan areas and the natural systems that support them: not strictly urban systems but hybrid urban/natural systems, with some regard for cultural factors in their delineation. The final Penn London map showed eight (or nine, if you counted the "emerging" Front Range/Wasatch) somewhat whimsically shaped protomegaregions, indicated by a large blob containing, in most case, an ellipsoidal urban core. (Florida's core resembled a crab claw; the urbanized "Texas Triangle," was, of course, triangular.) The megaregions were shown in color on a gray field with shaded relief and a scattering of nonmega urban areas indicated by isolated red splotches. Later work by future generations of Penn students and at the Regional Plan Association (RPA) along with national consultations has refined these initial megaregions, adding the rapidly growing Phoenix/Tucson Sun Corridor and separating the Gulf and Texas Triangle megaregions.

As noted in this volume, there have been earlier attempts at delineating large regional systems for the country. In 1935, the National Resources Planning Board divided the 48 states into 16 possible planning regions based on "major metropolitan influence" (Fishman 2000). In another map, based on "composite planning problems," the board came up with 12 possible regions. With judicious squinting, and allowing for the consequences of development trends over the past 75 years, it is possible to view these maps alongside the most recent version of the megaregion map and see, if not congruence, at least a strong family resemblance. Also, as the authors point out, the journalist Joel Garreau later created a popular work, *The Nine Nations of North America*, with its own system of colorfully named contiguous regions.

There was a strong European influence on the early megaregion concept, based on our familiarity with European transnational planning, the concept of polycentricity, and global economic integration zones. In a Lincoln Institute volume edited by Andreas Faludi, we had earlier written on the possibility of translating the European spatial planning experience into a new American regional planning that could cross state boundaries as needed. With a further nod to the Europeans, this led to a sketch for an "American Spatial Development Perspective" published in the Lincoln Institute's *LandLines*. Asian precedents—including the planning of high-speed rail in Japan, development strategy in South Korea, and the response to rapid urbanization in China—were also seminal.

On returning to the United States from the London workshop, there was some debate about what to call these large new spatial units. "Megalopolis" appeared in antiquity, although with a different meaning than in Gottmann's famous 1961 work, and it has achieved some currency. But it carries an overly specific association with the Atlantic seaboard, as well as generally negative popular connotations. "Metropolitan" areas have been defined by the federal Bureau of the Budget and its successor, the Office of Management and Budget (OMB), since 1949 and gone through periodic redefinition and transformation, but they are focused on discrete urbanized areas and commuting patterns (although containing rural areas) and do not particularly relate to natural systems. "Supercity" region was a hit in Europe, but we abandoned it back home where it appeared to overemphasize the urban aspect and inadequately convey the importance of natural systems. (It also called to some minds the anathematized slogan "supersize me.") We toyed briefly with "macropolitan." The term of choice in this volume, megapolitan, was proposed by Rob Lang as a census-friendly category that reflects the growth in intermetropolitan commuting and other trends in metropolitan integration. The term is occasionally used as a synonym for "megaregion," but it should be clear that megapolitans are dominantly urban systems (borne out in the Nelson-Lang urban-rural continuum herein) and more akin to OMB's consolidated metropolitan statistical areas. Megapolitans are not coterminous with megaregions, lacking their larger natural context, although they can comfortably fit within them, with clusters of megapolitans forming the urban core of megaregions.

It has been observed that the initial megaregion map was more strongly influenced by morphology—that is, development patterns on the ground—than by function, as indicated by the flows of people, goods, transactions, or information. This physical planning bias has continued to have a strong influence on the mapping of megaregions, although flows of goods and people have increasingly figured in the analysis. The megapolitan, on the other hand, is strongly functional through its reliance on the employment interchange measure. As is always the case with megapolitans, which are by definition county-based, megaregions have often been mapped using counties as constituent units, providing a convenient means of tracking comparative statistics but creating an artifactual hard edge that conflicts with the fuzzy boundaries of the concept. Moreover, *any* mapping of megaregions creates "insiders" and "outsiders" and leaves troublesome white space on the map, some of which is inhabited by people who really care about their communities and have been understandably vocal in their displeasure at being left out.

Early responses to this "terra incognita" problem included identifying the more lightly populated quarters of the Intermountain West and Great Plains as "resource regions," bringing us closer to wall-to-wall coverage but carrying unfortunate overtones of exploitation by the more populous megas. A newer approach for these "wide open spaces" is to think in terms of large landscape conservation, and we have been developing that idea at the Lincoln Institute in conjunction with the presidential initiative known as "America's Great Outdoors." This approach looks at these vast areas of small population not as empty spaces but as a mosaic of communities, working lands, and wild lands that can be managed for mutual benefit. The Interior Department has issued a map of 21 landscape conservation cooperatives covering the entire country and including not just wilderness but urban areas as well, underlining a commitment to connecting cities (and urban dwellers) with nature.

It is best not to think too literally of megaregions as bounded, physical entities but as a vehicle for planning at larger scales when that is called for by the problem at hand. Megaregional planning then becomes a process

for tackling issues that occupy fluid and often overlapping territories of greater than metropolitan scale, such as major infrastructure projects like high-speed rail, electric grids, and large water systems; landscape scale conservation; and regional economic development.

In spite of the seeming complexity of the foregoing, it is possible to construct a fairly neat system of nested regional spaces at increasing scale, beginning with county-based metropolitan areas, with megapolitans in mid-position, and progressing up to the megaregion. Lang and Dhavale published such a diagram in *Planning* magazine, reflecting the consensus nomenclature and definitions, and an updated version is included here.

In the relatively short time since the current megaregion conversation was launched, it has been gratifying to see the completion of a number of academic research projects and publications, as well as the birth of a national infrastructure policy initiative, America 2050, that has grown out of a partnership of the Lincoln Institute, RPA, and others. Although it is difficult in 2011 to be buoyant about the immediate prospects for a coherent national development strategy based on megaregional thinking, we are beginning to see greater-than-metropolitan responses to planning for the challenges of climate change, demographic shifts, and economic restructuring. Looking beyond the moment to the coming century, the authors of this volume, both steeped in demography, have pondered the likelihoods and uncertainties surrounding how much the country will grow, what our society will look like, and where all those people will live. My own megaadventure began in that first Penn studio, when we looked out to 2050 and asked ourselves, as the authors of this volume argue we should, how to best plan for "where people live, not where they don't."

West Barnstable, Massachusetts, August 2011

ACKNOWLEDGMENTS

We gratefully acknowledge many people who have helped us through our journey researching and preparing this book.

We acknowledge first several students who provided key assistance to us on this project over the years. From our days at the Metropolitan Institute at Virginia Tech, we thank especially Dawn Dhavale and Dwayne Guthrie (now at Catholic University). At the Metropolitan Research Center at the University of Utah, we thank Grace Bjarnson and Doug Woodruff. At Brookings Mountain West at the University of Nevada, Las Vegas, we thank Chrissy Nicholas.

In no particular order, we thanks many colleagues who have helped us conceptualize and then apply the "megapolitan" concept including:

Armando Carbonell, Gregory K. Ingram, Anthony Flint, and colleagues at the Lincoln Institute of Land Policy;

Robert D. Yaro of the Regional Plan Association and Petra Todorovich of America 2050, along with their colleagues;

Mark Muro, Bruce Katz, Anthony Downs, Robert Puentes, Amy Liu, Andrea Sarzynski, Christopher B. Leinberger, and colleagues at the Brookings Institution;

John Hall and his public-policy studio class at Arizona State University for their work on the Sun Corridor, and Hall's colleagues at the Morrison Institute including Grady Gammage Jr., Rob Melnick, and Nancy Welch;

Paul Knox at Virginia Tech, especially for helping with initial conceptualizations and early, critical review of our work, and Casey Dawkins (now at University of Maryland), Mariela Alfonzo, Thomas W. Sanchez, Rebecca Sohmer, and colleagues at the Metropolitan Institute at Virginia Tech;

Timothy Mennel, Sylvia Lewis, and colleagues at the American Planning Association;

Christopher H. Cole for his early support of our work;

Catherine Ross and our many other colleagues who collaborated in her book, *Megaregions: Planning for Global Competitiveness* (2009) including Adjo A. Amekudzi, William Ankner, Tridib Banerjee, Jason Barringer, Scott Campbell, Cheryl K. Contant, Jessica L. Harbour Doyle, Norman Fainstein, Susan S. Fainstein, Andreas K. F. Faludi, Richard Florida, Shirley Franklin, Karen Leone de Nie, Thomas F. Luce, Michael D. Meyer, Myron Orfield, and Saskia Sassen.

We thank Woods & Poole Economics, Inc. (www.woodsandpoole.com), in Washington, D.C., for use of data from its Complete Economic and Demographic Data Source for 2010, which we assembled into megapolitan cluster and region format throughout the book; the conclusions drawn from that data are our own. We also thank the Regional Plan Association for allowing us to use Figure 1.13, as well as the Urban Land Institute for allowing us to adapt material in Nelson and Lang (2009) for use in Table 2.1.

Finally, books such as this are simply not possible without a productive office environment, which in our case was provided ably by Jeannette Benson of the Metropolitan Research Center at the University of Utah and Miriam Lechuga of the Urban Affairs and Planning Program at Virginia Tech's Alexandria Center.

PROLOGUE: FROM CITIES TO MEGAPOLITANS

In a space as large as France and the Low Countries, the Netherlands and Belgium—considered some of the world's most densely settled regions—America's "megapolitan" areas house more than 2.5 times as many people. In fact, although they occupy only 17 percent of the contiguous 48 states' land base, America's megapolitan areas are more densely settled than Europe as a whole. Or the United Kingdom. Or Japan. Or India. Table P.1 lists the 10 megapolitan clusters we define in this book; the principal cities in each; and the comparably dense industrialized country in 2010 and projected for 2040 (holding these industrialized countries' 2010 population constant). The 10 megapolitan clusters we propose would, as a group, form the world's third most populous country, behind China and India. The sooner the United States recognizes it has evolved into a nation of 20-some very densely settled economic engines, the better able it will be to sustain long-term economic development to midcentury and beyond.

The New Kid in Town: Megapolitan Areas and Clusters

A common misconception about the United States is that it has low population density. This view is held even by some public policy experts, who argue that because we are so spread out, the country cannot support European-style passenger rail. Economist Paul Samuelson is one such expert. His 2009 *Washington Post* op-ed captures this view:

> What works in Europe and Asia won't in the United States. Even abroad, passenger trains are subsidized. But the subsidies are more justifiable because geography and energy policies differ.
>
> Densities are much higher, and high densities favor rail with direct connections between heavily populated city centers and business districts. In Japan, density is 880 people per square mile; it's 653 in Britain, 611 in Germany and 259 in France. By contrast, plentiful land in the United States has led to suburbanized homes, offices and factories. Density is 86 people per square mile. Trains can't pick up most people where they live and work and take them to where they want to go. Cars can.

Table P.1. American Megapolitan Clusters and Comparably Dense European Countries

Megapolitan Cluster	Principal Cities	Comparably Dense Industrial Country in 2010	Comparably Dense Industrial Country by 2040
Cascadia	Seattle–Portland	Switzerland	Great Britain
Sierra Pacific	San Francisco–Sacramento	>United Kingdom	<The Netherlands
Southwest	Los Angeles–San Diego–Las Vegas–Phoenix	The Netherlands	<Taiwan
Mountain	Denver–Salt Lake City	>Great Britain	<The Netherlands
Texas Triangle	Dallas–Fort Worth–Austin–San Antonio–Houston	Switzerland	United Kingdom
Twin Cities	Minneapolis–St. Paul	Portugal	>Denmark
Great Lakes	Chicago–Detroit–Cleveland–Pittsburgh	United Kingdom	<Japan
Florida	Tampa–Orlando–Miami	Belgium	South Korea
Piedmont	Atlanta–Charlotte	>Denmark	Germany
Megalopolis	New York–Boston–Philadelphia–Washington, D.C.	<The Netherlands	The Netherlands

Note: The sign < means the megapolitan area density is about 50–200 fewer persons per square mile than in the comparable nation, while > means the density is about 50–200 more persons per square mile; no sign indicates the density is within about 50 persons per square mile. Figures compare developed nation population in 2010 to megapolitan cluster population in 2010 and 2040. All ranges are illustrative.

We disagree. Certainly, the overall average population density of the United States—about 100 persons per square mile—is roughly half that of Western European countries, but the comparison is misguided. The contiguous 48 states extend about 3,000 miles east-west and about 1,000 miles north-south, for about three million square miles total. If federally owned land is excluded, as well as the sparsely populated states of the northern plains, the population density would rival Western Europe's. In our view, we need to target many long-range planning and public policy efforts to where people live, not where they don't. As we show in this book, two-thirds of the U.S. population lives on less than 20 percent of the privately owned land. The United States is not so much a collection of 50 states, more than 3,000 counties, or more than 30,000 cities and places as it is a federation of 23 megapolitan areas composed of networks of multiple large metropolitan areas. This is America's new economic geography.

As early as the 1880s, geographers and demographers understood there were two Americas, one as densely settled as Europe and the other open frontier. As Deborah Popper, Robert Lang, and Frank Popper (1997, 2001) have shown, the 1870 Census imposed the frontier concept to remove the vast American wilderness from any calculation of how settled or developed the nation had become. Henry Gannett, the census's original geographer, is the first social scientist to explicitly argue that only the developed parts of the United States should be used in determining infrastructure demand and type, and for urban comparisons with Western Europe. He even showed an explicit disdain for those who failed to recognize this fact:

I was asked not long ago, by a foreigner, "What is the density of settlement in your country?" to which I was obliged [to give] the true Yankee rejoinder, "What portion of my country?" The average density of settlement of such a country as this some parts of which are peopled as fully as the oldest parts of Europe, while great stretches, empires in extent are as yet almost without inhabitants, means nothing, and the question of my friend implied an ignorance. (Gannett 1882, 70)

Gannett might as well have been speaking directly to Samuelson, who, despite not being foreign, nonetheless misses this basic point about America: the settled parts of the United States are often as densely built as Europe.

A big difference, however, is that Europe has stopped growing, while the United States is on track to gain 90 million more residents between 2010 and 2040. That is the equivalent of adding a nation more populous than Germany to the United States, and the vast majority of the increase will be in megapolitan areas. Thus, in the spirit of Henry Gannett, one of the most insightful geographers of the 19th century, we propose to look at the parts of the United States that are as settled as Europe and seek solutions that may in fact borrow from Germany or France.

From Megalopolis to Megapolitan

The Megapolitan concept seems to have popularized the idea that the modern cities are better reviewed not in isolation, as centers of a restricted area only, but rather as parts of "city-systems," as participants in urban networks revolving in widening orbits.

—**Jean Gottmann**, *Megalopolis Revisited*

Geographer Jean Gottmann, writing more than two decades after publishing his influential book, *Megalopolis* (1961), understood the impact that his thinking had had on urban theory.[1] Today, two decades later still, a new transmetropolitan geography is emerging that advances many of Gottmann's ideas. Researchers in the United States and Europe are proposing new methods for classifying and tracking the megalopolis (Faludi 2002; Yaro and Carbonell 2004; Yaro, Carbonell, and Barnett 2004; Carbonell and Yaro 2005). And while Gottmann was specifically referring to the northeastern United States, the latest research extends the concept to clusters of networked metropolitan areas around the world. For example, European researchers argue that large-scale urbanized areas are the primary geographic unit for integration into the world economy (Faludi 2002). The European Union currently has one well-defined "global integration zone"—the area inside the "Pentagon" that runs from London to Hamburg to Munich to Milan to Paris, and back to London (Schon 2002).

Our book expands on Gottmann's megalopolis themes and insights to account for trends in American transmetropolitan development.[2] Gottmann's original study of the Northeast's megalopolis (1961) held that the region was unique in several ways, including its large size and commercial inventiveness. When Gottmann

revisited his earlier thoughts on the megalopolis in the late 1980s (Gottmann 1987; Gottmann and Harper 1990), he acknowledged that several other U.S. regions could qualify as megapolitan. He pointed in particular to the Midwest and West Coast, but he also saw a nascent megalopolis forming in the South around Atlanta. This study identifies 10 megapolitan areas across the country, not just in the Northeast.

Gottmann's work influenced academics but had no impact on the way the U.S. Census Bureau defines space, probably in part because his 1961 work discussed a single, unique region. But the idea of a functional transmetropolitan geography is one that warrants the Census Bureau's attention. Regional economies now clearly extend beyond an individual metropolitan area. The megapolitan concept recognizes this fact and suggests a new geography to show which regional economies are linked.

A geographic concept, once formally recognized by the Census Bureau, gains power. As an example, rural development advocates lobbied the Census Bureau for years to redefine more heavily settled rural areas as quasi-metropolitan places (Lang and Dhavale 2004). In 2003 the U.S. Office of Management and Budget, which oversees the Census Bureau, responded with the designation "Micropolitan Area." Now micropolitans are literally on the map. Businesses, government agencies, and planners have new geography to work with. Publications took notice— *Site Selection Magazine*, for example, started a list of "Top Micropolitans" in which to locate businesses (Starner 2005).

Megapolitan areas have a similar potential. Once megapolitan areas are officially recognized, private industries and government agencies will embrace them.[3] And there are clearly cases in which the megapolitan scale is the most logical one at which to address problems. An example here is the debate over the fate of Amtrak—America's National Railroad Passenger Corporation—during the George W. Bush administration, which wanted to eliminate all Amtrak funding in the 2006 federal budget. Defending this action, former U.S. secretary of transportation Norman Mineta wrote in the February 23, 2005, *New York Times*, "The problem is not that Americans don't use trains; it is that Amtrak has failed to keep up with the times, stubbornly sticking to routes and services, even as they lose money and attract few users." Amtrak is a national rail system with one profitable line connecting big northeastern cities that offsets losses on service to remote rural areas. As shown in Figure P.1, megapolitan areas have two qualities, concentrated

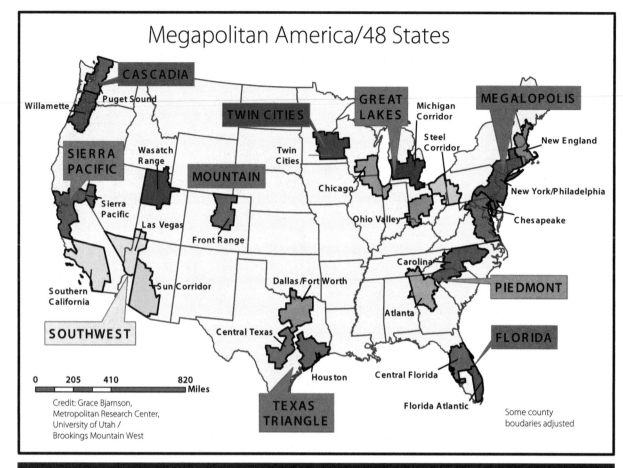

Figure P.1. The 10 megapolitan clusters and 23 megapolitan areas of the contiguous 48 states by 2040

populations and often corridor form, that make them excellent geographic units in which high-speed rail could be feasible.

The Evolving Megapolitan Idea

The concept of a large-scale, transmetropolitan urban structure has been debated among planners since the early 20th century. The idea can be traced to a famous exchange in the pages of the *New Republic* during the summer of 1932 between noted theorist and critic Lewis Mumford and Thomas Adams, director of the Region Plan of New York and Environs (now the Regional Plan Association, or RPA).[4] The debate pitted what Fishman (2000) calls "regionalists" (led by Mumford) against "metropolitanists" (led by Adams). Metropolitanists believed that

20th-century cities would maintain their 19th-century form even as they grew to 10 or 20 million residents and extended 50 or more miles from the center (Thomas 2000). They also argued that most investment should therefore go to fixing the metropolitan core.

Regionalists saw a radical shift in metropolitan structure, away from a monocentric metropolis and toward a more dispersed network of cities and villages arrayed across a vast—although integrated—space they called the "urban region" (Fishman 2000). After the mid-20th century, most new urban growth occurred outside the regional core, which fueled the development of sprawling and often connected metropolitan areas. The proposed urban region concept is thus the progenitor of the megapolitan area.

In the year following the Mumford-Adams debate, urban sociologist R. D. McKenzie (1933) published *The*

Metropolitan Community. This book formally laid out the regionalist's thinking. McKenzie argued that American metropolitan development "is tending to concentrate more and more in large regional aggregates. In every such aggregate, the population tends to subdivide and become multinucleated in a complex of centers that are economically integrated into a larger unity" (1). According to John L. Thomas (2000, 50), Gottmann's *Megalopolis* "effectively completed the analysis of metropolitan regionalism undertaken by R. D. McKenzie three decades earlier." Like McKenzie, Gottmann emphasized economic integration.

The RPA's Second Regional Plan in the 1960s (the first appeared in the 1920s under Adams) produced a series of reports on growth patterns in the New York metropolitan area. One such report, *The Region's Growth* (1967), had a section titled "The Atlantic Urban Region."[5] This region stretched from Virginia to Maine and covered essentially the same area as Gottmann's megalopolis.[6] The RPA report extended Gottmann's work by including new data analysis to show regional integration. It also projected the spread of urbanization to the year 2000 (which looks very similar to current patterns).[7] The RPA report featured an aerial photo-portrait that documented variation in growth patterns from the cores to the edges of the region.

Interestingly, *The Region's Growth* appeared just before the explosion of suburban office development in the early 1970s (Garreau 1991; Lang 2003; Lang, Blakely, and Gough 2005). For example, Dulles airport and its accompanying access road through Fairfax County, Virginia, are shown as the "metropolitan fringe" in the photo-essay. Today, the Dulles Corridor anchors one of the nation's biggest high-tech concentrations.[8]

The Region's Growth raised an important point: Is the Atlantic urban region a "super-city or a chain of cities?" The report found that:

> The main difference between an urban area at the scale of the Atlantic Urban Region and the traditional metropolitan scale is that the emerging larger form has a multitude of major nodes whose areas are likely to be largely autonomous. Nevertheless, the individual urban centers benefit from mutual proximity, and there is bound to be increased integration. (RPA 1967, 35)

As we show in this book, the continuing spread and growing integration of large-scale urban space since 1967 now confirm the Northeast as a supercity. We call such a supercity a "megapolitan" area, with combinations of them constituting "megapolitan clusters." There are several of them.

While Gottmann's and the RPA's works were influential in the 1960s, and Gottmann's definition has a prominent place in geography dictionaries, the megalopolis concept had little lasting impact outside academic geography (Baigent 2004, 687). But that is now starting to change. The current RPA president, Robert Yaro, has kept the idea of the megalopolis alive in recent years. Yaro argues that Americans should do large-scale European-style "spatial planning" (Yaro and Carbonell 2004; Yaro, Carbonell, and Barnett 2004). To that end, Yaro and Armando Carbonell from the Lincoln Institute of Land Policy organized a meeting at the Rockefeller Brothers Foundation headquarters in Tarrytown, New York, to begin a coordinated effort at advancing this idea. The RPA's role in promoting the megalopolis makes sense. Greater New York is the nation's most populous metropolitan area, and it lies at the center of the oldest and largest megalopolis. The RPA also has the deepest history with the concept, which dates to the Adams-Mumford exchanges of the 1930s.

Progression of Thought

In this book, we develop various ways of looking at a new metropolitan geography that has established itself in the contiguous 48 states. Specifically, we consider *megapolitan areas*, composed of at least one metropolitan area with an estimated population of two million by 2040 that connects, via commuting patterns, at least one metropolitan area of more than 250,000 people in 2040 creating a string of such metropolitan areas, with no more than 180 miles between these anchors; and *megapolitan clusters*, composed of megapolitan areas that are networked either by commuting, trucking, or commuter airline to one another but where there is no more than three times the distance used to define a megapolitan area between anchor metropolitan areas at their furthest distance (essentially 550 miles), all such areas in the cluster having reasonably similar terrain, climate, culture, economic base, and sociopolitical orientations.

In all, we derive 10 megapolitan clusters and 23 megapolitan areas (see Figure P.1). We limit our analysis to the United States in large part because of data comparability; over time, we hope to expand the construct to all of North America, though perhaps no farther south than Mexican metropolitan areas adjacent to the U.S. border.

Organization of *Megapolitan America*

This book is organized into five thematic areas. The first area, the structural and historical background germane to subsequent arguments in the book, reviews alternative views of American urban, metropolitan, and regional spatial constructs leading to the megapolitan construct (Chapter 1), suggests that megapolitan areas present new governance challenges (Chapter 2), and shows how we define and apply the megapolitan construct in a manner that may guide future data collection efforts by such agencies as the Census Bureau (Chapter 3). (The Appendix details the progression of Census Bureau thought in defining urban, metropolitan, micropolitan, and combined metropolitan area concepts.) The next thematic area, the interplay of urban and rural landscapes, explores the megapolitan landscape in terms of a rural-megapolitan continuum (Chapter 4), the rise of the megapolitan area as the new economic core or center of America (Chapter 5), and its relative attractions for sustained growth (Chapter 6). The third theme has to do with numbers, such as population trends (Chapter 7) and development (Chapter 8). The fourth thematic area, the key implications of a megapolitan America, takes up transportation issues (Chapter 9) and land, water, and air resource use (Chapter 10). The last thematic area, a synthesis of data, analyzes megapolitan measures and trends for each of the 10 megapolitan clusters, covering all 23 megapolitan areas (Chapters 11 through 20). We conclude with an epilogue calling the 21st century the megapolitan century in the progression of America's evolution.

FROM CITIES TO MEGAREGIONS

*A Brief History of the Progression
of Thought on How the Built
Landscape Is Organized*

In this book, we pose a new way of looking at America's landscape. From its colonial beginnings as a loose confederation of merchant towns, America's urban landscape has evolved considerably. In this chapter, we synthesize the progression of thought about the urban landscape from the simplistic monocentric urban form to the extended metropolis to megaregions. The next chapter reviews how the Census Bureau has wrestled with defining America's changing urban landscape in ways useful for its purposes.

We start this chapter with a walk through standard models of city form. We progress to alternative forms that consider how multiple cities create a special region, one that might be called a metropolitan area. As transportation and telecommunication technology has advanced, we find the idea of spatially delimited regions to be anachronistic, so we explore the idea of diffuse regions defined largely by extended commuting sheds. We conclude with concepts of a nation composed of regions defined according to certain shared affinities.

City and Metropolitan Form

Cities are defined by their spatially integrated functions, not by their political boundaries. The suburbs and even exurbs of a city are elements of the city writ large. For instance, the "city" of Atlanta is not the 500,000 people living within its 60-square-mile jurisdictional limits but the extended commuting range, which includes more than 20,000 square miles.

Historically, cities arose because their location gave them least-cost access to farming, or they were at the crossroads of trading routes, or they were least-cost locations from which to ship goods, often by water. Cities arose mostly in isolation from one another, dominating surrounding trade areas. Over time, successful cities grow because of agglomeration and scale economies. Many become major, independent centers of commerce and manufacturing, such as modern-day Atlanta (McCarthy and Knox 2005). Others grow into each other, creating multicity regions that share interdependencies. Jean Gottmann's (1961) megalopolis, extending from Boston to Washington, D.C.—called "BosWash" by some—is an example.

Cities also sort themselves into a hierarchy of trading areas, with the largest cities being in the center, where they are also closest to all other cities. This is known as the hierarchy of markets comprising a "system of cities," conceptualized by Christaller (1933) and Lösch (1954). The "system" can be at any scale. For instance, in the Northeast, New York City would be the dominant or "capital" city, while Philadelphia and Boston, both of about equal size and distance from New York, would be secondary or "regional" cities. (This is only a schematic representation, however, since ocean port cities do not extend into the ocean.) For the nation as a whole, New York would remain the capital city in a system of cities, but the major second-tier regional cities across the breadth of the continent would be Chicago and Los Angeles. At a smaller scale, systems of cities form metropolitan areas, usually with a central city at the geographic center of accessibility.

While the hierarchy of cities describes how they arise, how they are organized internally is another matter. We will not review the evolution of city form but instead focus on different conceptualizations of that form since the early 20th century with the advent of modern transportation and telecommunication technologies. There are three general city forms: concentric ring or monocentric, sector, and multinuclear or polycentric.

Concentric Ring or Monocentric City and Metropolitan Form

Park, Burgess, and McKenzie (1925) applied natural ecology to urban areas and created the urban ecology school

of thought. Their theory describes what happens when a city grows. Generally, growth results in more activity in the downtown area, pushing it outward. As the downtown area penetrates the next ring, it absorbs or overtakes the business activities, terrain, and population, becoming spatially larger. At the same time, activities in the invaded zone grow because of overall growth and invade the next ring, succeeding uses that were previously there. The overall process extends the city outward and, with modern technology, results in an extensive commuting zone surrounding the built-up area. Figure 1.1 illustrates the theory. In Chicago, the concentric theory of growth seems to explain the distribution of land uses that creates the city's overall form.

Sector City and Metropolitan Form

Cities are more complex than the simple model conceptualized by Park, Burgess, and McKenzie. To further understanding of city form, Hoyt (1939) conceptualized the sector theory. Generally, cities organize themselves around a center not in concentric rings but in sectors, as illustrated in Figure 1.2. Sometimes this occurs because of geography, but more often it occurs as a natural ordering of land uses based on principal uses. For instance, manufacturing and warehousing might occur along riverfronts (as in early Pittsburgh) or along railroads (as in early Atlanta). Residential areas in particular would sort

1 Central business district
2 Zone of transition
3 Zone of independent workers' homes
4 Zone of better residences
5 Commuter zone

Figure 1.1. Concentric ring theory of urban form
Credit: Doug Woodruff

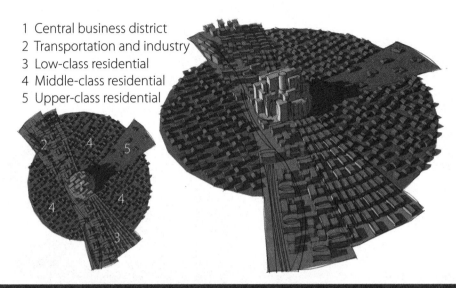

1 Central business district
2 Transportation and industry
3 Low-class residential
4 Middle-class residential
5 Upper-class residential

Figure 1.2. Sector theory of urban form
Credit: Doug Woodruff

themselves out demographically by race or socioeconomic class (or both) based substantially on income. Early on, a "favored" sector might emerge. Many factors facilitate the rise of a favored quarter; some important ones include elevation above flood-prone or polluted lowlands, location upwind from manufacturing plants, and the original settlement of upper-class families away from downtown. For instance, in Atlanta, Georgia, there was a settlement north of downtown called Buckhead where business and financial leaders chose to live in the mid-1800s when Atlanta had but a few tens of thousands of residents. Buckhead was a few miles away from the railroads that terminated in downtown (Atlanta's original name was Terminus) and slightly elevated from downtown itself. Almost two centuries later, Atlanta's favored sector has created a kind of northern arc that has been dubbed the "favored quarter" in recent times (Leinberger 1995).

Multinuclear or Polycentric City and Metropolitan Form
As urban areas grow and transportation costs decline, new, satellite suburban centers rise up, leading to multiple centers, or what some call a polycentric city form. Harris and Ullman (1945) were the first to conceptualize this form (Figure 1.3).

Vance (1964, 1977, 1986) expanded on the polycentric form to characterize large urban areas as composed of "urban realms" (Figure 1.4). Vance points out that the large geographic scale of modern urban areas limits personal routine interactions (for shopping, personal services, and social networks) to smaller areas, which he calls "realms." Realms often have their own large commercial centers and, as we observe, a population base within a defined geography of about one quarter to one million people. The geographic space is defined by terrain and topographic barriers, the overall size of the metropolitan area, the amount and type of economic activity the area can support, and the geography of transportation within the region, such as the presence of transit nodes, freeway interchanges, and the like.

A variant of the polycentric form, and of the urban realm concept, is the edge city (Figure 1.5), popularized by Garreau (1991). Edge cities are seen as completely automobile-driven, suburban activity centers comprising more than five million square feet of office space, more than 600,000 square feet of retail space, having more jobs than bedrooms, perceived by the local population as a definable place, and could not have had any urban features 30 years earlier. Some well-known edge cities include Tysons Corner in suburban northern Virginia, King of Prussia in suburban Philadelphia, the Galleria in

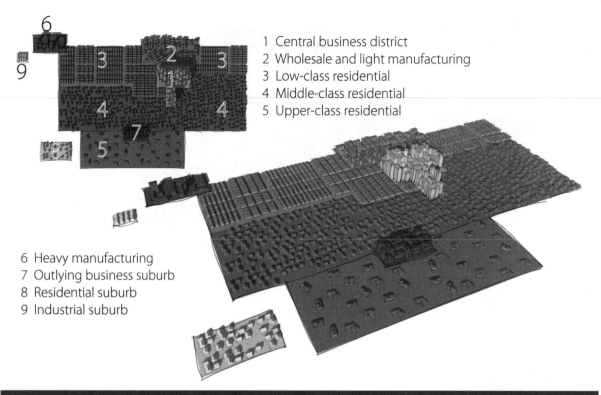

1 Central business district
2 Wholesale and light manufacturing
3 Low-class residential
4 Middle-class residential
5 Upper-class residential

6 Heavy manufacturing
7 Outlying business suburb
8 Residential suburb
9 Industrial suburb

Figure 1.3. Polycentric theory of urban form
Credit: Doug Woodruff

suburban Houston, Bloomington in suburban Minneapolis–St. Paul, and Bellevue in suburban Seattle. Lang (2003) advanced Garreau's concept of edge cities by suggesting that many will evolve into true downtowns in their own right (Figure 1.6).

The Extended Metropolis

All these characterizations of cities and metropolitan areas seem to suppose that a large share of business activity actually occurs in downtowns, edge cities, or the like. Lang (2003) showed this is not the case. In fact, roughly 80 percent of all business activity is not found in central locations but rather is dispersed along corridors, in office and industrial parks, or simply elsewhere. As Lang notes, "a revolution in metropolitan form occurred in the past several decades—the regional office hierarchy has been turned upside down" (2003, 56). He concludes that the United States is composed substantially of edgeless cities (Figure 1.7).

Lang's work builds on the extended metropolis literature. Friedmann and Miller (1965), for instance, described how American metropolitan areas were evolving so that their reach among commuters (via commuter train or even automobile) was up to 100 miles from large central cities They called this large space the "urban field" (Figure 1.8). Blumenfeld (1986) went further by suggesting continued dispersion of population, facilitated by a combination of technological improvements and some innate desire of humans to settle in or near lower-density spaces (see also Nelson 1992). There would be little distinction on the built-up landscape: "It seems likely that within the next century the entire ecumene will be transformed into a mosaic of contiguous metropolitan orbits. This is not a 'reversal of the trend to the metropolis.' It is something far more significant: the end of the age-old distinction between urban and rural forms of human settlements" (Blumenfeld 1986, 348).

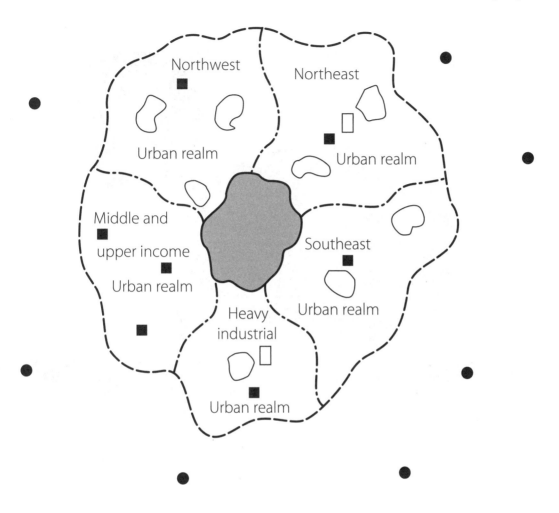

Northwest

Northeast

Urban realm

Urban realm

Middle and

upper income

Southeast

Urban realm

Urban realm

Heavy
industrial

Urban realm

■ 18th- and 19th-century extent of metropolis and present-day traditional core

☐ Late 19th- and 20th-century suburban growth

⬭ Initially outlying industrial satellite now surrounded by suburbs, often
serving as administrative center for realm

■ Post–World War II integrated shopping centers

☐ Major professional sports facilities

● Freestanding small town

— — Edge of built-up metropolis

—·— Interrealm boundary

Figure 1.4. Urban realms as conceptualized by Vance (1964)
Credit: Doug Woodruff

1 Central city
2 Suburban residential area
3 Shopping mall
4 Industrial district
5 Office park
6 Service center
7 Airport complex
8 Combined employment
   and shopping center

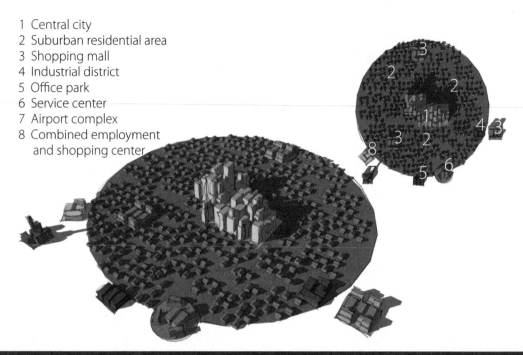

Figure 1.5. The edge city urban form (Garreau 1991)
Credit: Doug Woodruff

Life Cycle of a Big Edge City

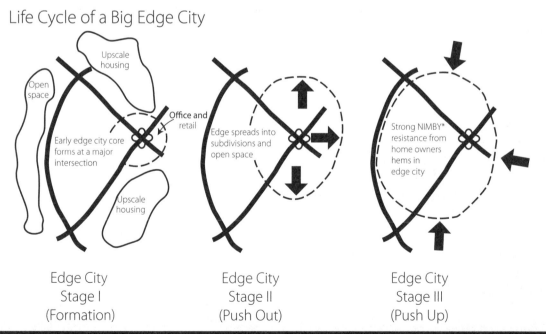

Figure 1.6. Evolution of an edge city (Lang 2003)
Credit: Doug Woodruff
* "not in my backyard"

Office Location Types

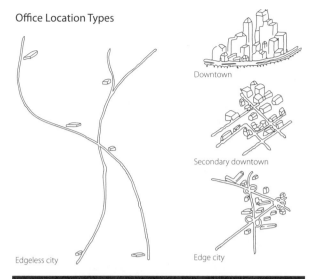

Figure 1.7. The edgeless city in the context of other conceptualizations of city and metropolitan form (Lang 2003)
Credit: Doug Woodruff

Yet proximity to place still matters, according to Nelson and colleagues. They (Nelson 1992; Nelson and Sanchez 1997, 1999) explored whether the attractiveness of exurban or rural living was driven by something other than the standard theories of land use (see Alonso 1968, Mills 1972). If so, a logical extension of one aspect of Lang's edgeless city concept would seem to imply the continuing demise of the importance of centrality of place, at least in its share of economic and social interaction. Nelson and colleagues concluded that the rise of exurban living merely conformed to standard urban form theory, and exurbs were nothing more than the suburbs of the suburbs. In other words, proximity to place still matters. Nonetheless, Nelson's work led to a refined conceptualization of America's extended metropolis, illustrated in Figure 1.9.

Megaregions and National Regions

From systems of cities creating metropolitan areas to the extended metropolis, we finally arrive at the concept of

Figure 1.8. The urban field (Friedmann and Miller 1965)
Credit: Doug Woodruff
* Standard Metropolitan Statistical Areas

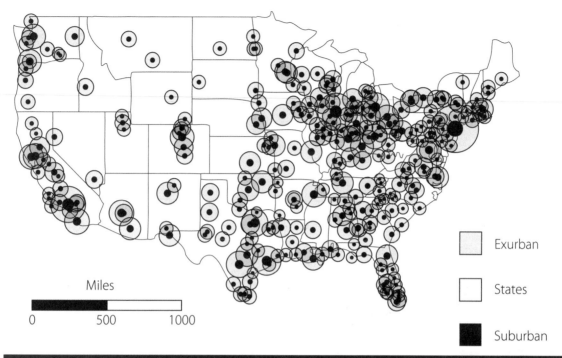

Miles

0   500   1000

Exurban

States

Suburban

Figure 1.9. Urban (dots not shown), suburban (black), and exurban (gray) regions defining metropolitan spaces for all Census-defined Metropolitan Statistical Areas in 1990 (Nelson et al. 1995)
Credit: Doug Woodruff

megaregions composed of multiple overlapping metropolitan areas. From our perspective, the seminal work here is Jean Gottmann's *Megalopolis* (1961). How he coined the term is instructive for our purposes. Gottmann credits the ancient Alexandrian philosopher Philo Judaeus, who used the name "Megalopolis," with characterizing the great city of ideas that commands our material world. Gottmann applied this concept to the string of metropolitan areas extending from Boston to northern Virginia along the northeastern seaboard (Figure 1.10). Gottmann showed how wealth and knowledge are concentrated in this contemporary megalopolis. The growth and increasing power of a megalopolis are sustained through macroscale transportation and communications investment that further integrates each part of the whole.

Without using the term, Jerome Pickard (1966, 3) described urban regions as the "continuous grouping, clustering and linking of cities and towns in close proximity with the majority of the population living in urban settlements." He described the current geography and demography of 21 urban regions, with

projections of future conditions in 1980 in which 25 urban regions would contain approximately two-thirds of the nation's population but cover only 10 percent of the land area of the contiguous 48 states. In 1970, Pickard published an article in *Futurist* magazine titled "Is Megalopolis Inevitable?" In defining "urban regions" as areas with at least one million residents and a population density at least three times the national average, Pickard extended his forecast of urban regions to the year 2000 and produced a map showing where they would be (Figure 1.11). He concluded by noting that "regional planning for clusters of urbanized areas in close proximity will become an absolute necessity" (1970, 154).

We conclude this review with two characterizations of how the United States is composed of very large, national-scale regions. The first is Joel Garreau's *Nine Nations of North America* (1981), in which he assigns all the space on the North American continent to one of nine regions sharing historical, social, cultural, and economic affinities (Figure 1.12). Garreau argues that

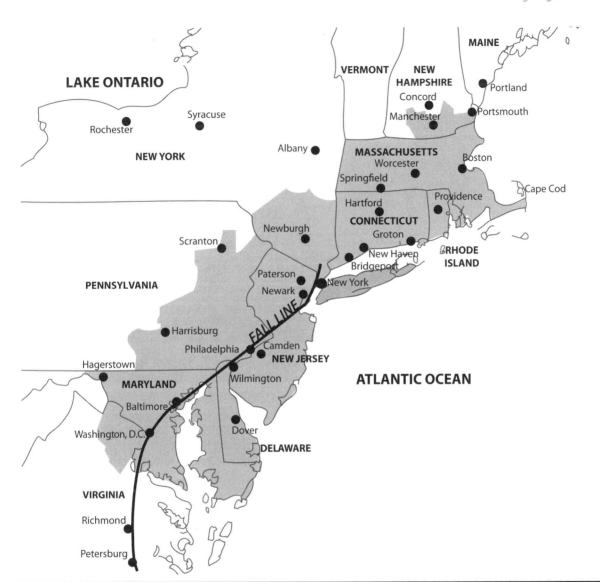

Figure 1.10. Gottmann's (1961) megalopolis was the original conceptualization of multiple metropolitan areas operating as an integrated economic, social, cultural, and political unit. From New York City southward, it spanned both sides of the "fall line" demarcating uplands and the coastal plain.
Credit: Doug Woodruff

local, state, and national borders are irrelevant and that viewing each region as its own nation advances an understanding of how North American society functions. From our perspective, however, Garreau's nine regions are much too large spatially to properly characterize America's emerging economic geography. More to the point, each of the nine nations would likely not

enjoy economic vitality without the systems of metropolitan areas functioning in each of them.

The second characterization is Armando Carbonell and Robert D. Yaro's "megaregions," based on their article "American Spatial Development and the New Megalopolis" (2005). Their work borrows from the spatial development policies of the European Union (see Faludi

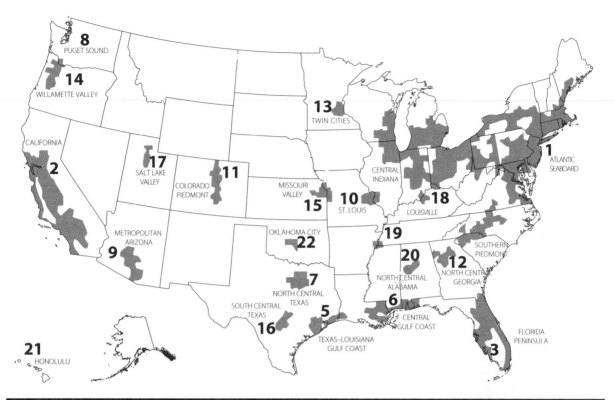

Figure 1.11. Pickard's (1970) 25 urban regions by 2000 would account for about two-thirds of the nation's population, occupying a land base of 10 percent of the contiguous 48 states.
Credit: Doug Woodruff

2002). The authors make the connection between the American megalopolis (Boston–Washington, D.C.) and similar networks of metropolitan areas in Europe and Asia. Carbonell and Yaro argue that "Major public and private investments are being made in high-speed rail, broadband communications and other infrastructure to strengthen transportation and economic synergies" (2005, 2), the precedent being national infrastructure systems already facilitated by the federal government, such as freight railroads, airports and interstate highways.

The megaregion concept has evolved over time (Figure 1.13). It was initially explored during a University of Pennsylvania planning studio taught in 2005 by Carbonell, at the Lincoln Institute of Land Policy, and Yaro, of the Regional Plan Association. In 2006, those two organizations jointly convened the National Committee for America 2050, a coalition of planners and civic leaders, to develop a national framework for rapid population

growth in the United States and the emergence of what they call megaregions. Catherine Ross's edited volume, *Megaregions: Planning for Global Competitiveness* (2009), synthesized this school of thought. Carbonell and Yaro's 2005 article, "American Spatial Development and the New Megalopolis," concludes with a call for governance and funding changes to acknowledge that megaregions "capture the true economic and social geography of their communities. And they have the size, capacity and expertise to undertake complex planning strategies" (4).

Our megapolitan construct differs somewhat from the concept of megaregion as published and endorsed by previous workers in the field. It is rooted in defining geographic spaces that create multiple metropolitan economic regions that are components of megaregions. Our method is a bottom-up strategy, as shown in the next chapter.

To be sure, the nine nations concept and the megaregions address different concerns from ours. The scales of

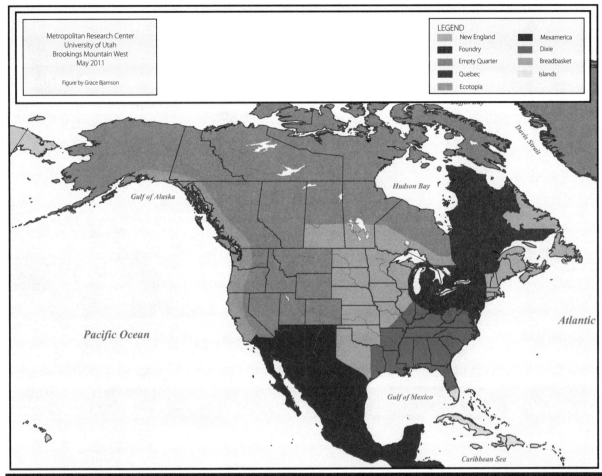

Metropolitan Research Center
University of Utah
Brookings Mountain West
May 2011

Figure by Grace Bjarnson

LEGEND

New England
Foundry
Empty Quarter
Quebec
Ecotopia
Mexamerica
Dixie
Breadbasket
Islands

Figure 1.12. Garreau's (1981) nine nations of North America, adapted from http://en.wikipedia.org/wiki/File:9nations.png

those conceptualizations fit nicely into broad attempts to create homogeneous spaces based on terrain, weather, culture, politics, history, and common economic foundations. What is needed, however, is a middle-ground conceptualization that recognizes that America's emerging economic geography is far larger than cities or their metropolitan areas but smaller than broad-brush multistate regions.

Summary Observations

That the urban areas of the United States are linked to each, often creating systems of metropolitan areas functioning as their own economic engines, has long been accepted. That such systems of metropolitan areas are of growing importance to the nation's long-term economic health also seems increasingly accepted. What is missing, however, is a clear, predictable method to describe and define these unique combinations of places and spaces to guide the next generation of planning and policy making. In the next chapter, we examine how the federal government, through the Census Bureau, has attempted to classify different levels and combinations of urban settlement. As we show, however, this categorization, too, falls short of recognizing contemporary realities.

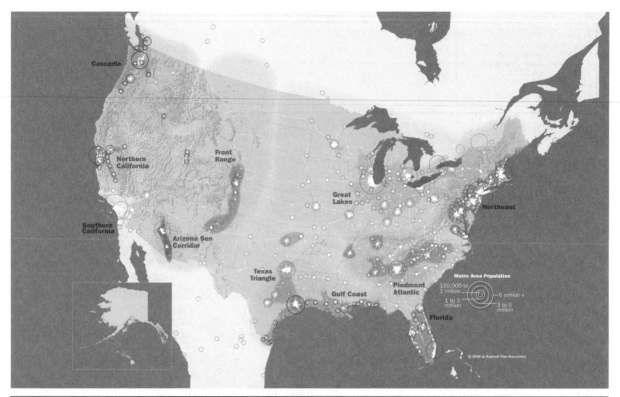

Figure 1.13. Megaregions (Carbonell and Yaro 2005)
Credit: America 2050, Regional Plan Association

2

MEGAPOLITAN CONVERGENCE

*Soft-Nosed Planning and the
New Regional Governance*

Regionalism is too often thought to require government initiative. As a result, progress is associated with full-on structural reform—and so the controversy (and usually frustration) begins. Look to the Intermountain West, however, and it becomes immediately clear that regionalism need not require top-down government overhaul, and especially need not require it at the "super-regional" scale of the "megapolitan" spaces.

—Mark Muro (2010)

How shall we manage our emerging megapolitan areas? By our definition, they are composed of multiple large metropolitan areas, some crossing state lines. There is a rich literature, especially since the mid-20th century, calling for the formation of general-purpose, regional governments to address metropolitan-scale issues (see Hamilton and Atkins 2008). Yet thus far, only one metropolitan area has a regionally elected governing body—the Metro Council of Portland, Oregon, created in the early 1980s. A key issue is how many regions would likely follow the Portland model. In our view, the question has now been answered—*none*. Yet even as formal, full-rigged regional government failed to take hold across the United States, a less formal and more voluntary form of regionalism emerged. It, too, is "functionally" based—that is, selected megapolitan-scale issues are addressed through a variety of governance structures. Few if any of those structures require the direct election of public officials to administer those functions.[1] We believe this trend will accelerate as we now move to the megapolitan scale. We review our arguments relating to key governance functions in this chapter.

Soft-Nosed, Self-Organized Planning

We are guided in our view of the future of metropolitan-scale governance by the work of Popper and Popper (1996), who argue for an alternative direction for regional, large-scale governance. Old-style bureaucracies, they hold, are not really needed because a new paradigm has emerged that can produce effective planning without an official structure. Popper and Popper call the new paradigm "soft-nosed planning," in contrast to the "hard-nosed planning" of some state agencies and selected federal agencies tasked with regional management, such as the Tennessee Valley Authority

The Poppers see the soft-nosed planning model as having emerged when people in the Great Plains states took up the Buffalo Commons idea at the grassroots level. In their original proposal for the commons, the Poppers assumed the federal government would need to organize the vast agricultural lands that were being abandoned on the western Great Plains into national grasslands. But to their surprise, the real energy for planning the commons came from the local level. It was also a creative and entrepreneurial effort.

Another key dimension of soft-nosed planning is the use of language—in particular, metaphor and storytelling. The reason why the Buffalo Commons idea gained traction at the grassroots level is that it captured in a single and flexible concept a notion that most local residents understood intuitively. Anyone living for decades on the western Great Plains understood the basic disconnect between the way the land was settled (as an eastern-style farming region) and the reality of nature. The Poppers used the buffalo as a metaphor—a hardy creature well adapted to the plains that had nearly been eradicated to pave the way for far less adaptive cattle. The core of the idea was a rebalancing between nature and land use, with the goal of long-term sustainability.

Can a form of soft-nosed planning work for megapolitans? We think so, but we also expect that the results will vary widely. Some places will see a good deal of effective soft-nosed planning efforts, while other regions will have little success. Perhaps the most important criterion for success will be the extent to which these regions are "organic places." Large-scale metropolitan areas today are so gigantic that at first glance they seem anything but organic. Simply comprehending a place such as Southern California as a unit seems impossible. Yet there clearly is a distinct region that runs along the California coast from Santa Barbara to San Diego. Any traveler on the Pacific Coast Highway can see it—and can distinguish Northern California from Southern California in the process. Partly it's environment, partly it's mood, but there is a visible, distinct place that local residents also refer to as the "Southland." Thus, Southern California begins with an advantage. It is a place in the public mind and not merely a statistical artifact cooked up by government analysts running numbers in a dark room at the Census Bureau back in Suitland, Maryland.

This is not to say that a sense of place per se will guarantee good soft-nosed planning results. Rather, it is a good starting point because the public more readily accepts the concept that a very large area of varied terrain that crosses jurisdictional boundaries forms one distinct region. Moreover, the public (and business leadership) can more easily accept that an identifiable region exists if it constitutes a reasonable extension of an already well-established place. An example is the Dallas–Fort Worth Metroplex. Census data showed that Dallas and Fort Worth had merged into a unified region by the 1970s, but local residents at first would have none of it. The two anchor cities had a historically rooted distaste

for one another, one that would not be ameliorated by statistics. But with federal aid formulas forcing a single airport on the region, there began a process of eventual acceptance and later a celebration of this metropolitan integration. Area residents even devised a cool name that conjured up an expansive, Texas-sized metropolis—or, in booster parlance, "metroplex." A Google search of the term *metroplex* yields nearly four million hits, with almost all referring to Dallas–Fort Worth. What was once a PR tag for the region, developed to offset the more generic-sounding moniker "North Texas," is now fully embedded in the public mind.

Other parts of the United States could soon follow the Metroplex example. The Arizona Sun Corridor, to take one example, seems poised for such a merger of cities. In the spring of 2006, while team teaching a public policy studio course at Arizona State University (ASU), Robert Lang and John Hall devised the name "Sun Corridor" to refer to the urban complex joining Phoenix and Tucson. The label was a play on the existing local name for the Phoenix area, "Valley of the Sun." Given the aridity of the whole region, keeping the word *sun* made sense. Pairing this older and common reference for Phoenix with the word *corridor* to connote urban form made the region distinct from the state's largest metropolitan area. The Sun Corridor is bigger than any one valley (in fact, it contains parts of a dozen valleys). Also, the sun shines brightly in Tucson and throughout urban Arizona, so why not apply it to the whole megapolitan area? Interestingly, while not every resident bought the concept of the Sun Corridor, no one has ever specifically challenged the name, even those outside the original Valley of the Sun.

The Sun Corridor concept was launched by a 2008 publication (Gammage et al. 2008), and since that time the name seems to have taken hold. There are now more 75,000 Google references to the region. The majority of these references do not direct a searcher specifically to the original ASU report, which means the concept has some legs. In addition, there is now an economic development initiative under the motto Arizona Sun Corridor: Open for Business that is marketing the whole megapolitan area. Finally, one key business sector that the entire region hopes to develop is solar energy. Thus, the word *sun* may be more important to the region as an economic metaphor (as the word *silicon* is to the San Francisco Bay Area) than as a designator of a historical place. The soft-nosed planning prospects for the Sun Corridor now seem bright because the region makes sense, and its acceptance as a unit facilitates organizing regionwide economic development efforts.

We believe what holds true for the Dallas–Fort Worth Metroplex and the Phoenix–Tucson Sun Corridor applies to the megapolitan areas writ large. Places with an organic basis, where a case for unified action is manifest and compelling, will see a boom in soft-nosed planning efforts. On Colorado's Front Range, there is a growing sense that the entire region from Denver north to the Wyoming border is now increasingly unifying economically (this is in fact the operating assumption of Metro Denver, the nonprofit organization charged with economic development on the Front Range). Mark Muro (2010) of the Brookings Institution in an article in the *New Republic* refers to these efforts as regional "governance" as opposed to "government." Muro's point, like the Poppers', is that we do not need formal, full-rigged, Portland-style government to get effective regional governance. Voluntary action based on self-interest will also suffice—at least in places where these interests are well known and there is a habit of cooperation. Muro refers to these efforts as "self-organizing."

The New Metropolitan Governance: Tied to Federal Formula

Unfortunately, the United States is also replete with places that see little cooperation, even when all parties would benefit. We do not advocate developing command-and-control mechanisms that would force such places to plan at the regional scale. Given the structure of land-use regulation in the United States, which is a federal republic comprised of states, there is no European-style central government that can make regions do right and essentially eat their planning spinach. As Americans, we think that is a good thing. Yet at the same time, the federal government does have an obligation to see that taxpayer money is well spent on infrastructure improvements in sprawling regions where divided government may produce inefficient outcomes.

By the 1990s, transportation experts recognized that money directed to some metropolitan areas was going to waste because localities were not coordinating their transportation plans. Regional mobility transcends any single city or suburb, especially for economies on the scale of a metropolitan area. Commutes to work, goods flows, and even shopping may cross multiple local boundaries. If localities do not unify some of their planning, the whole region could face greater congestion, increased energy consumption, and lower productivity. Therefore, starting with the landmark 1991 Intermodal Surface Transportation Efficiency Act (ISTEA), local governments were required to form regional transportation councils in order to receive their full share of federal funding. While metropolitan planning organizations (MPOs) were first required in 1962 for all "urbanized areas," these entities had virtually no power or purpose. ISTEA led to a very specific power and purpose, and MPOs revived and flourished. Thus, metropolitan planning today owes less to the inspiration of places such as Portland and more to a charge given to transportation organizations by Congress.

There is wide variation in how regional transportation bodies have been organized across the United States, but the general impact on metropolitan planning has been significant. We think that the limited scope of these councils has been essential in taking some of the sting out of what can be seen as an intrusive federal edict via ISTEA. It is a form of soft-nosed planning in that it allows local innovation and interpretation, while backed by a hard-nosed funding requirement at the federal level. The manifest purpose of these councils was the formation and implementation of regional plans for transportation. Yet in many regions, they have come to represent much more. In some cases, it was the first time that cities, suburbs, and counties sat down to talk about regional problems and solutions. The dialogue led to improved cooperation on other fronts, especially those concerned with such broad interests as land preservation, resource management, and economic development.

From the experience of existing metropolitan areas, we see the megapolitan future. The governance of metropolitan areas should follow and extend the existing pattern of soft-nosed planning practices, spurred on by federal funding requirements. In fact, a main reason why we based our criteria for megapolitan areas in this book on the census definition of Combined Statistical Areas (CSAs) was to link them to federal funding policies—especially those concerned with transportation and infrastructure investment. The megapolitan areas are really a reasonable estimate of the CSAs at mid-century. All Congress need do is insert the term CSA for MSA (or Metropolitan Statistical Area) in a transportation authorization bill, and we will have the basic framework for 21st-century megapolitan planning in America. As with metropolitan area planning, wide variants will emerge in the actual structures developed. Some locales will simply go through the motions; others will begin a much broader effort at region planning. It is up to each region what it decides to make of it.

The Business of Megapolitans: Cooperating on Economic Development

Another key basis for mid-century megapolitan planning is the increasing realization that megapolitans are the zones by which the United States integrates into the global economy. Megapolitans contain every major land, sea, and air link in the nation, including every international hub airport (Puentes and Tomer 2009). If, as the Brookings Institution (Katz 2000) predicts, the United States shifts from a consumer-led economy to one that puts more emphasis on exports and innovation, megapolitan areas with the most efficient infrastructure and research capacity will be advantaged. We expect much greater regional cooperation as some regions move beyond local differences to access the global economy. Such a transformation is occurring in the Sun Corridor as Phoenix and Tucson work together on common economic development strategies that seek to position the entire megapolitan area as a global leader in solar technology.

Like Dallas and Fort Worth, Tucson and Phoenix are not natural partners. The two regions have a history of rivalry that extends back to the territorial days. Tucson sees Phoenix as illegitimate, as its residents have constructed a human-made world in defiance of the desert. The region is sometimes referred to by residents of its southern neighbor as a "Disney Desert" in that it is overstylized, overplanted, and overly reliant on water for its "lush" desert look. It is also derided as a "little L.A." because of its expansive freeways and subdivisions. To many living in Phoenix, Tucson looks like a dusty cow town that is too laid back for its own good. To many outsiders, the rivalry seems silly. In the global scheme of things, these two desert metropolises share the same state and even the same physical region, the Sonoran Desert. There are similar rivalries between proximate metropolitan areas throughout the United States. But as happened with the now joined-at-the-hip Dallas–Fort Worth area, many of these antagonisms may fade as a common stake in economic development emerges.

Phoenix and Tucson have ample reason to cooperate. Their collective assets and markets can produce a synergistic rise to world city and global gateway status. Phoenix is a large-scale region and has an airport that is a key domestic hub, with a high potential for enhanced global links. Aptly named Sky Harbor, the airport is this inland region's port to the world. Tucson had the good fortune to receive the state's original land grant university, the University of Arizona, which has a strong research capacity in fields such as space science and optics. The university is also home to the main branch of Arizona's only medical school. Phoenix and the entire Sun Corridor are seeking opportunities for diversification away from industries such as tourism and home construction and toward an export economy based on emerging technologies. Roughly speaking, Phoenix has the global access and Tucson has the technology.

Phoenix, in its bid to gain a toehold in the biotechnology sector, borrowed some of Tucson's assets in the form of a branch of the medical school (which now lies in downtown Phoenix). ASU could have started a medical school from scratch, but the accreditation process would have taken years, and the new institution would have lacked the research capacity of the already well-established institution in Tucson. The relative closeness of the two cities made the medical school branching practical and should lead to more areas of cooperation between the bookends of the Sun Corridor megapolitan area.

Phoenix and Tucson could, in fact, partner in numerous economically viable ways. Tucson's optics research capacity is world class as a result of NASA's investment in the Kitt Peak National Observatory. Yet the region never developed a private, spin-off optics industry around this government-led effort in the way that Rochester, New York, did. Because of the prominence of imaging and optical science in industry and the academy, Rochester has become known as the world capital of imaging, and industry supports research activity at the Rochester Institute of Technology. Through being part of a large extended metropolis, Tucson would be in good position to develop links to world markets and venture capital to bootstrap a bigger optics-led economy. In other emerging industry sectors, such as renewable energy, Tucson and Phoenix could cooperate from the start. In this spirit, the Arizona Sun Corridor: Open for Business campaign is targeting several key industries for megapolitan-wide growth, among them aerospace, optics, bioscience, information technology, renewable energy, and logistics.

The Sun Corridor is well along the path toward working out a megapolitan-level economic development strategy, and other areas are following suit. A case in point is the Florida Corridor (Orlando–Tampa). Orlando's regional economy is far too reliant on tourism. The Brookings Institution report estimates that after Las Vegas, Orlando is the second major metropolitan area where an economy based on a combination of tourism and real estate construction led to growth. Orlando took a hard fall in the recession of 2007–2009, when real estate collapsed and discretionary income dried up. By contrast, Tampa fared a bit better. Tampa contains a major port, and industries tied to logistics softened its economic fall. Orlando and Tampa are closer to one another than are Phoenix and Tucson. Orlando, because of tourism, has a globally connected airport. Paired with Tampa's ocean port, the possibilities for a larger share of trade in the Florida Corridor are clearly present.

Like the Sun Corridor, the Florida Corridor will likely see an official convergence based on commuter patterns by mid-century. In anticipation of this day, cooperation between Tampa and Orlando has already begun. The Tampa Bay Partnership, a nonprofit organization promoting Tampa's economy, has started holding joint conferences with its megapolitan peer, the Central Florida Partnership. One of us, Robert Lang, has spoken at these meetings and shared data on the region. The immediate goal of the conferences was to promote improved rail and highway capacity. The announcement in the spring of 2010 of a high-speed rail link between the two was enthusiastically greeted in both regions, and the benefits of greater business integration are now manifestly apparent. One strategy that Orlando has for economic diversification is convergence with Tampa. For Tampa, Orlando's global brand, a result of Disney World's presence, helps with tourism and trade. Cooperation is expected to result in a joint organization that promotes both regions as a unified space. Again, these efforts are all voluntary (rather than mandated by legislative fiat) and are led by a business community that sees a direct benefit from ending parochial infighting as it seeks world city status for the entire megapolitan area.

The Megapolitan Footprint: Managing Land and Water

Megapolitan areas are large, expansive regions. As urban zones converge, the loss of farmland and the degradation of natural resources accelerate. The old notion of a regional greenbelt becomes moot as one metropolitan area's open space becomes another's exurbs. Thus, another area for potential cooperation concerns the environmental impact of megapolitans. There are multiple areas where such coordinated planning efforts apply, including habitat conservation, open-space preservation, watershed resource management, air quality monitoring, and recreation planning.

The need to preserve vital habitats for endangered species has a direct impact on metropolitan development. Reports such as "Endangered by Sprawl" (Ewing et al. 2005), put out by Smart Growth America and the National Wildlife Federation, show that the nation's largest urban counties are home to numerous endangered species. The Endangered Species Act (ESA) of 1973 gives the U.S. government broad power to preserve habitats that often lie in the path of urban growth. The federal government can halt projects to protect habitats. A 1978 amendment to the ESA created an Endangered Species Committee of seven members, comprising cabinet officials in the executive branch, such as the head of the Environmental Protection Agency. The committee has been dubbed the "God Squad" because of its power and ability to literally play God and save some species from extinction. The committee can bring development to a screeching halt in cases where it sees an immediate danger to a critical habitat, as in the hills surrounding San Diego, where the sagebrush provides a home to hummingbirds.

Because megapolitan areas are simply larger and extended versions of metropolitan areas, there is an even greater likelihood that endangered species will be found within their borders. Leaders in these regions have a self-interest in coordinating planning to avoid the wrath of the God Squad. The current pattern of growth, in which decentralization leads to dispersal, is a major part of the problem. The regions that make up a megapolitan area can reverse this trend by promoting a more focused peripheral development practice. In place of sprawl there could be nodal development, in which decentralized growth is refocused in urban villages. This tactic would reduce the risk of running afoul of federal laws protecting habitats.

On the other hand, the pressure to develop in megapolitan areas can lead to regional (including multistate) approaches to protecting habitats. Mason (2008), for instance, identifies numerous regional habitat and landscape preservation initiatives that affect large shares, if not all the land, in several megapolitan areas. These include the Everglades Restoration Plan in the Florida Atlantic megapolitan area, numerous habitat preservation plans in the Southern California megapolitan area, the New York/New Jersey/Pennsylvania/Connecticut highlands preservation efforts in the New York–Philadelphia megapolitan area, and the Chesapeake Bay watershed restoration initiatives.

Water resource management is another area where cooperation within and between megapolitan areas should prove beneficial. The major watersheds in the United States are massive in scale, and the issue of water supply and quality is now a key concern in most large, fast-growing U.S. metropolitan areas. Water systems throughout the nation are under stress, and in some areas the lack of water may limit future growth. *Fortune* magazine in its March 19, 2007, issue called water the oil of the 21st century—"the precious commodity that determines the wealth of nations"—and water will play a greater role in determining the degree to which a metropolitan area or country can grow. People concerned about water are no longer limited to the arid West. Some of the biggest water challenges may be found in the East, in particular the Atlanta megapolitan area.

Water transcends the old model of the stand-alone metropolitan area. Atlanta's water demand can affect large patches of the urban and rural south in Georgia, Alabama, and Florida. Likewise, the entire Southwest is integrated into a common water system dependent on the Colorado River. The Sun Corridor's water capacity requires consideration of places such as Las Vegas. The problems Las Vegas faces in securing an alternative water supply to the Colorado River (which the city is now attempting to do in the Great Basin) will determine the extent to which it competes with the Sun Corridor for this resource in the future. The point is that these two regions are linked and have an imperative to coordinate on water policy. The good news is that they are now doing so, and that makes water an example of a transmegapolitan area of governance. Water is a megaregional, even national, issue.

Even with cooperation, some megapolitan areas, such as Las Vegas, face the very real prospect of running out of water. And there are places with plenty of rainfall where the management of water is so poor and the infrastructure investment so minimal that they are simply wet versions of Las Vegas. The federal government needs to take a far more active role in mediating among the interests that now compete over water. Such policy efforts may include a decision to redirect large-scale agriculture to regions with sufficient rainfall so that the supply to urban populations is not imperiled. But that is only one dimension of the need for federal action. Another major concern is the need for direct, national-level investment in water systems that have not kept up with population growth. Megapolitan clusters and megapolitan areas are the right scale for this investment. The federal hand is also needed in incentivizing governance structure to match this investment.

The State and the Megapolitan: Conflict and Convergence

Megapolitan areas have a complex and often combative relationship with states. Many big megapolitans reach into multiple states, adding even more complexity to this relationship. The link between the nation's biggest regions and their home states will be an important determinant of how growth is managed and supported. Large-scale urbanization has challenged planning models and produced an evolution in land-use regulation.

In our recent book for the Urban Land Institute, *The New Politics of Planning* (Nelson and Lang 2009), we describe a "convergence" or a "common ground" emerging on key issues attending metropolitan growth. We describe a movement toward soft-nosed planning. States that have a formal planning structure in place, such as Oregon, have seen challenges to their approach in recent years, while places with a history of light regulation, such as Georgia, now mandate some form of comprehensive planning. The convergence refers to the midpoint in regulation: More states now require planning, but the structure is open to local interpretation and negotiation. The main tool for promoting good planning is incentives tied to aid formulas. In a way, the states mimic the federal government's method of inducing planning based on funding. Let us explore this further.

In *The New Politics of Planning*, we assessed states according to the rigor and content of planning enabled by or required of local governments by state statutes. Our assessment was based on the *Growing Smart Legislative Guidebook* (Meck 2002), published by the American Planning Association. The APA guidebook includes a compendium of state planning legislation, focusing on planning rigor (such as whether plans were mandatory and included state-level review) and content (such as mandatory or optional planning elements). We developed the Nelson-Lang Planning Index and ranked states based on overall planning commitment (Table 2.1).

Table 2.1. Ranking of States by Planning Rigor and Content Requirements of Local Government, 2002

State	Plan Mandated	State Land-Use Policy Basis	Strength of State Role	Internal Consistency Required	Structure Score	Total Elements	Total Score	Nelson-Lang Planning Index
Alabama	1		1		2	4	6	41
Alaska	3		2		5	4	9	31
Arizona	1		1		2	12	14	16
Arkansas	2	1	2		5	6	11	22
California	3		2	1	6	9	15	12
Colorado	1		1		2	4	6	41
Connecticut	1		2		3	12	15	12
Delaware	3	1	3	1	8	11	19	5
Florida	3	1	3	1	8	15	23	1
Georgia	3	1	3	1	8	12	20	3
Hawaii	3	1	3		7	5	12	20
Idaho	3		2		5	12	17	8
Illinois	2		1		3	5	8	36
Indiana	1		1		2	7	9	31
Iowa	2		1		3	7	10	25
Kansas	2		1		3	6	9	31
Kentucky	3		2	1	6	10	16	10
Louisiana	1		1		2	7	9	31
Maine	1	1	3	1	6	10	16	10
Maryland	1	1	3	1	6	7	13	18
Massachusetts	3		2	1	6	8	14	16
Michigan	1		1		2	6	8	36
Minnesota	1		2		3	7	10	25
Mississippi	1		2		3	7	10	25
Missouri	1		1		2	4	6	41
Montana	1		1		2	9	11	22
Nebraska	3		2		5	3	8	36
Nevada	3		2		5	10	15	12
New Hampshire	1	1	3		5	7	12	20
New Jersey	2		2		4	9	13	18
New Mexico	1		1		2	3	5	47
New York	2		2		4	11	15	12
North Carolina	2		1		3	0	3	49
North Dakota	2		1		3	5	8	36
Oregon	3	1	3	1	8	12	20	3

(continued)

Table 2.1. Ranking of States by Planning Rigor and Content Requirements of Local Government, 2002 *(continued)*

State	Plan Mandated	State Land-Use Policy Basis	Strength of State Role	Internal Consistency Required	Structure Score	Total Elements	Total Score	Nelson-Lang Planning Index
Pennsylvania	1		2		3	7	10	25
Rhode Island	3	1	3	1	8	10	18	6
South Carolina	1		2		3	7	10	25
South Dakota	3		2		5	4	9	31
Tennessee	1		1		2	5	7	40
Texas	2		1		3	1	4	49
Utah	2		2		4	13	17	9
Vermont	1	1	3		5	13	18	7
Virginia	1		1		2	8	10	25
Washington	3	1	3	1	8	14	22	2
West Virginia	1		2		3	8	11	22
Wisconsin	1		1		2	4	6	41
Wyoming	1		1		2	3	5	47

Source: Adapted by Nelson and Lang (2009) from Meck (2002)

Note: Column definitions (for details on APA's approach, see Meck (2002)):

Plan Mandated—From Meck (2002), table 7.5: 3 = mandated plan; 2 = mandated plan if jurisdiction meets certain conditions (such as having a planning commission, having a certain size or growth rate, or other factors); 1 = optional, that is, plan simply being enabled

State Land-Use Policy Basis—From Meck (2002), table 7.5: 1 = yes, blank = no

Strength of State Role—From Meck (2002), table 7.5: 3 = strong (such as state review and approval of plans before being eligible for certain state programs); 2 = significant (such as state review and approval in an advisory capacity or limited, if any, loss of eligibility for certain state programs); 1 = weak (no state review)

Internal Consistency Required—From Meck (2002), table 7.5: 1 = yes; blank = no

Structure Score—Unweighted sum of the preceding columns

Total Elements—The number of elements mandated, mandated if conditions are met, or optional through enablement regardless of the rigor needed to address the element. (There are 20 standard elements considered: land use, growth limits, housing, economic development, agriculture/forest/open space land preservation, critical and sensitive areas, natural hazards, redevelopment, recreation, energy, air quality, transportation, community facilities, human services, community design, historic preservation, implementation, policy, visioning or public participation, and local coordination.)

Total Score—Sum of Structure Score and Total Elements

Nelson-Lang Planning Index—Rank of state by Total Score, with 1 being the highest and 49 (because of ties) the lowest

The index is useful for appreciating the kinds of planning efforts local governments may undertake in megapolitan areas, but it is not a definitive predictor of outcomes. For instance, Georgia ranked third when evaluated according to the Nelson-Lang Planning Index because of its planning mandates, state oversight, internal consistency, and required planning elements. Yet as a practical matter it is difficult to see tangible outcomes for the landscape since the Georgia Planning Act was adopted in 1989 because the state or its metropolitan areas have among the nation's highest levels of vehicular-based air pollution, water limitations have not been addressed, and the state is a leader in losing farmland to urban sprawl. On the other hand, Texas, at 49th, has seen little change in farmland among its megapolitan areas—indeed, it has seen an increase in the largest one (Greater Metroplex), while New Mexico, at 47th place, has ensured that its largest metropolitan area, Albuquerque, is among the nation's most contained as a result of local planning policies. Throughout the book, we refer to the Nelson-Lang Planning Index in our assessment of the individual megapolitan clusters and their megapolitan areas.

While the convergence of state and local planning efforts in a more common set of practices is a positive development, problems remain in the relationship between megapolitans and states that produce inefficiencies in how the United States grows. The biggest area of concern is state legislatures. State legislatures seem to have a very different agenda from the practical need to fix megapolitan areas. Robert Lang and Jennifer LeFurgy in their book *Boomburbs* (2007) found that local officials were fed up with legislatures that took up a set of wedge issues as their business rather than address the critical needs of cities. Interestingly, these comments came from both Republican and Democratic officeholders. The divide is mostly between those who are elected on the basis of how well they deliver local services (typically mayors and council members) and those who win elections by firing up a partisan base (more often state assemblypersons and senators).

While local officials in megapolitans look for partnership and support from the states in areas such as infrastructure improvement, the legislature may find its time taken up with bills to limit gay marriage, extend gun rights, or act on dozens of other hot-button issues. This was true even when the nation faced the worst economic downturn since the Great Depression. While global competitors invest in new ports, improved airports, and high-speed rail, American megapolitan areas choke on congestion. The frictions of movement that mostly go unaddressed reduce efficiency and drive up costs. The problems faced by the largest metropolitan areas are not even part of a national discussion. Yet the megapolitans account for more than 70 percent of the nation's gross domestic product, almost all its exports, and an equally large share of its innovation.

Most states also seem to have a rural-urban divide that may reduce the resources directed to megapolitan areas. In some cases the political gap between the big city and the small town is stark. There may be no better example of this divide than in Nevada. Even though the Las Vegas metropolitan area drives the state's economy and is home to nearly 73 percent of Nevada's population, it is on the short end of multiple political decisions that involve allocating state resources. The region's schools receive less funding per capita than the rest of the state, even though it has greater costs from providing instruction in multiple languages and teaching low-income students. Northern Nevada's branch of the state university—the University of Nevada, Reno—also receives far more funding per capita than the University of Nevada, Las Vegas. The list goes on and on, and every item on it is buttressed by a rationale that somehow justifies the differential expenditures, yet the net effect is the same: The state's emerging megapolitan area must do with less than its fair share even as it seeks to diversify Nevada's economy. The same process, with perhaps a bit less dramatically skewed results, is occurring in much of the United States.

The United States is an urban nation with a frontier ethos. This observation has been made by numerous observers and is perhaps best characterized in a book, *The Urban Wilderness* (1995), by Sam Bass Warner Jr. Warner shows that despite a parallel legacy of urbanization, the logic and imagery for U.S. development come from the wilderness. As Warner and others show, even the West began as an urban society. To this day, the region with the highest percentage of urban residents remains the West. But somehow this entire national project to build great cities and now megapolitan areas remains less quintessentially American than the yeoman family farm. Nations need myths, but it would be helpful if these did not come at the expense of solving problems and improving conditions in the places where the vast majority of people live.

3

DEFINING WHAT IS MEGAPOLITAN

In this chapter we explore the features of a new urban unit of analysis, the megapolitan area, and the grouping of such areas into megapolitan clusters. Megapolitan areas we consider to be bigger than existing metropolitan areas but smaller than the recently identified "megaregions" (Carbonell and Yaro 2005; Ross 2009). Lang and Dhavale (2005) use the term *megapolitan* to describe an extended urban area similar to a megaregion. However, in this chapter we characterize megapolitan areas as smaller and more narrowly defined units of analysis, and provide evaluative reasoning.

In our view, megapolitan areas are those with projected populations of more than four million people, anchored by at least one metropolitan area of more than one million people that is connected through current or projected commuting patterns with at least two and often several other metropolitan areas of more than about a quarter million people. Megapolitan areas are big, but not so large that they cannot be traversed by car in a day, round-trip—about 200 miles in distance. We also introduce megapolitan clusters, or groups of megapolitan areas characterized by a distance of no more than about 500 miles between the centers of their major metropolitan areas (each of more than one million population) that historically composed an economically similar region, such as the Great Lakes cluster.

The sense of a large-scale metropolitan convergence under way has been brought home forcefully by the merging of once distinct metropolitan areas into very large urban complexes. Such megapolitan areas have economic linkages, as demonstrated through evolving commuter patterns. Indeed, our megapolitan construct is similar to the Combined Statistical Area (CSA) of the U.S. Census as these areas may emerge by 2040; our construct is limited to just the largest ones. Table 3.1 shows the relationships among the Census Bureau's Metropolitan Statistical Areas (MSAs), CSAs, megapolitan areas, and megapolitan clusters.

The main criterion for a census-defined CSA is economic interdependence as evidenced by overlapping commuting patterns. The same holds true for megapolitans. Based on projections of commuting patterns, by the 2020 Census we should find that the Phoenix–Tucson and Washington, D.C.–Baltimore–Richmond, Virginia, areas qualify as CSAs. By then, several more metropolitan

Table 3.1. The Evolving Regional Hierarchy

Types	Descriptions	Examples
Metropolitan Statistical Area	An "urban area" or "principal city" with at least 50,000 people plus surrounding counties with a 25% employment interchange measure (EIM) in 2000	Pittsburgh, Denver
Combined Statistical Area	Two or more adjacent micro- and metropolitan areas that had an EIM of at least 15% in 2000	Washington, D.C.–Baltimore, Cleveland–Akron
Megapolitan area	By 2040, two or more metropolitan areas anchored by one metropolitan area of more than one million population plus at least two metropolitan areas of at least 250,000 population each, no more than 200 miles apart, that will have an EIM of at least 15% by 2040 based on our projections	Sun Corridor (Phoenix–Tucson), Chesapeake (Richmond–Washington, D.C.–Baltimore)
Megapolitan clusters	Large, connected networks of megapolitan areas that maintain environmental, cultural, and functional linkages	Carolina and Atlanta megapolitan areas composing the Piedmont megapolitan cluster

areas will have passed this threshold, and before mid-century all the megapolitan areas we have identified should officially be CSAs (Lang and Nelson 2006).

Generally, American megaregions (see Chapter 1) exhibit broad, common geophysical, climate, and cultural attributes but are not necessarily independent economic geographic units. Megapolitan areas and megapolitan clusters have a common economic foundation, as observed principally through commuting patterns.

This chapter begins with a background on metropolitan theory by covering the literature relevant to large-scale urban development. The analytic basis for megapolitans derives from theories that Lang and Knox (2007) categorize as the "new metropolis" thinking. The theory background is followed by a methods section that defines the terms in which megapolitans are measured. Next are selected case studies that test the theory and methods throughout the United States. The concluding section discusses the meaning of the development of megapolitans.

Metropolitan Evolution

The Metroplex Model

To say that megapolitan areas are "beyond the metroplex" means they exceed the size of a metroplex. The term *Metroplex* as a proper noun refers to the Dallas–Fort Worth, Texas, metroplex.

The metroplex is a precursor of today's megapolitan areas. A metroplex is a large, extended metropolitan area that has two or more key anchor urban cores, such as Dallas and Fort Worth. Unlike twin cities, such as Minneapolis and St. Paul, the anchor cities of a metroplex do not touch. Dallas and Fort Worth lie about 35 miles apart from downtown to downtown, 30 miles as the crow flies. Thus, the Metroplex was the first true megapolitan area.

The Dallas–Fort Worth region, the first metropolitan area to join two relatively distant urban cores, has an instructive history. The two regions were long bitter rivals that competed for business. What brought the region together was the federal government. First, the census found that Dallas and Fort Worth had suburbs that so overlapped and interpenetrated that they formed one statistical region. Then, in 1964, when Dallas and Forth Worth both sought federal aid to improve their airports, the Federal Aviation Administration contended that the improved airports would be too close together and recommended that the region build one large airport at the midpoint between Dallas and Fort Worth. And so, with its runways located right on the county line, the Dallas–Fort Worth airport was born.

The Dallas–Fort Worth region then began to think regionally about other issues, including economic development. It first tried marketing itself as "North Texas," but focus groups revealed that most people associated the name with places such as Amarillo and the Texas Panhandle, so the label "Metroplex" was developed. It is meant to imply that Dallas and Fort Worth are not twin cities but rather proximate places that are joined across an urban complex—or metroplex. Multiple metroplexes have now sprung up around the United States, and the scale of many considerably exceeds that of the progenitor Dallas–Fort

Worth Metroplex, but they are characterized by much the same connectivity. In the 1960s, Dallas and Fort Worth were clearly converging, as were Washington, D.C., and Baltimore two decades later. Today, regions with more distant urban cores, such as Phoenix and Tucson, Tampa and Orlando, and San Antonio and Austin, are exhibiting the same pattern, only on a more massive scale.

Urban Realms

Within metropolitan areas there is another phenomenon emerging: urban realms. Until the mid-20th century, urban and metropolitan form could safely be conceptualized in terms of the outcomes of competition for land and the ecological processes of congregation and segregation, all pivoting tightly around a dominant central business district and transportation hub (Figure 3.1.a). During the middle decades of the 20th century, however, U.S. metropolises were unbound by the combination of increased automobile use, massive federal outlays on highway construction, and federal mortgage insurance programs created in the 1930s that facilitated lending for home purchases on long-term contacts with small down payments (Checkoway 1980; Harvey 1985; Lake 1995). The result was a massive spurt of city building, the evolution of dispersed, polycentric spatial structure, and the emergence of urban realms (Figure 3.1.b).

Initially, the shift to an expanded polycentric metropolis was most pronounced in the northeastern United States, and Gottmann captured the moment with his conceptualization of the megalopolis. It was not long, however, before observers noted the change elsewhere. Peter Muller (1976) was among the first to note the emergence of a new type of outer city. James E. Vance Jr. (1977) proposed that major metropolitan areas in the United States, such as Los Angeles, New York, and San Francisco, had grown so decentralized that they had become a series of semiautonomous subregions, or "urban realms."

Vance's (1964) basis for identifying different realms within metropolitan areas rests on several criteria. The first is the overall size of the region: the bigger the metropolis, the more plentiful and differentiated the realms. Next is an area's terrain and topography. Physical features such as mountains, bays, and rivers often serve to delimit realms by directing the spread of urbanization into distinct, geographically defined areas. The third variable is the amount and type of economic activity contained within it. Urban realms can also be distinguished by either an overriding economic unification, such as that seen with Silicon

Valley in California, or shared employment centers, such as are identified by commuter sheds. Finally, the regional geography of transportation, as originally recognized by Homer Hoyt (1939), also plays a role in separating urban realms. This process began with trolley cars but is now centered on interstate highways, in particular metropolitan beltways. Beltways can either define the boundary of an area, as reflected in the expression "inside the Washington beltway," or unify a realm, as in the case of the LBJ Corridor north of downtown Dallas.

According to Vance, urban realms come about naturally as a function of the growth of cities; the city changes structurally as a collection of realms and grows "one stage beyond that of a metropolis" (1964, 78). The core-periphery relationship weakens as realms become more equal. The basic organization of the region becomes more cooperative as the shared urban and cultural identity of the urban realms creates what Vance calls a "sympolis" rather than a metropolis.

These concepts are illustrated by the relationship between Orange County and Los Angeles. Orange County is clearly part of Greater Los Angeles, but it also maintains a distinct and semiautonomous identity as the South Coast. Orange County contributes significantly to the region's larger economy but for the most part does not compete with Los Angeles. Industries such as automotive design, with several companies found at the Irvine Spectrum, a master planned high-tech office park in the center of the county, show this pattern. The auto companies chose the Spectrum for access to California trends and regard Orange County as "the next capital of cool" (Sklar 2003). Orange County's association with Los Angeles helps makes this once sleepy suburban county cool, and the larger Southern California region gains from the additional economic activity.

Urban realms have their own subregional identities—in the Los Angeles region, for example, the South Coast (or Orange County) and the Inland Empire (Riverside and San Bernardino Counties). The realms around Los Angeles are so distinct that the South Coast and the Inland Empire have their own subregional newspapers and airports. On a smaller but emerging scale, a place such as the East Valley of Phoenix, Arizona (with such major suburbs as Mesa, Tempe, Chandler, and Gilbert), has its own newspaper and will soon have a separate national airport from Phoenix's. Finally, urban realms show up in business names, such as South Coast Plaza, Inland Empire National Bank, or the *East Valley Tribune*.

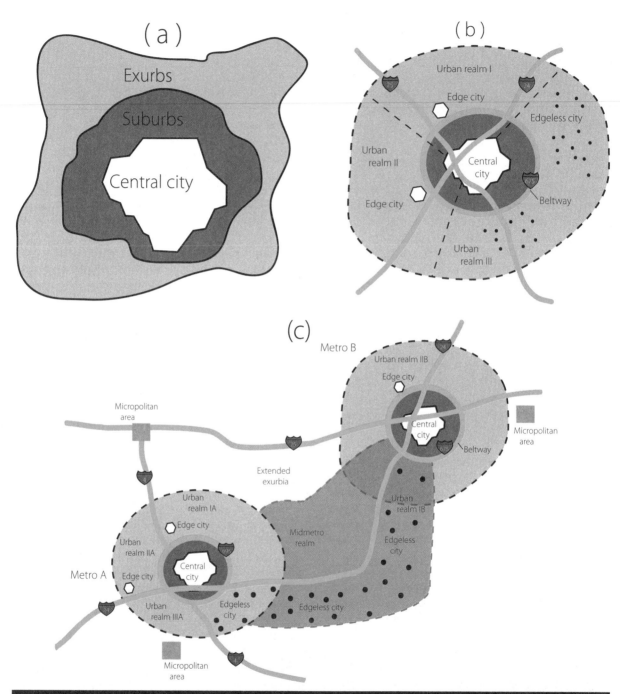

Figure 3.1. The development and evolution of American metropolitan areas follow reasonably predictable paths. **a.** The urban form starts as organized tightly around a dominant central business district and transportation hub. **b.** With growth and improvements in transportation leading to highways serving automobiles, urban areas since about 1950 have evolved into dispersed, polycentric forms, accompanied by the rise of urban realms. **c.** The merging of metropolitan areas over time into essentially one megapolitan unit
Credit: Robert E. Lang

Lang and Hall (2007) synthesize thinking on urban realms and offer four realm types, based on a mix of social characteristics, built densities, and development age. The four types are:

Urban core realms—the original places of substantial 19th- and 20th-century development, including the region's major principal city and downtown.
Favored quarter realms—the most affluent wedge of a metropolitan area, containing upscale communities, luxury shopping, and high-end office districts.
Maturing suburban realms—the areas of substantial late 20-century and early 21st-century development that are rapidly filling in and will ultimately extend the edges of the metropolis.
Emerging exurban realms—extended, rapidly growing, lower-density spaces that exhibit leapfrog development and will not be full extensions of the main metropolitan development for decades to come. Yet commuting from these realms often serves as the link between metropolitan areas that leads to the formation of census-defined CSAs.

The relationship between and among these realm types plays a role in determining the overall megapolitan dynamic. Favored quarters, such as Southern California's South Coast (Orange County), are often job-rich, but have expensive housing. A less affluent maturing suburban realm, such as the Inland Empire (Riverside and San Bernardino Counties), can develop a dependence on the favored quarter. Thus, an important traffic pattern in Southern California is the commute between these two suburban realms. In fact, one of the biggest bottlenecks in the region's freeway system is along a mountain pass (known locally as "the 91") that divides the two realms. Without alluding to it, Peter Gordon, Harry W. Richardson, and Yeol Choi (1992) characterize the Los Angeles basin as a series of urban realms, each serving a population base of around one-half to one million residents, with about half to twice as many jobs centered in each.

Exurban realms also serve a critical role in megapolitan formation. The "mid" exurban realms that emerge between two proximate metropolitan areas lie in the crosshairs of regional growth. Figure 3.1.c graphically depicts the new megapolitan form based on extended urban realms, including the development of mid-corridor realms. It is these places, where commuters go in both directions and provide the linkages, based on

a shared economy, that join metropolitan areas. These mid-exurban realms are of principal interest in this chapter. We focus specifically on the counties that make up these realms to see if their divided commuter patterns indicate an emerging CSA. The methods section details how commuting data were used to predict megapolitan formation.

The New Metropolitan Form

Paralleling the development of urban realm theory were models of a new metropolitan form (Lang and Knox 2007). These concepts captured the ever expanding scale and fracturing nature of the late 20th-century metropolis. In 1962, a now obscure urban thinker, Jerome Pickard, took Jean Gottmann's megalopolis idea a step further and created a national map of "urban regions." Pickard (1966) then followed up with an analysis of how U.S. migration patterns were expanding these regions. In 1970, Pickard projected growth in urban regions to the year 2000 (Figure 1.11). With remarkable precision, Pickard predicted the basic frame of the nation's current pattern of urbanization. He also cleanly delineated an urban region from a metropolitan area. An urban region, according to Pickard (1970), is "not necessarily a contiguous 'super city' but rather it is a region of high concentrations of urban activities and urbanized population" (154). From even his original work on urban regions, Pickard (1966, 3; emphasis in original) argued that urban regions were not simply an extended city:

> Our largest urban region, sometimes called "Megalopolis," extends along the northern Atlantic seaboard from Portland, Maine to Washington, DC. A popular misconception has led to calling this a "city 500 miles long." It most definitely is *not* a single city, but a region of concentrated urbanism—a continuous zone of metropolises, cities, towns and exurban settlement within which one is never far from a city.

Pickard (1970, 154) also noted that "urban regions have evolved during the automobile era form multiple urban nodes that expanded very rapidly toward regional cities." By Pickard's definition, an urban region has a total population of one million and an average population density at least three times the national average (Pickard 1962).

Pickard was indeed a seer, but he was not alone in noting the role that postwar metropolitan expansion played in changing basic regional form. Friedmann and Miller

(1965) crafted the concept of the "urban field," suggesting that the reach of the largest central cities was upward of 100 miles. Blumenfeld (1986) envisioned an "extended metropolis" composed of urban areas stitched together by vast exurban commuting sheds. These views, however, were merely extensions of the *New York Times* journalist Auguste Spectorsky's (1955) pioneering observations that modern transportation technology allowed some downtown Manhattan workers to live in eastern Pennsylvania and traverse the entire state of New Jersey in commuting to and from work daily. Nelson (1992) and Nelson, Dawkins, and Sanchez (2007) observe that by the end of the 20th century, the exurban landscape (as they define it) was home to about a quarter of all Americans and accounted for a fifth of the nation's growth in the 1990s.

Recognizing these spatial trends, Peirce Lewis (1983) coined the term "galactic metropolis" to capture the disjointed and decentralized urban landscapes of late 20th-century North America. To Lewis, the galactic metropolis is vast, with varying sized urban centers, subcenters, and satellites. It is also fragmented and multinodal, with mixed densities and unexpected juxtapositions of form and function. Looking at U.S. cities established after 1915, Lewis found that all had evolved in the "galactic" form rather than with a traditional nucleated morphology (Lewis 1995). This pattern applied to all metropolitan areas regardless of their age.

The megapolitan spatial model used in this study extends elements of Gottmann's, Vance's, Pickard's, and Lewis's thinking. When the notion was first proposed several decades ago that super, multimetropolitan regions were emerging, the focus clearly lay on the vast physical extent of development. We now add a vital functional component to this analysis—a strong economic interdependency as defined by the U.S. Census Bureau. In the 1960s and 1970s, commuting was still mostly confined to a relatively limited set of core cities and counties. But the explosion of suburban and exurban employment into edge cities and even edgeless cities (Lang 2003) projected commuter sheds into a much wider hinterland. The metropolitan space that now exhibits economic interdependence has grown exponentially since the 1960s. The physical convergence of large regions, apparent even in the early post–World War II period, now has an accompanying functional reality. By the middle of the 21st century a decades-long process of decentralization and metropolitan interpenetration is expected to result in functionally connected spaces that dwarf today's big regions.

Metropolitan and Megapolitan Commuting

Many millions of Americans live in one metropolitan area but work in another. The prevalence of this trend has been growing steadily since the interstate highway system was completed in the 1980s. It became so prevalent by the end of the 1980s, for instance, that the Census Bureau created a new metropolitan category, the Consolidated Metropolitan Statistical Area, or CMSA. This geographic designation was included in the 1990 and 2000 Census tabulations.

In 2003, however, the Census Bureau reconsidered the role of commuting in forming networks of metropolitan areas. The upshot was a wholesale change in how regions are defined (Frey et al. 2006) based on new commuting formulas. The idea of a consolidated area in which one core dominated was thrown out and replaced with the concept that multicenter regions could overlap and share commuter sheds. The updated model opens the door to even larger regional networks with a daisy chain of overlapping interdependencies, which provides the basis of megapolitan areas.

Urban economies are successful if they do many things. One is to capitalize on the economies of agglomeration. Another is to capitalize on comparative advantages. A third is to create efficient means of connecting them to larger landscapes in ways that facilitate both agglomeration economies and comparative advantages. Arthur O'Sullivan (2007) observes that there is a fourth ingredient that is uniquely 21st century: high-quality social interaction. Indeed, O'Sullivan argues that not only have place-centric models run their course, so also have deconcentration models (in which jobs follow people into the suburbs and beyond). The economy is now becoming homocentric. This means that because of technology, flexible working conditions, and so forth, people have unprecedented residential location options. But they also depend on social interaction. For instance, the 1990s saw the advent of Internet-based shopping, which some thought would doom the retail sector. Others foresaw the rise of telecommuting as the antidote to traffic congestion and pollution through reducing work-based trips and the demand for office space. Yet Nelson (2006) has found that more retail and office space per capita exists today than in the 1990s. Census data also reveal that urbanized land area density is rising for the first time in half a century. We speculate that regardless of technological advances—or perhaps because of them—people pursue personal interaction.

There is another feature. As people have congregated into settlements that have become cities and metropolitan regions, transmetropolitan networks have emerged. While people may shop and receive personal services close to home, and certainly in the same urbanized area where they live, their livelihood is less bounded but nonetheless constrained spatially. The principal source of that constraint is mobility—being able to conduct business efficiently. A growing literature is showing that this is done in situations where person-to-person exchanges are possible, even though most actual business may be conducted on the telephone, by e-mail, or over the Internet.[1]

To understand why this is so, we turn to the location and work behavior of information workers. Richard Bolan and Peng Xu (2004) asked, Do information workers locate in concentrated fashion or in a highly dispersed fashion? Do they congregate in central downtown areas or in edge city areas, or do they disperse randomly throughout a metropolitan area? Their central findings are worthy of repeating here:

> The study has reinforced the notion that information workers thrive best on proximity to other information workers to a significant degree but with the substantial growth and dynamic of the 1990's, proximity is a relative characteristic mediated by limits of land markets. Thus, the workplaces of information workers were more dispersed in 2000 than in 1990, but in that suburban movement, such workplaces tended to be clustered. Overall, the speculative thinking during the 1990's that information technology would change the shape, form and function of the contemporary city has not been borne out in this study. Indeed, there seems to be some reinforcement of traditional urban form. (Bolan and Xu 2004, 92)

This brings us to the supposition that despite technological advances, economies of agglomeration remain important, but across a larger space than conventionally perceived. How large? That is the research question to be addressed.

The Census Bureau sees commuting patterns as the key variable to identify an economically integrated space. It has used this measure since metropolitan areas were first officially defined by the bureau, in 1949. Commuting is taken as a proxy for a host of other variables, such as retail and housing markets. For example, if job losses occur in one metropolitan county, then the residents of a neighboring metropolitan county that commute to these jobs may be displaced. It will also affect their ability to purchase goods and services and afford housing. Commuting therefore reveals much larger patterns of economic integration. These relationships at the metropolitan scale should hold for megapolitans as well.

Data showing commutes of 50 and 100 miles each way indicate there are several million people who journey to work between big megapolitan metros. According to the Census Bureau, the number of these "extreme commuters" (or those who travel 90 or more miles to work) doubled between 1990 and 2005, to about 3.4 million. In addition, the fastest growing commuting departure time is between 5 and 6 a.m., indicating a boom in long journeys to work (Naughton 2006). The percentage of people who participate in a regional economy without technically living in its officially designated metropolitan area is correspondingly rising (Morrill, Cromartie, and Hart 1999). But one question the Census Bureau does not ask is the frequency of commutes, or the number of days in an average week that a worker reports to the place of employment. It may be that as commuting distances grow, the number of trips drops (Lang and Nelson 2007). Although the 2007–2009 recession likely dampened some extreme commuting, time will tell whether it will rebound.

The changing nature of work is also fueling the emergence of megapolitan areas. In many fields, workers need not be present in the office five days a week. The practice of "hoteling," whereby employees "visit" work infrequently and mostly work at home or on the road, is common in high-tech firms and will soon spread to other sectors. This work mode gives people the flexibility to live at a great distance from their workplace, in remote exurbs or even in a neighboring metropolitan area. Over the next several decades the very nature of metropolitan connectivity is likely to shift from a situation in which only local workers contribute to an economy to a condition in which a significant share of local jobs is held by people living outside the region. The megapolitan research anticipates this change by analyzing the scale at which the 21st-century economy will emerge. The shift also reflects the changing nature of metropolitan form.

Methods

The Census Bureau has very specific criteria for defining regions. As noted above, the most important criterion is commuting. The bureau provides population projections to the mid-21st century but does not extend its current geography forward to reflect new growth. Yet the bureau does provide a set of rules that allows researchers to (mostly) construct such a geography that conforms in rough approximation to the federal government's officially defined metropolitan spaces. In a nutshell, that is what we do in this study.

Here, we explore potential future linkages between metropolitan areas by examining the commuting patterns in mid-corridor urban realms. Because the Census Bureau uses county commuting data, we identify the key counties that approximate these realms. For example, in the case of the Phoenix–Tucson megapolitan area (known also as the Sun Corridor), the key county is Pinal, which lies between Maricopa County (Phoenix) and Pima County (Tucson). After looking at multiple regions around the country to test for linking counties where future commuter patterns would predict convergence, we adduce 10 case studies here to explore this process of change in more detail.

Our method locates key counties between metropolitan areas that lie 50–200 miles apart core to core, checks current commuting patterns in these places, determines the direction and velocity of changes in commuting patterns there, and examines local development conditions and projected growth to predict future commuting. If these key counties show (1) a commuter pattern well on its way to the 15 percent employment interchange measure (EIM) with two proximate metropolitan areas or (2) have high projected growth rates that will produce spillover commuting patterns likely to generate a 15 percent EIM by 2040, then the two adjacent metropolitan areas form a megapolitan area. We now review our method in detail.

One of our former doctoral students, Dwayne Guthrie (now on the faculty at Catholic University), worked with us to refine and apply our analytic method. Much of the foregoing is attributable to him. A rigorous methodology was developed to determine the geographic extent of future metropolitan-scale commuter sheds. This was based on county-to-county Internal Revenue Service (IRS) migration data, principally to evaluate metropolitan connectivity.

Lawrence Frank (1994) demonstrated the effects of urban form on travel behavior, which is based on factors such as employment density at the census tract level. At the urban scale, it is the concentration of population and jobs that creates the sense of space associated with urban environments. Methodologies that examine only residential density do not accurately depict the extent of urban areas and reflect only one end of home-based

work trips. Guthrie's (2007) dissertation methodology expanded this approach.

Guthrie (2007) took advantage of the Longitudinal Employer-Household Dynamics (LEHD) program, which is formulating cooperative arrangements with federal, state, and private sector sources to provide detailed job data necessary for understanding commuter flows at the subcounty level. The primary data source for this effort is the quarterly workforce report required of employers as part of the federal unemployment insurance program. LEHD data were used to evaluate metropolitan-scale connectivity, as described further in the following section.

Urban areas, or realms, can be aggregated into metropolitan-scale commuter sheds. Guthrie recognized that modern metropolitan areas are polycentric in form, and thus set out to determine net worker inflow and outflow for each county, summing flows to identify commuter sheds based on polycentricity. As a general rule of thumb, researchers have identified a 100-mile radius as indicative of metropolitan commuter sheds (Friedmann and Miller 1965; Sudjic 1992; Davis, Nelson, and Dueker 1994). Nelson, Drummond, and Sawicki (1995) extended this analysis to show long-distance commuting sheds of up to 200 miles for regular though not daily travel, or truck-based freight traffic from manufacturing firms located in exurban areas to metropolitan markets. The expected geographic pattern for metropolitan commuter sheds should be similar to CSAs but larger than most metropolitan planning organization areas.

Using available data, Guthrie developed a composite list of projected population plus jobs in 2030 for each CSA and MSA in the United States (using the Office of Management and Budget's 2005 definitions). Multiple GIS files were downloaded from various federal government websites for use in his analysis. The GIS files were decompressed, edited to remove areas outside the continental United States, and converted to the Albers equal-area projection (U.S. Geological Survey continental) to provide consistent spatial alignment of the various data layers. Data sets used in this analysis include Counties, CSAs, MSAs, Urbanized Areas, and the National Highway Planning Network line segments. Data were then edited and aggregated to match the Woods and Poole geography, which we use in this book to project megapolitan area growth and changes in key social and economic respects.

Past (1990 and 2000) and projected population, median age, and jobs (i.e., employment by place of work) for each county in the continental United States were obtained from Woods and Poole Economics. Additional exogenous variables were used in the logistic regression models to develop the spatial parameters such as gross regional product (GRP) and a proprietary Woods and Poole "Wealth Index" for each county in the continental United States. The Wealth Index is "a measure of the relative total personal income per capita, weighted by source of income.... Relative income per capita is weighted positively for a relatively high proportion of income from dividends, interest and rent, and negatively for a relatively high proportion of income from transfer payments. Since dividends, interest, and rent income are a good indicator of assets, the Woods & Poole Wealth Index attempts to measure relative wealth" (Woods & Poole Economics 2010, 33–34).

The Census Bureau's long-form responses on commuting patterns provide data for the bureau's County-to-County Worker Flow files. We thus have detailed data on workers (16+ years old) and the county in which they worked during the week prior to the census date. In addition to indicating journey-to-work patterns, the data are summarized by place of work to yield the number of jobs in each county. A concise, county-level summary of the worker flow data is available from the Census Bureau under the title "Estimated Daytime Population and Employment-Residence Ratios" (U.S. Bureau of the Census 2002).

A key metric for analysis is the concept of net worker exchange, which builds on the daytime population analysis. In terms of complexity, net worker exchange occupies the middle ground between the simple concept of jobs-housing balance and the complex commuter-flow data needed for the classic four-step computerized transportation model (Meyer and Miller 2001). A static picture of jobs and housing units in a community has limited utility because of dynamic commuting patterns. For example, Alexandria, Virginia, has a balanced jobs-housing ratio, yet there is significant commuting because many service jobs are filled by workers who cannot afford to live in Alexandria and many of the higher-income residents of Alexandria have jobs in the greater Washington, D.C., area.

Guthrie observed that the Census Bureau's core-based statistical areas are essentially conceived as concentric rings, with counties used as boundaries to delineate the geographic area either inside or outside the statistical area. In contrast, metropolitan commuter sheds might include multiple employment centers in a large geographic area in which counties form "seams" or "links" between trip attractors. Because of the different concepts, metropolitan

commuter shed evaluations are not concerned with the details of specific county-to-county flows but with the overall balance between worker inflows and outflows.

Net worker exchange, illustrated in Figure 3.2, is a useful measure for identifying the geographic extent of commuter sheds. For each county, worker outflow is subtracted from worker inflow to yield the net worker exchange. To reveal the extent of the commuter shed, the net worker flow for each county is summed until the counties that function as employment centers (i.e., net inflow of workers) are balanced with the counties that serve as bedroom communities (i.e., net outflow of workers).

As shown in Figure 3.2, the number of nonresident workers (i.e., inflow) is derived by subtracting resident workers (i.e., those working within their county of residence) from the total number of workplace jobs. For consistency in deriving the commuter shed balance, inflow workers are assigned a positive number and outflow workers are assigned a negative number.

A large database was created for Guthrie's analysis. It included all 3,076 "counties" in the Woods and Poole database[2] plus 159 variables for population, employment, economic, and socioeconomic characteristics, with the large number of variables partly a result of the several time periods studied for each variable type. For example, for most variables, historical data for 1990, 2000, and 2005 are available, plus projected data for 2010, 2015, 2020, 2025, and 2030.

After the net worker exchange database was created, aggregate comparisons were made of worker inflow and outflow for each of the projection years. Conceptually, the aggregate number of workers for the entire continental United States should roughly match the number of workplace jobs. Also, the number of workers that leave their county of residence for work (i.e., outflow) should be approximately the same as the number of nonresident workers that flow into another county.

Figure 3.2 illustrates key relationships and the components used to derive the net worker exchange for each county. We start with population (1) and estimate those who work (2). For each county, worker outflow (3) is subtracted from worker inflow (5) to yield the net worker exchange. Not all workers occupy building space, so a further adjustment is made (6), which feeds into the total jobs projection (7). To reveal the extent of the commuter shed, the net worker flow for each county is summed until the counties that function as employment centers (i.e., net inflow of workers) are balanced

Net Worker Exchange Model

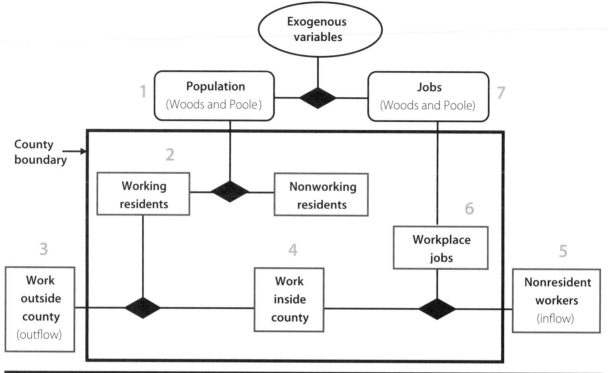

Figure 3.2. Net worker exchange model
Credit: Guthrie (2007)

with the counties that serve as bedroom communities (i.e., net outflow of workers).

The diamond shapes represent individual county adjustments that account for demographic changes over time. The net worker exchange model includes three demographic adjustment calculations that extrapolate past trends (based on actual 1990, 2000, and 2005 data) into the future. These demographic adjustments derive ratios for workers to population, outflow workers to resident workers (i.e., outflow percentage), and Census Transportation Planning Package (CTPP) workplace jobs to Bureau of Economic Analysis (BEA) jobs.

The first demographic adjustment accounts for the changing ratio of workers to total population from 1990 to 2000. For larger counties, Guthrie used American Community Survey data to derive a trend line forecast of the worker percentage for 2010, 2015, 2020, 2025,

and 2030. A similar process was followed to project outflow worker percentage, which is the second demographic adjustment. As illustrated in the net worker exchange model diagram, subtracting the number of outflow workers from the total number of working residents yields the number of people who work in their county of residence.

A third demographic adjustment accounts for the difference between CTPP jobs used in the daytime population methodology published by the Census Bureau and the typically larger number of jobs reported by Woods and Poole. Using actual county data for 1990 and 2000, Guthrie used a logarithmic curve to project the ratio of CTPP to BEA jobs for each county in 2010, 2015, 2020, 2025, and 2030.

The five major analytic processes Guthrie used are described below. First, a logistic regression yielding predicted employment centers was applied to counties with a positive net worker exchange in 2030 and was used to indicate the likelihood of an individual county becoming a future statistical area. The model included independent variables for workplace jobs, nonresident workers (inflow), inbound worker share, and GRP.

Second, a logistic regression ranking of the bedroom communities model was used to predict the likelihood of an individual county becoming part of a statistical area by applying a logistic regression to counties with negative net worker exchange in 2030. The four independent variables included in this model were place of residence of workers, outflow percentage, outflow of workers (absolute), and the Woods and Poole Wealth Index.

The next three analytic steps evaluated the net worker exchange major commuter sheds. Tasks included (1) using SPSS software to create a case summary report that sums net worker exchange by statistical area in the year 2030; (2) using SPSS software to create and save in the database a predicted probability score for bedroom counties (i.e., those with net outflow of workers in 2030) using the logistic regression model described above; and (3) saving the SPSS database as a DBF file, switching to ArcMap, and joining the DBF file to the shapefile of Woods and Poole county equivalents.

A key ingredient of Guthrie's analysis is county-level migration data, which are available from the IRS. Files are organized by state, with detailed data for each county indicating both inflows and outflows of the number of returns and exemptions. The number of returns is roughly equivalent to census data on households and the number of exemptions is an approximation of persons. By comparing addresses from one year to the next, the IRS figures the number of nonmigrants and county-level migration data.

As Guthrie notes, IRS migration data are useful in two distinct ways. First, migration data help identify "linking counties" that form the seams between metropolitan areas. For example, in Florida Corridor, Polk County functions as a linking county between the dominant metropolitan areas of Orlando on the east and Tampa on the west. A second utility for IRS migration data is to help evaluate the geographic extent of a megapolitan area. Households tend to migrate over time from a more urban location to either suburban or exurban locations, with the primary wage-earner often retaining his or her same job (Davis, Nelson, and Dueker 1994). Therefore, IRS data should identify outlying counties that are connected by intramegapolitan migration.

The importance of movement in understanding urban-scale development (Hillier 1999) was the genesis of the worker flow index Guthrie developed to characterize multiple metropolitan commuting networks. To help visualize the movement of workers and define megapolitan-scale development, Guthrie created a worker flow index for each county in the continental United States. The index takes into account the share of workers flowing in and out of a county, as well as the absolute number of workers coming and going. In combination, the outflow and inflow percentages help reduce, or normalize, the amount of variation in worker outflow plus inflow.

On the other hand, Guthrie's bedroom communities model (i.e., net outbound workers) only indicates relative rankings, or scores, for the selection of additional counties needed to achieve commuter shed balance. The bedroom communities logistic regression model for counties found a negative worker exchange in 2030 that successfully increased the overall percentage correct from 56.3 percent to 80.4 percent.

Guthrie's analysis (2007) extended to 2030 and provided statistical reasoning for 22 megapolitan areas. Extending the analysis to 2040 found 23 megapolitan areas, which are the ones we assess throughout this book (Figure P.1).

4

THE RURAL-MEGAPOLITAN CONTINUUM

It goes without saying that megapolitan clusters and their megapolitan areas are among the most urbanized and least likely to be considered "rural." However, as Jean Gottmann observed in *Megalopolis* (1961), megapolitan areas include extensive rural landscapes, along with lagging as well as leading areas. This chapter develops the construct of a rural-megapolitan continuum. We begin by reviewing the U.S. Department of Agriculture's "rural-urban continuum" and "urban influence" constructs. We then adapt those constructs to create the rural-megapolitan continuum, principally as a way to illustrate how megapolitan clusters and megapolitan areas differ from America's remaining landscapes.[1]

The Rural-Urban Continuum

The USDA has developed a set of Rural-Urban Continuum Codes that allows analysts to distinguish among metropolitan counties by the population size of their metropolitan area, and nonmetropolitan counties by their degree of urbanization and proximity to a metropolitan area. The metropolitan and nonmetropolitan categories have been subdivided into three metropolitan and six nonmetropolitan groups, respectively, resulting in nine Rural-Urban Classification Codes. The codes allow researchers working with county data to break such data into finer residential groups beyond a simple metropolitan-nonmetropolitan distinction.

All U.S. counties and their county equivalents are classified by the USDA according to their official metropolitan-nonmetropolitan status, published by the Office of Management and Budget (OMB) in June 2003 and based on the 2000 Census data. Metropolitan counties are categorized by the population size of the Metropolitan Statistical Area in which they are assigned. Nonmetropolitan counties are classified based on the total size of their urban population. Within the three urban categories, nonmetropolitan counties are sorted by whether they have some functional adjacency to a metropolitan area or areas, as determined by the USDA. A nonmetropolitan county is considered adjacent to a metropolitan area if it physically adjoins one or more metropolitan areas and at least 2 percent of its employed labor force commutes to the central county of a metropolitan area.

Nonmetropolitan counties that do not meet these criteria are classed as nonadjacent.[2] Table 4.1 summarizes the rural-urban coding scheme, while Figure 4.1 shows the resulting national map. The 2003 rural-urban continuum scheme assigned 1,089 counties to the metropolitan category and 2,052 counties to the nonmetropolitan category. (Independent cities of Virginia were merged with their counties of origin.)

Urban Influence Codes

A variant of the rural-urban continuum developed by the USDA is the urban influence construct.[3] Generally, it is based on the notion that geographic context has a significant effect on an area's development. That is, economic opportunities are associated with an area's size and its access to larger economies. Access to larger economies providing information, communication, trade, and finance resources helps a smaller economy connect to markets. The construct is comparable to central place theory in understanding regional economic structure. The USDA's 2003 Urban Influence Codes assigns 3,141 counties, county equivalents, and independent cities to 12 groups (Table 4.2). Although it has more categories than the rural-urban continuum scheme, the urban influence scheme has only two categories for metropolitan counties—location in metropolitan areas of more than one million residents ("large" metropolitan areas) or location in areas of less than one million residents ("small" metropolitan areas)—and 10 categories for nonmetropolitan counties. The nonmetropolitan areas are sorted into three groups based on their classification as a Micropolitan Statistical Area and their adjacency to large or small metropolitan areas, plus seven more groups into which are placed all other nonmetropolitan counties based on their adjacency to core-based metropolitan or micropolitan areas and whether they have their own urban place of at least 2,500 residents. Figure 4.2 illustrates how the Urban Influence Codes are applied nationally.

Table 4.1. USDA 2003 Rural-Urban Continuum Codes

Code and Description

Metropolitan Counties

1 Counties in metropolitan areas of 1 million+ population

2 Counties in metropolitan areas of 250,000 to 1 million population

3 Counties in metropolitan areas of fewer than 250,000 population

Nonmetropolitan Counties

4 Urban population of 20,000 or more, adjacent to a metropolitan area

5 Urban population of 20,000 or more, not adjacent to a metropolitan area

6 Urban population of 2,500 to 19,999, adjacent to a metropolitan area

7 Urban population of 2,500 to 19,999, not adjacent to a metropolitan area

8 Completely rural or less than 2,500 urban population, adjacent to a metropolitan area

9 Completely rural or less than 2,500 urban population, not adjacent to a metropolitan area

Source: U.S. Department of Agriculture

Table 4.2. USDA 2003 Urban Influence Codes

Code and Description

Metropolitan Counties

1 In large metropolitan area of 1+ million residents

2 In small metropolitan area of less than 1 million residents

Nonmetropolitan Counties

3 Micropolitan area adjacent to large metropolitan area

4 Noncore adjacent to large metropolitan area

5 Micropolitan area adjacent to small metropolitan area

6 Noncore adjacent to small metropolitan area and contains a town of at least 2,500 residents

7 Noncore adjacent to small metropolitan area and does not contain a town of at least 2,500 residents

8 Micropolitan area not adjacent to a metropolitan area

9 Noncore adjacent to micropolitan area and contains a town of at least 2,500 residents

10 Noncore adjacent to micropolitan area and does not contain a town of at least 2,500 residents

11 Noncore not adjacent to metropolitan or micropolitan area and contains a town of at least 2,500 residents

12 Noncore not adjacent to metropolitan or micropolitan area and does not contain a town of at least 2,500 residents

Source: U.S. Department of Agriculture

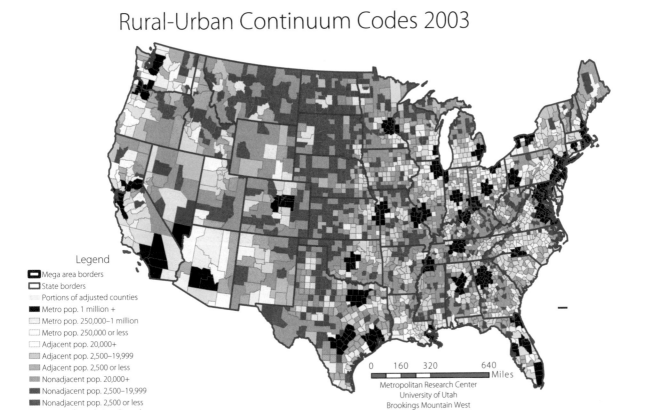

Rural-Urban Continuum Codes 2003

Legend
- Mega area borders
- State borders
- Portions of adjusted counties
- Metro pop. 1 million +
- Metro pop. 250,000–1 million
- Metro pop. 250,000 or less
- Adjacent pop. 20,000+
- Adjacent pop. 2,500–19,999
- Adjacent pop. 2,500 or less
- Nonadjacent pop. 20,000+
- Nonadjacent pop. 2,500–19,999
- Nonadjacent pop. 2,500 or less

Some county boundaries adjusted

0   160   320   640 Miles

Metropolitan Research Center
University of Utah
Brookings Mountain West
May 2010
Figure by Grace Bjarnson

Figure 4.1. USDA 2003 rural-urban continuum map of the United States
Credit: Adapted from USDA (2003)

Rural-Megapolitan Continuum

We combine elements of both spatially based assignment schemes and simplify them to create a *rural-megapolitan continuum*. Our purpose is principally to help understand differences in scale between megapolitan areas and the rest of the nation. The construct is simple: the closer a county is to the center of metropolitan areas, and the larger the metropolitan area, the more apt it is to be part of the network of metropolitan, micropolitan, and nonmetropolitan areas that creates the engine of economic activity alluded to in earlier chapters. Our rural-megapolitan continuum borrows from both the rural-urban continuum and the urban influence coding approach. In particular, the three metropolitan size

categories used in the USDA's rural-urban continuum are combined with the micropolitan areas adjacent to metropolitan areas, other noncore counties also adajcent to metropolitan areas, and all others. Our rural-megapolitan continuum is described in Table 4.3 and illustrated in Figure 4.3, which also shows megapolitan boundaries.

Table 4.4 reports the distribution of counties, population, and shares of population within classes of the rural-metropolitan continuum and in relation to total 2010 U.S. population. It is no surprise that megapolitan areas account for a very large share of the total population of the nation in metropolitan areas of more than one million people—73 percent. Yet in every other rural-megapolitan category, the nonmegapolitan landscape

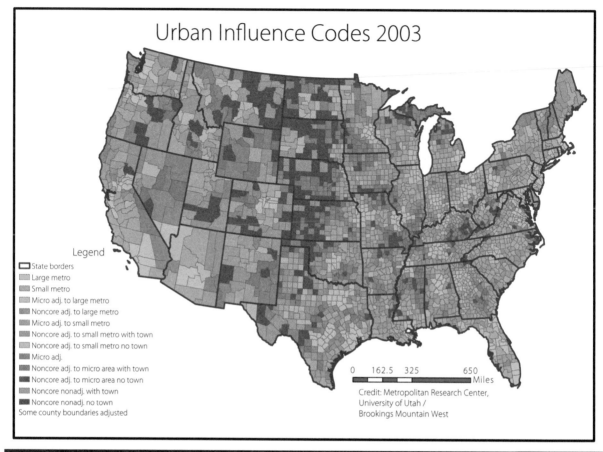

Figure 4.2. USDA 2003 urban influence map of the United States
Credit: Adapted from USDA (2003)

Table 4.3. Nelson-Lang Rural-Megapolitan Continuum

Code and Description

Metropolitan Counties

1 Counties in metropolitan areas of 1 million+ population

2 Counties in metropolitan areas of 250,000 to 1 million population

3 Counties in metropolitan areas of less than 250,000 population

Nonmetropolitan Counties

4 Micropolitan area adjacent to a metropolitan area

5 Noncore counties adjacent to a metropolitan area

6 All other nonmetropolitan counties

has more counties and usually more people than megapolitan areas, even though many counties are also within megapolitan areas.

Summary Observations

Not surprisingly, the definition of megapolitan areas results in a skewed distribution of counties based on a particular geographic space. For one, they need to have a minimum 2040 projected population of four million (rounded). For another, they are defined as a collection of two or more metropolitan areas at least 20 and no more than 180 miles apart (as the crow flies). They also include land area between metropolitan areas and often adjacent to them. Their particular design

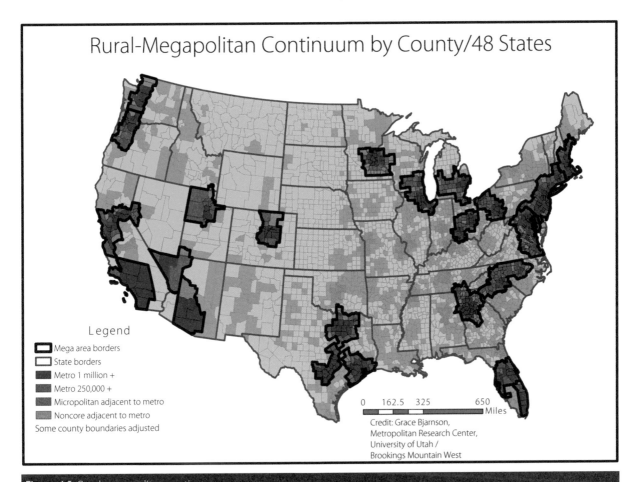

Figure 4.3. Rural-megapolitan continuum

is based on regional development theory. The distribution of population among megapolitan and nonmegapolitan counties based on the rural-megapolitan continuum is illustrated in Figure 4.3. It shows that, whereas the distribution of the contiguous 48 states' population in megapolitan counties falls steeply (from Code 1 to Code 6) along the continuum, for nonmegapolitan counties the distribution is decidely more even—meaning it is more scattered and tending toward isolation from major economic centers. This phenomenon is taken up in subsequent chapters.

Table 4.4. Rural-Megapolitan Continuum Distributions, 2010

Continuum Category, Comparisons	Megapolitan	Nonmegapolitan
Counties in Metropolitan Areas 1,000,000+		
Counties in category (N)	294	109
Share of counties in classification (%)	73.0	27.0
Ratio of mega-/nonmegapolitan population in class (%)	89.1	10.9
Share of population in contiguous states (N)	47.7	4.8
Counties in Metropolitan Areas 250,000–1,000,000		
Counties in category (N)	125	196
Share of counties in classification (%)	38.9	61.1
Ratio of mega-/nonmegapolitan population in class (%)	56.2	43.8
Share of population in contiguous states (%)	11.1	8.6
Counties in Metropolitan Areas <250,000		
Counties in category (N)	82	260
Share of counties in classification (%)	24.0	76.0
Ratio of mega-/nonmegapolitan population in class (%)	30.1	69.9
Share of population in contiguous states (%)	3.0	7.0
Micropolitan Areas Contiguous to Metropolitan Areas		
Counties in category (N)	112	702
Share of counties in classification (%)	13.8	86.2
Ratio of mega-/nonmegapolitan population in class (%)	23.6	76.4
Share of population in contiguous states (%)	2.4	7.8
Noncore Counties Contiguous to Metropolitan Areas		
Counties in category (N)	8	531
Share of counties in classification (%)	1.5	98.5
Ratio of mega-/nonmegapolitan population in class (%)	2.5	97.5
Share of population in contiguous states (%)	0.1	4.6
All Other Counties		
Counties in category (N)	19	638
Share of counties in classification (%)	2.9	97.1
Ratio of mega-/nonmegapolitan population in class (%)	8.9	91.1
Share of population in contiguous states (%)	0.2	1.7

5

MEGAPOLITAN AREAS AS AMERICA'S NEW ECONOMIC CORE

Classic regional economic literature divides regions, and indeed nations, into a core-periphery (or center-hinterland) dichotomy. The core-periphery model describes the economic, political, and social relationships between an advanced, metropolitan "center" and a less developed, often dependent "periphery."[1] Generally, the periphery is dependent on core markets for survival.

Advancement of the periphery, however, can be beneficial to both it and the core. For instance, for two centuries, public policy in the United States has been geared to settling and exploiting the periphery to elevate the national economy. Settlement of the Great Lakes combined with innovations in water transportation allowed raw goods to be shipped to such core markets as New York, Boston, and Philadelphia. Soon the Great Lakes region saw its own core markets emerge, especially in Chicago and Cleveland. As the continent was settled, new core markets emerged. By the middle of the 20th century, virtually all the core markets had been established. Since then regional development, especially in the contiguous 48 states, can best be characterized as sorting out the relative prominence among core markets.

Core markets give rise to metropolitan areas. For a time during the latter part of the 20th century, scholars would consider "nonmetropolitan" areas as the periphery, resulting in a metropolitan-metropolitan dichotomy as an alternative for core and periphery. This unraveled in part when analysts discovered people relocating from metropolitan to nonmetropolitan areas, in a kind of back-to-the-country movement (see Nelson 1992). The argument posed was that millions of households valued location and lifestyle differently than standard urban economic theory allowed, resulting in "inefficient" location decisions that maximized different values. It was not that those households resettled deep in the rural hinterland, however; they would settle in the nonmetropolitan counties between urbanized ones and truly rural ones, dubbed "exurban" areas (Nelson 1992). Nelson and Sanchez (1999) then debunked the back-to-the-country constructs by showing that (1) those households remained within commuting distance of the core and (2) their self-satisfying location decisions were consistent with urban economic theory after all, meaning that the exurbs were essentially the suburbs of the suburbs.

Our megapolitan characterization allows exurban areas to be included *within* the core geography of modern urbanized America. As we demonstrated in Chapter 3, it also allows multiple metropolitan areas linked into an economic network to be accessible via surface transportation modes from anywhere to anywhere within that network, in a round-trip conveniently completed in the same day.

In effect, our construct creates a broad dichotomy for the 48 states, the new core being megapolitan areas and the periphery being everything else. We concede this is a sweeping generalization. In future work, we will refine this dichotomy, principally by incorporating what Wallerstein (1988) calls the "semiperiphery," which is an economy dominated by the core but dominating other landscapes. We anticipate developing a new construct composed of the core, comprising megapolitan areas; a newly defined periphery, consisting of larger metropolitan areas not linked to a megapolitan area (such as Nashville, Tennessee; Memphis, Tennessee; New Orleans; Kansas City, Missouri; Oklahoma City; Indianapolis; Louisville, Kentucky; and St. Louis); and the hinterland, comprising the remaining area of the contiguous 48 states (and likely including such sizable metropolitan areas as Des Moines, Iowa; Omaha, Nebraska; Tulsa, Oklahoma; Wichita, Kansas; Jackson, Mississippi; and Little Rock, Arkansas).

In this chapter we show that the economic and socioeconomic structures of megapolitan areas differ rather remarkably from those structures as found in nonmegapolitan areas. We begin with economic differences and proceed to socioeconomic distinctions.

Major Economic Differences Between Megapolitan and Nonmegapolitan Areas

Generally, an area's economic characteristics have significant effects on its development. In 2004, the USDA's Economic Research Service (2004a) developed a new county-level typology to better understand economic differences among counties. It created an economic dependence typology that was applied to all 3,141 counties and their county equivalents plus independent cities.[2]

The USDA codes sort counties by their degree of dependence on particular economic sectors, including agriculture, mining, manufacturing, federal and state employment, and services; all others not assigned to one of these codes are considered "nonspecialized." (If a county qualified for more than one of mining, federal/state government, or manufacturing types, it was classified in the industry in which it was above the threshold by the largest number of percentage points.) Selection of these sectors

was guided by regional economic theory. Farming, mining, manufacturing, and federal or state government sectors produce goods or services for "export" outside the local economy and thus stimulate economic development. In regional economics, exporting industries, such as automobile manufacturing, are considered "basic" activities since they can be sources of greater growth (or decline) in local economies than local-serving activities such as food stores. Service industries may produce for either the local economy (such as dentists) or the export economy (such as brain surgery). The advantage of using the economic dependence codes is that they are mutually exclusive.

However, for our purposes, we have combined the service and nonspecialized categories into one, which we call nonbasic economic sector dependency. There are three reasons. First, services dominate the national economy; in 2010, it was estimated that about 57 percent of all jobs were in the service sector. Indeed, service sector dominance is viewed as an important element of a diversified economic base. Second, nonspecialization implies an economy that is diversified, with no single industry dominating and thus skewing its long-term performance. Third, generally, an economy that is not dependent on an export-based economic sector is considered to be more resilient to economic cycles than are economies that depend on export-based sectors. We thus combine USDA's service and nonspecialization codes into one. Our five-code economic dependence scheme, adapted from the USDA's six-code scheme, is applied to all counties in the 48 states in Figure 5.1.

We divide this chapter into two analytic sections, basic economic sector dependency and nonbasic economic sector dependency, with summary observations.

Basic Economic Sector Dependency

This section reviews the USDA's method for sorting counties according to their dependency on four basic economic sectors: farming, mining, manufacturing, and federal and state government employment. The discussion for each basic sector includes an overview of the USDA's coding criteria, summary data reporting the distribution of dependency on each basic sector by megapolitan status, and a map of the 48 contiguous states illustrating that distribution.

Farming Dependency

The USDA-based county-level farming dependence denotes farm earnings accounting for an annual average of 15 percent or more of total county earnings (during 1998–2000) or

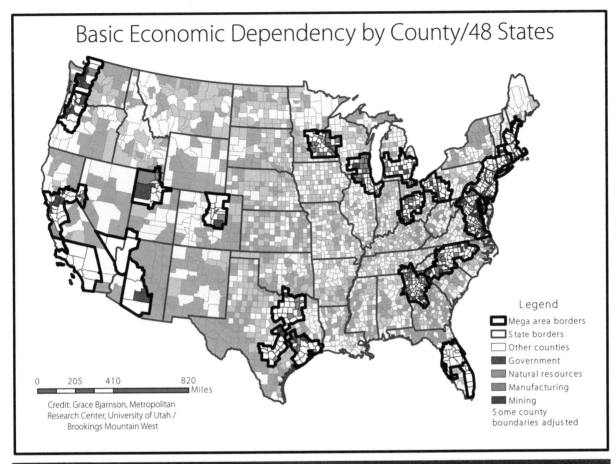

Figure 5.1. Nelson and Lang adaptation of the USDA Economic Dependence Codes applied to counties in the 48 states, with megapolitan areas in bolder shades within boundaries as shown
Credit: Adapted from U.S. Department of Agriculture 2004a.

farm occupations accounting for 15 percent or more of all employed residents in 2000. The farming occupation option was adopted to allow into the farming-dependent group counties that had highly farming-oriented economies but did not meet the earnings threshold, most often as a result of negative farm earnings estimates for some or all of the analyzed years. Farming dependence was determined first and takes precedence over all the other economic sector dependence types.

Table 5.1 reports the distribution of farming-dependent counties by megapolitan status, while Figure 5.2 illustrates this distribution among the 48 states. Clearly, farming dependency is restricted almost entirely to non-megapolitan areas. On the other hand, the population of

farming-dependent counties is less than 3.5 percent of the total 48-state population.

Mining Dependency

Mining includes the extraction and processing of metals; coal; oil and gas; stone; sand and gravel; clay, ceramic, and refractory minerals; chemical and fertilizer minerals; and miscellaneous nonmetallic minerals, such as gemstones, diatomaceous earth, peat, and talc. The USDA classifies counties as mining dependent if mining accounted for 15 percent or more of total county earnings during 1998–2000.

Table 5.2 reports the distribution of mining-dependent counties by megapolitan status, while Figure 5.3 shows

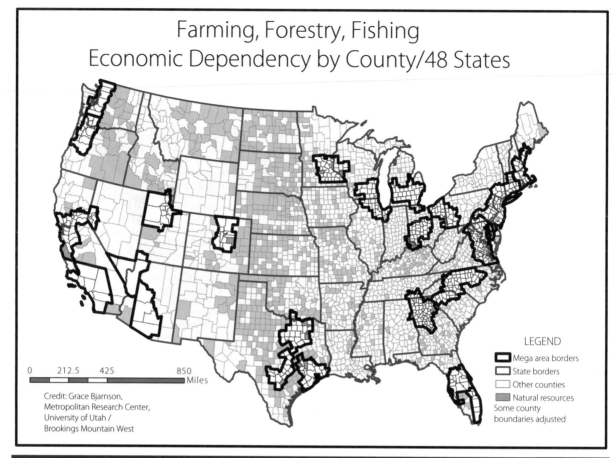

Farming, Forestry, Fishing
Economic Dependency by County/48 States

0   212.5   425   850
                             Miles

Credit: Grace Bjarnson,
Metropolitan Research Center,
University of Utah /
Brookings Mountain West

LEGEND

▭ Mega area borders
▯ State borders
▢ Other counties
▩ Natural resources
Some county
boundaries adjusted

Figure 5.2. Farming-dependent counties in relation to megapolitan areas
Credit: Adapted from Economic Research Service, U.S. Department of Agriculture, www.ers.usda.gov/briefing/rurality/typology/
Maps/Econtype.htm

Table 5.1. Farming-Dependent Counties by Megapolitan Status

Megapolitan County Class	Counties (N)	Population Share in Megapolitan Category (%)
Nonmegapolitan	432	3.3
Megapolitan	8	0.1
Megapolitan share	1.8%	

this distribution across the 48 states. Clearly, like farming dependency, mining dependency occurs almost entirely outside megapolitan areas. But also like farming, it accounts for a small share of the entire population of the contiguous 48 states—in the case of mining, less than 2.5 percent.

Manufacturing Dependency
Manufacturing dependence is based on whether 25 percent or more of average annual laborers' and proprietors' earnings were derived from manufacturing during 1998–2000.

Table 5.3 summarizes the distribution of manufacturing-dependent counties by megapolitan status, and Figure 5.4 maps their distribution across the contiguous 48 states. About a quarter of the population outside megapolitan areas lives in manufacturing-dependent counties compared to about 16 percent in megapolitan areas. It used

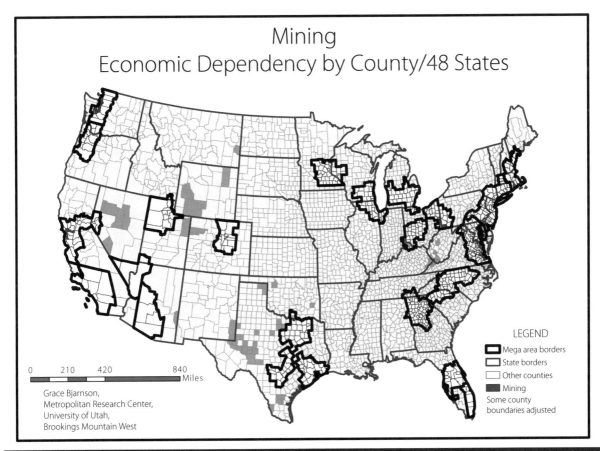

Mining
Economic Dependency by County/48 States

LEGEND
- ■ Mega area borders
- □ State borders
- □ Other counties
- ■ Mining

Some county boundaries adjusted

0   210   420   840 Miles

Grace Bjarnson,
Metropolitan Research Center,
University of Utah,
Brookings Mountain West

Figure 5.3. Mining-dependent counties in relation to megapolitan areas
Credit: Adapted from Economic Research Service, U.S. Department of Agriculture, www.ers.usda.gov/briefing/rurality/typology/Maps/Econtype.htm

Table 5.2. Mining-Dependent Counties by Megapolitan Status

Megapolitan County Class	Counties (N)	Population Share in Megapolitan Category (%)
Nonmegapolitan	119	2.3
Megapolitan	6	0.1
Megapolitan share	95.2%	

to be that manufacturing was found mostly in urban and metropolitan areas, where the labor force lived and goods could be shipped easily via water and rail. Over the past half century, however, manufacturing has been converted from a vertical to a linear process requiring vastly more land area, labor has become more productive, and roads have replaced water as a transport medium and reduced the advantage of locating near rail. Even inside megapolitan areas, manufacturing is usually found in the exurban countryside, outside built-up urban areas.

Federal and State Government Employment Dependency

Dependence on the federal and state government is based on whether 15 percent or more of average annual laborers' and proprietors' earnings were derived from those sources during 1998–2000. In this case, dependency implies that a county has a disproportionate number of federal and state workers employed in it, such as Washington, D.C., or counties of state capitals in small metropolitan

Figure 5.4. Manufacturing-dependent counties in relation to megapolitan areas
Credit: Adapted from Economic Research Service, U.S. Department of Agriculture, www.ers.usda.gov/briefing/rurality/typology/Maps/Econtype.htm

Table 5.3. Manufacturing-Dependent Counties by Megapolitan Status

Megapolitan County Class	Counties (N)	Population Share in Megapolitan Category (%)
Nonmegapolitan	687	24.4
Megapolitan	199	15.1
Megapolitan share	22.5%	

or nonmetropolitan areas, or major federal and state installations such as military bases and penitentiaries.

Federal and state government dependency is summarized in Table 5.4. Figure 5.5 shows the distribution of federal- and state-dependent counties by megapolitan status. Nearly 17 percent of the population outside megapolitan areas is dependent on federal or state government employment compared to less than 8 percent within megapolitan areas.

Basic Economic Dependency Review

The overall pattern of basic economic sector dependency is provided with a "big picture" look. Table 5.5 summarizes information contained in the previous four tables to compare overall dependency on economic sectors between megapolitan and nonmegapolitan areas. It shows that nearly half the population living outside megapolitan areas resides in counties that are in some way dependent

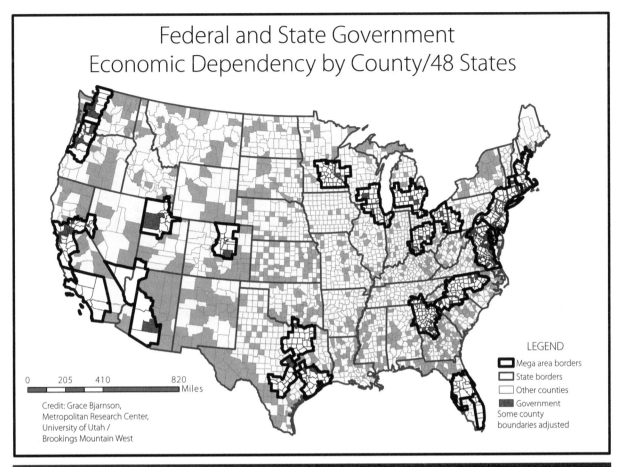

Figure 5.5. Federal and state government–dependent counties in relation to megapolitan areas
Credit: Adapted from Economic Research Service, U.S. Department of Agriculture, www.ers.usda.gov/briefing/rurality/typology/Maps/Econtype.htm

Table 5.4. Federal and State Government–Dependent Counties by Megapolitan Status

Megapolitan County Class	Counties (N)	Population Share in Megapolitan Category (%)
Nonmegapolitan	298	15.5
Megapolitan	62	7.7
Megapolitan share	17.2%	

on a single export-base economic sector, compared to about a quarter residing in megapolitan areas. Figure 5.6 maps this distribution in relation to megapolitan areas.

Nonbasic Economic Sector Dependency

All other counties are classified as service dependent or nonspecialized, which we combine into one category called nonbasic economic sector dependency. Let us first review how the USDA addresses service dependency.

The USDA identifies as service dependent those counties where service-based employment (in retail trade, finance, insurance, real estate, and other services as defined by the Standard Industrial Classification System) was 45 percent or more of total earnings during the period 1998–2000.

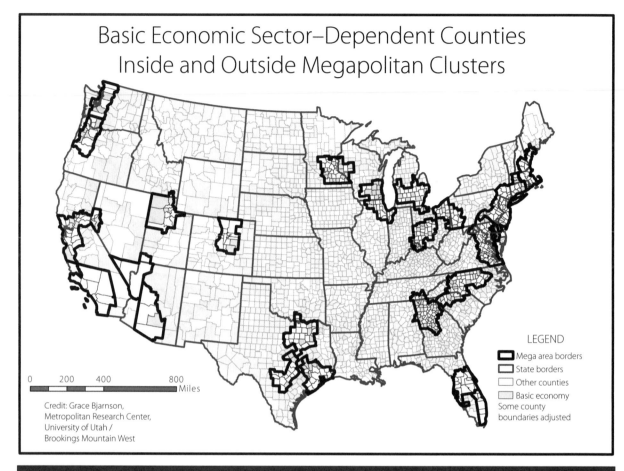

Basic Economic Sector–Dependent Counties Inside and Outside Megapolitan Clusters

LEGEND
- Mega area borders
- State borders
- Other counties
- Basic economy
Some county boundaries adjusted

0   200   400   800 Miles

Credit: Grace Bjarnson,
Metropolitan Research Center,
University of Utah /
Brookings Mountain West

Figure 5.6. Basic sector–dependent counties in relation to megapolitan areas

Table 5.5. Basic Economic Sector Dependency by Megapolitan Status

Megapolitan County Class	Counties (N)	Population Share in Megapolitan Category (%)
Nonmegapolitan	1,536	45.4
Megapolitan	275	24.1
Megapolitan share	15.2%	

As noted earlier, if a county qualified for more than one category among mining, manufacturing, or federal and state government employment, it was classified in the industry in which it was the largest number of percentage points above the threshold. Services were not allowed to take such precedence over those industries, however. Nearly 60 percent of the population living in megapolitan areas lived in service-dependent counties compared to 20 percent of the population living in counties outside megapolitan areas.

By combining the service and nonspecialized categories into one category called nonbasic economic sector dependency, we recognize that both are an indicator of economic diversity. The category is also a better indicator of nondependency on basic industries, which makes counties registering high in this category less vulnerable to business cycles.

Table 5.6 presents information on nonbasic economic sector dependency by megapolitan status, while Figure 5.7 maps this relationship for the contiguous 48 states. Three quarters of the population living inside megapolitan areas live in counties that are not dependent on major export-based sectors, compared to a little more than half

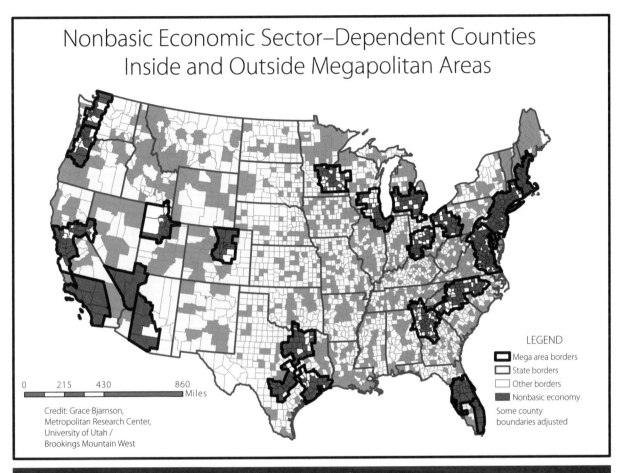

Nonbasic Economic Sector–Dependent Counties Inside and Outside Megapolitan Areas

LEGEND
- Mega area borders
- State borders
- Other borders
- Nonbasic economy

Some county boundaries adjusted

0   215   430   860
Miles

Credit: Grace Bjarnson,
Metropolitan Research Center,
University of Utah /
Brookings Mountain West

Figure 5.7. Nonbasic sector–dependent counties in relation to megapolitan areas

Table 5.6. Nonbasic Economic Sector Dependency by Megapolitan Status

Megapolitan County Class	Counties (N)	Population Share in Megapolitan Category (%)
Nonmegapolitan	951	53.6
Megapolitan	314	75.9
Megapolitan share	24.8%	

the population living outside megapolitan areas. While the nation as a whole is less dependent on export-based economies than in the past, megapolitan areas would appear to be better poised to weather economic cycles than nonmegapolitan areas.

Socioeconomic Dichotomies

We turn now to exploring socioeconomic dichotomies between the core, meaning megapolitan areas, and the periphery, which is everything else.

As the nation headed into the 21st century, much of the population faced various forms of socioeconomic stress, such as poor housing conditions, lack of education, underemployment, and poverty. As the first decade of the 21st century closed, it was unclear whether those stresses had changed much. The housing bubble and along with it record-low unemployment and record-low interest rates may have remedied some stresses. Yet the latter part of the 2000s saw the nation's longest recession since the Great Depression—called by some the Great Recession—which likely reversed many advances. Moreover, many forms of stress are structural in the sense that they are a product of underlying, long-lasting dynamics that are difficult to reverse even in the best of times. It may be useful to assess the spatial pattern of socioeconomic stress reported in the 2000 Census (and earlier in some cases) in terms of megapolitan and nonmegapolitan status. The reason is related to policy-making triage. Megapolitan areas may provide more opportunities for resolving stress than other areas. If so, different policies may be needed to address stress, depending on geographic location with respect to megapolitan status.

In this part, we adapt the USDA's prior assessments of various indicators of socioeconomic stress to help characterize challenges and opportunities facing megapolitan areas. We look at housing stress, low education, low employment, persistent poverty, and child poverty. We characterize this as a comparison between the megapolitan and the nonmegapolitan milieu.

Housing Stress

The USDA considers a county "stressed" in terms of housing if 30 percent or more of the housing units had at least one of the following four attributes: lacking complete plumbing, lacking complete kitchen facilities, gross rent or selected owner costs greater than 30 percent of household income, and more than one person per room (USDA, Economic Research Service 2004b).

Table 5.7 reports the distribution of counties by megapolitan status in relation to housing stress. It shows that roughly 70 percent of all counties meeting the USDA's housing stress definition were found outside megapolitan areas. However, more than half the population inside megapolitan areas faced some form of housing stress, likely in the form of housing costs. In contrast, about a fifth of the population in nonmegapolitan areas endured some form of housing stress, likely poor housing conditions. Figure 5.8 illustrates the distribution of housing stress by megapolitan status.

Figure 5.8. Counties under substantial housing stress inside and outside megapolitan areas. Inside megapolitan areas, white areas are moderately stressed and dark blue ones are stressed. Outside megapolitan areas, gray areas are moderately stressed and amber ones are not stressed.

Table 5.7. Housing Stress

County Megapolitan Category	Housing Stress Counties (N)	County Population in Megapolitan Category (%)
Nonmegapolitan	348	21.4
Megapolitan	157	58.1
Megapolitan share	31.1%	

Table 5.8. Low Education

County Megapolitan Category	Low-Education Counties (N)	County Population in Megapolitan Category (%)
Nonmegapolitan	544	13.3
Megapolitan	67	11.6
Megapolitan share	11.0%	

Low Education

We turn next to educational levels. Using the 2000 Census, the USDA classified as "low education" those counties where 25 percent or more of the residents between the ages of 25 and 64 had neither a high school diploma nor a GED. Table 5.8 summarizes the distribution of these counties by megapolitan status, while Figure 5.9 maps it. Whereas overall, low educational attainment may be a modest concern, it may be an important concern in more than a third of the nonmegapolitan counties.

Low Employment

Generally, educational attainment and employment are related. The USDA considered low employment in a given county to mean that less than 65 percent of residents between the ages of 21 and 64 were employed in

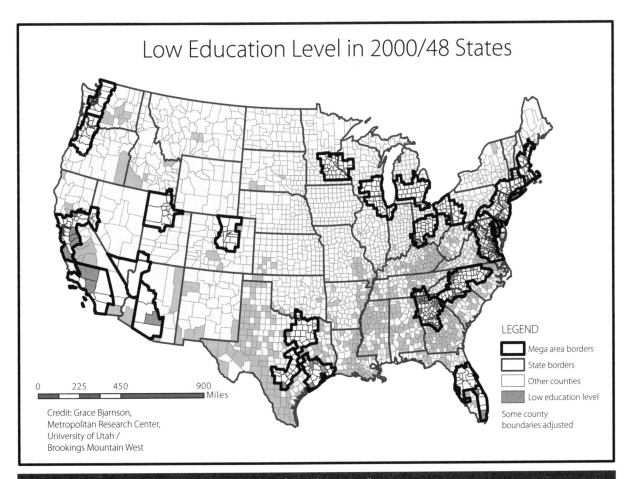

Low Education Level in 2000/48 States

0   225   450   900 Miles

Credit: Grace Bjarnson,
Metropolitan Research Center,
University of Utah /
Brookings Mountain West

LEGEND
Mega area borders
State borders
Other counties
Low education level
Some county boundaries adjusted

Figure 5.9. Counties with low education levels inside and outside megapolitan areas

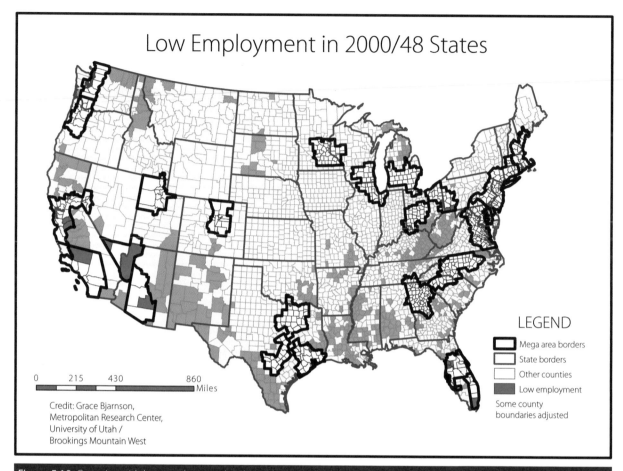

Figure 5.10. Counties with low employment levels inside and outside megapolitan areas

2000. Table 5.9 reports the distribution of those counties by megapolitan status and Figure 5.10 illustrates it with a national map. The year 2000 saw a near record-low unemployment rate, which had more than doubled a decade later. However, the relative distribution of unemployment regardless of business cycles may be an important way to compare megapolitan and nonmegapolitan areas. In this respect, megapolitan counties may be more resilient to economic stresses than nonmegapolitan areas.

Persistent Poverty

Persistent poverty signals certain social and economic structures that, along with isolation from markets, compromise social and economic advancement. The USDA determines that if a county has had 20 percent or more of its residents in poverty as measured on each of the 1970,

1980, 1990, and 2000 Censuses, it faces persistent poverty. Another indicator developed by the USDA identifies counties where more than 15 percent of children are enrolled in some form of poverty-related program, such as subsidized school lunches. Table 5.10 summarizes the distribution of these counties by megapolitan category, while Figure 5.11 illustrates the distribution on a map.

Table 5.9. Low Employment

Megapolitan County Category	Low-Employment Counties (N)	County Population in Megapolitan Category (%)
Nonmegapolitan	420	11.5
Megapolitan	22	5.0
Megapolitan share	5.0%	

Table 5.10. Counties with Persistent Poverty by Megapolitan Status

Megapolitan County Category	Persistent Poverty Counties (N)	County Population Share in Megapolitan Category (%)
Nonmegapolitan	377	10.2
Megapolitan	5	0.2
Megapolitan share	1.3%	

Table 5.11. Counties with Persistent Child Poverty by Megapolitan Status

Megapolitan County Category	Child Poverty Counties (N)	County Population Share in Megapolitan Category (%)
Nonmegapolitan	691	21.4
Megapolitan	36	5.5
Megapolitan share	5.0%	

Table 5.10 shows clearly that persistent poverty is a concern limited substantially to nonmegapolitan areas, where nearly 99 percent of such counties are found. Table 5.11 shows that child poverty is a more extensive problem by a multiple, though megapolitan counties compare considerably more favorably than nonmegapolitan counties.

Summary Observations

Classic regional economic literature divides regions into core-periphery or center-hinterland dichotomies. Generally, the periphery and the hinterlands are dependent on markets located in the core or center for their livelihood—and are often equated with being colonies of those markets. Various federal and state policies have

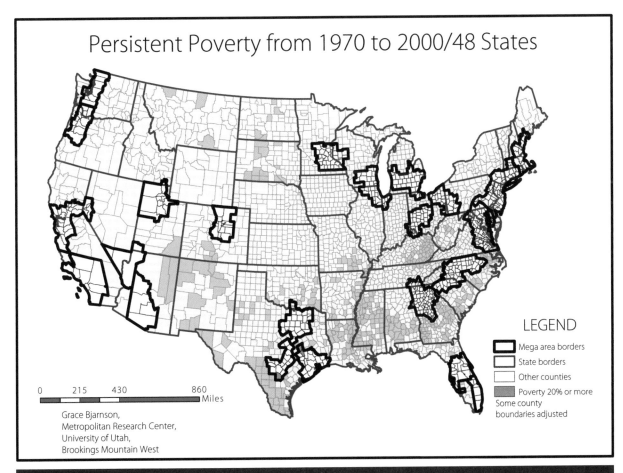

Persistent Poverty from 1970 to 2000/48 States

0   215   430   860 Miles

LEGEND
Mega area borders
State borders
Other counties
Poverty 20% or more
Some county boundaries adjusted

Grace Bjarnson,
Metropolitan Research Center,
University of Utah,
Brookings Mountain West

Figure 5.11. Counties with 20 percent or more of residents classified as in persistent poverty

attempted to make the periphery or hinterland less dependent on the core or center through improved transportation, decentralization of key investments (e.g., military bases, penitentiaries, public institutions of higher education, research and development facilities), and a variety of commodity subsidies (e.g., for crops, land conservation, rural electrification, and telecommunications). While dependency on markets would continue—and indeed, in many instances dependency was strengthened—the overall objective of these policies was to make these areas less dependent on the cores or centers of the nation.

To some extent, these policies may have been successful, at least as measured by the rise of small metropolitan and micropolitan areas in the periphery/hinterland. Yet what may seem to be a loosening grip on the core/center may be masked by larger phenomena, as suggested in Table 5.12. It may be not so much that dominance of the core over the periphery has been lessened as that the geography of the core has itself changed with the rise of megapolitan areas. For instance, in 1970, megapolitan areas, comprising 17 percent of the accessible landscape in the contiguous 48 states, accounted for about 59 percent of the population. By 2010, megapolitan areas' share of the 48 states' population had risen to 63 percent, despite efforts to decentralize economic activity. Even more impressive is that megapolitan areas absorbed 70

Table 5.12. Distribution and Share of Population Growth by Megapolitan Status, 1970–2010

Classification	1970 (N)	2010 (N)	Growth (N)
Nonmegapolitan areas	82,270	114,173	31,903
Megapolitan areas	120,627	194,393	73,766
Megapolitan share	59.5%	63.0%	69.8%

percent of the 48 states' growth. If anything, the new characterization of the core-periphery or center-hinterland relationship advanced by the megapolitan scheme shows America's newly defined core or center as tightening its grip on the nation's economy. The next chapter, on megapolitan attractiveness, bolsters this assertion.

There are important socioeconomic differences as well. Except in housing, megapolitan counties are less stressed than nonmegapolitan ones. This is especially the case with respect to persistent poverty and children living in poverty. In a sense, the nation could be moving toward two Americas rather than the many that presently exist. One, megapolitan America, would have the advantages of economic scale and highly networked spaces, and the other, nonmegapolitan America, would be composed mostly of smaller, isolated places outside the reach of economically productive networks.

6

MEGAPOLITAN ATTRACTIVENESS

Many things can make one area more conducive to growth than other areas. Certainly included are features that fuel growth such as comparative and competitive advantages over alternatives. But classic growth-inducing influences have lessened in their importance in attracting growth as the United States has emerged as a postindustrial society. Two new influences have gained in prominence in recent decades: the attractiveness of natural amenities and the growing "knowledge class," consisting of nonlocation-bound white-collar workers. The first section of the chapter explores the extent to which megapolitan area amenities provide growth advantages. The second assesses the comparative advantages of megapolitan areas in attracting the knowledge class. Summary observations follow.

Megapolitan Natural Amenity Attractiveness

To an increasingly important extent, an area's amenities drive long-term economic development, in large part because people are attracted to them. Amenities in turn fuel the rise and sustainability of the knowledge class. Both work to influence growth, and both may be found among megapolitan areas and regions. We consider the role of amenities first, then how the rise of the knowledge class is expected to fuel megapolitan growth more so than growth in nonmegapolitan areas.

The U.S. Department of Agriculture (USDA), through its Economic Research Service, has developed what it calls the Natural Amenities Scale. It is a measure of the physical characteristics of a county that may improve it as a place to live. The scale was devised initially to assess the economic development prospects of nonmetropolitan counties associated with their natural amenities, but the scale itself is applicable more broadly.

The Natural Amenities Scale was constructed by David McGranahan (1999). The scale combines six measures of climate, typography, and water area, on the assumption that these are the environmental features most people prefer. These measures are a warm winter, winter sun, a temperate summer, low summer humidity, topographic variation, and water area, using the following particular interpretations:

- *Climate*: Four measures are used, including the average number of days of sun in January, the average January temperature, the lowness of average July humidity, and the temperateness of July weather. Temperateness is measured in such a way that locales with the warmest winters and coolest summers score highest on the scale.
- *Topography*: This measure is based on a 1937 *National Geographic* map with 26 categories ranging from flat with no hills to highly mountainous.
- *Water area*: This measure is based on the proportion of county area classified as water by the U.S. Census Bureau. Because county boundaries extend offshore, ocean front as well as lakes and ponds are reflected in this measure.

The resulting seven-point scale, with 1 representing the fewest natural amenities and 7 the most, was applied to all U.S. counties. We collapse the seven-point scale into three ordinal groups: high amenity (Natural Amenities Scale scores of 5, 6, and 7), moderate amenity (scores of 3 and 4), and low amenity (scores of 1 and 2). Counties in the 48 states are thus grouped into a pattern resembling a nearly bell-shaped curve with low- and high-amenity counties accounting for 15 percent and 13 percent of all counties, respectively, and moderate-amenity counties accounting for 72 percent (Figure 6.1).

The distribution of counties based on megapolitan status by amenity level is interesting. Table 6.1 shows this distribution based on number of counties. Nonmegapolitan counties accounted for 84 percent of all counties classified as low amenity and 80 percent of counties classified as moderate amenity. In contrast, despite being outnumbered 4 to 1, megapolitan counties accounted for more than 40 percent of the high-amenity counties. The sheer number of counties outside megapolitan areas masks differences in population distribution, which is addressed in Table 6.2.

Table 6.1. Distribution of Counties by Amenity Level and Megapolitan Status

Megapolitan Category	Low Amenity	Moderate Amenity	High Amenity
Megapolitan (N)	72	502	66
Megapolitan share (%)	16	20	43
Nonmegapolitan (N)	376	1,973	87
Nonmegapolitan share (%)	84	80	57

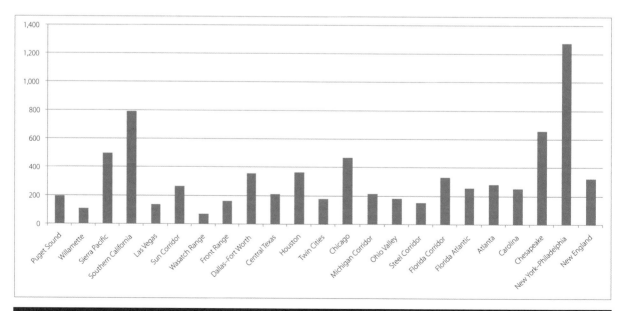

Figure 6.1. Distribution of counties in the contiguous 48 states by amenity category—high, moderate, or low

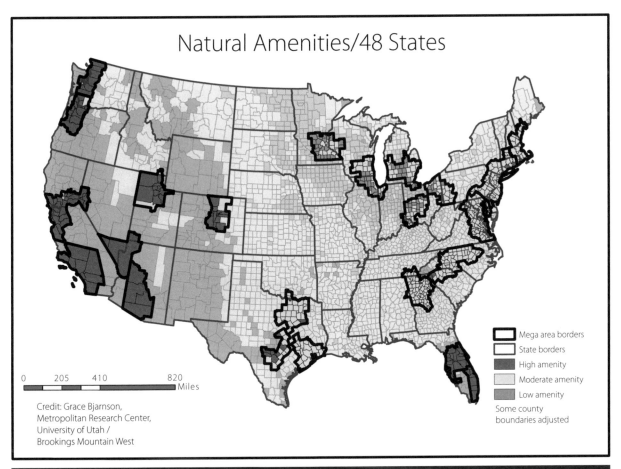

Figure 6.2. Distribution of counties in the contiguous 48 states by amenity level—high, moderate, or low—in relation to megapolitan areas

Table 6.2. Share of Population within Megapolitan Category by Amenity Level

Megapolitan Category	Low Amenity	Moderate Amenity	High Amenity
Megapolitan (N)	11,993	135,630	50,280
Megapolitan share (%)	45	60	90
Nonmegapolitan (N)	14,486	89,963	5,692
Nonmegapolitan share (%)	55	40	10

Table 6.2 shows how the population within each amenity level is distributed between megapolitan and nonmegapolitan counties. Here we see that of the people living in low-amenity counties, more than half (55 percent) live in nonmegapolitan counties. At the other end of the spectrum, megapolitan counties account for 90 percent of the people living in high-amenity counties. Thus, the population appears to be attracted to areas with moderate to high levels of amenities, and especially to megapolitan counties with those amenities. Figure 6.2 shows the distribution of high-, moderate-, and low-amenity counties in relation to megapolitan areas in the contiguous 48 states.

Let us now assess differences between megapolitan and nonmegapolitan counties in terms of their attractiveness to knowledge workers.

Megapolitan Knowledge Class Attractiveness

Richard Florida's *The Rise of the Creative Class* (2002) argues that contemporary economic development depends on new combinations of knowledge and ideas, and further, that only selected occupations affect economic development. Moreover, people in those occupations are drawn to areas that offer a high quality of life, both natural and man-made. Modern economic development strategy is thus to take advantage of natural assets and invest in man-made ones (cultural attractions, education systems, modern transit, etc.) that attract and retain knowledge workers.

Some have questioned the analytic rigor of the knowledge class concept. For instance, Edward Glaeser, Joseph Gyourko, and Raven E. Saks (2005) found that educational attainment, and not the presence of artistic or alternative lifestyle people (bohemians and gays, according to Florida), is correlated with metropolitan economic development. Second, Lang and LeFurgy (2007) argue that preconditions matter more to predicting future economic development than do changes in percentage of knowledge class persons: High-quality institutions of higher education, for instance, attract the knowledge class, not vice versa.

Still, Florida's knowledge class construct is a useful way to compare the attractiveness of different geographies. Florida's conceptualization of the knowledge class is discussed in his book, *The Rise of the Creative Class*. It includes occupational classes that he has judged to reflect differing levels of creativity, which coincide with educational levels. The foundation of the knowledge class concept is offered in the following excerpt:

> The distinguishing feature of the Knowledge Class is that its members engage in work whose function is to "create meaningful new forms." I define the knowledge class as consisting of two components. The Super Knowledge Core of this new class includes scientists and engineers, university professors, poets and novelists, artists, entertainers, actors, designers and architects, as well as thought leadership of modern society: nonfiction writers, editors, cultural figures, think-tank researchers, analysts and other opinion-makers. . . . Beyond this core group, the Knowledge Class also includes "knowledge professionals" who work in a wide range of knowledge-intensive industries such as high-tech sectors, financial services, the legal and healthcare professions, and business management. These people engage in knowledge problem solving, drawing on complex bodies of knowledge to solve specific problems. (Florida 2002, 68–69)

McGranahan and Wojan (2007) of the USDA's Economic Research Service expand on Florida's knowledge class measures and apply them to all counties among the contiguous 48 states. Their reconceptualization includes recasting knowledge class measures by excluding from Florida's original measure several occupations with low creativity scores and those engaged in merely "economic production" (such as health care delivery) rather than true economic development (such as research, inventions leading to patents, etc.). They claim, with statistical evidence, that their measure is more consistent with the knowledge class concept and is more predictive of development than Florida's measure. Their predictive model includes, at the county level, various interactions among the following county attributes:

Natural amenities (from the Natural Amenities Scale)

Size of or change in knowledge class (based on occupation)

Change in jobs

Net migration

Natural amenities (from the Natural Amenities Scale)

Their refinements resulted in an estimated knowledge class share of the workforce of 21 percent in 1990, rising to 25 percent in 2000. We use the 25 percent figure as the floor to distinguish between counties that are composed substantially of knowledge class workers and those that are not.

In all, we find that megapolitan counties account for about 60 percent of all counties with more than 25 percent knowledge class employment. More astonishing, those counties account for more than 80 percent of the people who live in knowledge class counties (Table 6.3). The knowledge class counties are illustrated in Figure 6.3.

Clearly, megapolitan counties dominate the knowledge class distribution. Although based on the refined data provided by McGranahan and Wojan, this is consistent with Florida's proposition that larger metropolitan areas with attractive central cities and high-quality natural amenities attract the knowledge class. As America's demographic profile continues to change,

megapolitan counties may expect to increase their share of knowledge class jobs. For instance, between 2000 and 2030, roughly 85 percent of the net gain in

Table 6.3. Distribution of Counties with Knowledge Class Employment >25% in 2000 and Share of Population by Megapolitan Category in 2010

Megapolitan Category	Counties	Population
Megapolitan (N)	229	137,940
Megapolitan share (%)	59	82
Nonmegapolitan (N)	161	29,550
Nonmegapolitan share (%)	41	18

Source: Adapted from McGranahan and Wojan (2007)

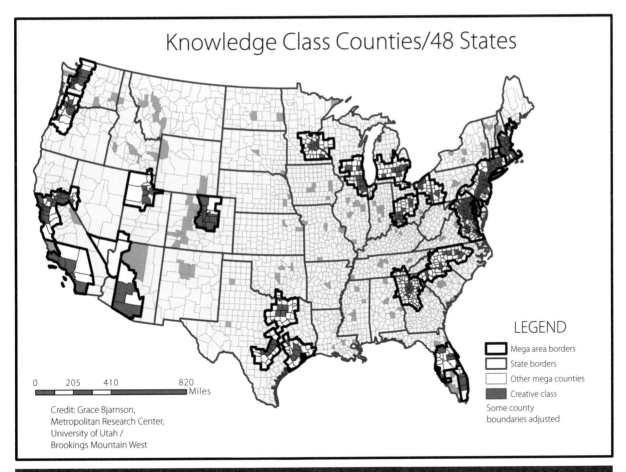

Knowledge Class Counties/48 States

0   205   410   820
Miles

Credit: Grace Bjarnson,
Metropolitan Research Center,
University of Utah /
Brookings Mountain West

LEGEND

Mega area borders
State borders
Other mega counties
Creative class
Some county
boundaries adjusted

Figure 6.3. Distribution of knowledge class counties in the contiguous 48 states in relation to megapolitan status

the total number of households is predicted to come from households without children (Nelson 2006). While many will be young professionals who have not yet had children, the larger share will be those who have already had children and are thus empty nesters. A large share will likely be drawn to attractive central cities (Leinberger 2007), and especially those with attractive natural amenities.

Summary Observations

Because of their natural amenities and economic advantages, which are likely related, megapolitan areas are favored for growth compared to other areas. Growth, of course, is not exclusive to megapolitan areas, as discussed in the next chapter. However, megapolitan areas will see the dominant share of the U.S. population growth toward mid-century.

7

KEY POPULATION TRENDS

America's megapolitan clusters and megapolitan areas will dominate the country's growth from 2010 to 2040. This chapter reviews major demographic trends, including population growth and changes in density, and how ethnicity will change—in some regions and areas, dramatically.

Population

The United States is a growing nation. Among industrialized nations, it is the fastest growing. By contrast, Germany, Italy, and Japan are losing population. Indeed, Japan's population is expected to fall from a peak of 128 million in 2005 to 105 million by mid-century, or just about its population at the end of World War II. In contrast, the United States will add 100 million new residents, a faster pace than any other country except India and China, and China only barely.[1]

Unless noted otherwise, we focus on demographic characteristics over the period 2010–2040. Our principal source of data is Woods and Poole Economics, the only commercial data widely available that include key demographic and economic data for the nation, regions, states, and counties.[2] We use Woods and Poole Economics (2010) county-level data aggregated to megapolitan areas and megapolitan clusters.

We organize the data on a loosely designed spatial continuum in reverse order as the census reports regions (Northeast–Midwest–Southeast) and regions (New England–Middle Atlantic–East North Central–West North Central–South Atlantic–East South Central–West South Central–Mountain–Pacific). This provides a left-to-right ordering as one might read a page. Megapolitan clusters and their associated megapolitan areas are ordered beginning with Cascadia through the Sierra Pacific and the mountains to the southwest, then east to the Texas Triangle, followed by Florida and the Piedmont, north to the Great Lakes, and concluding with Megalopolis.

Between 2010 and 2040, the entire U.S. population will increase from 310 million to 407 million. In the contiguous 48 states, the population over this period is expected to grow from 308 million to 404 million. The distribution of the population growth will be skewed, both regionally and favoring megapolitan clusters and megapolitan areas. The population projections for 2010, 2025, and

2040 are shown in Table 7.1 for megapolitan clusters and in Table 7.2 for megapolitan areas. We provide 15-year projection intervals to illustrate both middle-range and long-range trends.

Megapolitan clusters and megapolitan areas will account for more than about 70 percent of the nation's growth between 2010 and 2040, with their share of the total population rising from less than 65 percent in 2010 to about 66 percent in 2040. The 67 million new megaregion and megapolitan area residents will occupy about 17 percent of the privately owned land in the contiguous 48 states (Table 7.1).

Both tables show populations for 2010, 2025, and 2040, as well as growth and growth rates between periods and the share of the contiguous states' growth megapolitan clusters and megapolitan areas will absorb. The fastest growing megaregion will be the Mountain megaregion, followed closely by the Texas Triangle and Florida megapolitan clusters (Figure 7.1). Among megapolitan areas, the fastest growing will be Las Vegas, followed by Central Texas, the Sun Corridor, and the Wasatch Range (Figure 7.2). The Great Lakes megaregion will be the least fast-growing, with the Steel Corridor and the Michigan Corridor having the slowest growth among megapolitan areas.

Growth rates can be deceiving. A small growth rate on a large base can still be a big number. Thus, the Megalopolis megaregion will add the largest number of people, followed closely by the Southwest megaregion (Figure 7.3). Among megapolitan areas, Southern California will add the most, followed by New York–Philadelphia and the Chesapeake megapolitan areas (Figure 7.4).

Density

Measuring density and comparing density between places is fraught with limitations. Often, county-level population density is used as a measure of relative urbanization: The higher the county density, the more "urbanized" it must be. This is a simple but useful tool when counties are roughly the same size, as they are east of the states of Montana, Wyoming, Colorado, and New Mexico. But in the Mountain and Pacific coast states, counties are often very large. At 20,000 square miles, San Bernardino County, California, is larger than six states. One reason for large counties in the West is that so much of the land is owned by federal and state agencies and tribal nations (Figure 7.5).

Even if not publicly owned, much of the land in the West is poorly suited for development because of slope, aridity, and lack of accessible groundwater. Once public ownership and marginal land are accounted for, resulting in a base of privately owned land, population density

Table 7.1. Megapolitan Cluster Population, 2010, 2025, 2040 (in thousands)

Megapolitan Cluster	2010	2025	2040	Change, 2010–2040	Percent Change, 2010–2040
Cascadia	7,993	9,637	11,333	3,340	41.8
Sierra Pacific	12,381	14,345	16,386	4,005	32.3
Southwest	30,552	36,826	43,296	12,744	41.7
Mountain	6,545	8,267	10,033	3,489	57.3
Texas Triangle	18,456	23,247	28,158	9,702	52.6
Twin Cities	5,002	5,858	6,745	1,744	34.9
Great Lakes	34,710	37,331	40,149	5,439	15.7
Florida	14,304	17,673	21,138	6,834	47.8
Piedmont	15,763	19,167	22,672	6,909	47.8
Megalopolis	53,343	59,534	66,040	12,697	27.8
Megapolitan clusters	199,048	231,887	265,950	66,902	37.6
Rest of contiguous states	108,996	123,320	138,300	29,304	26.9
Megapolitan share of 48 states	64.6%	65.3%	65.8%	69.5%	

Source: Based on Woods & Poole Economics (2010)

Table 7.2. Megapolitan Area Population, 2010, 2025, 2040 (in thousands)

Megapolitan Area	2010	2025	2040	Change, 2010-2040	Percent Change, 2010–2040
Puget Sound	4,472	5,363	6,283	1,811	40.5
Willamette	3,521	4,274	5,049	1,528	47.4
Sierra Pacific	12,381	14,345	16,386	4,005	32.3
Southern California	22,469	26,217	30,105	7,636	34.0
Las Vegas	2,352	3,180	4,025	1,673	71.1
Sun Corridor	5,730	7,429	9,166	3,436	60.0
Wasatch Range	2,479	3,212	3,962	1,484	59.9
Front Range	4,066	5,055	6,071	2,005	49.3
Dallas–Fort Worth	7,445	9,264	11,129	3,684	49.5
Central Texas	4,287	5,640	7,022	2,735	67.8
Houston	6,723	8,343	10,007	3,284	48.8
Twin Cities	5,002	5,858	6,745	1,744	34.9
Chicago	13,452	14,990	16,607	3,155	27.5
Michigan Corridor	8,991	9,429	9,917	926	10.3
Ohio Valley	5,436	6,017	6,630	1,195	22.0
Steel Corridor	6,831	6,895	6,994	163	2.4
Florida Corridor	8,130	10,078	12,081	3,952	48.6
Florida Atlantic	6,174	7,596	9,057	2,882	46.7
Atlanta	7,792	9,605	11,470	3,677	47.2
Carolina	7,971	9,562	11,203	3,232	40.5
Chesapeake	10,986	13,435	15,956	4,969	45.2
New York–Philadelphia	33,901	36,830	39,954	6,053	17.9
New England	8,456	9,269	10,130	1,675	19.8

Source: Based on Woods & Poole Economics (2010)

comparisons become more realistic. To do this, we used a variety of sources to adjust land area in western states for public ownership and marginal development suitability. While not precise, we were able to distill privately owned land area in western states, by county, comparable to what is available in other states. With this done, we were able to calculate county-based densities and aggregate them for all megapolitan clusters and megapolitan areas, allowing for improved comparisons. Table 7.3 reports population and Figure 7.6 shows densities for megapolitan clusters as well as the rest of the contiguous 48 states. Table 7.4 and Figure 7.7 do the same for megapolitan areas.

Overall, about 65 percent of the U.S. population now lives in megapolitan clusters and their megapolitan areas, on roughly 17 percent of what we call the accessible land base (that which is not publicly owned or marginal for development purposes). The overall population density is more than 12 times the density of the rest of the contiguous states on similar land. By 2040, megapolitan clusters will approach 750 people per square mile, about 13 times greater than the average population density in the rest of the 48 states. Nearly 270 million Americans will live on a landscape comprising about 360,000 square miles.

Clearly, while the population density for the nation as whole is increasing, as expected with growth

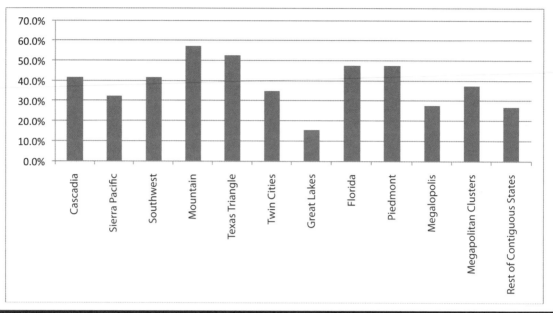

Figure 7.1. Growth rates of megapolitan clusters and balance of 48 states, 2010–2040

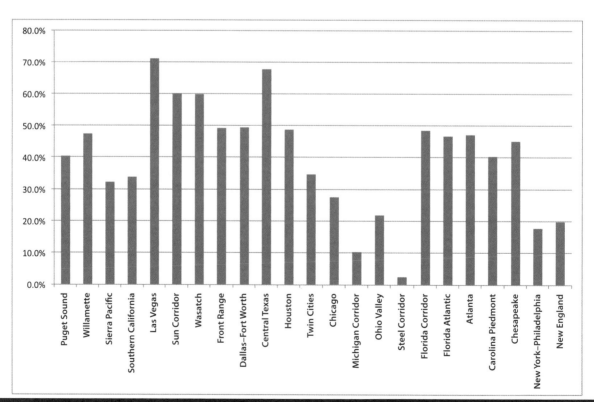

Figure 7.2. Growth rates of megapolitan areas, 2010–2040
Credit: Based on Woods & Poole Economics (2010)

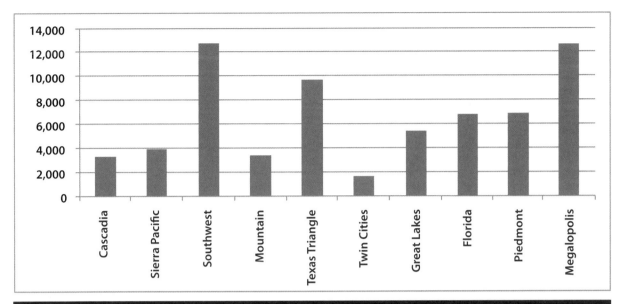

Figure 7.3. Megapolitan cluster growth, 2010–2040
Credit: Based on Woods & Poole Economics (2010)

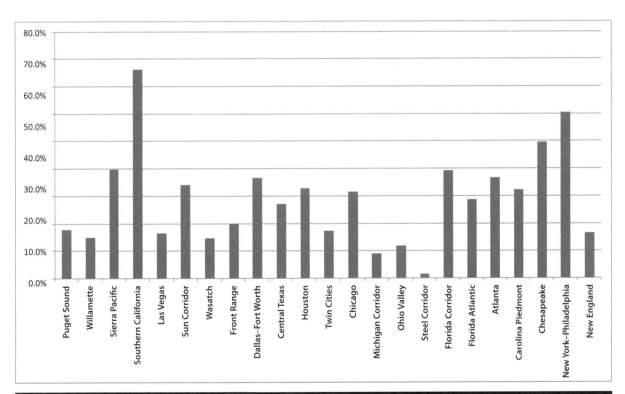

Figure 7.4. Megapolitan area growth, 2010–2040
Credit: Based on Woods & Poole Economics (2010)

U.S. Federal Lands/Western States

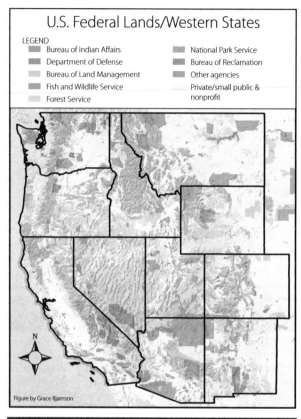

LEGEND
- Bureau of Indian Affairs
- Department of Defense
- Bureau of Land Management
- Fish and Wildlife Service
- Forest Service
- National Park Service
- Bureau of Reclamation
- Other agencies
- Private/small public & nonprofit

Figure by Grace Bjarnson

Figure 7.5. Federal and tribal lands in western states
Credit: Lang, Sarzynski, and Muro 2008

Table 7.3. Persons Per Square Mile for Megapolitan Clusters and Contiguous 48 States, 2010, 2025, 2040

Megapolitan Cluster	Density 2010	Density 2025	Density 2040
Cascadia	461	553	649
Sierra Pacific	394	456	521
Southwest	757	912	1,073
Mountain	284	359	436
Texas Triangle	378	476	577
Twin Cities	245	289	335
Great Lakes	544	585	629
Florida	925	1,143	1,367
Piedmont	358	436	515
Megalopolis	975	1,089	1,210
Megapolitan clusters	558	650	745
Rest of contiguous states	44	50	56
Contiguous 48 states	110	127	144

Table 7.4. Persons Per Square Mile for Megapolitan Areas, 2010, 2025, 2040

Megapolitan Area	Density 2010	Density 2025	Density 2040
Puget Sound	576	690	809
Willamette	364	438	514
Sierra Pacific	394	456	521
Southern California	887	1,035	1,188
Las Vegas	344	464	588
Sun Corridor	700	907	1,120
Wasatch Range	211	274	338
Front Range	359	447	536
Dallas–Fort Worth	346	431	517
Central Texas	412	543	676
Houston	398	494	593
Twin Cities	245	289	335
Chicago	720	802	888
Michigan Corridor	515	540	568
Ohio Valley	386	427	471
Steel Corridor	502	507	514
Florida Corridor	782	969	1,162
Florida Atlantic	1,218	1,498	1,786
Atlanta	388	478	571
Carolina	334	400	469
Chesapeake	643	781	924
New York–Philadelphia	1,294	1,406	1,526
New England	798	874	956

generally, the pace of densification in almost all megapolitan clusters and megapolitan areas is faster. The Florida megaregion and its megapolitan areas will lead the nation in densities in all three time periods. In terms of rate of change, however, the Mountain megaregion is densifying the most quickly, followed closely by Florida and the Texas Triangle. Among megapolitan areas, Las Vegas will nearly double its population density, while the Wasatch Range, Texas Corridor, and Sun Corridor will increase densities by more than 60 percent.

Only two megapolitan clusters, the Great Lakes and Megalopolis, will increase density at a pace slower than the rest of the contiguous 48 states, although because of its sheer size, Megalopolis will still be the nation's second most densely settled megaregion (Figure 7.8). All

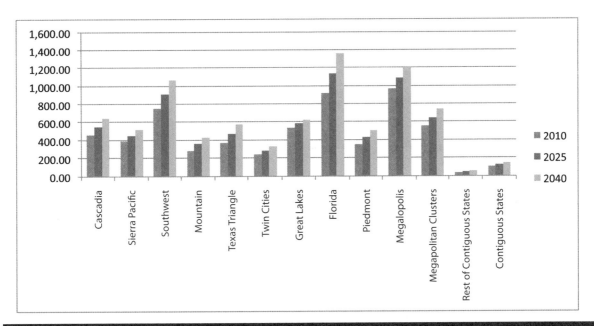

Figure 7.6. Population densities for megapolitan clusters and the rest of the contiguous 48 states for 2010, 2025, and 2040

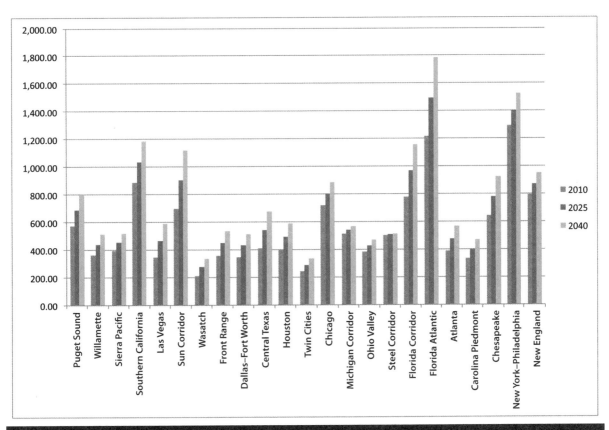

Figure 7.7. Population densities for megapolitan areas and the rest of the contiguous 48 states for 2010, 2025, and 2040

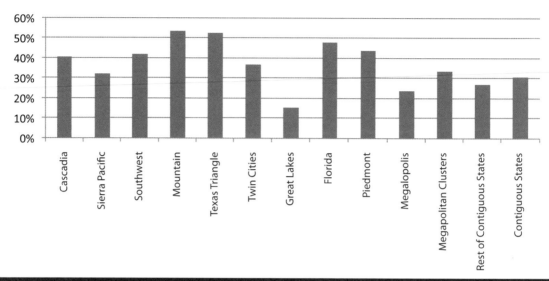

Figure 7.8. Change in population density 2010–2040 among megapolitan clusters and the rest of the contiguous 48 states

four of the Great Lakes megapolitan areas—the Chicago megapolitan area, Michigan Corridor, Ohio Valley, and Steel Corridor—will densify more slowly than the contiguous states, as will two of the megapolitan areas in Megalopolis, New England and the New York–Philadelphia megapolitan area. However, the Chesapeake megapolitan area will be among the leaders in the pace of densification (Figure 7.9).

Let us put this into perspective. In 2010, France, Germany, Belgium, and the Netherlands had about 260 million people living on a comparable land base of 360,000 square miles. Densities in those countries clearly support important transportation options, and also create economic synergies. We discuss these and related issues later.

Ethnicity

The face of America is changing. In 1990, more than three quarters of the population in the contiguous 48 states was white (non-Hispanic). By 2040, barely more than half will be. The census projects that by 2042, America will become majority minority, although non-Hispanic whites will retain a plurality.[3]

Overall trends are impressive. Megapolitan clusters and megapolitan areas will see the most dramatic changes. In the contiguous 48 states, minorities will account for about 90 percent of the population growth.

In megapolitan clusters and megapolitan areas, however, minorities will account for virtually all the growth (Tables 7.5 and 7.6). In the rest of the 48 states, minorities will account for about 70 percent of the growth. Figures 7.10 and 7.11 illustrate these trends.

Among megapolitan clusters, four will actually lose non-Hispanic white population between 2010 and 2040, the Sierra Pacific, Southwest, Great Lakes, and Megalopolis. In some megapolitan areas the change will be even more dramatic. The New York–Philadelphia megapolitan area will lose about 3.4 million non-Hispanic whites, but because it will add nearly 9 million minorities, its total growth will be among the megapolitan leaders, at 6 million. Likewise, Southern California will lose about 2.4 million non-Hispanic whites but will gain nearly 10 million minorities, for a total population gain of nearly 8 million. The slowest-growing megapolitan area will see similar trends: the Steel Corridor will grow by less than 200,000 people but will lose more than 400,000 non-Hispanic whites while it will gain 600,000.

The trends will be equally impressive among megapolitan clusters that in 2010 had the smallest shares of minority populations. The minority share of the population will grow by more than 80 percent in the Mountain and Twin Cities megapolitan clusters between 2010 and 2040 (Table 7.7). The Wasatch Range and Willamette

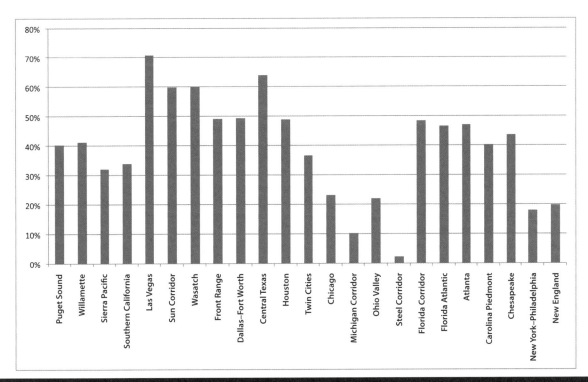

Figure 7.9. Change in population density 2010–2040 among megapolitan areas and the rest of the contiguous 48 states

Table 7.5. White and Minority Share of Population Change by Megapolitan Cluster and the 48 States, 2010–2040 (in thousands)

Megapolitan Cluster	Population Change, 2010–2040 (N)	White Non-Hispanic Population Change, 2010–2040 (N)	Minority Population Change, 2010–2040 (N)	Minority Share of Growth, 2010–2040 (%)
Cascadia	3,200	335	2,865	89.5
Sierra Pacific	4,005	(602)	4,607	115.0
Southwest	12,744	(973)	13,717	107.6
Mountain	3,505	1,040	2,465	70.3
Texas Triangle	9,702	1,417	8,286	85.4
Twin Cities	1,605	589	1,016	67.3
Great Lakes	5,439	(566)	6,005	110.4
Florida	6,834	267	6,567	96.1
Piedmont	6,911	1,387	5,524	79.9
Megalopolis	13,206	(2,672)	15,878	120.2
Megapolitan clusters	67,151	222	66,929	99.7
Rest of contiguous states	29,055	8,683	20,372	70.1
Contiguous 48 states	96,206	8,905	87,301	90.7
Megapolitan share of contiguous states	69.8%	2.5%	76.7%	

Note: "White" means non-Hispanic white; "minority" means all other.
Source: Based on Woods & Poole Economics (2010)

Table 7.6. White and Minority Share of Population Change by Megapolitan Area, 2010–2040 (in thousands)

Megapolitan Area	Population Change, 2010–2040 (N)	White Non-Hispanic Population Change, 2010–2040 (N)	Minority Population Change, 2010–2040 (N)	Minority Share of Growth, 2010–2040 (%)
Puget Sound	1,811	127	1,685	97.0
Willamette	1,389	208	1,181	85.0
Sierra Pacific	4,005	(602)	4,607	115.0
Southern California	7,636	(2,358)	9,994	130.9
Las Vegas	1,673	541	1,132	67.7
Sun Corridor	3,436	845	2,591	75.4
Wasatch Range	1,484	524	960	64.7
Front Range	2,021	516	1,505	74.5
Dallas–Fort Worth	3,684	827	2,857	77.6
Central Texas	2,735	654	2,081	76.1
Houston	3,284	(64)	3,348	102.0
Twin Cities	1,605	589	1,016	67.3
Chicago	3,155	(52)	3,207	101.7
Michigan Corridor	926	(252)	1,178	127.2
Ohio Valley	1,195	176	1,019	85.3
Steel Corridor	163	(438)	601	368.1
Florida Corridor	3,952	365	3,587	90.8
Florida Atlantic	2,882	(98)	2,980	107.4
Atlanta	3,679	963	2,716	77.8
Carolina	3,232	424	2,808	86.9
Chesapeake	5,478	737	4,741	86.5
New York–Philadelphia	6,053	(3,376)	9,430	155.8
New England	1,675	(33)	1,707	102.0

Note: "White" means non-Hispanic white; "minority" means all other.
Source: Based on Woods & Poole Economics (2010)

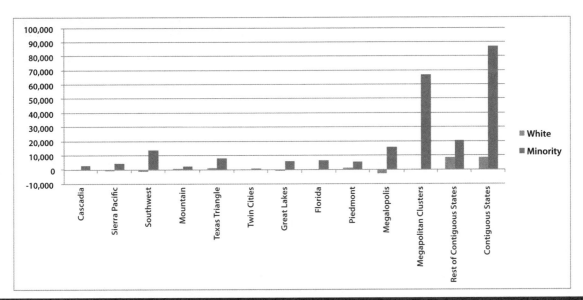

Figure 7.10. Shares of growth among minorities and non-Hispanic whites by megapolitan cluster, all 48 states, and rest of 48 states, 2010–2040

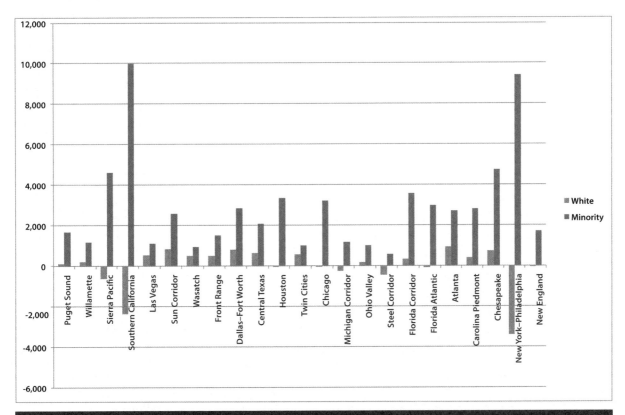

Figure 7.11. Shares of growth among minorities and non-Hispanic whites by megapolitan area, 2010–2040

Table 7.7. Share of Minority Population by Megapolitan Cluster, 2010–2040

Megapolitan Cluster	Minority Share of Population, 2010 (%)	Minority Share of Population, 2025 (%)	Minority Share of Population, 2040 (%)	Minority Share of Growth in Population, 2010–2040 (%)
Cascadia	27.2	32.2	42.5	82.8
Sierra Pacific	51.0	59.3	66.6	30.7
Southwest	57.0	65.2	71.9	26.1
Mountain	25.5	37.2	41.1	61.1
Texas Triangle	50.8	57.4	62.8	27.4
Twin Cities	15.5	20.6	28.3	82.8
Great Lakes	27.0	32.2	38.3	41.8
Florida	47.3	52.3	60.3	39.5
Piedmont	35.9	41.9	49.3	37.5
Megalopolis	37.0	45.0	57.1	47.7
Megapolitan clusters	39.4	47.1	54.6	38.4
Rest of contiguous states	24.8	29.3	34.3	38.6
Contiguous 48 states	34.3	41.0	47.7	39.2

Sources: Metropolitan Research Center, University of Utah, and Brookings Mountain West

megapolitan areas will see their minority population shares increase by more than 90 percent (Table 7.8).

Over the period 2010–2040, minorities collectively will become the majority population among megapolitan clusters as a whole, at nearly 55 percent. In contrast, the rest of the 48 states will see the minority share of the population rise from about a quarter to just a bit more than a third (34 percent). In a very real sense, there will be two Americas demographically: one dominated, or nearly so, by minorities—the megapolitan clusters and most megapolitan areas, the other dominated by non-Hispanic whites—the rest of the contiguous 48 states.[4]

The distribution of the change in minority population by major ethnic group is also interesting. For the contiguous states as a whole, Hispanics will dominate the change in minority share of population growth, followed by Asians and African Americans least (Table 7.9). Indeed, Hispanics will dominate the growth of minorities in nearly all megapolitan areas as well (Table 7.10). Hispanics will especially dominate minority growth in the Mountain, Southwest, Texas Triangle, and Florida megapolitan clusters and their respective megapolitan areas. Asians will have the next dominant share in the Cascadia, Sierra Pacific, and Megalopolis megapolitan

clusters and their respective megapolitan areas. The African American share of minority growth will exceed the Asian share in the Piedmont and Florida megapolitan clusters and their megapolitan areas, but African Americans will also exceed the Asian growth share in the Ohio Valley, the Steel Corridor, and the Chesapeake megapolitan areas. The African American share of minority growth will exceed the Asian share in areas outside the megapolitan clusters as well. The role of minorities, especially Hispanics, in reshaping the ethnic base of the Steel Corridor will be remarkable, mostly because this megapolitan area will lose non-Hispanic white population.

Aging

The United States is aging. The principal reason is the aging of the baby boom cohort, which turns 65 between 2011 and 2029.[5] Between 2000 and 2030, for instance, the share of the population age 65 and older will increase from about 12 percent to about 20 percent. But patterns of the aging population are not intuitive. For instance, although megapolitan clusters are expected to account for nearly 70 percent of the

Table 7.8. Share of Minority Population by Megapolitan Area, 2010–2040

Megapolitan Area	Minority Share of Population, 2010 (%)	Minority Share of Population, 2025 (%)	Minority Share of Population, 2040 (%)	Minority Growth in Population Share, 2010–2040 (%)
Puget Sound	25.2	34.4	44.7	77.6
Willamette	20.6	29.2	39.5	91.5
Sierra Pacific	51.0	59.3	66.6	30.7
Southern California	62.7	72.1	80.0	27.6
Las Vegas	42.8	49.6	57.1	24.2
Sun Corridor	40.6	47.8	57.7	32.1
Wasatch Range	18.8	27.1	36.0	91.1
Front Range	29.6	37.0	44.4	50.2
Dallas–Fort Worth	45.2	51.2	55.9	27.7
Central Texas	52.7	57.6	61.8	17.3
Houston	56.0	64.2	71.0	27.0
Twin Cities	15.5	20.6	28.3	82.8
Chicago	37.7	47.6	49.9	32.2
Michigan Corridor	24.8	29.0	34.3	38.6
Ohio Valley	17.8	22.8	30.0	68.2
Steel Corridor	16.3	20.1	24.5	50.4
Florida Corridor	30.9	41.0	50.5	67.4
Florida Atlantic	59.5	67.3	77.5	27.4
Atlanta	40.3	45.6	51.1	26.6
Carolina	31.5	38.1	47.4	50.8
Chesapeake	40.4	47.1	54.5	35.1
New York–Philadelphia	40.4	49.2	57.9	47.3
New England	18.1	24.6	32.0	76.6

Table 7.9 Distribution of Minority Population Change by Megapolitan Cluster, Contiguous States, and Rest of 48 States, 2010–2040

Megapolitan Cluster	Hispanic Share of Population Change, 2010–2040 (%)	African American Share of Population Change, 2010–2040 (%)	Asian Share of Population Change, 2010–2040 (%)
Cascadia	56.7	7.9	24.4
Sierra Pacific	77.7	2.7	38.5
Southwest	92.2	1.3	12.8
Mountain	56.8	5.8	7.3
Texas Triangle	67.1	7.0	15.1
Twin Cities	24.7	16.7	22.0
Great Lakes	65.4	17.8	26.8
Florida	70.8	17.1	8.2
Piedmont	41.8	21.6	16.5
Megalopolis	66.7	17.8	35.8
Megapolitan clusters	67.2	11.4	20.7
Rest of contiguous states	46.9	14.6	6.2
Contiguous 48 states	61.1	12.4	16.3

Note: The Asian category includes Pacific Islanders.
Source: Based on Woods & Poole Economics (2010)

population growth in the contiguous 48 states, their share of the growth in the senior population will be slightly less, about 68 percent. Moreover, such apparent retirement havens as Florida will actually see about an average rate of growth in the senior population relative to the nation's rate (44 percent for both). The Great Lakes, Megalopolis, and Sierra Pacific megapolitan clusters will have substantially higher rates of growth of the senior population (Tables 7.11 and 7.12). Two megapolitan clusters stand out for their relatively small change in population growth share attributable to seniors, the Mountain and Texas Triangle megapolitan clusters.

Among the megapolitan areas, the Steel Corridor and the Michigan Corridor stand out In both cases, growth of the senior population is expected to eclipse total population growth (Tables 7.13 and 7.14). At the other end of the spectrum are the Wasatch Range, Front Range, and Central Texas megapolitan areas, where growth of the aging population is around half the national rate.

For the most part, all megapolitan clusters and megapolitan areas will see substantial increases in the share of the population that is over 65. The role

of aging is a factor in changing dependency rates, as discussed next.

Changing Dependency

Demographers are interested in what is called the "dependency ratio" because it is an important measure of the extent to which the working-age population may be burdened with raising children and caring for the elderly. The usual formula is:

$$[(\text{Population Aged } 0\text{–}14 + \text{Population Aged } 65+) / (\text{Population Aged } 15\text{–}64)] \times 100$$

The lower the ratio, the better able (in theory) the population is to support children and seniors. In contrast, the higher the ratio, the more likely it is that the economy will be stressed because of a small labor force relative to population. In particular, children would need schooling, which may stress the tax base, while seniors are not only out of the labor force but drawing pensions, which may dampen economic investment.

The dependency ratio is growing in the United States, as would be expected with an aging population. As seen

Table 7.10. Distribution of Minority Population Change by Megapolitan Area, 2010–2040

Megapolitan Area	Hispanic Share of Population Change, 2010–2040 (%)	African American Share of Population Change, 2010–2040 (%)	Asian Share of Population Change, 2010–2040 (%)
Puget Sound	49.7	11.1	31.5
Willamette	65.8	7.7	15.1
Sierra Pacific	77.7	2.7	38.5
Southern California	117.9	-0.7	12.6
Las Vegas	39.0	5.5	27.1
Sun Corridor	61.0	7.8	8.5
Wasatch Range	52.3	6.4	6.0
Front Range	60.1	5.4	8.3
Dallas–Fort Worth	54.2	5.4	17.7
Central Texas	57.3	6.1	12.8
Houston	78.0	9.6	14.0
Twin Cities	24.7	16.7	22.0
Chicago	77.2	7.6	20.4
Michigan Corridor	54.8	24.3	47.4
Ohio Valley	39.3	26.4	19.5
Steel Corridor	165.8	117.5	87.5
Florida Corridor	68.9	12.6	9.3
Florida Atlantic	77.3	27.3	6.6
Atlanta	37.2	22.1	18.3
Carolina	51.5	21.1	14.4
Chesapeake	45.4	27.6	18.8
New York–Philadelphia	91.1	12.4	51.6
New England	47.9	18.6	34.7

Note: The Asian category includes Pacific Islanders.
Source: Based on Woods & Poole Economics (2010)

Table 7.11. Megapolitan Cluster Senior Population Change and Share of Total Population Change, 2010–2040 (in thousands)

Megapolitan Cluster	Total Population Change, 2010–2040 (N)	Senior Population Change, 2010–2040 (N)	Seniors as Share of Population Change, 2010–2040 (%)
Cascadia	3,200	1,158	36.2
Sierra Pacific	4,005	1,993	49.8
Southwest	12,744	5,205	40.8
Mountain	3,505	813	27.2
Texas Triangle	9,702	2,834	29.2
Twin Cities	1,605	630	39.3
Great Lakes	5,439	3,731	68.6
Florida	6,834	3,014	44.1
Piedmont	6,911	2,100	30.4
Megalopolis	13,206	7,089	57.7
Megapolitan clusters	67,151	28,568	42.5
Rest of contiguous states	29,055	13,638	46.9
Contiguous 48 states	96,206	42,206	47.9
Megapolitan share of 48 states	69.8%	67.7%	

Source: Based on Woods & Poole Economics (2010)

Table 7.12. Megapolitan Area Senior Population Change and Share of Total Population Change, 2010–2040 (in thousands)

Megapolitan Area	Total Population Change, 2010–2040 (N)	Senior Population Change, 2010–2040 (N)	Seniors as Share of Population Change, 2010–2040 (%)
Puget Sound	1,811	710	39.2
Willamette	1,389	448	32.3
Sierra Pacific	4,005	1,993	49.8
Southern California	7,636	3,558	46.6
Las Vegas	1,673	557	37.3
Sun Corridor	3,436	1,090	31.7
Wasatch Range	1,484	268	18.0
Front Range	2,021	546	27.0
Dallas–Fort Worth	3,684	1,094	29.7
Central Texas	2,735	742	27.1
Houston	3,284	998	30.4
Twin Cities	1,605	630	39.3
Chicago	3,155	1,550	49.1
Michigan Corridor	926	964	104.1
Ohio Valley	1,195	514	47.0
Steel Corridor	163	703	430.6
Florida Corridor	3,952	1,527	38.6
Florida Atlantic	2,882	1,487	51.6
Atlanta	3,679	1,143	31.1
Carolina	3,232	957	29.6
Chesapeake	5,478	2,018	36.8
New York–Philadelphia	6,053	3,920	64.8
New England	1,675	1,151	68.8

Source: Based on Woods & Poole Economics (2010)

in Table 7.15, only the Mountain and Texas Triangle megapolitan clusters will see substantially lower increases in the dependency ratio than the nation as a whole.

A closer look at dependency ratios is offered for megapolitan areas in Table 7.16. Here we see several megapolitan areas at the extremes. For instance, the Florida Atlantic megapolitan area will grow from about half its population dependent to more than 80 percent from 2010 to 2040, and the rate of change will also be the highest among megapolitan areas. The Steel Corridor is not far behind. On the other hand, although the Wasatch Range has a very high rate of dependency in 2010, the rate of change to 2040 will be the least. The

reason is a large population base comprised of children. Others with small rates of change resulting in among the lowest dependency ratios include the Front Range, Dallas–Fort Worth, Central Texas, Houston, and Ohio Valley megapolitan areas.

Observations

Our construct of megapolitan clusters and megapolitan areas, presented in the first part of this book, was based on a series of factors that link multiple metropolitan areas together into a cohesive geographic network. We argued that "megas" are and will remain an important

Table 7.13. Seniors as Share of Total Population in Megapolitan Clusters, 2010–2040

Megapolitan Cluster	Seniors as Share of Population, 2010 (%)	Seniors as Share of Population, 2025 (%)	Seniors as Share of Population, 2040 (%)
Cascadia	12.0	17.9	19.0
Sierra Pacific	12.2	17.9	21.4
Southwest	11.5	16.3	20.1
Mountain	9.3	17.5	14.2
Texas Triangle	9.4	17.9	16.3
Twin Cities	11.2	17.1	18.7
Great Lakes	12.8	18.2	20.4
Florida	18.1	22.9	26.5
Piedmont	11.1	15.7	17.0
Megalopolis	17.1	18.2	21.0
Megapolitan clusters	12.4	17.4	20.0
Rest of contiguous states	14.5	19.5	21.3
Contiguous 48 states	17.1	18.1	20.4

Table 7.14. Seniors as Share of Total Population in Megapolitan Areas, 2010–2040

Megapolitan Area	Seniors as Share of Population, 2010 (%)	Seniors as Share of Population, 2025 (%)	Seniors as Share of Population, 2040 (%)
Puget Sound	11.9	18.0	19.8
Willamette	12.1	17.7	18.0
Sierra Pacific	12.2	17.9	21.4
Southern California	11.0	15.8	20.0
Las Vegas	12.7	17.2	21.3
Sun Corridor	17.0	17.7	20.0
Wasatch Range	8.4	11.3	12.0
Front Range	9.9	14.9	15.5
Dallas–Fort Worth	9.5	17.8	16.2
Central Texas	9.8	14.0	16.5
Houston	9.1	14.0	16.1
Twin Cities	11.2	17.1	18.7
Chicago	11.7	16.5	18.8
Michigan Corridor	12.6	18.7	21.2
Ohio Valley	12.2	16.6	17.8
Steel Corridor	15.9	22.6	25.6
Florida Corridor	18.6	22.6	25.2
Florida Atlantic	17.5	27.3	28.3
Atlanta	10.1	15.0	16.8
Carolina	12.0	16.4	17.1
Chesapeake	12.0	17.2	19.5
New York–Philadelphia	17.4	18.2	21.2
New England	17.6	19.7	22.7

Table 7.15. Megapolitan Cluster Total Dependency Ratios and Changes in Ratios, 2010–2040

Megapolitan Cluster	Total Dependency Ratio, 2010	Total Dependency Ratio, 2025	Total Dependency Ratio, 2040	Percent Change in Total Dependency Ratio, 2010–2040
Cascadia	44.9	58.3	61.7	37.2
Sierra Pacific	46.8	58.8	66.1	41.2
Southwest	49.1	58.6	66.1	34.6
Mountain	48.0	57.0	57.2	19.2
Texas Triangle	47.9	55.8	59.5	24.2
Twin Cities	45.7	58.4	61.7	34.9
Great Lakes	48.3	59.9	64.3	37.1
Florida	56.0	67.7	76.9	37.5
Piedmont	47.4	56.8	61.4	29.6
Megalopolis	47.4	57.9	64.3	35.7
Megapolitan clusters	48.3	58.8	64.4	37.4
Rest of 48 states	52.6	65.5	68.5	30.3

Source: Based on Woods & Poole Economics (2010)

Table 7.16. Megapolitan Area Total Dependency Ratios and Changes in Ratios, 2010–2040

Megapolitan Area	Total Dependency Ratio, 2010	Total Dependency Ratio, 2025	Total Dependency Ratio, 2040	Percent Change in Total Dependency Ratio, 2010–2040
Puget Sound	44.0	57.3	62.2	41.5
Willamette	46.3	59.7	61.0	31.7
Sierra Pacific	46.8	58.8	66.1	41.2
Southern California	47.6	56.9	65.2	37.0
Las Vegas	52.6	61.3	68.5	30.2
Sun Corridor	54.0	67.9	68.2	26.3
Wasatch Range	54.5	59.9	58.3	7.1
Front Range	44.4	55.3	56.6	27.4
Dallas–Fort Worth	48.2	55.4	59.5	27.4
Central Texas	48.3	54.7	58.3	20.6
Houston	47.3	57.1	60.5	27.7
Twin Cities	45.7	58.4	61.7	34.9
Chicago	47.7	57.7	62.1	30.2
Michigan Corridor	47.5	59.9	64.4	35.5
Ohio Valley	48.5	58.7	61.7	27.2
Steel Corridor	50.5	66.1	72.5	47.5
Florida Corridor	56.9	68.0	74.1	30.2
Florida Atlantic	54.7	67.3	80.9	47.8
Atlanta	46.7	55.5	60.4	29.3
Carolina	48.0	58.1	62.4	30.0
Chesapeake	46.7	58.2	67.6	36.2
New York–Philadelphia	48.0	57.7	64.3	34.1
New England	45.9	58.5	65.4	42.4

Source: Based on Woods & Poole Economics (2010)

factor in the nation's long-term economic and social vitality. In this chapter, we have gone into detail concerning major demographic trends affecting megas and the landscape outside them, in the contiguous 48 states. We find that megas are gaining in share of total U.S. population, are densifying faster, and are becoming more ethnically diverse. Indeed, a new kind of America may be in the making. By 2040, two-thirds of the population will live on a land mass comparable in density to Western Europe—but will have about half again as much population. Megas will also be more ethnically diverse than the rest of the nation, again, by quite a large margin. By 2040, 55 percent of mega residents will be minority, compared to 34 percent for the rest of the nation. On the whole, mega residents will also be slightly younger and slightly less dependent than the rest of the nation.

The following several chapters will explore other differences between megas—megapolitan clusters and their megapolitan areas—and the rest of the nation in terms of social and economic stress, creative opportunities, economic structure, and overall development.

8

MEGAPOLITAN DEVELOPMENT

In this chapter we hazard projections of residential and nonresidential development for the megapolitan clusters and their megapolitan areas over the periods 2010–2025, 2025–2040, and 2010–2040. We do not estimate precisely where in megapolitan areas this development will occur, or in what mix. And other than estimating total residential demand and demand for industrial and commercial/institutional space, we do not specify the type or kind of construction. In effect, we are projecting broad, overarching development demand.

Our projections include "growth-related" development and "replacement" development. Growth-related development is that needed to accommodate population and employment change. Replacement development is that development replacing existing development. Projections of future development needs often do not consider replacement development, likely because it is an area of land-use projection that is not understood well.

A home, for instance, may last centuries or a day. The same is true for nonresidential development. The type of development, however, dictates how long it will last, barring catastrophe. Homes are built for families, and they are built in areas reserved solely for residential use. Home mortgages extend 30 years but may often be refinanced as older mortgages are repaid. Of the 25.6 million homes existing in 1970 that were built before 1940, by 2007, 19.5 million, or 76 percent, were still standing. This equates to an average annual loss rate of just 0.73 percent—a rate that implies homes built before 1940 will last nearly 140 years.[1] For all housing, the average annual rate of loss is about 0.61 percent, implying a useful life of about 160 years (Figure 8.1). Housing is a durable commodity indeed!

For nonresidential development, the situation is very different. Here we find three kinds of space, but one clearly dominates. The first kind of space is public institutional, such as capitol buildings, city halls, county courthouses, libraries, schools, and so forth. These are built to be durable, and indeed will last centuries. A second kind of space is private-sector, investment-intensive space, such as office towers. Combined, public institutional and private-sector spaces account for less than 10 percent of all nonresidential structures. The rest are built to meet the needs of the next few decades, such as strip shopping centers, warehouses, low-rise/low-intensity office buildings, assembly operations, and so forth. Retail stores, for instance, last only 15–20 years before being replaced, and warehouses and distribution buildings not much longer. The average duration of all nonresidential structures is about 40 years (see Figure 8.1).[2] Nonresidential development is not a durable commodity. Roughly speaking, a community's entire privately owned nonresidential built environment will be replaced about every 40 years, and of course, the total stock will expand to meet the needs of growth.

In this chapter we consider residential construction needs of megapolitan clusters and megapolitan areas first, then nonresidential needs.

Residential Development

We divide residential development needs into growth-related and replacement needs, based on the assumptions and data analyses described next.

Growth-Related Housing Needs

We project growth-related housing needs for each of the megapolitan clusters and their megapolitan areas. The projections are based on the number of total residential units per capita for each geographic area from the 2000 Census, adjusted annually based on the smoothed compounded change in the number of persons per household estimated by Woods and Poole Economics (2010). For instance, in 2000 there were 0.4119 total dwelling units per capita in the United States and 2.59 persons per household. In part because the number of single-person households as a share of total households increases to about 2025 before leveling off, Woods and Poole Economics estimates there will be 2.50 persons per household in 2040.

This technique may overestimate housing units in any given year but may be reasonable over long-term planning horizons. For instance, this technique would estimate 125.6 million total residential units in 2007, but the census reports 127.9 million units,[3] or about 2.3 million more units than projected. The difference turns out to reflect the excess amount by which the housing market had overbuilt from the early to mid-2000s (Nelson 2008).

We estimate housing needs for 2010, 2025, and 2040. The difference between housing needed in 2025 and supported in 2010 is what we call "growth-related" housing. We use the term "supported" as it is based on our assumptions of housing needed per capita within a geographic area (such as a particular

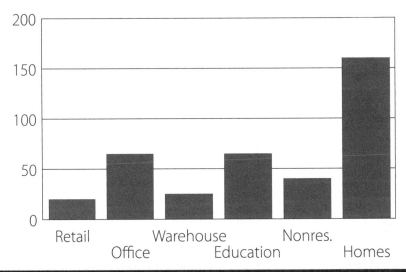

Figure 8.1. Life spans of residential and selected nonresidential structures (years)
Credit: Nonresidential life spans estimated from the 1992 and 2001 samples of the Commercial Buildings Energy Consumption Survey of the Energy Information Administration of the U.S. Department of Energy; residential life span estimated from the 1990 and 2000 Census of Housing for the United States.

megapolitan area), incorporating vacancies, second homes, homes in transition, and other factors from the 2000 Census. Growth-related needs are estimated for each of the time periods 2010–2025, 2025–2040, and 2010–2040.

It is important to qualify that the estimates do not separate units by tenancy or by type, such as attached or small- or large-lot detached. They also include those that are occupied, seasonal, or vacant for any reason. There may also be changes in housing market dynamics that could affect the number of units, such as an increasing share of households occupying the same dwelling, an increasing number of households composed of multigenerational families (parents taking care of their parents and children for example), changes in demand for seasonal units, and, in cases where housing markets are tight, perhaps lower vacancy rates in the future than seen in 2000. Of course, the actual number of units seen in any given year will differ from the projections, and the difference will be more pronounced in 2040 than in 2025. Analysts may revise projections for 2025 and 2040 based on actual housing units existing in 2010, and further considering important local dynamics that appear to be emerging.

Table 8.1 shows our estimate of change in household size for megapolitan clusters, and Table 8.2 reports these figures for megapolitan areas. As household size changes, so will the demand for new housing units relative to the base year, 2010. Tables 8.3 and 8.4 (and Figures 8.2 and 8.3) show our estimates of total housing units needed by megapolitan cluster and area, respectively. Megapolitan clusters and megapolitan areas will see their growth-related housing needs expand as their populations do, accounting for about 65 percent of the 48-state growth-related housing needs between 2010 and 2040.

Replacement Housing

Nearly all structures wear out over time and need to be replaced, or they are destroyed, or they are replaced to make way for different development. In most situations, these structures need to be replaced to continue to provide services to the population. But with a structural lifetime averaging about 160 years, the pace of replacement is slow.[4] There are reasons for this. First, most conventional homes are indeed built to last longer than conventional nonresidential structures. Second, owners of residential structures usually reinvest in their homes far more frequently than owners

Table 8.1. Household Size by Megapolitan Cluster and the Contiguous 48 States, 2010–2040				
Megaregion	Household Size, 2010	Household Size, 2025	Household Size, 2040	Change in Household Size, 2010–2040	Percent Change in Household Size, 2010–2040
Cascadia	2.49	2.43	2.46	−0.02	−0.9
Sierra Pacific	2.72	2.71	2.80	0.08	2.9
Southwest	2.85	2.84	2.95	0.10	3.5
Mountain	2.72	2.69	2.76	0.04	1.4
Texas Triangle	2.71	2.68	2.76	0.06	2.1
Twin Cities	2.53	2.44	2.45	−0.08	−3.2
Great Lakes	2.53	2.45	2.47	−0.06	−2.3
Florida	2.96	2.97	3.09	0.13	8.4
Piedmont	2.56	2.50	2.54	−0.01	−0.6
Megalopolis	2.57	2.49	2.51	−0.06	−2.2
Megaregion total	2.65	2.60	2.66	0.01	0.4
Rest of 48 states	2.52	2.44	2.46	−0.06	−2.3

Source: Based on Woods & Poole Economics (2010)

Table 8.2. Change in Household Size for Megapolitan Areas, 2010–2040

Megapolitan Area	Household Size, 2010	Household Size, 2025	Household Size, 2040	Change in Household Size, 2010–2040	Percent Change in Household Size, 2010–2040
Puget Sound	2.47	2.40	2.43	−0.03	−1.4
Willamette	2.51	2.46	2.51	−0.01	−0.2
Sierra Pacific	2.72	2.71	2.80	0.08	2.9
Southern California	2.95	2.96	3.08	0.14	8.6
Las Vegas	2.62	2.62	2.72	0.11	8.0
Sun Corridor	2.61	2.59	2.68	0.07	2.6
Wasatch Range	3.11	3.05	3.10	−0.01	−0.5
Front Range	2.53	2.51	2.58	0.05	1.8
Dallas–Fort Worth	2.67	2.65	2.74	0.08	2.9
Central Texas	2.68	2.62	2.68	0.01	0.3
Houston	2.77	2.75	2.84	0.07	2.6
Twin Cities	2.53	2.44	2.45	−0.08	−3.2
Chicago	2.63	2.57	2.62	−0.02	−0.6
Michigan Corridor	2.53	2.42	2.43	−0.10	−3.9
Ohio Valley	2.46	2.35	2.35	−0.11	−8.6
Steel Corridor	2.41	2.33	2.36	−0.06	−2.4
Florida Corridor	2.36	2.30	2.33	-0.03	−1.1
Florida Atlantic	2.56	2.55	2.65	0.09	3.6
Atlanta	2.64	2.60	2.66	0.03	1.0
Carolina	2.48	2.40	2.43	−0.05	−2.2
Chesapeake	2.50	2.41	2.41	−0.09	−3.7
New York–Philadelphia	2.62	2.55	2.59	−0.02	−0.9
New England	2.49	2.39	2.39	−0.10	−3.9

Source: Based on Woods & Poole Economics (2010)

of most nonresidential structures. Third, homes are the "vessels" of families, so owners have some incentive to keep the ship afloat. Finally, homes are usually built in areas reserved for residential use, so owners will likely oppose conversions of residential neighborhoods to other land uses—they become NIMBYs ("not in my backyard"). On this latter point, once residential development occurs, land-use changes are unlikely to occur for decades and even centuries.

Loss rates for residential structures vary, of course. Some regions of the country will lose homes at a faster rate than others because of natural disasters, especially hurricanes, which can devastate large swaths of urban areas. More rapidly growing areas will likely lose homes at a faster pace than slower-growing ones because the demand for conversion may be more intense. On the other hand, even slow-growing areas may see relatively high loss rates if older housing is

Table 8.3. Housing Units by Megapolitan Cluster and the Contiguous 48 States, 2010–2040 (in thousands)

Megaregion	Housing Units, 2010	Housing Units, 2025	Housing Units, 2040	Change in Housing Units, 2010–2040	Percent Change in Housing Units, 2010–2040
Cascadia	3,246	4,099	4,733	1,487	45.8
Sierra Pacific	4,740	5,545	6,123	1,383	29.2
Southwest	11,621	13,865	15,693	4,072	35.0
Mountain	2,510	3,235	3,826	1,317	52.5
Texas Triangle	6,673	9,316	10,941	4,268	68.0
Twin Cities	1,722	2,192	2,528	805	46.8
Great Lakes	13,908	15,990	17,038	3,131	22.5
Florida	5,174	6,733	7,730	2,556	49.4
Piedmont	6,412	8,242	9,577	3,165	49.4
Megalopolis	21,876	26,341	28,981	7,105	32.5
Megaregion total	77,882	95,499	107,082	29,201	37.5
Rest of 48 states	47,342	57,252	63,620	16,278	38.4
Contiguous states	125,223	152,870	170,860	45,636	36.4
Megaregion share	62.2%	62.5%	62.7%	68.0%	

Source: Based on Woods & Poole Economics (2010)

easier to replace (perhaps abandoned) with new homes than to rehabilitate.

Table 8.5 reports our estimate of replacement units for megapolitan clusters, and Table 8.6 shows these for megapolitan areas. (See also Figures 8.4 and 8.5.) It should be noted that megapolitan clusters and megapolitan areas account for only about half the replacement of existing homes in the contiguous 48 states. This is due principally to the relatively small base of homes existing in 2010 compared to homes that are needed by 2040, especially in the Cascadia, Mountain, Southwest, Texas Triangle, Florida, and Piedmont megapolitan clusters.

Total Housing Needs

Total projected residential units constructed by megapolitan cluster and the rest of the 48 states are reported in Table 8.5, and total by megapolitan area is reported in Table 8.6. At 9 million units, the Megalopolis megapolitan cluster will lead the nation in total housing construction, followed by the Southwest at 7.7 million. It is the New York–Philadelphia megapolitan area, however, that will lead the nation in total growth-related and replacement housing units constructed, with slightly more than about 8.5 million units, followed closely by Southern California, with 8.5 million units.

The percentage of growth-related and replacement residential units constructed in relation to units existing in 2010 is telling. In Table 8.5, we see that, on the whole, there will be more residential units constructed in the rest of the 48 states outside megapolitan clusters as a percentage of units existing in 2010, 60 percent, than in megapolitan clusters, 50 percent. The principal reason is the very large base of existing homes outside megapolitan clusters that will need to be replaced, in addition to new construction to meet growth needs. Indeed, in some situations outside megapolitan clusters, virtually all new homes built will be to replace existing homes, unless those existing homes are simply abandoned. Among the megapolitan clusters, we see that in the Florida megapolitan cluster, total new housing constructed will come to about 86 percent of units existing in 2010, the highest ratio among the megapolitan clusters. At the other

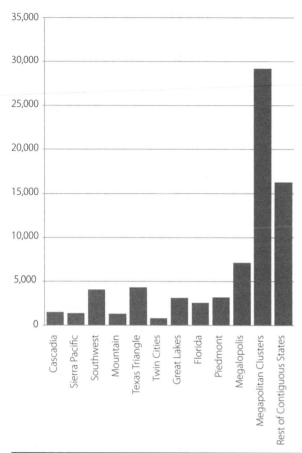

Figure 8.2 Net change to housing inventory by megapolitan cluster, 2010–2040 (in thousands)

end of the scale, new housing built in the Great Lakes megapolitan cluster will come to about a third of units existing in 2010.

Table 8.6 takes a closer look at megapolitan areas. Here we see that total housing construction in the Las Vegas and Texas Gulf megapolitan areas will be more than all the units existing in 2010—residential construction will essentially double the existing supply. Not far behind are the Florida Corridor (89 percent); Sun Corridor (88 percent), Wasatch Range (88 percent), and Texas Corridor (87 percent) megapolitan areas. At the other end of the spectrum is the Steel Corridor, where total new residential construction will be equivalent to just 21 percent of units existing in 2010, followed by

the Michigan Corridor at 31 percent and the Chicago megapolitan area at 39 percent.

Nonresidential Development

Nonresidential development essentially denotes the structures not intended primarily for permanent or seasonal human occupancy. We divide nonresidential development into industrial and commercial/institutional components. Industrial development includes structures needed for such activities as manufacturing, warehousing, transportation, utilities, and communication. Commercial/institutional development includes structures needed for retail, service, finance, government, and related activities. Commercial/institutional uses account for by far the largest share of all nonresidential land uses.

Nonresidential development projections are based on employment estimates published by Woods and Poole Economics (2010). Employment in both broad categories is based on the two-digit North American Industry Classification System (NAICS) industry codes. Following the convention of the Bureau of Economic Analysis (BEA), employment in a given industry is based on the principal activity of the establishment. Our analysis excludes natural resource–based jobs such as farming, forestry, fishing, and mining, as well as construction. We focus principally on structures where the workers' primary activity is conducted inside the structures.

Each analysis includes employment projections, the assumptions relating to space needs and loss rates, and estimated space to be constructed for the periods 2010–2025, 2025–2040, and 2010–2040.

Industrial Development

Here we describe the kinds of jobs comprising the industrial sectors for which we synthesize employment projections published by Woods and Poole Economics for megapolitan clusters and megapolitan areas, review our assumptions of space needs per worker and loss rates for space, and estimate industrial space needs for the projection periods. Our employment and associated space needs for industrial development estimate includes the following NAICS two-digit codes, published in Woods and Poole Economics (2010) based on BEA data:

Table 8.4. Housing Units by Megapolitan Area, 2010–2040 (in thousands)

Megapolitan Area	Housing Units, 2010	Housing Units, 2025	Housing Units, 2040	Change in Housing Units, 2010–2040	Percent Change in Housing Units, 2010–2040
Puget Sound	1,878	2,364	2,733	855	45.5
Willamette	1,368	1,735	2,000	632	46.2
Sierra Pacific	4,740	5,545	6,123	1,383	29.2
Southern California	8,140	9,389	10,331	2,191	26.9
Las Vegas	1,065	1,345	1,637	572	53.7
Sun Corridor	2,416	3,172	3,785	1,369	56.7
Wasatch Range	847	1,119	1,356	508	60.0
Front Range	1,662	2,118	2,473	811	48.8
Dallas–Fort Worth	2,786	3,729	4,329	1,543	55.4
Central Texas	1,482	2,283	2,777	1,295	87.4
Houston	2,404	3,301	3,830	1,426	59.3
Twin Cities	1,722	2,192	2,528	805	46.8
Chicago	5,054	5,923	6,450	1,395	27.6
Michigan Corridor	3,658	4,143	4,355	697	19.1
Ohio Valley	2,256	2,731	3,019	763	33.8
Steel Corridor	2,940	3,175	3,188	248	8.4
Florida Corridor	3,690	4,990	5,897	2,207	59.8
Florida Atlantic	2,587	3,366	3,865	1,278	49.4
Atlanta	3,010	3,940	4,585	1,575	52.3
Carolina	3,403	4,300	4,990	1,588	46.7
Chesapeake	5,018	6,729	7,942	2,925	58.3
New York–Philadelphia	13,354	15,437	16,477	3,123	23.4
New England	3,505	4,168	4,550	1,045	29.8

Source: Based on Woods & Poole Economics (2010)

Utilities

Establishments engaged in the provision of electric power, natural gas, steam supply, water supply, and sewage removal. Utilities include electric power generation, electric power transmission, electric power distribution, natural gas distribution, steam supply provision, steam supply distribution, water treatment, water distribution, sewage collection, sewage treatment, and disposal of waste through sewer systems and sewage treatment facilities. Excluded are establishments primarily engaged in waste management services that collect, treat, and dispose of waste materials but do not use sewer systems or sewage treatment facilities. Also excluded from this sector are federal or state or local government–operated establishments.

Manufacturing

Establishments engaged in the mechanical, physical, or chemical transformation of materials, substances, or components into new products. The assembling of component parts of manufactured products is considered manufacturing, except in cases where the component parts are associated with structures. Manufacturing establishments can be plants, factories, or mills, as well as bakeries, candy stores, and custom tailors. Manufacturing establishments may either process materials or contract with other establishments to process their materials for them. Broadly defined, manufacturing industries include the following: food processing, such as canning, baking, meat processing, and beverages; tobacco products; textile mill products, such as fabric, carpets, and rugs;

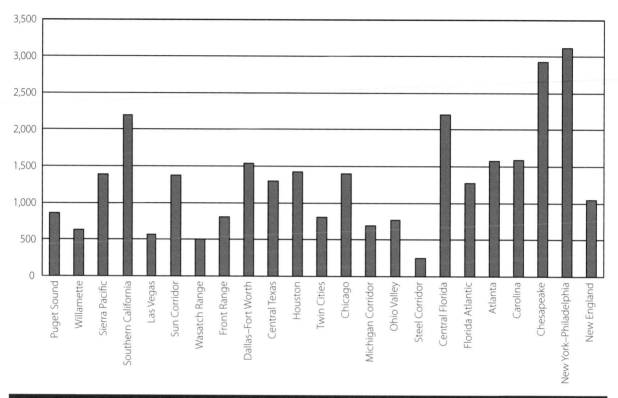

Figure 8.3. Net change to housing inventory by megapolitan area, 2010–2040 (in thousands)

Table 8.5. Housing Construction by Megapolitan Cluster, 2010–2040 (in thousands)

Megaregion	Net Additions to Housing Inventory, 2010–2040	Housing Units Replaced, 2010–2040	Total Housing Construction, 2010–2040	Housing Constructed as Share of Units in 2010 (%)
Cascadia	1,487	413	1,900	58.5
Sierra Pacific	1,383	603	1,986	41.9
Southwest	4,072	1,479	5,551	47.8
Mountain	1,317	319	1,636	65.2
Texas Triangle	4,268	1,312	5,580	83.6
Twin Cities	805	278	1,083	62.9
Great Lakes	3,131	2,245	5,375	38.7
Florida	2,556	1,017	3,573	69.1
Piedmont	3,165	1,260	4,426	69.0
Megalopolis	7,105	2,783	9,888	45.2
Megaregion total	29,201	11,709	40,910	52.5

Table 8.6. Housing Construction by Megapolitan Area, 2010–2040 (in thousands)

Megapolitan Area	Net Additions to Housing Inventory, 2010–2040	Housing Units Replaced, 2010–2040	Total Housing Construction, 2010–2040	Housing Constructed as Share of Units in 2010 (%)
Puget Sound	855	239	1,094	58.3
Willamette	632	174	806	58.9
Sierra Pacific	1,383	603	1,986	41.9
Southern California	2,191	1,036	3,226	39.6
Las Vegas	572	135	707	66.4
Sun Corridor	1,369	307	1,677	69.4
Wasatch Range	508	108	616	72.7
Front Range	811	211	1,022	61.5
Dallas–Fort Worth	1,543	548	2,090	75.0
Central Texas	1,295	291	1,586	107.0
Houston	1,426	473	1,898	79.0
Twin Cities	805	278	1,083	62.9
Chicago	1,395	816	2,211	43.7
Michigan Corridor	697	590	1,288	35.2
Ohio Valley	763	364	1,127	50.0
Steel Corridor	248	474	722	28.6
Florida Corridor	2,207	725	2,932	79.5
Florida Atlantic	1,278	509	1,786	69.1
Atlanta	1,575	592	2,167	72.0
Carolina	1,588	669	2,256	66.3
Chesapeake	2,925	638	3,563	71.0
New York–Philadelphia	3,123	1,699	4,822	36.1
New England	1,045	446	1,491	42.6

apparel; wood equipment; transportation equipment, such as cars, trucks, ships, and airplanes; instruments; and miscellaneous industries, such as jewelry, musical instrument, and toy manufacture. Excluded from manufacturing is the publishing of printed materials.

Wholesale trade
Establishments engaged in wholesaling merchandise, generally without transformation, and rendering services incidental to the sale of merchandise. The merchandise described in this sector includes the outputs of agriculture, mining, manufacturing, and certain information industries, such as publishing. Wholesale establishments are primarily engaged in selling merchandise to retailers; or to industrial, commercial, institutional, farm, or construction contractors; or to professional business users; or to other wholesalers or brokers. The merchandise sold by wholesalers includes all goods used by institutions, such as schools and hospitals, as well as virtually all goods sold at the retail level. Wholesalers can be merchant wholesalers that purchase goods from manufacturers or other wholesalers and sell them; sales branches of manufacturing, mining, or farm companies engaged in marketing the products of the company to retail establishments; or agents, merchandise or commodity brokers, and commission merchants.

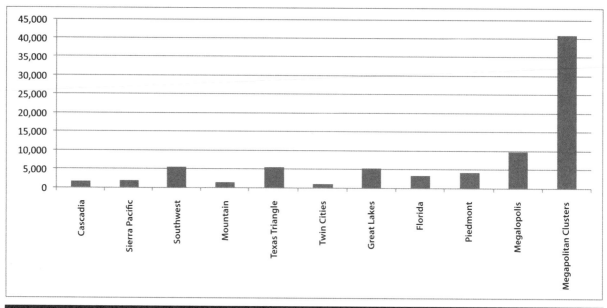

Figure 8.4. Total housing construction by megapolitan cluster, 2010–2040 (in thousands)

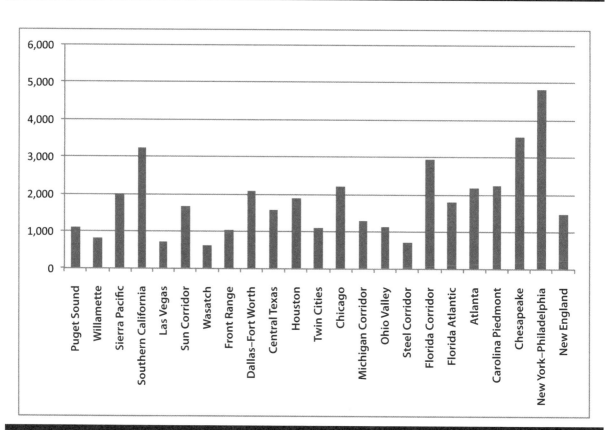

Figure 8.5. Total housing construction by megapolitan area, 2010–2040 (in thousands)

Transportation and warehousing

Industries providing transportation of passengers and cargo, and warehousing and storage for goods. Establishments in these industries use transportation equipment or transportation-related facilities as a productive asset. Transportation includes railroads, highway passenger transportation, trucking, shipping, air transportation, pipelines, and transportation services. Transportation also includes private postal services and courier services but excludes the U.S. Postal Service. Warehousing includes refrigerated storage and grain elevators.

Employment projections are based on total, as opposed to part-time, jobs in each sector, summed for the industrial category; they also include independent contractors or others not registered for state health or employment compensation purposes. This is based on the BEA's convention for reporting jobs.[5] We report industrial employment for megapolitan clusters in Table 8.7 and for megapolitan areas in Table 8.8, along with employment change, for the periods 2010–2025, 2025–2040, and 2010–2040. (See also Figures 8.6 and 8.7.) For the most part, a megapolitan cluster's share of industrial employment matches its share of total population. However, its share of employment change

is projected by Woods and Poole Economics (2010) to decline slightly relative to the rest of the 48 states to 2040. One reason is simply that industrial jobs are a declining share of all jobs. While such jobs increase from about 31.8 million in 2010 to about 36.8 million in 2040, or about 17 percent, total U.S. jobs increase from 174.8 million to 248.6 million, or about 42 percent. Another is that many industrial activities, because of their demand for large tracts and need to be remote from population centers for environmental reasons, choose rural or exurban locations away from metropolitan centers.

Among megapolitan clusters, the Southwest and Texas Triangle megapolitan clusters will lead the nation in industrial job growth. Among megapolitan areas, Southern California will dominate industrial job growth (principally in the outer counties east and north of Los Angeles). New England, however, is projected to see a small decline in the total number of industrial jobs.

Commercial and Institutional Employment

We now describe the kinds of jobs comprising the commercial and institutional sectors for which we synthesize employment projections published by Woods

Table 8.7. Industrial Employment by Megapolitan Cluster and Contiguous States, 2010–2040 (in thousands)					
Megaregion	*2010*	*2025*	*2040*	*Change*	*Percent Change*
Cascadia	906	973	1,053	148	16.3
Sierra Pacific	1,158	1,265	1,384	226	19.5
Southwest	2,792	3,066	3,380	588	21.1
Mountain	695	795	912	217	31.3
Texas Triangle	2,091	2,340	2,627	536	25.6
Twin Cities	567	603	640	73	12.8
Great Lakes	3,853	3,953	4,077	225	5.8
Florida	1,140	1,288	1,462	323	28.3
Piedmont	1,814	1,939	2,085	271	18.9
Megalopolis	4,877	5,182	5,535	658	13.5
Megaregion total	19,893	21,405	23,156	3,263	16.4
Rest of contiguous states	11,684	12,589	13,645	1,961	16.8
Contiguous 48 states	31,577	33,994	36,801	5,223	16.5
Megaregion share of 48 states	63.0%	63.0%	62.9%	62.5%	

Source: Based on Woods & Poole Economics (2010)

Table 8.8. Industrial Employment by Megapolitan Area, 2010–2040 (in thousands)

Megapolitan Area	2010	2025	2040	Change	Percent Change
Puget Sound	530	576	631	101	19.0
Willamette	376	397	422	47	12.5
Sierra Pacific	1,158	1,265	1,384	226	19.5
Southern California	2,083	2,237	2,400	317	15.2
Las Vegas	200	262	342	142	71.3
Sun Corridor	509	568	638	129	25.3
Wasatch Range	289	342	406	117	40.4
Front Range	406	453	506	101	28.8
Dallas–Fort Worth	869	965	1,072	204	23.4
Central Texas	408	463	529	121	29.7
Houston	814	912	1,025	211	25.9
Twin Cities	567	603	640	73	12.8
Chicago	1,568	1,623	1,691	124	7.9
Michigan Corridor	912	921	933	21	2.4
Ohio Valley	595	621	650	55	9.3
Steel Corridor	778	789	803	24	3.1
Florida Corridor	638	732	850	212	33.2
Florida Atlantic	502	556	613	111	22.1
Atlanta	825	902	987	162	19.6
Carolina	989	1,037	1,098	109	11.0
Chesapeake	1,064	1,182	1,312	248	23.3
New York–Philadelphia	2,934	3,088	3,266	332	11.3
New England	879	912	957	78	8.9

Source: Based on Woods & Poole Economics (2010)

and Poole Economics (2010) for megapolitan clusters and megapolitan areas, review our assumptions of space needs per worker and loss rates for space, and estimate commercial and institutional space needs for the projection periods. The employment and associated space needs for industrial development data are reported for the following NAICS two-digit codes, published in Woods and Poole Economics (2010) based on BEA data, excluding federal military employment.

Retail trade

Establishments engaged in retailing merchandise, generally without transformation, and rendering services incidental to the sale of merchandise. Retail trade includes store retailers such as motor vehicle and parts dealers, including automobile, motorcycle, and boat dealers, as well as tire and automobile parts stores; furniture and home furnishing stores; electronics and appliance stores; food and beverage stores, including supermarkets, convenience stores, butchers, and bakeries; health and personal care stores such as pharmacies and optical goods stores; gasoline stations; clothing and clothing accessory stores; sporting goods, hobby, book, and music stores; department stores; and miscellaneous establishments, including office supply stores, mobile home dealers, thrift shops,

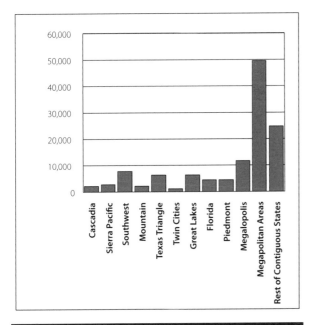

Figure 8.6. Total new jobs by megapolitan cluster, 2010–2040 (in millions)

florists, tobacco stores, and pet shops. Retail trade also includes nonstore retailers such as Internet and catalog sellers, as well as home delivery establishments such as heating oil dealers. Retail trade excludes eating and drinking places, including restaurants, bars, and takeout stands.

Information

Establishments engaged in producing and distributing information and cultural products; providing the means to transmit or distribute these products as well as data or communications; and processing data. The main components of this sector are the publishing industries, including software publishing, and both traditional publishing and publishing exclusively on the Internet; the motion picture and sound recording industries; movie theaters; the broadcasting industries, including traditional broadcasting and those broadcasting exclusively over the Internet; the telecommunications industries; the industries known as Internet service providers and Web search portals;

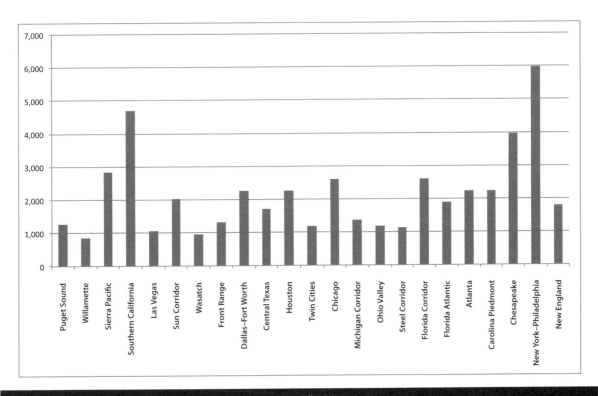

Figure 8.7. Total new jobs by megapolitan area, 2010–2040 (in millions)

data processing industries; and the information services industries.

Finance and insurance

Establishments primarily either engaged in or facilitating financial transactions (e.g., transactions involving the creation, liquidation, or change in ownership of financial assets). Establishments include depository institutions, such as commercial banks, credit unions, savings and loans, and foreign banks; credit institutions; credit card processing companies; investment companies; brokers and dealers in securities and commodity contracts; security and commodity exchanges; carriers of all types of insurance; and insurance agents and insurance brokers. Also included are central banks and monetary authorities charged with monetary control.

Real estate and rental and leasing

Establishments primarily engaged in renting, leasing, or otherwise allowing the use of tangible or intangible assets, and establishments providing related services. Real estate includes real estate leasing establishments, real estate agencies and brokerages, property management establishments, appraisals establishments, and escrow agencies. Rental and leasing includes car and truck rental companies, consumer goods rentals such as video stores and formal wear rental stores, and commercial equipment renting and leasing construction, transportation, office, and farm equipment. Also included are establishments that lease nonfinancial and noncopyrighted intangible assets such as patents and trademarks.

Professional and technical services

Establishments that specialize in performing professional, scientific, and technical activities for others. These activities include legal advice and representation; accounting, bookkeeping, and payroll services; architectural, engineering, and specialized design services; computer services; consulting services; research services; advertising services; photographic services; translation and interpretation services; veterinary services; and other professional, scientific, and technical services. Excluded are establishments primarily engaged in providing office administrative services, such as financial planning, billing and recordkeeping, personnel, and physical distribution and logistics.

Management of companies and enterprises

Bank holding establishments, other holding establishments, and corporate management establishments, as well as regional and subsidiary management establishments. Company or enterprise headquarters are included.

Administrative and waste management

Establishments engaged in office administration, hiring and placing of personnel, document preparation and similar clerical services, solicitation, collection, security and surveillance services, cleaning, and waste disposal services. Among many other establishments, administrative includes call centers, telemarketers, janitorial services, armored cars, temporary employment agencies, locksmiths, landscaping, and travel agencies. Waste management includes, among other establishments, those involved in solid waste collections and disposal, landfill operations and septic tank maintenance. Excluded from administrative and waste management are establishments involved in administering, overseeing, and managing other establishments of the company or enterprise. Also excluded are government establishments engaged in administering, overseeing, and managing governmental programs.

Educational services

Private elementary schools, junior colleges, colleges, universities, and professional schools. Also included are trade and vocational schools, business and secretarial schools, computer training services, language schools, fine arts training centers, sports training establishments, driving schools, flight schools, and establishments that provide test preparation and tutoring. Educational services may be provided in educational institutions, the workplace, or the home through correspondence, television, or other means. Public schools, including colleges and universities, are excluded from educational services.

Health care and social assistance

Establishments providing health care and social assistance for individuals. Health care establishments include those providing ambulatory care services (e.g., physician offices, dentists, specialists, HMO care centers, dialysis centers, blood banks, ambulance services), hospitals, and nursing and residential care facilities. Social assistance establishments include those providing individual and family services (e.g., adoption agencies and youth centers) and community services, such as food banks and homeless shelters. Excluded from this sector are those providing aerobic classes and nonmedical diet and weight-reducing centers. Also excluded are public hospitals and clinics.

Arts, entertainment, and recreation

Establishments involved in producing, promoting, or participating in live performances, events, or exhibits intended for public viewing; establishments that preserve and exhibit objects and sites of historical, cultural, or educational interest; and establishments that operate facilities or provide services that enable patrons to participate in recreational activities or pursue amusement, hobby, and leisure time interests. The sector includes establishments engaged in the performing arts, sporting events, museums, zoos, amusement and theme parks, golf courses, marinas, casinos, and gambling. Excluded are movie theaters.

Accommodation and food services

Hotels, motels, casino hotels, bed-and-breakfasts, campgrounds and recreational vehicle parks, and other lodging places, as well as eating and drinking places, including restaurants, bars, and takeout stands. Also included are caterers and food service contractors.

Other services, except public administration

Churches and establishments engaged in equipment and machinery repairing, promoting or administering religious activities, grant-making, advocacy, and establishments providing dry cleaning and laundry services, personal care services, death care services, pet care services, photofinishing services, temporary parking services, and dating services. Private households that engage in employing workers on or about the premises in activities primarily concerned with the operation of the household are included in this sector.

Federal civilian

All federal government workers regardless of their establishment classification. Federal civilian employment includes that in executive offices and legislative bodies; courts; public order and safety institutions; correctional institutions; taxation; administration and delivery of human resource programs, such as health, education, and public assistance services; housing and urban development programs; environmental programs; regulators, including air traffic controllers and public service commissions; the U.S. Postal Service; and other federal government agencies.

State and local government

The same as federal civilian except that the activities are run by state and local governments. At the local level, this includes all public schools, as well as police and fire departments; at the state level, it includes all public junior colleges, colleges, and universities.

Commercial/institutional employment projections are based on total, as opposed to part-time, jobs in each sector. They include independent contractors or others not registered for state health or employment compensation purposes. In Table 8.9, we report commercial/institutional employment for megapolitan clusters and in Table 8.10 we do so for megapolitan areas. The megapolitan cluster share of commercial/institutional employment is higher than that for industrial employment, and somewhat higher than the population growth. It would seem that megapolitan clusters are gaining employment share in commercial/institutional employment faster than population growth while areas outside megapolitan clusters are gaining industrial employment at a faster pace.

At 11.0 million new jobs, Megalopolis dominates commercial/institutional growth among megapolitan clusters. The Southwest follows, with 7.2 million new jobs, with the Great Lakes adding another 6.0 million jobs. Not coincidentally, these are the nation's largest megapolitan clusters as well. The largest megapolitan areas in each of these megapolitan clusters also lead megapolitan employment change, with the New York–Philadelphia megapolitan area adding 5.7 million jobs, Southern California 4.4 million, and Chicago 2.5 million.

What about the space needed to support these jobs? Using estimates by Nelson (2006) based on such sources as the U.S. Department of Energy's Energy Consumption Survey series, we estimate the total volume of space that would be supported for megapolitan clusters (Table 8.11) and megapolitan areas (Table 8.12). This includes a vacancy factor. In the next two tables (Table 8.13 for megapolitan clusters and Table 8.14 for megapolitan areas), we estimate the total amount of new space needed to accommodate job growth, as well as space

Table 8.9. Commercial/Institutional Employment by Megapolitan Cluster and Contiguous States, 2010–2040 (in thousands)

Megaregion	2010	2025	2040	Change	Percent Change
Cascadia	3,768	4,656	5,729	1,961	52.0
Sierra Pacific	6,108	7,327	8,712	2,605	42.6
Southwest	13,890	17,152	21,082	7,192	51.8
Mountain	3,324	4,245	5,390	2,065	62.1
Texas Triangle	8,492	10,979	14,155	5,663	66.7
Twin Cities	2,335	2,845	3,436	1,101	47.1
Great Lakes	15,846	18,707	21,891	6,045	38.1
Florida	6,743	8,603	10,904	4,161	61.7
Piedmont	7,003	8,864	11,214	4,211	60.1
Megalopolis	28,085	33,241	39,138	11,053	39.4
Megaregion total	95,595	116,619	141,651	46,056	48.2
Rest of contiguous states	47,660	57,924	70,186	22,526	47.3
Contiguous 48 states	143,255	174,542	211,837	68,582	47.9
Megaregion share of 48 states	66.7%	66.8%	66.9%	67.2%	

Source: Based on Woods & Poole Economics (2010)

Table 8.10. Commercial/Institutional Employment by Megapolitan Area, 2010–2040 (in thousands)

Megapolitan Area	2010	2025	2040	Change	Percent Change
Puget Sound	2,243	2,771	3,411	1,168	52.1
Willamette	1,526	1,884	2,318	793	52.0
Sierra Pacific	6,108	7,327	8,712	2,605	42.6
Southern California	10,130	12,157	14,500	4,370	43.1
Las Vegas	1,162	1,555	2,077	916	78.8
Sun Corridor	2,598	3,440	4,505	1,906	73.4
Wasatch Range	1,192	1,557	2,034	842	70.7
Front Range	2,133	2,687	3,356	1,223	57.3
Dallas–Fort Worth	3,500	4,414	5,541	2,041	58.3
Central Texas	2,014	2,700	3,606	1,592	79.1
Houston	2,978	3,864	5,008	2,030	68.2
Twin Cities	2,335	2,845	3,436	1,101	47.1
Chicago	6,276	7,450	8,752	2,475	39.4
Michigan Corridor	3,749	4,385	5,090	1,341	35.8
Ohio Valley	2,640	3,163	3,768	1,128	42.7
Steel Corridor	3,181	3,710	4,281	1,100	38.6
Florida Corridor	3,701	4,751	6,073	2,372	68.1
Florida Atlantic	3,042	3,852	4,831	1,789	58.8
Atlanta	3,490	4,413	5,564	2,074	59.4
Carolina	3,513	4,451	5,650	2,137	60.8
Chesapeake	6,890	8,576	10,598	3,708	53.8
New York–Philadelphia	16,750	19,419	22,400	5,650	33.7
New England	4,445	5,246	6,140	1,695	38.1

Source: Based on Woods & Poole Economics (2010)

Table 8.11. Nonresidential Space Supported by Megapolitan Cluster and the Contiguous States, 2010–2040 (in millions of square feet)

Megaregion	2010	2025	2040	Change	Percent Change
Cascadia	2,233	2,654	3,165	932	41.7
Sierra Pacific	3,455	4,051	4,724	1,269	36.7
Southwest	7,965	9,572	11,498	3,533	48.4
Mountain	1,897	2,363	2,938	1,040	58.8
Texas Triangle	5,362	6,716	8,430	3,068	57.2
Twin Cities	1,537	1,813	2,130	594	38.6
Great Lakes	10,388	11,847	13,475	3,087	29.7
Florida	3,999	4,996	6,224	2,225	55.6
Piedmont	4,550	5,530	6,766	2,216	48.7
Megalopolis	14,507	16,784	19,402	4,895	33.7
Megaregion total	55,893	66,327	78,751	22,858	40.9
Rest of contiguous states	29,001	34,133	40,250	11,249	38.8
Contiguous 48 states	84,893	100,460	119,001	34,108	40.2
Megaregion share of 48 states	65.8%	66.0%	66.2%		

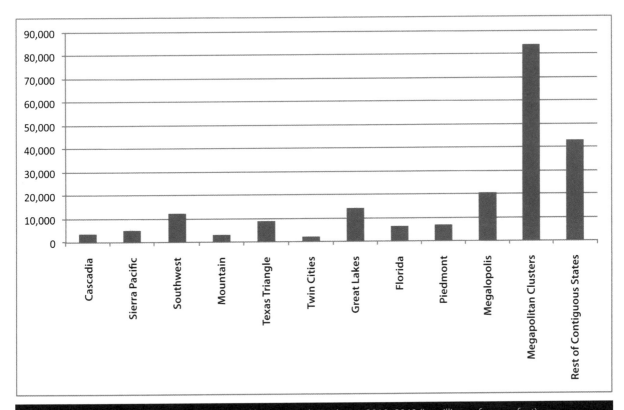

Figure 8.8. Total nonresidential space constructed by megapolitan cluster, 2010–2040 (in millions of square feet)

Table 8.12. Nonresidential Space Supported by Megapolitan Area, 2010–2040 (in millions of square feet)

Megapolitan Area	2010	2025	2040	Change	Percent Change
Puget Sound	1,317	1,569	1,874	557	42.3
Willamette	916	1,085	1,291	375	40.9
Sierra Pacific	3,455	4,051	4,724	1,269	36.7
Southern California	5,878	6,873	8,015	2,137	36.4
Las Vegas	620	824	1,095	475	76.7
Sun Corridor	1,468	1,875	2,388	920	62.7
Wasatch Range	705	897	1,144	439	62.3
Front Range	1,192	1,465	1,794	601	50.4
Dallas–Fort Worth	2,233	2,728	3,331	1,098	49.2
Central Texas	1,217	1,587	2,073	856	70.3
Houston	1,912	2,401	3,027	1,114	58.3
Twin Cities	1,537	1,813	2,130	594	38.6
Chicago	4,134	4,735	5,405	1,271	30.7
Michigan Corridor	2,469	2,788	3,143	674	27.3
Ohio Valley	1,702	1,976	2,291	589	38.6
Steel Corridor	2,083	2,349	2,636	553	26.5
Florida Corridor	2,201	2,766	3,476	1,275	57.9
Florida Atlantic	1,798	2,230	2,748	950	52.8
Atlanta	2,219	2,715	3,328	1,109	50.0
Carolina	2,330	2,815	3,438	1,107	47.5
Chesapeake	4,012	4,904	5,968	1,956	48.8
New York–Philadelphia	8,250	9,322	10,522	2,272	27.5
New England	2,245	2,558	2,912	667	29.7

that we estimate will be recycled, also based on methods developed by Nelson (2006). (See also Figures 8.8 and 8.9.) Recycled space includes space that is demolished and rebuilt, or repurposed, such as loft conversions for residential development. There is no definitive study on the pace of nonresidential space recycling, but our estimates are based on best available federal data. In all cases, we estimate there will be more construction of nonresidential spaces to meet growth or recycling needs between 2010 and 2040 than existed in 2010.

Megapolitan America and the Nation's Gross Regional Product

We turn now to megapolitan clusters' and megapolitans' share of the nation's growth. Table 8.15 shows for

megapolitan clusters and Table 8.16 for megapolitan areas how much megapolitan America dominates the nation's economy (see Figures 8.10 and 8.11). In 2010, megapolitan America accounted for about 71 percent of the nation's GDP, and by 2040 this figure will grow to about 72 percent. Indeed, megapolitan America will account for about 73 percent of the change in the nation's GDP.

Summary Observations

Two-thirds of America's growth over the next generation and beyond will be concentrated in specific landscapes that are reasonably well defined and comprise a relatively small share of the privately owned land in the contiguous 48 states. In the heyday of the mid-2000s, new

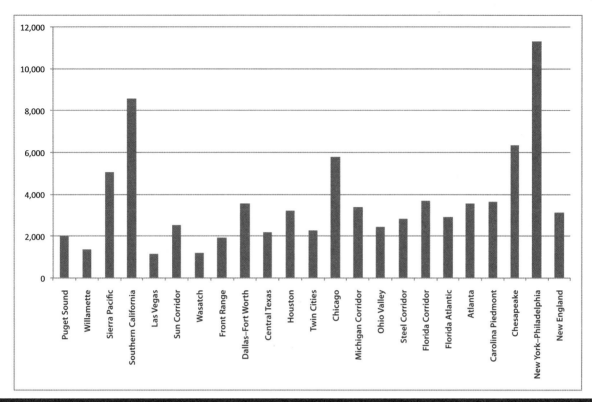

Figure 8.9. Total nonresidential space constructed by megapolitan area, 2010–2040 (in millions of square feet)

Table 8.13. Total Space Constructed by Megapolitan Cluster and the Contiguous States, 2010–2040 (in millions of square feet)

Megaregion	Space Added to Inventory, 2010–2040	Space Recycled, 2010–2040	Total Space Constructed, 2010–2040	Percent of Space in 2010
Cascadia	932	2,450	3,382	151.5
Sierra Pacific	1,269	3,792	5,061	146.5
Southwest	3,533	8,742	12,275	158.1
Mountain	1,040	2,082	3,123	168.6
Texas Triangle	3,068	5,885	8,953	167.0
Twin Cities	594	1,687	2,280	148.4
Great Lakes	3,087	11,402	14,489	139.5
Florida	2,225	4,389	6,614	165.4
Piedmont	2,216	4,993	7,209	158.5
Megalopolis	4,895	15,922	20,817	143.5
Megaregion total	22,858	61,346	84,204	150.7
Rest of contiguous states	11,249	31,830	43,080	148.5
Contiguous 48 states	34,108	63,670	97,778	115.2
Megaregion share of 48 states	67.0%	96.3%	86.1%	

Table 8.14. Total Space Constructed by Megapolitan Area, 2010–2040 (in millions of square feet)

Megapolitan Area	Space Added to Inventory, 2010–2040	Space Recycled, 2010–2040	Total Space Constructed, 2010–2040	Percent of Space in 2010
Puget Sound	557	1,445	2,003	152.1
Willamette	375	1,005	1,380	150.7
Sierra Pacific	1,269	3,792	5,061	146.5
Southern California	2,137	6,451	8,589	146.1
Las Vegas	475	680	1,155	186.4
Sun Corridor	920	1,611	2,531	172.4
Wasatch Range	439	774	1,213	172.1
Front Range	601	1,309	1,910	160.2
Dallas–Fort Worth	1,098	2,451	3,549	158.9
Central Texas	856	1,336	2,192	180.1
Houston	1,114	2,099	3,213	168.0
Twin Cities	594	1,687	2,280	148.4
Chicago	1,271	4,537	5,808	140.5
Michigan Corridor	674	2,710	3,384	137.1
Ohio Valley	589	1,868	2,457	148.4
Steel Corridor	553	2,287	2,839	136.3
Florida Corridor	1,275	2,416	3,690	167.7
Florida Atlantic	950	1,974	2,924	162.6
Atlanta	1,109	2,436	3,545	159.7
Carolina	1,107	2,557	3,665	157.3
Chesapeake	1,956	4,403	6,359	158.5
New York–Philadelphia	2,272	9,055	11,327	137.3
New England	667	2,464	3,131	139.5

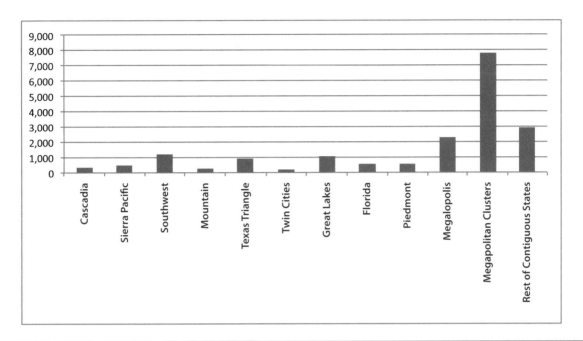

Figure 8.10. Gross regional product by megapolitan cluster and contiguous states, 2010–2040 (in billions of US$)

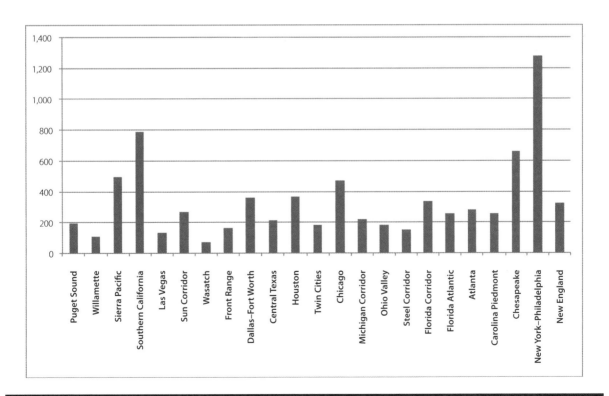

Figure 8.11. Gross regional product by megapolitan area, 2010–2040 (in millions of US$)

Table 8.15. Gross Regional Product by Megapolitan Cluster and the Contiguous States, 2010–2040 (in billions of US$)

Megaregion	Gross Regional Product, 2010	Gross Regional Product, 2025	Gross Regional Product, 2040	Change in Gross Regional Product, 2010–2040	Percent Change in Gross Regional Product, 2010–2040
Cascadia	358	488	668	309	86.2
Sierra Pacific	658	873	1,156	497	75.6
Southwest	1,245	1,741	2,440	1,196	96.1
Mountain	277	377	511	234	88.2
Texas Triangle	874	1,256	1,814	939	107.4
Twin Cities	206	282	386	180	87.2
Great Lakes	1,400	1,844	2,425	1,025	73.2
Florida	521	761	1,112	591	113.4
Piedmont	611	833	1,147	536	87.7
Megalopolis	2,854	3,825	5,113	2,259	79.1
Megaregion total	9,006	12,280	16,772	7,766	86.2
Rest of contiguous states	3,689	4,920	6,623	2,934	79.5
Contiguous 48 states	12,695	17,200	23,395	10,700	88.3
Megaregion share of 48 states	70.9%	71.4%	71.7%	72.6%	

Table 8.16. Gross Regional Product by Megapolitan Area and the Contiguous States, 2010–2040 (in millions of US$)

Megapolitan Area	Gross Regional Product, 2010	Gross Regional Product, 2025	Gross Regional Product, 2040	Change in Gross Regional Product, 2010–2040	Percent Change in Gross Regional Product, 2010–2040
Puget Sound	227	311	425	198	87.1
Willamette	131	178	242	111	88.8
Sierra Pacific	658	873	1,156	497	75.6
Southern California	940	1,278	1,731	791	88.1
Las Vegas	97	150	234	137	141.8
Sun Corridor	208	312	475	267	128.7
Wasatch Range	89	118	160	71	78.8
Front Range	188	258	351	163	86.8
Dallas–Fort Worth	352	500	711	359	101.9
Central Texas	173	258	388	215	128.6
Houston	349	498	714	365	108.5
Twin Cities	206	282	386	180	87.2
Chicago	605	808	1,076	470	77.7
Michigan Corridor	317	412	535	218	68.6
Ohio Valley	215	293	398	183	88.8
Steel Corridor	262	330	417	155	59.1
Florida Corridor	276	409	609	333	120.5
Florida Atlantic	245	352	503	258	105.5
Atlanta	300	418	582	282	93.9
Carolina	311	416	565	254	81.6
Chesapeake	639	913	1,298	658	103.0
New York–Philadelphia	1,807	2,364	3,084	1,277	70.7
New England	408	547	731	323	79.2

Source: Based on Woods & Poole Economics (2010)

construction for all purposes, including infrastructure, topped $1 trillion annually. As the nation absorbs over-development in selected sectors and in selected parts of the country, development will rise to this level by about the mid-2010s, for two reasons. First, the nation is still growing—it is the fastest-growing industrialized nation in the world—and second, much of the existing built stock needs to be rehabilitated, if not replaced entirely, at a fairly rapid pace. We estimate that between 2010 and 2040, the nation will spend more than $40 trillion on development, with up to $30 trillion of that spent on megapolitan clusters and their megapolitan areas. Implications for the nation's transportation system and natural resources are discussed in the next two chapters.

9

TRANSPORTATION PLANNING AND THE MEGAPOLITANS

Megapolitan areas need more transportation capacity to serve the millions of new people America will be adding in the coming decades. The policy debate over funding major public works projects such as transportation is in full swing, as evidenced by Senator Charles Schumer's 2011 observation: "If we do not continue to build grand projects, to seek the solutions that are necessary for ensuring our economic future . . . we will end up paralyzed . . . as our competitors overseas pull further and further ahead."

This chapter advances Schumer's theme by covering the planning and politics of adding significant new transportation capacity to megapolitan areas. In our view, there are two key areas of ground-based transportation investments that most megapolitan areas may see by mid-century: enhancements to the current interstate highways and the development of regional high-speed (or at least higher-speed) rail.

In addition, the megapolitan areas are the global gateways through which the United States engages the global economy. These regions are home to all of the major international airports and virtually every high-volume port in the nation. Improving and maintaining this infrastructure will become an important priority as the United States seeks more trade and exports as a way to shift its economy from consumption and real estate speculation to technology, innovation, and high-value manufacturing. The megapolitan capacity for trade is a key element in this economic transition. Failure to establish adequate infrastructure to move people and goods around the country could significantly constrain future economic growth.

Yet the politics of infrastructure investment, once characterized by a broad bipartisan consensus, are now an area of increased political conflict. A large number of politicians at the state and national levels see major infrastructure projects such as highways, transit systems, and high-speed rail (HSR) as too costly, especially during the protracted economic slowdown from the late 2000s into the mid-2010s. Indeed, some major transportation projects with federal appropriation were canceled for lack of state matching funds. For the sake of long-term economic competitiveness in a global economy, this may prove to have been shortsighted.

Advocates for major infrastructure improvements have not made a sufficiently compelling case for their value in economic development to gain the type of public support that would insulate such efforts from the charge that they are simply pork. Meanwhile, the United States, once the leader in cutting-edge transportation technology, from canals to freeways, is now falling far behind global competitors such as China and the European Union in areas such as HSR.

The Megapolitan Interstates

The Interstate Highway System began in the mid-1950s with the goal of connecting all metropolitan areas in the United States with populations above 50,000 via four lanes of limited-access highway. The interstate highways were sold with the tag line "coast to coast without a light" and supposedly facilitated national defense, which is why the system's formal label still refers to it as a "defense highway." The reality is that interstates had limited utility in military operations, in part because the bridges were not high enough to clear missile carriers and other defense equipment. Nonetheless, interstates transformed the nation's regions and their economies by providing a much higher-capacity system than the old two-lane highways they replaced.

When the first interstate highway appeared in the 1950s, the United States had a population of just 150 million residents. It now has more than 310 million people and is well on the path to having 400 million by 2040. What were once the wide-open highways of the 1960s and 1970s are the congested roads of the 2010s. Much of the intrametropolitan capacity of the interstate system has been expanded considerably. The sections of I-85 and I-75 that converge and pass through the Atlanta region are illustrative. As the highway approaches Atlanta's core, it opens up to no less than 14 lanes. Yet much of I-85, which forms the transportation spine for the Piedmont region from Raleigh, North Carolina, in the east to Atlanta in the west, remains unimproved. On busy days, especially during holiday weekends, long stretches of the I-85 corridor are completely jammed. Interestingly, much of this congestion is found in rural areas, with no major city or suburb proximate. This is also true for the other interstates that link up big metropolitan areas such as I-95 from Maine to Virginia and I-35 in Texas. There are also nearby metropolitan areas that have some of the worst "rural" traffic in the United States. Most of the rural

highways really lie in megapolitan areas that have yet to be designated CSAs. Examples include I-4 between Orlando and Tampa, I-10 between Phoenix and Tucson, and I-25 from Fort Collins to Colorado Springs (passing through metropolitan Denver).

Clearly, the United States needs to rethink the interstate system and make it work for a nation that has more than doubled its population since the mid-20th century, when the interstates were begun. To start, we need a "megapolitan plan" for the interstates. This includes two elements. The first is simply recognizing that significant stretches of the system have evolved from linking metropolitan areas to now lying within expanded megapolitan complexes. The interstates between places such as Tampa and Orlando, Phoenix and Tucson, and San Antonio and Austin should be treated as intramegapolitan highways.

Recognizing the status of megapolitan interstates leads to the next element, an expansion of major linking highway in these zones. It is in the national interest that the increased frictions of movement in these spaces be addressed so that goods and people can flow better across the entire country. The megapolitan system needs redundancy and perhaps specific capacities such as passenger-only and freight-only lanes. Instead of the earmarks that suck up funding in every recent surface transportation bill, the United States should have an empirically based policy that ranks road projects on their ability to both integrate large-scale regional economies and relieve severe bottlenecks in the national road network. We note again that the original interstate system was not a product of earmarks but was based on a plan to link all major metropolitan areas. The same model should apply to the next generation of interstate improvements, with the guiding principle being to fund projects that would (1) fix regional megapolitan congestion and (2) smooth the flow of people and goods at the national scale.

Finally, we need to actually finish parts of the interstate network to reflect 21st-century urban geography. The interstate system was originally planned using the 1950 Census. The United States at the mid-20th century had a completely different metropolitan development pattern than it does today. In 1950, virtually all large American cities were in the Midwest and Northeast and formed part of an extended national urban complex that ran from St. Louis and Minneapolis in the west to Boston and Washington, D.C., in the east. Reflecting this reality, there was not one baseball franchise west of St. Louis or south of Washington until the Brooklyn (trolley) Dodgers moved to Los Angeles in the late 1950s. A quick look at Major League Baseball franchises today clearly shows the emergence of the modern Sun Belt. California alone has five teams, and Florida and Texas have two each.

The Sun Belt and especially the Southwest have an underdeveloped interstate highway network that does not even meet current demand. There are also key segments missing in the system. For example, Phoenix and Las Vegas, the two largest metropolitan areas in the interior Southwest, lack an interstate connection. The two regions are also the largest proximate metropolitan areas in the United States not directly linked by an interstate. By contrast modest-sized places such as Lubbock and Amarillo in Texas have a direct interstate highway connection, while sections of a two-lane road built by the Works Progress Administration (WPA) in the 1930s still link southern Nevada to central Arizona.[1] Proponents of a newly designated "Interstate 11" are proposing a road that connects I-10 in Phoenix and I-15 in Las Vegas. In addition to passenger traffic, this highway would help move the enormous flow of goods that is expected when a planned Chinese-built port is finished in Mexico in the Gulf of California. An essential part of the proposed I-11 project was completed in October 2010 when a high-capacity bridge opened crossing the Colorado River just south of Hoover Dam. The federal government should step up and finish key missing segments in the interstate system. One place to begin is by *finally* funding the road between Las Vegas and Phoenix.

High-Speed and Regional Rail

Many megapolitan areas may see new rail projects in the next several decades. This work has already started in several places and more projects are in the planning stages. President Barack Obama included HSR projects as part of the 2009 American Renewal and Reinvestment Act (ARRA), but these plans are now under attack from both Republican legislators and governors. So far, Ohio and Wisconsin have rejected federal money offered to build rail, while Illinois and California have green-lighted their federally supported projects. The verdict is still out on Florida's HSR line between Tampa and Orlando; the state will decide the issue in February 2011.

A comprehensive plan for building a national network of HSR lines was proposed by Regional Plan Association of New York (RPA) in 2009 (Todorovich and Hagler 2009) and updated in 2011 (Todorovich and Hagler 2011). The plan is based on an analytic model developed by the RPA that uses several criteria to predict where HSR will do the most good. The model also uses the RPA's "megaregion" geography, which matches the megapolitan clusters proposed in this book. Thus, the RPA model is highly relevant for megapolitan areas and remains the best planning tool so far offered in how to prioritize HSR projects.

The RPA method starts with pairs of major cities separated by a distance of 100–500 miles. These cities are assessed on measures of population size, economic activity, transit connections, existing travel markets, urban spatial form, and density to determine the success of HSR (Hagler and Todorovich 2009). The RPA criteria are weighted and then calculated to create an index ranking the top 50 corridors with the greatest demand for HSR. The corridors are concentrated primarily in the Northeast, Midwest, and California. The Megalopolis (New England, New York–Philadelphia, and Chesapeake) megapolitan cluster accounted for the top four links, which is unsurprising, given the current population size and economic output in this region.[2] In addition, links within California and connecting Los Angeles to major cities in the Southwest ranked high. A corridor connecting Los Angeles to San Francisco ranked fifth, Los Angeles to Phoenix ranked 15th, and Las Vegas to Los Angeles ranked 23rd. The Midwest had seven corridor connections among the top 25 city pairs, including Chicago to Detroit, ranked 11th, Chicago to the Ohio Valley, ranked 13th, and Chicago to the Steel Corridor, ranked 16th.

Two geographic scales are analyzed in this book, megapolitan areas and megapolitan clusters (or megaregions, in RPA's term). HSR lines should be organized at both scales. In fact, the Federal Railroad Administration (FRA), the U.S. agency charged with planning HSR, provides a useful template for separating megapolitan rail projects from megaregional ones. The FRA sees both regional HSR and express HSR as possible in the United States. Express HSR is true HSR based on the European model in that it travels at speeds in excess of 150 mph and makes few stops. Regional HSR can be achieved by improving both the rail and the rolling stock along many existing Amtrak lines. The regional HSR trains could include next-generation diesel engines that exceed 80 mph and are less expensive than fully electrical systems.

The regional-express HSR typology roughly matches the divide between distances and speed needed within both megapolitan areas and megapolitan clusters. Megapolitan areas are mostly continuous urban corridors and are best served by regional HSR. Megapolitan clusters are proximate but discrete urban complexes that need express HSR to bridge the gaps between multiple megapolitan areas. In megapolitan areas, trains mostly compete with automobiles and should make multiple stops at key centers along the route. In megapolitan clusters, trains mostly compete with short-haul air service and should make very few stops in order to maintain maximum speed.

Consider the application of these different rail systems in California in the Mountain West.

Megapolitan-scale, or regional HSR, projects might include the following:

- Front Range: Fort Collins to Colorado Springs (through Denver)
- Sun Corridor: Phoenix to Tucson
- Wasatch Range: Logan to Provo, Utah (through Salt Lake City)
- Southern California: Los Angeles to San Diego
- Sierra Pacific: Bay Area to Sacramento

Megaregion-scale, or express HSR, could include the following:

- Southern California to Las Vegas
- Southern California to Sierra Pacific
- Southern California to Sun Corridor

The key point is that not all rail corridors need the fastest HSR capability. In fact, many could work off a megapolitan-wide regional HSR. There are already several projects in the West that utilize this grade of rail, such as the commuter line to Salt Lake City from Ogden in the Wasatch Range. However, faster rail is needed over the long distances that connect one megapolitan area to another, such as the proposed Desert Express line between Las Vegas and Southern California. The Desert Express would utilize an Acela-type train that runs at 150 mph and makes no stops between Victorville, California (near San Bernardino), and Las Vegas.[3] The train could make the run in 78 minutes station to station.

The reality is that the United States does not need all that much true HSR, or, as the FRA refers to it, express HSR. Regional HSR could serve as the main intramegapolitan rail capacity. This means that extensive development

of HSR could be achieved at much lower cost than is commonly perceived. Ironically, one of the main tests of express HSR under the Obama administration's plan is the link between Orlando and Tampa. The train as proposed could whisk passengers between these two proximate cities (separated by only 80 miles) at true express HSR speeds. Yet there is really no need to rush, in that the primary alternative would be an automobile that is stuck in traffic along I-4. By contrast, the proposed next phase rail from Orlando to Miami should be express HSR because it is between megapolitan areas rather than within one. The truth is that the Orlando–Tampa connection should be a regional HSR that, while fast, need not compete with air travel.

In a follow-up study by the RPA in 2011, HSR feasibility was evaluated by length of corridor: short corridors are defined as 150 miles or less, mid-length corridors are defined as 150–300 miles, and long corridors are defined as greater than 300 miles (Todorovich and Hagler 2011). Again, these distances roughly approximate the megapolitan-megaregion geographies. All short corridors lie within megapolitan areas, while all long ones bridge them and are thus megaregional in scale. Table 9.1 illustrates the top six short corridor connections. All corridors are within megapolitan areas and are less than HSR. Tables 9.2 and 9.3 highlight the top three mid-length corridors and long corridors, drawing attention to the importance of connections between megapolitans.

The top three medium-defined RPA corridors as shown in Table 9.2 all run *between* megapolitan areas, as do the so-called long-corridors (the top three of which are indicated in Table 9.3). It is interesting to note that all of these connections are either in the Northeast or originate in

Table 9.1. Top Six Intramegapolitan or Short Rail Corridors

Megapolitan Area	From	To	Miles
New York–Philadelphia	New York	Philadelphia	91
Southern California	Los Angeles	San Diego	150
Chicago	Chicago	Milwaukee	86
Chesapeake	Washington, D.C.	Richmond	110
Sierra Pacific	Sacramento	Bay Area	139
Florida Corridor	Tampa	Orlando	84

Source: Todorovich and Hagler (2011)

Table 9.2. Top Three High-Speed Rail Corridors of 150–300 Miles

Beginning Megapolitan Area	Ending Megapolitan Area	From	To	Miles
Chesapeake	New York–Philadelphia	Washington, D.C.	New York	224
New England	New York–Philadelphia	Boston	New York	231
Willamette	Puget Sound	Portland	Seattle	185

Source: Todorovich and Hagler (2011)

Table 9.3. Top Three High-Speed Rail Corridors Greater Than 300 Miles

Beginning Megapolitan Area	Ending Megapolitan Area	From	To	Miles
Chesapeake	New England	Washington, D.C.	Boston	455
Southern California	Sierra Pacific	Los Angeles	San Francisco	453
Southern California	Las Vegas	Los Angeles	Las Vegas	338

Source: Todorovich and Hagler (2011)

California, except the link between the Willamette and Puget Sound megapolitan areas in Cascadia. All six of the short corridors could work off regional HSR (including Tampa–Orlando), while all medium and long corridor projects would require express (or true) HSR.

Air Travel and the Megapolitans

Megapolitan areas link the nation to the global economy. Perhaps the most important connections are the megapolitans' international hub airports. Every globally reaching U.S. airport lies in a megapolitan area. Research on U.S. urban overseas connections by Taylor and Lang (2005) shows that an airport with direct flights to foreign business centers often determines where a region ranks in the hierarchy of world cities. Places with the densest air connections abroad score the highest in a ranking of world cities—and every leading city in the Taylor and Lang study is part of a megapolitan area with an international hub airport.

Megapolitan areas also dominate domestic air routes. Links between megapolitans form a dense web of connections that carries the bulk of business travel in the nation. Proximate megapolitan areas with hub airports coalesce into larger megapolitan clusters based on an analysis of these connections. The best evidence for urban structure at the megaregional level lies in the pattern of megapolitan-to-megapolitan air linkages.

There are 19 U.S. "international and domestic airport hubs" as defined by the Brookings Institution Metropolitan Program (Tomer and Puentes 2009). The hubs are located in 18 metropolitan areas. Only one megapolitan area, New York–Philadelphia, has two hub airports. The smallest megapolitan area with an international-domestic airport is Las Vegas. On a megaregional scale, the Piedmont, Florida, and Texas Triangle megapolitan areas have two airports each. But there are five megapolitan areas in this study that lack a Brookings-defined international-domestic hub. Those megapolitan areas are the Wasatch Range, Steel Corridor, Willamette, Central Texas, and Ohio Valley; however, the Wasatch Range and Willamette do have domestic hubs. It should be noted that Las Vegas and Orlando, despite being modest-sized metropolitan areas, are so well connected owing to tourist and convention travel that they have a global reach. Both megapolitan areas have an opportunity to leverage their tourist linkages into business travel and move up the hierarchy as world city destinations.

An analysis of megapolitan-to-megapolitan international hub connections based on a less than 90-minute airline trip (or roughly less than 500 miles) produced five supermegapolitan "gateway" clusters:

- Midwest cluster (Chicago centered): Minneapolis–Chicago–Detroit
- Piedmont–Atlantic cluster (Orlando centered): Atlanta–Charlotte–Orlando–Miami
- Megalopolis cluster (New York centered): Boston–New York–Philadelphia–Washington, D.C.
- Texas Triangle cluster: Houston–Dallas
- Southwest cluster (Los Angeles centered): San Francisco–Los Angeles–Las Vegas–Phoenix

The global gateway megapolitan clusters are the key access points to the global economy and account for the vast majority of overseas flights. Global airports in the Front Range and Puget Sound are isolates in that they do not connect to nearby megapolitans to create 90-minute trips. Yet the Front Range lies in such a central location that its passengers have access to the Texas, Midwest, and Southwest clusters in about a two-hour flight. It is the only case in the United States with this type of longer range but still proximate air access to three gateway megapolitan clusters. Thus, the Front Range cannot truly be described as an isolate.

Table 9.4 highlights the top megapolitan gateway corridors by air passengers traveling 400 miles or less based on the Brookings analysis (Tomer and Puentes 2009). The Southwest cluster accounted for the top three spots—Los Angeles to San Francisco had 6.3 million passengers per annum, Las Vegas to Los Angeles had 3.7 million passengers per annum, and Los Angeles to Phoenix had 3.4 million passengers per annum—followed by the Texas Triangle's Dallas to Houston link and the Megalopolis's Boston to New York and New York to Washington connections.

The 400-mile or less airline connections also indicate an opportunity for HSR. Analysis of the intensity of air travel in just these corridors suggests there would be a high market demand for express HSR in California, Texas, and the Northeast. A Los Angeles–centered southwestern system with lines to San Francisco, Las Vegas, and Phoenix seems especially workable. Insofar as almost a third of the air traffic in Las Vegas and the Sun Corridor is heading to Southern California, HSR would replace a large number of regional flights and would clear the region's airspace for more international and long-distance domestic connections.

Assault on the Future

The United States became a world economic power in large part because of major federal and state investments in infrastructure. For the most part, massive investments in rail, shipping, airports, highways, and the like enjoyed bipartisan support. That seems to have changed in the 2010s. Indeed, one major holdup in transforming the megapolitan road, shipping, air, and rail networks is the political environment following Barack Obama's 2008 win in the presidential elections and the resurgence of the Democratic Party. Investment in infrastructure, which once enjoyed broad bipartisan support, now seems to be identified specifically with Democratic Party initiatives. While it is true historically that Democratic president Franklin Delano Roosevelt was perhaps the greatest builder of new infrastructure during the Great Depression, it is also the case that the interstate highways had their biggest advocate in Republican president Dwight David Eisenhower.

Yet since President Reagan, it seems that Republicans are little interested in building much of anything or even properly maintaining our existing systems. We now have an enormous infrastructure investment gap as one legacy of Reagan's "small government" ethos. As the Chinese rush boldly to fill their nation with new interstates, modern airports, expansive shipping terminals, and the world's most extensive HSR network, the United States has stalled on all these fronts. The sad irony is that the nation is indeed growing and, as pointed out earlier, will add its next 100 million new residents faster than China. Even Europe, which has practically no population growth, still invests more in new transportation infrastructure than the United States.

In the recent rounds of elections, conservative (or Tea Party) Republicans have taken to calling pork almost any

Table 9.4. Top Megapolitan Corridor Air Travel under 400 Miles

From Megapolitan Area	To Megapolitan Area	Passengers	Miles
Southern California	Sierra Pacific	6.3 million	347
Las Vegas	Southern California	3.7 million	229
Southern California	Sun Corridor	3.4 million	358
Dallas–Fort Worth	Houston	2.9 million	232
New England	New York–Philadelphia	2.7 million	185
New York–Philadelphia	Chesapeake	2.3 million	222

Source: Tomer and Puentes (2009)

transportation improvement, no matter how manifestly worthy of funding. Part of this has to do with the specific politics of the 2009 economic stimulus package, which included some infrastructure spending. As part of a newfound austerity in the face of large federal and state deficits, Republicans around the United States have begun trying to kill projects. One of the most notable examples of this is New Jersey Republican governor Chris Christie's efforts to defund the Hudson River tunnel project linking New York City and the Garden State. There is currently only one rail tunnel under the Hudson, and it dates from the early 20th century. For decades, groups such as the RPA of New York have been calling for a second tunnel to relieve congestion. The deal to build this tunnel was in place and ready to start in 2011 when at the last moment Governor Christie withdrew New Jersey's support. In a parallel action, Florida governor Rick Scott killed the HSR project connecting Tampa to Orlando in the heart of the Florida Corridor megapolitan area—most of the money was to come from the federal government.

The long-term economic development case to build this tunnel is so strong on virtually any metric that it seems almost incomprehensible that a politician from either major party would oppose its construction. The fuel saved, the trips shortened, and the development spurred are all easily identified in the data. Yet Governor Christie wants to redirect the money to fix potholes and will not even consider raising New Jersey's gasoline tax (among the lowest in the United States) as a source of funding. Governor Christie's behavior in this matter helped make him the darling of the small-government types in the Republican Party in the early 2010s. The party has since gone on record as being against the very investments that would improve the efficiency and productivity of megapolitan areas. In light of the high-profile nature of the Hudson River tunnel project and the opposition to the Tampa–Orlando HSR project that has become a hallmark of modern Republicanism, we worry that the Republican Party has launched an assault on the long-term economic competitiveness of the United States. As the nation adds more people in the next three decades than the current population of Germany, it remains to be seen whether proponents of the rail and road projects needed to accommodate this growth can overcome this assault on the future. If they cannot, the nation is at risk for a long-term decline.

10

IMPLICATIONS OF MEGAPOLITAN AMERICA FOR LAND, WATER, AND AIR RESOURCES

In this chapter we explore some of the implications of megapolitan cluster and megapolitan area development patterns for such key resources as land, air, and water. We point out some surprises as well as challenges.

Land

It almost goes without saying that development consumes land. The concern of planners and policy makers is whether land consumption is inefficient, resulting in more land being developed at costs that exceed benefits to society. In some quarters, the whole concern about land consumption is misplaced. For instance, the 2000 Census shows that urban development occupied about 60 million acres of land. While this is a large number, the contiguous 48 states contain about 1.5 billion acres of nonfederal land.[1] In effect, urban land accounts for just 3 percent of the land area. These estimates are based on census definitions of urbanized land, which understate the true effect of development patterns.

Other estimates are likely more accurate depictions of land that has been converted and committed to nonrural uses. The U.S. Department of Agriculture (USDA), for example, estimated that rural residential development—which is characterized simply as very low-density residential development, usually with on-site sewer systems and private wells—consumed another 94 million acres in 2002 (Lubowski et al. 2006). Still, this would bring total land committed to nonrural uses to about 150 million acres, or just 10 percent of the nonfederal land area.

The concern of planners and policy makers may not be so much the amount of land converted to urban uses of whatever density but where it is located and its configuration. Urban development often occurs on the highest-quality farmland, so its development could require more land of lesser quality elsewhere to meet society's agricultural needs—and likely at higher environmental cost (see Nelson 1992). The configuration of development can also lead to adverse outcomes (see Ewing et al. 2007).

Jean Gottmann (1961) was among the first to note the fragility of farmland especially in Megalopolis, and by extension in any metropolitan area. A large literature exists arguing that farmland of any quality ought to be preserved, for a variety of societal benefit reasons.[2] Usual reasons include such public good benefits as air cleansing, water purification, watershed services, and food production. Other reasons include preserving future options for the production of food or fiber or other services no one can anticipate; in recent years this last has been the production of crops for fuel.

We focus here on trends in the relationship between megaregion and megapolitan development and change in the supply of farmland. A cautionary note is in order. Our analysis is based on the Census of Agriculture for 1997 and 2007, or data based on a census of those claiming to be engaged in agriculture. Aside from potential but likely small inaccuracies in individual responses to census survey instruments, a significant factor in gauging the supply of farmland is simply economic: If the market supports more consumption of goods produced from farmland, prices will rise and more farmland will be used.

Finally, farmland competes with urban development. In growing regions, farmland is typically at a disadvantage relative to urban development because of urbanization subsidies roughly 10 times the subsidies for farming (Nelson 2000), inefficient pricing of public facilities and services (Nelson and Duncan 1995), and land-use externalities wherein what farmers do is inconsistent with what neighboring or nearby residents will accept as intrusions in terms of smells, hours of operation, noise,

and highway use (Nelson 1992). We would expect, generally, that growth among megapolitan clusters and megapolitan areas would compromise the use and preservation of farmland.

The farmland base in the contiguous 48 states is very large. In 1997 it was about 930 million acres in the contiguous 48 states, or about two-thirds of the nonfederal land base. Not all farmland is actually used, however. The figure is based on "land in farms" as defined by the USDA and includes land used for crops, pasture, or grazing, as well as for woodland and wasteland not under cultivation or used for pasture or grazing, if it was part of a total operation.[3] Between 1997 and 2007, however, farmland fell by about 9 million acres (1 percent) to about 920 million acres. During the same period, the U.S. population grew by about 30 million, implying that for each 1,000 new residents, the supply of farmland dropped by about 340 acres.

Trends are not the same around the nation, however, as seen in Table 10.1 and illustrated in Figure 10.1, which compare megapolitan clusters to themselves and the 48 contiguous states. For instance, megapolitan clusters lost farmland at half the rate of the rest of the 48 states, and less than the nation as a whole. On the other hand, megapolitan clusters tend to be located where some of the nation's best farmland is located, such as in California's

Megapolitan Cluster	Farmland, 1997 (acres)	Farmland, 2007 (acres)	Change in Farmland (acres)	Change in Farmland (%)	Change Per 1,000 New Residents (acres)
Cascadia	2,538,062	2,585,477	47,415	1.9	49
Sierra Pacific	9,364,997	8,956,162	(408,835)	−4.4	(365)
Southwest	13,125,614	10,638,408	(2,487,206)	−18.9	(584)
Mountain	10,214,061	9,826,459	(387,602)	−3.8	(332)
Texas Triangle	24,125,358	24,178,050	52,692	0.2	15
Twin Cities	8,359,938	7,933,787	(426,151)	−5.1	(1,007)
Great Lakes	22,115,680	22,106,310	(9,370)	−0.0	(9)
Florida	5,447,221	4,523,028	(924,193)	−17.0	(436)
Piedmont	8,104,985	7,648,407	(456,578)	−5.6	(159)
Megalopolis	9,732,947	9,368,371	(364,576)	−3.7	(113)
Megapolitan total	113,128,863	107,764,459	(5,364,404)	−4.7	(258)
Rest of 48 states	816,346,276	812,328,467	(4,017,809)	−0.5	(607)
Total, 48 states	929,475,139	920,092,926	(9,382,213)	−1.0	(342)

Table 10.1. Change in Farmland by Megapolitan Cluster and the 48 States, 1997–2007

Source: Based on data from the Census of Agriculture for 1997 and 2007

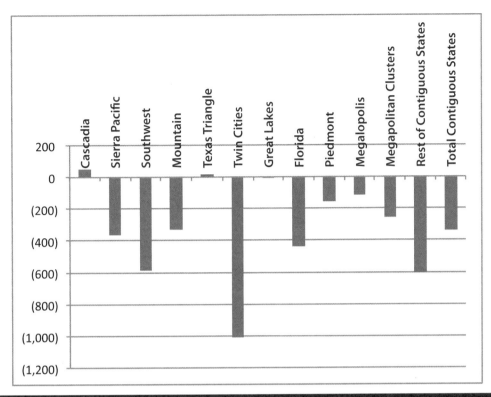

Figure 10.1. Change in farmland acres per new resident by megapolitan cluster, rest of contiguous 48 states outside megaregions, and total of 48 states, 1997–2007

Central Valley and much of Florida. For instance, in the Sierra Pacific megapolitan cluster, about 400,000 acres, or more than 4 percent of the farmland base, was lost—or about 370 acres per 1,000 new residents. While seemingly small, over a century this pace means Central Valley farmland could fall by up to half. Even worse is Florida, which saw its farmland base fall by 17 percent in just one decade—more than 900,000 acres, or about 440 acres lost per 1,000 new residents. At this pace, all of Florida's farmland will be lost by about mid-century. The Southwest megapolitan cluster is also losing farmland at a rapid pace—more than 580 acres per 1,000 new residents, or 2.5 million acres over the period 1997–2007. As in Florida, at this pace farmland in the Southwest cluster could disappear around mid-century.

Trends for megapolitan areas are shown in Table 10.2 and illustrated in Figure 10.2. Here we see some interesting trends. For the most part, growth results in removing farmland, but the pace varies remarkably. The Twin Cities megapolitan area leads the nation in rate of farmland

loss, at more than 1,000 acres lost per 1,000 new residents—or simply one acre per new resident. Southern California and the Sun Corridor megapolitan areas lost farmland at a rate of 650 to nearly 700 acres per 1,000 new residents. On the other hand, the Puget Sound and Dallas–Fort Worth megapolitan areas gained farmland at a rate of about 150 and 290 acres per 1,000 new residents, respectively. At the other end of the spectrum, the Steel Corridor megapolitan area added about 150,000 acres of farmland, but it also lost population during this period.

With just 17 percent of the nonpublic and accessible land base in the contiguous 48 states, megapolitan clusters and their megapolitan areas account for only 11 percent of the farmland base. On the other hand, they also accounted for more than half the loss of the farmland inventory and nearly 5 percent of its farmland base. At this rate, half of the farmland in megapolitan areas would be removed from the inventory by the end of the 21st century. Gottmann (1961) warned of the dangers of this trend in the middle of the 20th century.

Table 10.2. Change in Farmland by Megapolitan Area, 1997–2007

Megapolitan Area	Farmland, 1997 (acres)	Farmland, 2007 (acres)	Change in Farmland (acres)	Change in Farmland (%)	Change Per 1,000 New Residents (acres)
Puget Sound	579,196	655,273	76,077	13.1	147
Willamette	1,958,866	1,930,204	(28,662)	−1.5	(64)
Sierra Pacific	9,364,997	8,956,162	(408,835)	−4.4	(365)
Southern California	6,111,707	4,716,644	(1,395,063)	−22.8	(650)
Las Vegas	1,316,581	1,211,833	(104,748)	-8.0	(154)
Sun Corridor	5,697,326	4,709,931	(987,395)	−17.3	(689)
Wasatch	3,950,632	3,700,516	(250,116)	−6.3	(481)
Front Range	6,263,429	6,125,943	(137,486)	−2.2	(212)
Dallas–Fort Worth	10,061,870	10,464,503	402,633	4.0	287
Central Texas	7,498,058	7,230,593	(267,465)	−3.6	(289)
Houston	6,565,430	6,482,954	(82,476)	−1.3	(68)
Twin Cities	8,359,938	7,933,787	(426,151)	−5.1	(1,007)
Chicago	7,756,100	7,694,785	(61,315)	−0.8	(74)
Michigan Corridor	5,616,865	5,609,762	(7,103)	−0.1	(76)
Ohio Valley	5,870,697	5,782,347	(88,350)	−1.5	(246)
Steel Corridor	2,872,018	3,019,416	147,398	5.1	n/a
Florida Corridor	1,692,084	1,379,875	(312,209)	−18.5	(460)
Florida Atlantic	3,755,137	3,143,153	(611,984)	−16.3	(424)
Atlanta	2,919,592	2,817,662	(101,930)	−3.5	(65)
Carolina Piedmont	5,185,393	4,830,745	(354,648)	−6.8	(274)
Chesapeake	5,341,025	4,984,509	(356,516)	-6.7	(261)
New York–Philadelphia	3,686,716	3,663,995	(22,721)	−0.6	(15)
New England	705,206	719,867	14,661	2.1	45

Source: Based on data from the Census of Agriculture for 1997 and 2007

On the other hand, the rate of loss might be worse, and in some instances farmland supply is actually increasing. We surmise that farmland in megapolitan clusters is of higher quality (including some of the nation's most productive soils), is naturally closer to markets, and thus is of higher value than farmland outside megapolitan clusters. The higher value allows it to compete better against alternative uses such as rural residential subdivisions, though this is debatable.[4]

Moreover, we suspect that farmland preservation policies are working better in megapolitan clusters and megapolitan areas than elsewhere. For instance, Mason (2008), Nelson and Lang (2009), and Ingram et al. (2009) observe that while states may vary in their approach to land-use planning and especially the preservation of open spaces, including farmland, it is difficult to say with certainty whether any particular approach works best. For instance, in our analysis, in such areas as the Greater Metroplex (Dallas and Fort Worth), given Texas's relatively low ranking on preservation (see Nelson and Lang 2009), we would expect farmland inventory to fall, whereas it actually rose. And although it fell, it fell only by 0.07 acres per new resident in the Houston megapolitan area. Yet in the Willamette megapolitan area, dominated by Oregon, which has seen some of the nation's most stringent farmland preservation efforts, farmland inventory fell, although only by about 0.06 acres per new resident,

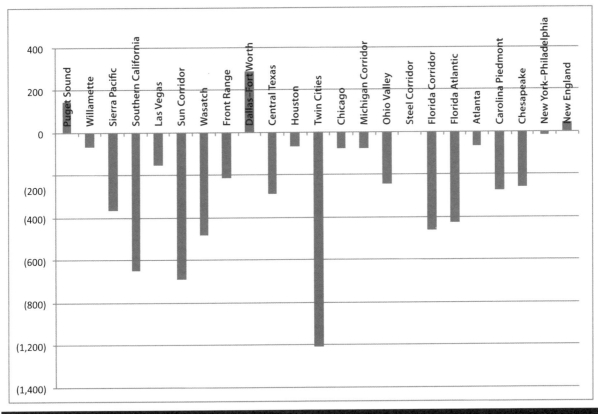

Figure 10.2. Change in farmland acres per new resident by megapolitan area, 1997–2007

and largely because farmland inside urban growth boundaries had been converted as planned.

Future analysis should delve into some of the structural differences in the farmland inventory, and farm productivity, between areas inside and outside megapolitan clusters, and between megapolitan clusters and their megapolitan areas. Our new way of perceiving the American urban geography lends itself to more structured analysis around these areas than simply comparing states, which is typically the case.

Water

People need water, and large assemblages of people, such as aggregate in megapolitan clusters, need lots of water. In this section we assemble and report data comparing water use among megapolitan clusters and their megapolitan areas, and compared to the 48 contiguous states. Our data come from the U.S. Geological Survey's

Estimated Use of Water in the United States for the years 1990 and 2005.[5] We analyzed only public use water withdrawals as they reflect best water consumption by the population as a whole. Public water is defined as water supplied to 15 or more residential customers from a public or publicly licensed source. We did not consider such specialized water uses as industrial, agriculture, mining, and so forth.[6] Table 10.3 reports average daily water consumption per capita for 1990 and 2005 and change per capita for each megapolitan cluster, while Table 10.4 reports figures for megapolitan areas. Change in water consumption per capita is illustrated in Figures 10.3 and 10.4, respectively.

Despite the overall consumption per capita falling over the period 1990–2005, we are surprised in several respects. First, per capita water consumption has been and remains the highest among the nation's most arid regions, the Southwest and Mountain megapolitan clusters. One reason is landscape irrigation several months of the year. Local

Table 10.3. Public Water Use and Change Per Capita by Megapolitan Cluster, 1990–2005

Megapolitan Cluster	Water Consumed Per Capita, 1990 (average daily gallons)	Water Consumed Per Capita, 2005 (average daily gallons)	Change in Water Consumed Per Capita, 1990–2005 (%)
Cascadia	190	148	−22.0
Sierra Pacific	189	192	1.3
Southwest	237	205	−13.3
Mountain	241	204	−15.6
Texas Triangle	185	193	4.1
Twin Cities	177	126	−28.8
Great Lakes	176	150	−14.7
Florida	166	155	−6.6
Piedmont	177	161	−9.3
Megalopolis	145	126	−13.7
Megapolitan total	179	161	−9.9
Rest of 48 states	193	192	−0.6
Total 48 states	184	171	−6.8

Source: U.S. Geological Survey, Water Use in the United States, 2009

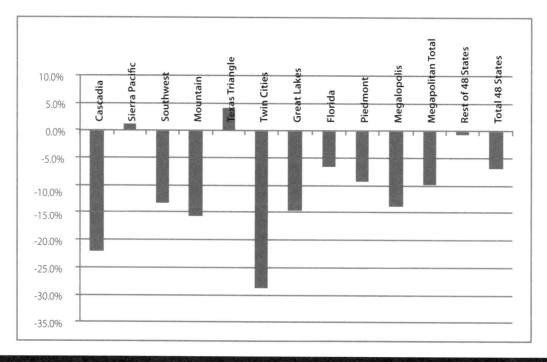

Figure 10.3. Change in per capita public water consumption by megapolitan cluster, 1990–2005

Table 10.4. Public Water Use and Change Per Capita by Megapolitan Area, 1990–2005

Megapolitan Area	Water Consumed Per Capita, 1990 (average daily gallons)	Water Consumed Per Capita, 2005 (average daily gallons)	Change in Water Consumed Per Capita, 1990-2005 (%)
Puget Sound	194	136	−29.6
Willamette	183	165	−10.1
Sierra Pacific	189	192	1.3
Southern California	235	194	−17.6
Las Vegas	359	324	−9.7
Sun Corridor	209	207	−1.0
Wasatch	300	237	−20.9
Front Range	206	183	−11.3
Dallas–Fort Worth	198	231	16.6
Central Texas	195	180	−7.3
Houston	166	159	−4.4
Twin Cities	177	126	−28.8
Chicago	193	145	−24.8
Michigan Corridor	181	158	−12.6
Ohio Valley	145	151	4.0
Steel Corridor	162	150	−7.9
Florida Corridor	157	143	−9.1
Florida Atlantic	183	170	−6.8
Atlanta	180	153	−15.3
Carolina Piedmont	173	169	−2.3
Chesapeake	164	145	−11.5
New York–Philadelphia	144	117	−19.1
New England	126	133	5.5

Source: U.S. Geological Survey, Water Use in the United States, 2009

and state governments in these regions have certainly worked to reduce per capita water consumption, but the megapolitan clusters are hardly leaders in conservation, as they remained at the top of consumption in 2005, with only slightly above-average reductions since 1990. In contrast, the Twin Cities and Cascadia megapolitan clusters reduced consumption by about a quarter. Two clusters, the Sierra Pacific and Texas Triangle, actually saw increases in per capita consumption.

We find similar trends among the megapolitan areas. We note especially that the nation's most densely settled megapolitan area, New York–Philadelphia, was not only the leader in low consumption per capita in both 1990 and 2005 but among the leaders in reducing per capita

water use. We surmise there may be a lot more that can be done to reduce water consumption over the next few decades as the United States grows from 310 million people in 2010 to as many as 500 million in 2050.

Air

We turn now to air, or more particularly air quality. Resources do not exist to allow us to estimate air quality for megapolitan clusters or their megapolitan areas, or thus to compare air quality implications between them and the rest of the nation. We are indebted to the Brookings Institution (Brown, Southworth, and Sarzynski 2008) for its analysis. Table 10.5 shows the automobile

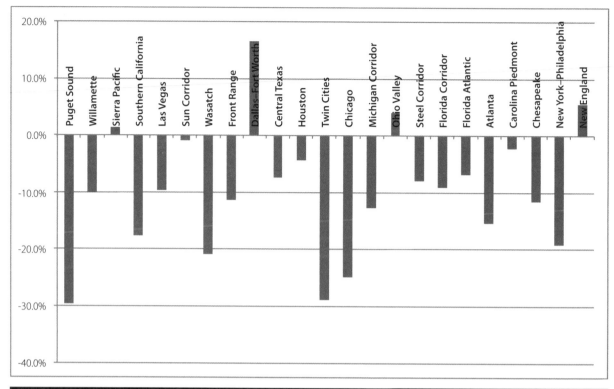

Figure 10.4. Change in per capita public water consumption by megapolitan area, 1990–2005

emissions per capita for the largest 100 metropolitan areas (measured by employment) in 2005, indicating megaregion and megapolitan area affiliation.

Interesting trends emerge. The largest metropolitan areas that also have extensive public transit systems fare the best in having the lowest emissions per capita, such as New York City, Philadelphia, Chicago, and Boston. Others rank well because they are isolated metropolitan areas with relatively small commuter sheds, such as Boise, Idaho; Buffalo, New York; Colorado Springs, Colorado; and Rochester, New York. There is another group that fares well primarily because of natural features that hem in commuting, such as Los Angeles, Honolulu, and New Orleans, or because of extensive public land ownerships, and in some cases mountains and deserts as well, such as Las Vegas, Phoenix, Salt Lake City, and Tucson. In a few cases, regional planning may have resulted in relatively low emissions, such as Portland and Seattle.

Because megapolitan clusters and megapolitan areas will continue to attract the largest share of the nation's

growth, but because public policy will require reductions in automobile-related air emissions, those areas will be challenged to comply. On the other hand, lessons have already been learned about the role of public transit and regional planning in reducing emissions, and in those areas that also have natural or ownership constraints, the challenge should be easier still to meet.

Concluding Observations

Like Jean Gottmann's megalopolis of the mid-20th century, the nation's megapolitan clusters and their megapolitan areas have similar challenges and opportunities.

Farmland is an instructive example. Most megapolitan clusters and their megapolitan areas have extensive farmlands, with soils among the nation's most productive. The Mid-Atlantic states especially have been active in using tax policies and land-use planning to preserve their farmland base (see Daniels and Daniels 2003). We suspect that by looking at America's urban geography

Table 10.5. Metric Tons of Greenhouse Gas Emissions Per Capita, 100 Largest Metropolitan Areas, 2005

Metropolitan Area	Megapolitan Cluster	Megapolitan Area	Auto Emissions (metric tons)	Rank Among Top 100 Metros
Megapolitan Metropolitan Areas				
Seattle–Tacoma–Bellevue, WA	Cascadia	Puget Sound	0.955	24
Portland–Vancouver–Beaverton, OR–WA	Cascadia	Willamette	0.860	13
San Jose–Sunnyvale–Santa Clara, CA	Sierra Pacific	Sierra Pacific	1.009	34
Sacramento–Arden–Arcade–Roseville, CA	Sierra Pacific	Sierra Pacific	1.063	47
San Francisco–Oakland–Fremont, CA	Sierra Pacific	Sierra Pacific	0.998	32
Bakersfield, CA	Southwest	Southern California	1.303	86
San Diego–Carlsbad–San Marcos, CA	Southwest	Southern California	1.078	48
Oxnard–Thousand Oaks–Ventura, CA	Southwest	Southern California	1.116	54
Riverside–San Bernardino–Ontario, CA	Southwest	Southern California	1.289	83
Los Angeles–Long Beach–Santa Ana, CA	Southwest	Southern California	0.882	17
Las Vegas–Paradise, NV	Southwest	Las Vegas	0.845	12
Phoenix–Mesa–Scottsdale, AZ	Southwest	Sun Corridor	0.940	22
Tucson, AZ	Southwest	Sun Corridor	0.924	20
Salt Lake City, UT	Mountain	Wasatch Range	0.981	29
Denver–Aurora, CO	Mountain	Front Range	1.116	55
Colorado Springs, CO	Mountain	Front Range	0.937	21
Dallas–Fort Worth–Arlington, TX	Texas Triangle	Dallas–Fort Worth	1.081	49
San Antonio, TX	Texas Triangle	Texas Corridor	0.969	27
Austin–Round Rock, TX	Texas Triangle	Texas Corridor	1.119	57
Houston–Sugar Land–Baytown, TX	Texas Triangle	Texas Gulf	1.030	41
Minneapolis–St. Paul–Bloomington, MN–WI	Twin Cities	Twin Cities	1.090	50
Milwaukee–Waukesha–West Allis, WI	Great Lakes	Chicago	1.038	43
Madison, WI	Great Lakes	Chicago	1.353	94
Chicago–Naperville–Joliet, IL–IN–WI	Great Lakes	Chicago	0.820	8
Grand Rapids–Wyoming, MI	Great Lakes	Michigan Corridor	1.197	69
Toledo, OH	Great Lakes	Michigan Corridor	1.190	68
Detroit–Warren–Livonia, MI	Great Lakes	Michigan Corridor	1.131	60
Lansing–East Lansing, MI	Great Lakes	Michigan Corridor	1.247	78
Dayton, OH	Great Lakes	Ohio Valley	0.898	18
Columbus, OH	Great Lakes	Ohio Valley	1.176	67
Cincinnati–Middletown, OH–KY–IN	Great Lakes	Ohio Valley	1.140	61
Akron, OH	Great Lakes	Steel Corridor	1.023	39
Youngstown–Warren–Boardman, OH–PA	Great Lakes	Steel Corridor	1.015	38
Cleveland–Elyria–Mentor, OH	Great Lakes	Steel Corridor	0.842	11

(continued)

Table 10.5. Metric Tons of Greenhouse Gas Emissions Per Capita, 100 Largest Metropolitan Areas, 2005 (*continued*)

Metropolitan Area	Megapolitan Cluster	Megapolitan Area	Auto Emissions (metric tons)	Rank Among Top 100 Metros
Pittsburgh, PA	Great Lakes	Steel Corridor	0.913	19
Orlando–Kissimmee, FL	Florida	Florida Corridor	1.277	81
Tampa–St. Petersburg–Clearwater, FL	Florida	Florida Corridor	1.212	71
Sarasota–Bradenton–Venice, FL	Florida	Florida Corridor	1.381	96
Palm Bay–Melbourne–Titusville, FL	Florida	Florida Corridor	1.295	85
Miami–Fort Lauderdale–Miami Beach, FL	Florida	Florida Atlantic	1.031	42
Chattanooga, TN-GA	Piedmont	Atlanta	1.272	80
Atlanta–Sandy Springs–Marietta, GA	Piedmont	Atlanta	1.224	73
Augusta–Richmond County, GA–SC	Piedmont	Atlanta	1.226	74
Durham, NC	Piedmont	Carolina Piedmont	1.119	56
Columbia, SC	Piedmont	Carolina Piedmont	1.216	72
Raleigh–Cary, NC	Piedmont	Carolina Piedmont	1.277	82
Greensboro–High Point, NC	Piedmont	Carolina Piedmont	1.104	53
Greenville, SC	Piedmont	Carolina Piedmont	0.874	15
Charlotte–Gastonia–Concord, NC–SC	Piedmont	Carolina Piedmont	1.256	79
Virginia Beach–Norfolk–Newport News, VA–NC	Megalopolis	Chesapeake	1.004	33
Baltimore–Towson, MD	Megalopolis	Chesapeake	1.044	44
Washington–Arlington–Alexandria, DC–VA–MD–WV	Megalopolis	Chesapeake	0.984	30
Richmond, VA	Megalopolis	Chesapeake	1.335	92
Lancaster, PA	Megalopolis	Philadelphia–New York	0.767	2
Harrisburg–Carlisle, PA	Megalopolis	Philadelphia–New York	1.320	89
Allentown–Bethlehem–Easton, PA–NJ	Megalopolis	Philadelphia–New York	0.964	26
Bridgeport–Stamford–Norwalk, CT	Megalopolis	Philadelphia–New York	0.972	28
Philadelphia–Camden–Wilmington, PA–NJ–DE–MD	Megalopolis	Philadelphia–New York	0.789	5
Trenton–Ewing, NJ	Megalopolis	Philadelphia–New York	1.483	100
New York–Northern New Jersey–Long Island, NY–NJ–PA	Megalopolis	Philadelphia–New York	0.664	1
Portland–South Portland–Biddeford, ME	Megalopolis	New England	1.097	51
Providence–New Bedford–Fall River, RI–MA	Megalopolis	New England	1.014	37
Boston–Cambridge–Quincy, MA–NH	Megalopolis	New England	0.872	14
Springfield, MA	Megalopolis	New England	0.948	23
New Haven–Milford, CT	Megalopolis	New England	0.876	16
Hartford–West Hartford–East Hartford, CT	Megalopolis	New England	1.046	45
Worcester, MA	Megalopolis	New England	1.242	77

(*continued*)

Table 10.5. Metric Tons of Greenhouse Gas Emissions Per Capita, 100 Largest Metropolitan Areas, 2005 (*continued*)

Metropolitan Area	Megapolitan Cluster	Megapolitan Area	Auto Emissions (metric tons)	Rank Among Top 100 Metros
Nonmegapolitan Metropolitan Areas				
Albany–Schenectady–Troy, NY			1.231	75
Albuquerque, NM			0.99	31
Baton Rouge, LA			0.956	25
Birmingham–Hoover, AL			1.335	93
Boise City–Nampa, ID			0.83	10
Buffalo–Niagara Falls, NY			0.801	6
Cape Coral–Fort Myers, FL			1.373	95
Charleston–North Charleston, SC			1.175	66
Des Moines, IA			1.206	70
El Paso, TX			0.83	9
Fresno, CA			1.146	62
Honolulu, HI			0.786	3
Indianapolis, IN			1.127	58
Jacksonville, FL			1.435	98
Jackson, MS			1.459	99
Kansas City, MO–KS			1.159	64
Knoxville, TN			1.402	97
Lexington–Fayette, KY			1.101	52
Little Rock–North Little Rock, AR			1.293	84
Louisville, KY–IN			1.129	59
Memphis, TN–MS–AR			1.162	65
Nashville–Davidson–Murfreesboro, TN			1.319	88
New Orleans–Metairie–Kenner, LA			0.789	4
Oklahoma City, OK			1.32	90
Omaha–Council Bluffs, NE–IA			1.147	63
Poughkeepsie–Newburgh–Middletown, NY			1.01	35
Rochester, NY			0.812	7
Scranton–Wilkes-Barre, PA			1.011	36
Stockton, CA			1.059	46
St. Louis, MO–IL			1.235	76
Syracuse, NY			1.333	91
Tulsa, OK			1.305	87
Wichita, KS			1.028	40

Source: Adapted from Brown, Southworth, and Sarzynski (2008)

in the way we have posed in this book, targeted farm-land preservation policies could be effective.

In the case of water, we find important variations in water use between megapolitan areas, but they are also reasonably easy to understand. The Southwest and Mountain megapolitan clusters especially have the combination of being attractive to tourists and, because of their aridity, receiving extensive domestic irrigation. It is likely that sustained growth in these megapolitan clusters will require reductions in domestic irrigation and new ways of economizing on water consumption in other respects. Lest one thinks other parts of the nation are better off, we are reminded that much of the Southern Piedmont centered around Atlanta may have a cap on water consumption that is less than its current use.[7]

Air quality is another area of concern, yet it is here that megapolitan clusters and megapolitan areas have a distinct advantage and opportunity to lead. All will likely have the density needed to support intermetropolitan rail transportation at least equivalent to commuter trains if not high-speed ones. The Acela already exists in Megalopolis, while California voters have approved funds to connect Southern California with Northern California via high-speed rail (HSR), and plans are under way to serve the Florida megaregion. While truly national-scale HSR service may not be practicable, systems based on megapolitan clusters may already be feasible in most cases. We discuss this in later chapters.

In the next part of the book we profile each of the megapolitan clusters and their megapolitan areas. The individual chapters for the megapolitan clusters follow a common format. For each megapolitan cluster, a detailed map shows the counties included in the megapolitan areas, along with an appendix listing the counties. The chapters on individual megapolitan clusters also show the county rankings according to the Nelson-Lang Rural-Megapolitan Continuum and report major demographic and housing trends, employment and development projections, the extent of economic dependency, and the level of attractiveness based on a refined application of the "knowledge class" concept. We considered exploring the extent to which megapolitan areas include geographic areas under various forms of stress. We discovered, however, that aside from high housing costs and their attractiveness, megapolitan areas are surprisingly free of low employment, low education, and persistent poverty, as measured by the USDA. Each chapter concludes with our perceptions of major planning and development challenges.

11

CASCADIA MEGAPOLITAN CLUSTER

Cascadia is the highly urbanized, metropolitan complex dominating the economy of the Pacific Northwest. The Puget Sound megapolitan area extends west of the Cascade Range to Puget Sound. The Willamette megapolitan area includes the Willamette Valley and several Washington counties north of Portland along the Columbia River (Figure 11.1). Appendix 11.1 lists the counties included in each megapolitan area. We profile the Cascadia megapolitan cluster in terms of major demographic and housing trends, employment and development projections, the extent of economic dependency, and attractiveness characteristics. We conclude with some assessment of major planning and development challenges.

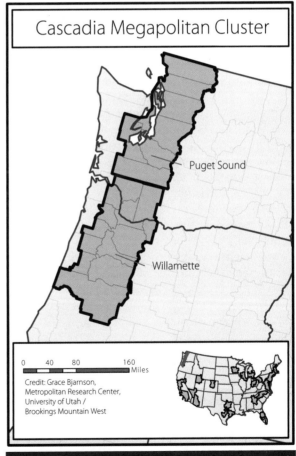

Figure 11.1. The Cascadia megapolitan cluster, composed of the Puget Sound and Willamette megapolitan areas

Table 11.1. Cascadia Megapolitan Cluster Rural-Megapolitan Continuum

Nelson-Lang Rural-Megapolitan Continuum Description	Counties	2010 Population (000s)
Counties in metropolitan areas of 1 million+ population	10	5,695
Counties in metropolitan areas of 250,000 to 1 million population	3	756
Counties in metropolitan areas of less than 250,000 population	6	1,016
Micropolitan area adjacent to a metropolitan area	5	358
Noncore counties adjacent to a metropolitan area	0	0
All other nonmetropolitan counties	0	0

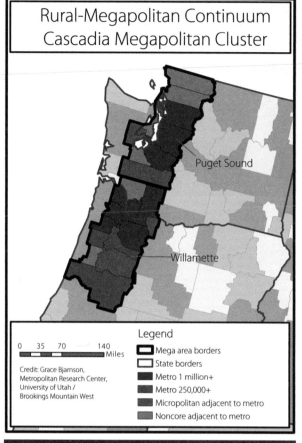

Figure 11.2. Nelson-Lang Rural-Megapolitan Continuum Codes applied to megapolitan cluster counties

Key Demographic Trends

About three-quarters of the megapolitan cluster's population lives in counties in metropolitan areas of more than 1 million residents and only about 5 percent of the population lives in nonmetropolitan counties (Table 11.1 and Figure 11.2). In 2010, its nearly 8 million inhabitants occupied about 16,000 square miles of privately owned, reasonably accessible land (Table 11.2), at a density of about 480 people per square mile (Table 11.3). This is roughly the density of Switzerland. By 2040, the Cascadia megapolitan cluster is expected to grow to about 11 million people (Table 11.4), and its density will exceed that of the United Kingdom. For its part, the density of the Puget Sound megapolitan area is expected to increase from roughly that of Germany in 2010 to that of Japan in 2040, and the Willamette Valley's density will increase from about that of Denmark in 2010 to about Germany's in 2040.

Table 11.5 shows the white non-Hispanic population for the Cascadia megapolitan cluster over the period 2010–2040. Growth in the Cascadia megapolitan cluster and its megapolitan areas will be dominated by minorities (Table 11.6), chiefly Hispanics (Table 11.7) followed by Asians (Table 11.8). On the other hand, the population of African Americans will actually decline (Table 11.9). Between 2010 and 2040, the region will add about 3.2 million people, of whom about 2.8 million, or nearly 90 percent, will be minorities, accounting for 93 percent of the population change in the Puget Sound megapolitan area and 85 percent of the change in the Willamette megapolitan area.

Table 11.10 shows the aging trend, headlined by aging baby boomers, who turn 65 between 2011 and 2029.

Table 11.2. Cascadia Megapolitan Cluster Land Area (in square miles)

Megapolitan Area	Total Land	Estimate of Privately Owned, Accessible Land
Puget Sound	14,448	7,768
Willamette	17,794	8,467
Total	32,241	16,235

Table 11.3. Cascadia Megapolitan Cluster Population Density, 2010–2040

Megapolitan Area	Persons Per Square Mile, 2010	Comparable Developed Nation	Persons Per Square Mile, 2040	Comparable Developed Nation
Puget Sound	576	<Germany	809	Japan
Willamette	396	>Denmark	560	Germany
Megapolitan cluster total	482	Switzerland	679	United Kingdom

Note: The sign < means the megapolitan area density is about 50–200 fewer persons per square mile than in the comparable nation, while > means the density is about 50–200 more persons per square mile; no sign indicates the density is within about 50 persons per square mile. Figures compare developed nation population in 2010 to megapolitan cluster population in 2010 and 2040. All ranges are illustrative.

Table 11.4. Cascadia Megapolitan Cluster Population, 2010–2040 (in thousands)

Megapolitan Area	Total Population, 2010	Total Population, 2025	Total Population, 2040	Total Change, 2010–2040	Percent Change, 2010–2040
Puget Sound	4,472	5,363	6,283	1,811	40.5
Willamette	3,353	4,037	4,742	1,389	41.4
Cascadia cluster	7,825	9,400	11,026	3,200	40.9

Source: Based on Woods & Poole Economics (2010)

Table 11.5. Cascadia Megapolitan Cluster White Non-Hispanic Population, 2010–2040 (in thousands)

Megapolitan Area	White Non-Hispanic Population, 2010	White Non-Hispanic Population, 2025	White Non-Hispanic Population, 2040	White Non-Hispanic Population Change, 2010–2040	White Non-Hispanic Population Percent Change, 2010–2040	White Non-Hispanic Share of Population Change, 2010–2040
Puget Sound	3,345	3,517	3,472	127	3.8	7.0
Willamette	2,662	2,857	2,870	208	7.8	15.0
Cascadia cluster	6,007	6,374	6,342	335	5.6	10.5

Source: Based on Woods & Poole Economics (2010)

Table 11.6. Cascadia Megapolitan Cluster Minority Population, 2010–2040 (in thousands)

Megapolitan Area	Minority Population, 2010	Minority Population, 2025	Minority Population, 2040	Minority Population Change, 2010–2040	Minority Population Percent Change, 2010–2040	Minority Share of Population Change, 2010–2040
Puget Sound	1,127	1,846	2,811	1,685	149.5	93.0
Willamette	691	1,180	1,872	1,181	170.8	85.0
Cascadia cluster	1,818	3,027	4,683	2,865	157.6	89.5

Source: Based on Woods & Poole Economics (2010)

Table 11.7. Cascadia Megapolitan Cluster Hispanic Population, 2010–2040 (in thousands)

Megapolitan Area	Hispanic Population, 2010	Hispanic Population, 2025	Hispanic Population, 2040	Hispanic Population Change, 2010–2040	Hispanic Population Percent Change, 2010–2040	Hispanic Share of Population Change, 2010–2040
Puget Sound	360	712	1,261	524	145.4	28.9
Willamette	393	753	1,307	516	131.4	37.1
Cascadia cluster	753	1,465	2,568	1,040	138.1	32.5

Source: Based on Woods & Poole Economics (2010)

Table 11.8. Cascadia Megapolitan Cluster Asian Population, 2010–2040 (in thousands)

Megapolitan Area	Asian Population, 2010	Asian Population, 2025	Asian Population, 2040	Asian Population Change, 2010–2040	Asian Population Percent Change, 2010–2040	Asian Share of Population Change, 2010–2040
Puget Sound	469	739	1,040	571	121.6	31.5
Willamette	178	278	387	209	117.8	15.1
Cascadia cluster	647	1,017	1,427	780	120.6	24.4

Source: Based on Woods & Poole Economics (2010)

Table 11.9. Cascadia Megapolitan Cluster African American Population, 2010–2040 (in thousands)

Megapolitan Area	African American Population, 2010	African American Population, 2025	African American Population, 2040	African American Population Change, 2010–2040	African American Population Percent Change, 2010–2040	African American Share of Population Change, 2010–2040
Puget Sound	235	324	436	(52)	−22.2	−2.9
Willamette	85	108	136	(252)	−297.9	−18.1
Cascadia cluster	319	433	572	(304)	−95.2	−9.5

Source: Based on Woods & Poole Economics (2010)

Table 11.10. Cascadia Megapolitan Cluster Population 65+, 2010–2040 (in thousands)

Megapolitan Area	Population 65+, 2010	Population 65+ as Share of Population, 2010	Population 65+, 2040	Population 65+ as Share of Population, 2040	Share of Population Change, 2010–2040
Puget Sound	531	11.9	1,241	19.8	39.2
Willamette	404	12.1	852	18.0	32.3
Cascadia cluster	935	12.0	2,094	19.0	36.2

Source: Based on Woods & Poole Economics (2010)

Indeed, more than a third (36 percent) of the change in population over the period 2010–2040 will be attributable to those over the age of 65.

Housing Trends

Between 2010 and 2040, the Cascadia megapolitan cluster will add more than 1.5 million residential units to its inventory. It will also see the rebuilding or replacement of about 0.4 million units, for a total of about 1.9 million residential units constructed or rebuilt during this period (Table 11.11). This is about 60 percent of all units existing in 2010.

Major Employment and Nonresidential Development Trends

The Cascadia megapolitan cluster will see impressive job growth (both part- and full-time). Data aggregated from Woods and Poole Economics to the megapolitan area and megapolitan cluster levels show the total number of jobs will grow from about 4.8 million in 2010 to nearly 7 million in 2040 (Table 11.12). Some of those jobs will be in natural resources, construction, or other activities that do not require that workers occupy space. We thus estimate "land-use" jobs will increase by about 2.1 million between 2010 and 2040 (Table 11.13).

In 2010, the Cascadia megapolitan cluster could support about 2.2 billion square feet of nonresidential space including industrial, commercial, and institutional uses. By 2040, it will support about 3.2 billion square feet of space, adding about a billion square feet over the

period (Table 11.14). However, counting space that will be replaced, sometimes twice (see Chapter 5), a total of 3.4 billion square feet is expected to be built. Growth-related and replaced space will be roughly equivalent to 1.5 times the nonresidential existing space in 2010. Very little of the new or replaced space will come from the industrial sectors. We estimate that more than 95 percent of the increase in total nonresidential space will be for commercial and institutional uses.

Economic Dependency

In Chapter 6, we noted that the U.S. Department of Agriculture has devised objective measures to determine whether counties are overly dependent on key economic sectors such as farming, mining, manufacturing, and federal and state government. We summarize these measures of economic dependency for the Cascadia megapolitan cluster and its megapolitan areas in Table 11.15 and illustrate them in Figure 11.3. Although manufacturing employment as a share of total jobs is small, the total population of counties dependent on manufacturing was about 20 percent of the megapolitan cluster's total population in 2010. This is attributable to the high-tech jobs found in the Willamette megapolitan area. Another area of dependency is in state and federal government employment, likely associated with major military bases located in the Puget Sound megapolitan area. Roughly 35 percent of the megapolitan cluster's population lives in an economically dependent county.

Table 11.11. Cascadia Megapolitan Cluster Residential Development, 2010–2040 (in thousands)

Megapolitan Area	Units Supported, 2010	Increase in Inventory, 2010–2040	Units Recycled, 2010–2040	Total Units Constructed, 2010–2040	Percent of Units Supported, 2010
Puget Sound	1,878	855	239	1,094	58.3
Willamette	1,368	632	174	806	58.9
Cascadia cluster	3,246	1,487	413	1,900	58.5

Table 11.12. Cascadia Megapolitan Cluster Total Employment, 2010–2040 (in thousands)

Megapolitan Area	Total Jobs, 2010	Total Jobs, 2025	Total Jobs, 2040	Change, 2010–2040	Percent Change, 2010–2040
Puget Sound	2,873	3,449	4,145	1,272	44.3
Willamette	1,977	2,361	2,824	848	42.9
Cascadia cluster	4,850	5,810	6,969	2,120	43.7

Source: Based on Woods & Poole Economics (2010)

Table 11.13. Cascadia Megapolitan Cluster Land-Use Employment, 2010–2040 (in thousands)

Megapolitan Area	Total Land-Use Employment, 2010	Total Land-Use Employment, 2025	Total Land-Use Employment, 2040	Change in Land-Use Employment, 2010–2040	Percent Change in Land-Use Employment, 2010–2040
Puget Sound	2,773	3,347	4,042	1,269	45.8
Willamette	1,901	2,281	2,741	840	44.2
Cascadia cluster	4,674	5,628	6,782	2,108	45.1

Source: Based on Woods & Poole Economics (2010)

Table 11.14. Cascadia Megapolitan Cluster Land-Use Employment Space Needs, 2010–2040 (millions of square feet)

Megapolitan Area	Total Land-Use Employment Space Supported, 2010	Total Land-Use Employment Space Supported, 2040	Increase in Land-Use Employment Space Inventory Supported, 2010–2040	Recycled Employment Land-Use Space, 2010–2040	Total Land-Use Employment Space Constructed, 2010–2040	Land-Use Employment Space Constructed in 2010–2040 as Percent of Space in 2010
Puget Sound	1,317	1,874	557	1,445	2,003	152.1
Willamette	916	1,291	375	1,005	1,380	150.7
Cascadia cluster	2,233	3,165	932	2,450	3,382	151.5

Table 11.15. Cascadia Megapolitan Cluster Economic Sector Dependence (in millions)

Megapolitan Area	Farming-Dependent Population, 2010	Mining-Dependent Population, 2010	Manufacturing-Dependent Population, 2010	Tourism and Entertainment–Dependent Population, 2010	Government-Dependent Population, 2010	Total Dependent Population, 2010	Total Population, 2010	Percent Dependent Population, 2010
Puget Sound	0	0	707	0	1,451	2,158	4,472	48.3
Willamette	22	0	102	3	496	620	3,353	18.5
Cascadia cluster	22	0	809	3	1,947	2,778	7,825	35.5

This does not suggest that such dependency is a form of economic instability, however. While the United States has been closing and realigning military bases, those in Washington appear to be of high priority for maintaining (especially the naval and air force operations in the only area outside California). In addition, the relatively low cost of housing in the Portland metropolitan area has attracted new high-tech jobs away from Silicon Valley. So long as demand for high-tech goods remains, the companies (such as Intel) remain innovative, and housing remains more attractive than in California, this industry would seem stable as well.

Attractiveness to the Knowledge Class

In Chapter 8, we reviewed the concept of the knowledge class and discussed how the USDA refined and applied it to classify every county in the United States. Table 11.16 summarizes the population and share of the population living in knowledge class counties for the megapolitan areas making up the megapolitan cluster. Roughly, about two-thirds of the Cascadia megapolitan cluster's population lives in a knowledge class county (Figure 11.4), and about 90 percent of the megapolitan cluster's population growth will occur in these counties. Further, almost all the knowledge class counties are high in natural amenities (Figure 11.5).

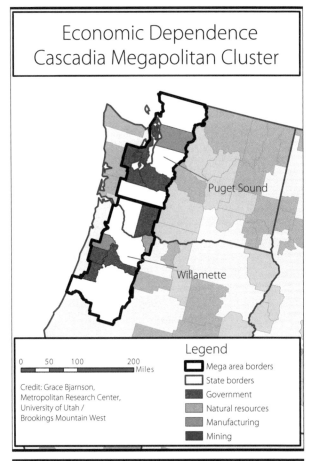

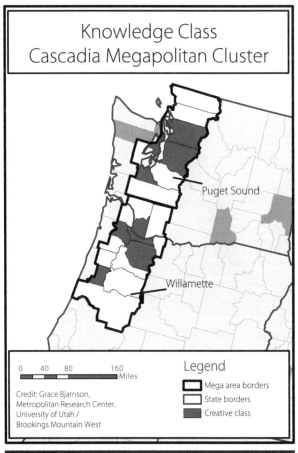

Figure 11.3. Megapolitan cluster counties identified by the USDA as dependent on selected economic sectors

Figure 11.4. Distribution of knowledge-class counties in the Cascadia megapolitan cluster

Table 11.16. Cascadia Megapolitan Cluster Knowledge Class Employment (in thousands)

Megapolitan Area	Knowledge Class Employment, 2010	Total Employment, 2010	Percent Knowledge Class Employment, 2010
Puget Sound	3,120	4,472	69.8
Willamette	2,192	3,353	65.4
Cascadia cluster	5,312	7,825	67.9

Source: Based on Woods & Poole Economics (2010)

Land, Water, and Air Resources

In this section we focus on the land, water, and air resource issues raised in Chapter 10.

In Table 11.17, we report the farmland, rate of change in farmland loss, and change per 1,000 new residents for the periods 1987–1997 and 1997–2007. Both the Puget Sound and the Willamette megapolitan areas lost farmland in the earlier period, though at a pace far less than the national average. This period was one of transition for both states. Oregon fully implemented its statewide land-use planning laws in the mid-1980s, and much of the loss of farmland during the 1990s could be attributable to farmland conversions

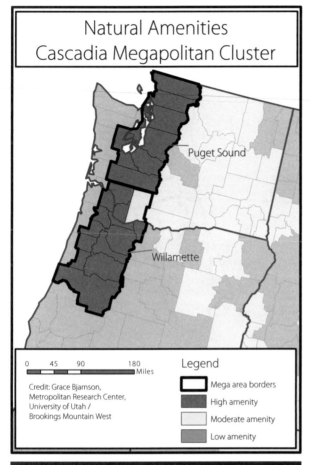

Figure 11.5. Distribution of counties based on natural amenities in the Cascadia megapolitan cluster

inside urban growth boundaries, as plans intended. Washington began implementing its statewide effort in the mid-1990s, so it is not surprising that its rate of farmland loss was substantially higher than Oregon's during this period.

Things changed in the later period, however: Farmland increased in the Puget Sound megapolitan area and losses were trivial in the Willamette megapolitan area. Both states have among the nation's most aggressive laws to preserve farmland, and both use urban growth boundaries and a variety of farmland preservation techniques to do so. The Cascadia megapolitan cluster as a whole saw an increase three times more than that of the only other megapolitan cluster to see an increase, the Texas Triangle.

Table 11.18 reviews changes in water consumption per capita for the Cascadia megapolitan cluster. Between 1990 and 2005, per capita consumption went from above the national average to substantially below it, reducing consumption by about 22 percent overall. While both megapolitan areas reduced per capita consumption, the Puget Sound area reduced consumption by nearly 30 percent.

Table 11.19 reports greenhouse gas production per capita from automobiles for the largest 100 metropolitan areas located in the Cascadia megapolitan cluster. Both metropolitan areas in the cluster are below the national average, with the Portland–Vancouver–Beaverton metropolitan area ranked 13th lowest.

Challenges

The Cascadia megapolitan cluster will approach the density of Great Britain by 2040, and its principal metropolitan areas, Seattle and Portland, will have about 5 million and 3.5 million residents, respectively. The megapolitan cluster itself will exceed 11 million residents by then. The

Table 11.17. Change in Farmland and Farmland Per 1,000 New Residents, 1987–2007, Cascadia Megapolitan Cluster (acres of land)

Megapolitan Area	Farmland, 1987	Farmland, 1997	Percent Farmland Change, 1987–1997	Farmland Change Per New 1,000 Residents, 1987–1997	Farmland, 2007	Percent Farmland Change, 1997–2007	Farmland Change Per New 1,000 Residents, 1997–2007
Puget Sound	633,721	579,196	−8.6	(121)	655,273	13.1	147
Willamette	2,048,757	1,958,866	−4.4	(357)	1,930,204	−1.5	(64)
Cascadia cluster	2,682,478	2,538,062	−5.4	(121)	2,585,477	1.9	49
National average				(425)			(342)

Source: Based on Woods & Poole Economics (2010)

Table 11.18. Change in Per Capita Water Consumption, 1990–2005, Cascadia Megapolitan Cluster (gallons per day)

Megapolitan Area	Water Consumed Per Capita, 1990	Water Consumed Per Capita, 2005	Percent Change in Water Consumed Per Capita, 1990–2005
Puget Sound	194	136	−29.6
Willamette	183	165	−10.1
Cascadia cluster	190	148	−22.0
National average	184	171	−6.8

Source: Based on Woods & Poole Economics (2010)

Table 11.19. Greenhouse Gas Emissions Per Capita, Cascadia Megapolitan Cluster MSAs, 2005 (in metric tons)

Metropolitan Area	Megaregion	Megapolitan Area	Auto Emissions	Percent Dispersion from Mean	Rank Among Top 100 Metros
Seattle–Tacoma–Bellevue, WA	Cascadia	Puget Sound	0.955	−4.9	24
Portland–Vancouver–Beaverton, OR–WA	Cascadia	Willamette	0.860	−14.3	13
Mean transportation footprint for the 100 largest metropolitan areas			1.004		

Source: Adapted from Brown, Southworth, and Sarzynski (2008)

populations of the major metropolitan areas would seem to support such major infrastructure investments as high-speed rail, extensive light rail, and perhaps high-capacity heavy- or third-rail (above- and belowground) options.

There will be land-use planning challenges as an additional 3 million people will need to occupy substantially already urbanized areas. In Oregon, despite decades of progressive planning to preserve farmland and other open spaces, there have also been attempts, some successful, to open up those areas to suburban-style low-density development (see Nelson and Lang 2009). Washington has addressed some of these pressures through spending hundreds of millions of dollars to acquire open spaces and the development rights to farmland. We suspect both states will continue to preserve open spaces and farmland, but they will also need to find ways to facilitate urban infill and redevelopment more aggressively.

Open-space and farmland preservation will likely be aided by demographic changes. Aging baby boomers will probably prefer smaller homes close to services, so they may not seek low-density options in sprawling communities. The biggest change, however, is among minorities. Nearly three-quarters of the population growth will be attributable to minorities. However, on average, they earn about one-third to one-half less than non-Hispanic whites, and own homes one-third as frequently. While assimilation and better education will

surely raise incomes, we are dubious that future income per household, in real terms, will be as high in 2040 as it was in 2000. This may lead to higher demand for smaller units, more attached units, higher densities, and access to transit options in the future than in the past, which bodes well for planning efforts to preserve open spaces and advance urban infill and redevelopment.

We have not explored water capacity in detail, but we suspect the capacity exists to accommodate the nearly 30 percent increase in population, especially if modest conservation efforts are made. For instance, the megapolitan cluster consumes about 10 percent more per capita than the national average, and even then there is likely room to conserve at least another quarter, which would meet future water needs without expanding current supplies.

Finally, with Washington in second place and Oregon in third place, we note the relatively high marks both states get on the Nelson-Lang Planning Index. We suspect that the social, economic, and political culture will be up to meeting the challenge of managing growth in the Cascadia megapolitan cluster in ways that will enhance affordable housing options, maintain environmental quality, expand economic development by facilitating megapolitan cluster networks that already exist and will emerge, and address the next generation of challenges such as reducing greenhouse gases to levels substantially lower than now.

Appendix 11.1. Counties in the Cascadia Megapolitan Cluster			
County, State	*Megapolitan Area*	*County, State*	*Megapolitan Area*
Island, WA	Puget Sound	Columbia, OR	Willamette
King, WA	Puget Sound	Hood River, OR	Willamette
Kitsa, WA	Puget Sound	Lane, OR	Willamette
Lewis, WA	Puget Sound	Linn, OR	Willamette
Mason, WA	Puget Sound	Marion, OR	Willamette
Pierce, WA	Puget Sound	Multnomah, OR	Willamette
Skagit, WA	Puget Sound	Polk, OR	Willamette
Snohomish, WA	Puget Sound	Washington, OR	Willamette
Thurston, WA	Puget Sound	Yamhill, OR	Willamette
Whatcom, WA	Puget Sound	Clark, WA	Willamette
Benton, OR	Willamette	Cowlitz, WA	Willamette
Clackamas, OR	Willamette	Skamania, WA	Willamette

12

SIERRA PACIFIC MEGAPOLITAN AREA

The Sierra Pacific megapolitan area is one of two stand-alone megapolitan areas. The Sierra Pacific megapolitan area is the highly populated agglomeration of metropolitan areas stretching from the Pacific Coast south of San Francisco to Sacramento, in the middle of the Central Valley, to Reno, just east of the Sierra Nevada range (Figure 12.1). Appendix 12.1 lists the counties included in the Sierra Pacific megapolitan area. We offer a vignette of this megapolitan area in terms of major demographic and housing trends, employment and development projections, the extent of economic dependency, and attractiveness characteristics. We conclude with an assessment of major planning and development challenges.

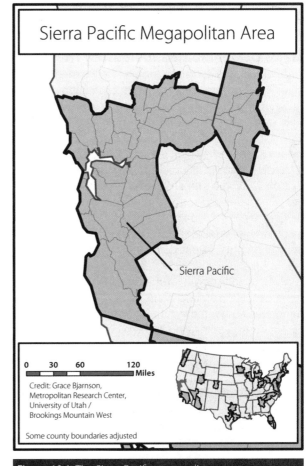

Figure 12.1. The Sierra Pacific megapolitan area

Table 12.1. Sierra Pacific Megapolitan Area Rural-Megapolitan Continuum

Nelson-Lang Rural-Megapolitan Continuum Description	Counties	2010 Population (000s)
Counties in metropolitan areas of 1 million+ population	11	8,348
Counties in metropolitan areas of 250,000 to 1 million population	8	3,215
Counties in metropolitan areas of less than 250,000 population	5	614
Micropolitan area adjacent to a metropolitan area	3	204
Noncore counties adjacent to a metropolitan area	0	0
All other nonmetropolitan counties	0	0

Major Demographic and Housing Trends

Nearly all the residents of the Sierra Pacific megapolitan area live in metropolitan counties, with about three-quarters living in metropolitan areas of more than 1 million residents (Table 12.1 and Figure 12.2). In 2010, its 12.4 million inhabitants occupied about 15,000 square miles of privately owned, reasonably accessible land, at a density of about 800 people per square mile (Table 12.2). In 2040 the Sierra Pacific megapolitan area is projected to have about 16.3 million people (Table 12.3), gaining nearly 4 million people over the period. Its population density will exceed 1,000 persons per square mile, approaching the population density of the Netherlands (Table 12.4).

Most of the growth in the Sierra Pacific megapolitan area will be among minority populations. In 2010, minorities accounted for more than 6.1 million of the 12.4 million people living in the region. Between 2010 and 2040, the region will add about 4.0 million people, yet the minority population will grow by more (Table 12.5)—in other words, more minorities will be living in the Sierra Pacific megapolitan area in 2040 than non-Hispanic whites did in 2010. In fact, the non-Hispanic white population is expected to decline (Table 12.6). Hispanics will dominate population growth (Table 12.7), followed by Asians (Table 12.8) and African Americans (Table 12.9). Moreover, about half the population

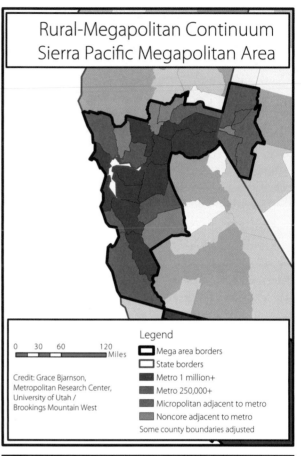

Rural-Megapolitan Continuum Sierra Pacific Megapolitan Area

Legend

0 30 60 120 Miles

Credit: Grace Bjarnson, Metropolitan Research Center, University of Utah / Brookings Mountain West

- ☐ Mega area borders
- ☐ State borders
- ■ Metro 1 million+
- ■ Metro 250,000+
- ■ Micropolitan adjacent to metro
- ■ Noncore adjacent to metro
- Some county boundaries adjusted

Figure 12.2. Nelson-Lang Rural-Megapolitan Continuum Codes applied to Sierra Pacific megapolitan area counties

Table 12.2. Sierra Pacific Megapolitan Area Land Area (in square miles)

Megapolitan Area	Total Land	Estimate of Privately Owned, Accessible Land
Sierra Pacific	33,641	15,380

change will be attributable to those older than 65 (Table 12.10).

Housing Development

Over the period 2010–2040, the Sierra Pacific megapolitan area will add about 1.4 million residential units to its inventory; it will also see the rebuilding or replacement of more than 600,000 units (Table 12.11). In all, more than

Table 12.3. Sierra Pacific Megapolitan Area Population, 2010–2040 (in thousands)

Megapolitan Area	Total Population, 2010	Total Population, 2025	Total Population, 2040	Total Change, 2010–2040	Percent Change, 2010–2040
Sierra Pacific	12,381	14,345	16,386	4,005	32.3

Source: Based on Woods & Poole Economics (2010)

Table 12.4. Sierra Pacific Megapolitan Area Population Density, 2010–2040

Megapolitan Area	Persons Per Square Mile, 2010	Comparable Developed Nation	Persons Per Square Mile, 2040	Comparable Developed Nation
Sierra Pacific	805	>United Kingdom	1,065	<The Netherlands

Note: The sign < means the megapolitan area density is about 50–200 fewer persons per square mile than in the comparable nation, while > means the density is about 50–200 more persons per square mile; no sign indicates the density is within about 50 persons per square mile. Figures compare developed nation population in 2010 to megapolitan cluster population in 2010 and 2040. All ranges are illustrative.

Table 12.5. Sierra Pacific Megapolitan Area Minority Population, 2010–2040 (in thousands)

Megapolitan Area	Minority Population, 2010	Minority Population, 2025	Minority Population, 2040	Minority Population Change, 2010–2040	Minority Population Percent Change, 2010–2040	Minority Share of Population Change, 2010–2040
Sierra Pacific	6,140	8,101	10,319	4,178	68.1	104.3

Source: Based on Woods & Poole Economics (2010)

Table 12.6. Sierra Pacific Megapolitan Area White Non-Hispanic Population, 2010–2040 (in thousands)

Megapolitan Area	White Non-Hispanic Population, 2010	White Non-Hispanic Population, 2025	White Non-Hispanic Population, 2040	White Non-Hispanic Population Change, 2010–2040	White Non-Hispanic Population Percent Change, 2010–2040	White Non-Hispanic Share of Population Change, 2010–2040
Sierra Pacific	6,241	6,244	6,067	(174)	−2.8	−0.3

Source: Based on Woods & Poole Economics (2010)

Table 12.7. Sierra Pacific Megapolitan Area Hispanic Population, 2010–2040 (in thousands)

Megapolitan Area	Hispanic Population, 2010	Hispanic Population, 2025	Hispanic Population, 2040	Hispanic Population Change, 2010–2040	Hispanic Population Percent Change, 2010–2040	Hispanic Share of Population Change, 2010–2040
Sierra Pacific	3,202	4,579	6,153	2,951	92.2	73.7

Source: Based on Woods & Poole Economics (2010)

2.0 million residential units will be built or rebuilt during this period, the equivalent of about 42 percent of all units existing in 2010. We estimate that two-thirds or more will be attached units.

Major Employment and Nonresidential Development Trends

The Sierra Pacific megapolitan area will see impressive job growth (both part- and full-time). Data aggregated from Woods and Poole Economics to the megapolitan area

Table 12.8. Sierra Pacific Megapolitan Area Asian Population, 2010–2040 (in thousands)

Megapolitan Area	Asian Population, 2010	Asian Population, 2025	Asian Population, 2040	Asian Population Change, 2010–2040	Asian Population Percent Change, 2010–2040	Asian Share of Population Change, 2010–2040
Sierra Pacific	2,240	2,998	3,782	1,542	68.8	38.5

Source: Based on Woods & Poole Economics (2010)

Table 12.9. Sierra Pacific Megapolitan Area African American Population, 2010–2040 (in thousands)

Megapolitan Area	African American Population, 2010	African American Population, 2025	African American Population, 2040	African American Population Change, 2010–2040	African American Population Percent Change, 2010–2040	African American Share of Population Change, 2010–2040
Sierra Pacific	788	838	897	109	13.9	2.7

Source: Based on Woods & Poole Economics (2010)

Table 12.10. Sierra Pacific Megapolitan Area Population 65+, 2010–2040 (in thousands)

Megapolitan Area	Population 65+, 2010	Population 65+ as Share of Population, 2010	Population 65+, 2040	Population 65+ as Share of Population, 2040	Share of Population Change, 2010–2040
Sierra Pacific	1,513	12.2	3,506	21.4	49.8

Source: Based on Woods & Poole Economics (2010)

Table 12.11. Sierra Pacific Megapolitan Area Residential Development, 2010–2040 (in thousands)

Megapolitan Area	Units Supported, 2010	Increase in Inventory, 2010–2040	Units Recycled, 2010–2040	Total Units Constructed, 2010–2040	Percent of Units Supported, 2010
Sierra Pacific	4,740	1,383	603	1,986	41.9

Table 12.12. Sierra Pacific Megapolitan Area Total Employment, 2010–2040 (in thousands)

Megapolitan Area	Total Jobs, 2010	Total Jobs, 2040	Change, 2010–2040	Percent Change, 2010–2040
Sierra Pacific	7,481	10,325	2,845	38.0

Source: Based on Woods & Poole Economics (2010)

level show the total number of jobs will grow from about 7.5 million in 2010 to about 10.3 million in 2040 (Table 12.12). Some of those jobs will be in natural resources, construction, or other activities that do not require that workers occupy space. We estimate "land-use" jobs will increase by about 2.8 million between 2010 and 2040 (Table 12.13).

In 2010, the Sierra Pacific megapolitan area could support about 3.5 billion square feet of nonresidential space, including industrial, commercial, and institutional uses. By 2040, it will support about 4.7 billion square feet of space, adding about 1.3 billion square feet over the period (Table 12.14). However, counting space that will be replaced, sometimes twice (see Chapter 5), a total of about 5.1 billion square feet is expected to be built. Growth-related and replaced space will be roughly equivalent to 1.5 times the nonresidential existing space in 2010.

Economic Dependency

Table 12.15 summarizes those economic sectors where the Sierra Pacific megapolitan area is dependent, and Figure 12.3 shows the sectors spatially. Although manufacturing employment as a share of total jobs is small, the total population of counties dependent on manufacturing was about 15 percent of the megapolitan area's total population in 2010. This is attributable to the high-tech jobs found in the Silicon Valley and nearby areas. Another area of dependency is in state and federal government employment, likely associated with major military bases located in the San Francisco Bay Area. Roughly a quarter of the megapolitan area's population lives in an economically dependent county.

Government employment is the primary sector of dependence, accounting for about 18 percent of the dependent county population.

Attractiveness to the Knowledge Class

Table 12.16 summarizes the population and share of the population living in knowledge class counties for the Sierra Pacific megapolitan area. About three-quarters of the megapolitan area lives in a knowledge class county (Figure 12.4), and about 90 percent of the megapolitan area's population growth will occur in those counties. Figure 12.5 illustrates where the highest-rated counties in terms of natural amenities are in the Sierra Pacific megapolitan area.

Table 12.13. Sierra Pacific Megapolitan Area Land-Use Employment, 2010–2040 (in thousands)

Megapolitan Area	Total Land-Use Employment, 2010	Total Land-Use Employment, 2025	Total Land-Use Employment, 2040	Change in Land-Use Employment, 2010–2040	Percent Change in Land-Use Employment, 2010–2040
Sierra Pacific	7,266	8,592	10,096	2,830	39.0

Source: Based on Woods & Poole Economics (2010)

Table 12.14. Sierra Pacific Megapolitan Area Land-Use Employment Space Needs, 2010–2040 (millions of square feet)

Megapolitan Area	Total Land-Use Employment Space Supported, 2010	Total Land-Use Employment Space Supported, 2040	Increase in Land-Use Employment Space Inventory Supported, 2010–2040	Recycled Employment Land-Use Space, 2010–2040	Total Land-Use Employment Space Constructed, 2010–2040	Land-Use Employment Space Constructed in 2010–2040 as Percent of Space in 2010
Sierra Pacific	3,455	4,724	1,269	3,792	5,061	146.5

Table 12.15. Sierra Pacific Megapolitan Area Economic Sector Dependence (in millions)

Megapolitan Area	Farming-Dependent Population, 2010	Mining-Dependent Population, 2010	Manufacturing-Dependent Population, 2010	Tourism and Entertainment–Dependent Population, 2010	Government-Dependent Population, 2010	Total Dependent Population, 2010	Total Population, 2010	Percent Dependent Population, 2010
Sierra Pacific	413	0	56	406	2,179	3,121	12,381	25.2

Table 12.16. Sierra Pacific Megapolitan Area Knowledge Class Employment (in thousands)

Megapolitan Area	Knowledge Class Employment, 2010	Total Employment, 2010	Percent Knowledge Class Employment, 2010,
Sierra Pacific	9,175	12,381	74.1

Source: Based on Woods & Poole Economics (2010)

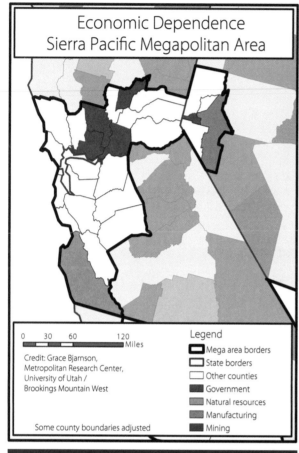

Figure 12.3. Sierra Pacific megapolitan area counties identified by the USDA as dependent on selected economic sectors

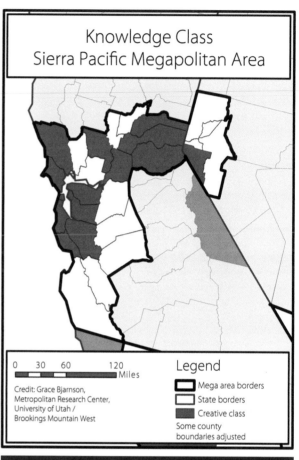

Figure 12.4. Distribution of knowledge-class counties in the Sierra Pacific megapolitan area

Table 12.17. Change in Farmland and Farmland Per 1,000 New Residents, 1987–2007, Sierra Pacific Megapolitan Area (acres of land)

Megapolitan Area	Farmland, 1987	Farmland, 1997	Percent Farm-land Change, 1987–1997	Farmland Change Per New 1,000 Residents, 1987–1997	Farmland, 2007	Percent Farm-land Change, 1997–2007	Farmland Change Per New 1,000 Residents, 1997–2007
Sierra Pacific	9,887,067	9,364,997	–5.3	(357)	8,956,162	–4.4	(365)
National average				(425)			(342)

Source: Based on Woods & Poole Economics (2010)

Land, Water, and Air Resources

Here we expand on the land, water, and air resource issues raised in Chapter 10 as they relate to the Sierra Pacific megapolitan area.

Table 12.17 shows the amount of farmland, rate of change in farmland, and change per 1,000 new residents for the periods 1987–1997 and 1997–2007. The rate of loss parallels that of the nation as a whole. Over the 20 years between 1987 and 2007, the megapolitan area lost nearly 1 million acres of farmland, or about 10 percent. The pace has changed little between the periods. At this pace, half the farmland in the Sierra Pacific megapolitan area could be lost by the end of the 21st century.

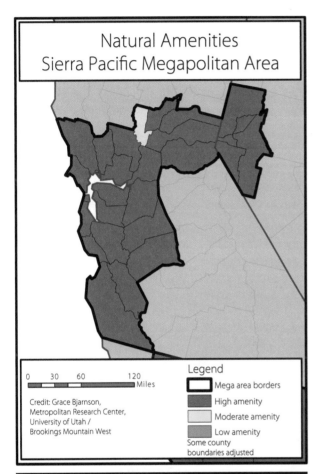

Figure 12.5. Distribution of counties based on natural amenities in the Sierra Pacific megapolitan area

In Table 12.18 we report changes in water consumption per capita for the Sierra Pacific megapolitan area. From 1990 to 2005, per capita consumption actually rose, with the Sierra Pacific megapolitan area joining the Texas Triangle megapolitan cluster as the only areas where this happened. Indeed, in 1990 the Sierra Pacific megapolitan area consumed about 189 gallons per capita per day, compared to the national average of 184, but in 2005 the per capita daily consumption was 192 and 171 gallons, respectively.

Table 12.19 presents greenhouse gas production per capita from automobiles for the largest 100 metropolitan areas located in the Sierra Pacific megapolitan area. Levels in all three metropolitan areas were around the national average, and these areas ranked in the top third to half of the larger metropolitan areas.

Challenges

The Sierra Pacific megapolitan area already has heavy rail and commuter rail serving the Bay Area and light rail serving Sacramento, and by the mid-2010s both metropolitan areas may be connected by European-style high-speed rail to Los Angeles.

Planning challenges lie ahead as 4 million more people will move into areas that are already urbanized. The supply of land available for new, greenfield development is falling steadily through public land acquisition or the purchase and transfer of development rights, and in the Central Valley land-use planning will likely prevent the development of vast farming areas. Indeed, it is largely because of farmland conversion, mostly from the Bay Area extending eastward but also from metropolitan areas in the Central Valley itself, that the supply of farmland fell by nearly 400,000 acres since 1990, or about one acre per new home built. At this pace, the Central Valley could lose more than a million more acres of farmland to development.

Table 12.18. Change in Per Capita Water Consumption, 1990–2005, Sierra Pacific Megapolitan Area (gallons per day)

Megapolitan Area	Water Consumed Per Capita, 1990	Water Consumed Per Capita, 2005	Percent Change in Water Consumed Per Capita, 1990–2005
Sierra Pacific	189	192	1.3
National average	184	171	−6.8

Source: Based on Woods & Poole Economics (2010)

Table 12.19. Greenhouse Gas Emissions Per Capita, Sierra Pacific Megapolitan Area MSAs, 2005 (in metric tons)

Metropolitan Area	Megaregion	Megapolitan Area	Auto Emissions	Percent Dispersion from Mean	Rank Among Top 100 Metropolitan Areas
San Jose–Sunnyvale–Santa Clara, CA	Sierra Pacific	Sierra Pacific	1.009	0.5	34
Sacramento–Arden–Arcade–Roseville, CA	Sierra Pacific	Sierra Pacific	1.063	5.9	47
San Francisco–Oakland–Fremont, CA	Sierra Pacific	Sierra Pacific	0.998	−0.6	32
Mean transportation footprint for the 100 largest metropolitan areas			1.004		

Source: Adapted from Brown, Southworth, and Sarzynski (2008)

Demographic changes present an opportunity to minimize loss of farmland and facilitate urban infill and redevelopment. As elsewhere, aging baby boomers will likely want smaller homes close to services and so may not seek low-density options in sprawling communities. The biggest change, however, is among minorities. Essentially all the growth will be attributable to minorities. However, on average, they earn about one-third to one-half less than non-Hispanic whites and own homes one-third as frequently. While assimilation and better education will surely raise incomes, we are dubious that future income per household, in real terms, will be as high in 2040 as it was in 2000. This may lead to higher demand for smaller units, more attached units, higher densities, and access to transit options in the future than the past, which bodes well for planning efforts to preserve open spaces and advance urban infill and redevelopment.

In terms of water, we suspect the capacity exists to accommodate the nearly one-third increase in population, especially if modest conservation efforts are undertaken. For instance, the Sierra Pacific megapolitan area consumes about 10 percent more per capita than the national average, and even then there is likely room to conserve at least another quarter, which would meet future water needs without expanding current supplies.

Finally, California's planning rigor is legendary. Although the state ranks 12th on the Nelson-Lang Planning Index, it is at the local government level where planning is rigorous. California jurisdictions routinely win national planning awards and pioneer new planning ideas. Perhaps the limiting factor in California's planning environment is truly regional-scale planning, let alone planning done at the megapolitan area scale.

Appendix 12.1. Counties and Independent Cities in the Sierra Pacific Megapolitan Area

County, State	Megapolitan Area
Alameda, CA	Sierra Pacific
Contra Costa, CA	Sierra Pacific
El Dorado, CA	Sierra Pacific
Marin, CA	Sierra Pacific
Merced, CA	Sierra Pacific
Monterey, CA	Sierra Pacific
Napa, CA	Sierra Pacific
Nevada, CA	Sierra Pacific
Placer, CA	Sierra Pacific
Sacramento, CA	Sierra Pacific
San Benito, CA	Sierra Pacific
San Francisco, CA	Sierra Pacific
San Joaquin, CA	Sierra Pacific
San Mateo, CA	Sierra Pacific
Santa Clara, CA	Sierra Pacific
Santa Cruz, CA	Sierra Pacific
Solano, CA	Sierra Pacific
Sonoma, CA	Sierra Pacific
Stanislaus, CA	Sierra Pacific
Sutter, CA	Sierra Pacific
Yolo, CA	Sierra Pacific
Yuba, CA	Sierra Pacific
Douglas, NV	Sierra Pacific
Lyon, NV	Sierra Pacific
Storey, NV	Sierra Pacific
Washoe, NV	Sierra Pacific
Carson City, NV	Sierra Pacific

13

SOUTHWEST MEGAPOLITAN CLUSTER

With nearly 13 million new residents expected between 2010 and 2040, the Southwest megapolitan cluster will see the nation's largest amount of growth. In many respects, it will also be the nation's most stressed megapolitan cluster.

The Southwest megapolitan cluster consists of the nation's most densely settled urban region, the Southern California megapolitan area; the nation's most rapidly growing megapolitan area of more than 1 million residents in 2010, Las Vegas; and the nation's most rapidly growing megapolitan area of more than 2 million residents in 2010, the Sun Corridor (Figure 13.1). The

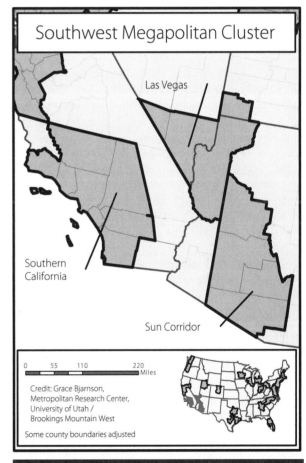

Southwest Megapolitan Cluster

Las Vegas

Southern California

Sun Corridor

0   55   110   220
                        Miles

Credit: Grace Bjarnson,
Metropolitan Research Center,
University of Utah /
Brookings Mountain West

Some county boundaries adjusted

Figure 13.1. The Southwest megapolitan cluster, composed of the Southern California, Las Vegas, and Sun Corridor megapolitan areas

Table 13.1. Southwest Megapolitan Cluster Rural-Megapolitan Continuum

Nelson-Lang Rural-Megapolitan Continuum Description	Counties	2010 Population (000s)
Counties in metropolitan areas of 1 million+ population	8	26,824
Counties in metropolitan areas of 250,000 to 1 million population	4	3,097
Counties in metropolitan areas of less than 250,000 population	2	379
Micropolitan area adjacent to a metropolitan area	2	252
Noncore counties adjacent to a metropolitan area	0	0
All other nonmetropolitan counties	0	0

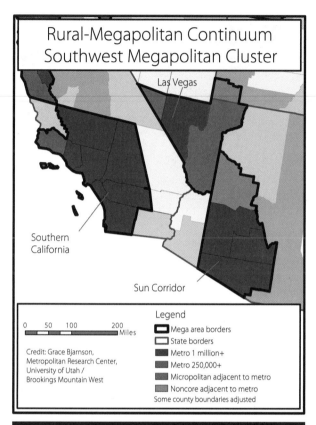

Figure 13.2. Nelson-Lang Rural-Megapolitan Continuum Codes applied to Southwest megapolitan cluster counties

Southwest megapolitan cluster extends from the Pacific Ocean east to the Sonoran Desert. Its principal metropolitan areas include Los Angeles, San Diego, San Bernardino, and Riverside in the Southern California megapolitan area, Las Vegas in the Las Vegas megapolitan area, and Phoenix in the Sun Corridor megapolitan area. Appendix 13.1 lists the counties included in each megapolitan area in the Southwest megapolitan cluster. In this chapter we profile the Southwest megapolitan cluster in respect to major demographic and housing trends, employment and development projections, the extent of economic dependency, and attractiveness characteristics. We conclude with our perceptions of major planning and development challenges.

Major Demographic and Housing Trends

The Southwest megapolitan cluster has one of the nation's highest percentages of population living in counties of metropolitan areas of more than 1 million residents, nearly 90 percent (Table 13.1 and Figure 13.2). It is also the area most affected by federal and tribal lands and by extensive, essentially uninhabitable land. Of its 123,000 square miles, we estimate that less than a third, about 24,000 square miles, are privately owned and reasonably accessible to development (Table 13.2). At more than 1,250 persons per square mile, it is the

Table 13.2. Southwest Megapolitan Cluster Land Area (in square miles)

Megapolitan Area	Total Land	Estimate of Privately Owned, Accessible Land
Southern California	49,051	11,325
Las Vegas	41,798	4,850
Sun Corridor	31,885	8,187
Total	122,733	24,363

nation's second most densely settled megapolitan cluster, after the Florida megapolitan cluster, and about as densely settled as the Netherlands (Table 13.3). By 2040, the megapolitan cluster will grow to about 44 million people (Table 13.4) and its density, at nearly 1,800 persons per square mile, will be greater than that of any European country (Table 13.4), far more than Japan's

Table 13.3. Southwest Megapolitan Cluster Density, 2010–2040

Megapolitan Area	Persons Per Square Mile, 2010	Comparable Developed Nation, 2010	Persons Per Square Mile, 2040	Comparable Developed Nation, 2040
Southern California	1,984	>Taiwan	2,658	Beyond comparison
Las Vegas	485	Italy	830	Belgium
Sun Corridor	700	>United Kingdom	1,120	<The Netherlands
Southwest cluster total	1,254	The Netherlands	1,777	<Taiwan

Note: The sign < means the megapolitan area density is about 50–200 fewer persons per square mile than in the comparable nation, while > means the density is about 50–200 more persons per square mile; no sign indicates the density is within about 50 persons per square mile. Figures compare developed nation population in 2010 to megapolitan cluster population in 2010 and 2040. "Beyond comparison" means the density is above peer among developed countries. All ranges are illustrative.

Table 13.4. Southwest Megapolitan Cluster Population, 2010–2040 (in thousands)

Megapolitan Area	Total Population, 2010	Total Population, 2025	Total Population, 2040	Total Change, 2010–2040	Percent Change, 2010–2040
Southern California	22,469	26,217	30,105	7,636	34.0
Las Vegas	2,352	3,180	4,025	1,673	71.1
Sun Corridor	5,730	7,429	9,166	3,436	60.0
Southwest cluster	30,552	36,826	43,296	12,744	41.7

Source: Based on Woods & Poole Economics (2010)

Table 13.5. Southwest Megapolitan Cluster Minority Population, 2010–2040 (in thousands)

Megapolitan Area	Minority Population, 2010	Minority Population, 2025	Minority Population, 2040	Minority Population Change, 2010–2040	Minority Population Percent Change, 2010–2040	Minority Share of Population Change, 2010–2040
Southern California	14,085	18,898	24,079	9,994	71.0	78.4
Las Vegas	1,006	1,577	2,138	1,132	112.5	8.9
Sun Corridor	2,327	3,553	4,918	2,591	111.4	20.3
Southwest cluster	17,419	24,028	31,135	13,717	78.7	107.6

Source: Based on Woods & Poole Economics (2010)

and nearly as much as Taiwan's but with about twice the population.

Especially in the Southwest megapolitan cluster, virtually all growth will be among minorities. In 2010, minorities accounted for about 17.4 million of the 35.6 million people living in the cluster (Table 13.5). Between 2010 and 2040, the region will add about 12.7 million residents, but because the non-Hispanic white population will actually fall (Table 13.6), minorities will account for all

the growth. The Hispanic population will about double in all megapolitan areas (Table 13.7), while the Asian population will more than double in the Las Vegas and Sun Corridor megapolitan areas (see Table 13.8). The African American population will grow only slightly, however (Table 13.9).

As the baby boomers turn 65, between 2011 and 2029, they will account for about 40 percent of the Southwest megapolitan cluster's population change (Table 13.10).

Table 13.6. Southwest Megapolitan Cluster White Non-Hispanic Population, 2010–2040 (in thousands)

Megapolitan Area	White Non-Hispanic Population, 2010	White Non-Hispanic Population, 2025	White Non-Hispanic Population, 2040	White Non-Hispanic Population Change, 2010–2040	White Non-Hispanic Population Percent Change, 2010–2040	White Non-Hispanic Share of Population Change, 2010–2040
Southern California	8,384	7,320	6,026	(2,358)	−28.1	−18.5
Las Vegas	1,346	1,603	1,887	541	40.2	4.2
Sun Corridor	3,403	3,876	4,248	845	24.8	6.6
Southwest cluster	13,133	12,798	12,160	(973)	−7.4	−7.6

Source: Based on Woods & Poole Economics (2010)

Table 13.7. Southwest Megapolitan Cluster Hispanic Population, 2010–2040 (in thousands)

Megapolitan Area	Hispanic Population, 2010	Hispanic Population, 2025	Hispanic Population, 2040	Hispanic Population Change, 2010–2040	Hispanic Population Percent Change, 2010–2040	Hispanic Share of Population Change, 2010–2040
Southern California	9,898	14,165	18,898	9,000	90.9	70.6
Las Vegas	618	968	1,271	653	105.6	5.1
Sun Corridor	1,808	2,813	3,905	2,097	116.0	16.5
Southwest cluster	12,324	17,946	24,074	11,750	95.3	92.2

Source: Based on Woods & Poole Economics (2010)

Table 13.8. Southwest Megapolitan Cluster Asian Population, 2010–2040 (in thousands)

Megapolitan Area	Asian Population, 2010	Asian Population, 2025	Asian Population, 2040	Asian Population Change, 2010–2040	Asian Population Percent Change, 2010–2040	Asian Share of Population Change, 2010–2040
Southern California	2,591	3,111	3,549	959	37.0	7.5
Las Vegas	172	342	559	387	224.4	3.0
Sun Corridor	169	290	460	291	171.9	2.3
Southwest cluster	2,932	3,743	4,569	1,636	55.8	12.8

Source: Based on Woods & Poole Economics (2010)

Housing Development

The Southwest megapolitan cluster will add about 4.1 million residential units to its inventory during the period 2010–2040 (Table 13.11), the second most of any megapolitan cluster, behind Megalopolis. Although it will add more people than any other megapolitan cluster, larger household size will mean demand for fewer homes than in Megalopolis. We also estimate that about 1.5 million units existing in 2010 will be rebuilt or replaced by 2040. In total, about 5.6 million residential units will be built or rebuilt between 2010 and 2040, equivalent to about half of all units existing in 2010. We further estimate that roughly three-quarters of those units will be attached units or very small-lot detached units.

Table 13.9. Southwest Megapolitan Cluster African American Population, 2010–2040 (in thousands)

Megapolitan Area	African American Population, 2010	African American Population, 2025	African American Population, 2040	African American Population Change, 2010–2040	African American Population Percent Change, 2010–2040	African American Share of Population Change, 2010–2040
Southern California	1,482	1,467	1,431	(51)	–3.4	–0.4
Las Vegas	196	246	287	92	46.7	0.7
Sun Corridor	228	292	358	130	56.8	1.0
Southwest cluster	1,906	2,005	2,076	170	8.9	1.3

Source: Based on Woods & Poole Economics (2010)

Table 13.10. Southwest Megapolitan Cluster Population 65+, 2010–2040 (in thousands)

Megapolitan Area/ Cluster	Population 65+, 2010	Population 65+ as Share of Population, 2010	Population 65+, 2040	Population 65+ as Share of Population, 2040	Share of Population Change, 2010–2040
Southern California	2,463	11.0	6,020	20.0	46.6
Las Vegas	299	12.7	857	21.3	33.3
Sun Corridor	745	13.0	1,836	20.0	31.7
Southwest cluster	3,507	11.5	8,713	20.1	40.8

Source: Based on Woods & Poole Economics (2010)

Table 13.11. Southwest Megapolitan Cluster Residential Development (in thousands)

Megapolitan Area	Units Supported, 2010	Increase in Inventory, 2010–2040	Units Recycled, 2010–2040	Total Units Constructed, 2010–2040	Percent of Units Supported, 2010
Southern California	8,140	2,191	1,036	3,226	39.6
Las Vegas	1,065	572	135	707	66.4
Sun Corridor	2,416	1,369	307	1,677	69.4
Southwest cluster	11,621	4,131	1,479	5,610	48.3

Major Employment and Nonresidential Development Trends

Among megapolitan clusters, the Southwest will be the leader in job growth, both part- and full-time jobs. Woods and Poole Economics data show that the total number of jobs will grow from about 16.9 million in 2010 to about 24.7 million in 2040 (Table 13.12). Subtracting jobs in natural resources, construction, or other activities that do not require that workers occupy space, we estimate "land-use" jobs will increase by about 7.8 million between 2010 and 2040 (Table 13.13).

Employment in the Southwest supported about 8.0 billion square feet of nonresidential space, including industrial, commercial, and institutional uses, in 2010. By 2040, it will be able to support about 11.5 billion square feet of space, adding about 3.5 billion square feet over the period (Table 13.14). Counting space that will be replaced, sometimes twice (see Chapter 5), a total of 12.3 billion square feet is expected to be built. Growth-related and replaced space will be roughly equivalent to 1.5 times the nonresidential space existing in 2010.

Economic Dependency

In Chapter 6, we presented the USDA's method of determining whether counties are overly dependent on key economic sectors, especially farming, mining,

Table 13.12. Southwest Megapolitan Cluster Total Employment, 2010–2040 (in thousands)

Megapolitan Area	Total Jobs, 2010	Total Jobs, 2040	Change, 2010–2040	Percent Change, 2010–2040
Southern California	12,394	17,090	4,696	37.9
Las Vegas	1,368	2,427	1,059	77.4
Sun Corridor	3,136	5,174	2,037	65.0
Southwest cluster	16,898	24,691	7,793	46.1

Source: Based on Woods & Poole Economics (2010)

Table 13.13. Southwest Megapolitan Cluster Land-Use Employment, 2010–2040 (in thousands)

Megapolitan Area	Total Land-Use Employment, 2010	Total Land-Use Employment, 2025	Total Land-Use Employment, 2040	Change in Land-Use Employment, 2010–2040	Percent Change in Land-Use Employment, 2010–2040
Southern California	12,214	14,394	16,900	4,687	38.4
Las Vegas	1,362	1,816	2,420	1,058	77.7
Sun Corridor	3,107	4,008	5,142	2,035	65.5
Southwest cluster	16,682	20,219	24,462	7,780	46.6

Source: Based on Woods & Poole Economics (2010)

Table 13.14. Southwest Megapolitan Cluster Land-Use Employment Space Needs, 2010–2040 (millions of square feet)

Megapolitan Area	Total Land-Use Employment Space Supported, 2010	Total Land-Use Employment Space Supported, 2040	Increase in Land-Use Employment Space Inventory Supported, 2010–2040	Recycled Land-Use Employment Space, 2010–2040	Total Land-Use Employment Space Constructed, 2010–2040	Land-Use Employment Space Constructed in 2010–2040 as Percent of Space in 2010
Southern California	5,878	8,015	2,137	6,451	8,589	146.1
Las Vegas	620	1,095	475	680	1,155	186.4
Sun Corridor	1,468	2,388	920	1,611	2,531	172.4
Southwest cluster	7,965	11,498	3,533	8,742	12,275	154.1

manufacturing, and federal and state government. Generally, if more than 20 percent of a county's jobs or earnings were in one sector in 2000, it was deemed to be dependent on it. We apply these measures of economic dependency to the Southwest megapolitan cluster and its megapolitan areas in Table 13.15 and illustrate them in Figure 13.3. The Southern California and Sun Corridor megapolitan areas are not heavily dependent on any economic sector. However, the Las Vegas megapolitan area is very heavily dependent on the tourist sector,

being the most dependent of any megapolitan area on any economic sector.

Attractiveness to the Knowledge Class

Figure 13.4 shows the knowledge class counties in the Southwest megapolitan cluster. Table 13.16 summarizes the population and share of the population living in knowledge class counties for the Southwest megapolitan cluster and its megapolitan areas. About three-quarters of the Southwest megapolitan cluster's population lives in a knowledge class county, but the distribution is skewed. The figure is 77 percent for Southern California and 90 percent for the Sun Corridor (the highest rate for an individual megapolitan area), but 0 percent for Las Vegas. Figure 13.5 shows the megapolitan cluster counties based on their natural amenities.

Table 13.15. Southwest Megapolitan Cluster Economic Sector Dependence (in millions)

Megapolitan Area	Farming-Dependent Population, 2010	Mining-Dependent Population, 2010	Manufacturing-Dependent Population, 2010	Tourism and Entertainment–Dependent Population, 2010	Government-Dependent Population, 2010	Total Dependent Population, 2010	Total Population, 2010	Percent Dependent Population, 2010
Southern California	0	0	0	0	0	0	22,469	0.0
Las Vegas	0	0	0	1,594	0	1,594	2,352	67.7
Sun Corridor	0	0	0	0	345	345	5,730	6.0
Southwest cluster	0	0	0	1,594	345	1,939	30,552	6.3

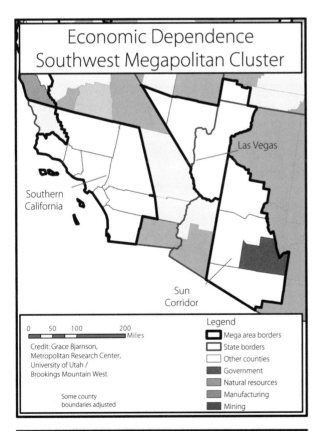

Figure 13.3. Southwest megapolitan cluster counties identified by the USDA as dependent on selected economic sectors

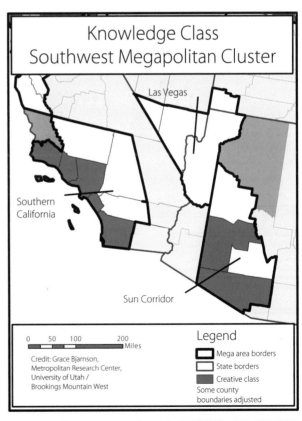

Figure 13.4. Distribution of knowledge class counties in the Southwest megapolitan cluster

Table 13.16. Southwest Megapolitan Cluster Knowledge Class Employment (in thousands)

Megapolitan Area	Knowledge Class Employment, 2010	Total Employment, 2010	Percent Knowledge Class Employment, 2010
Southern California	17,302	22,469	77.0
Las Vegas	0	2,352	0.0
Sun Corridor	5,159	5,730	90.0
Southwest cluster	22,460	30,552	73.5

Source: Based on Woods & Poole Economics (2010)

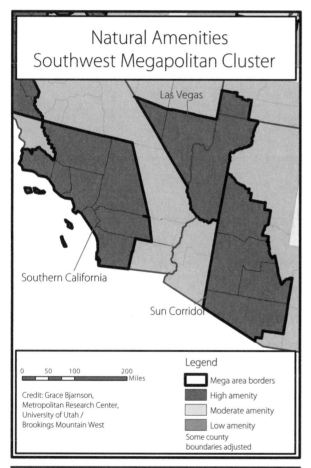

Figure 13.5. Distribution of counties based on natural amenities in the Southwest megapolitan cluster

Land, Water, and Air Resources

We conclude the analytic part of this chapter with an assessment of the land, water, and air resource issues raised in Chapter 10.

The farmland, rate of change in farmland, and change per 1,000 new residents is reported in Table 13.17 for the periods 1987–1997 and 1997–2007. All three megapolitan areas lost farmland in both periods. Between 1987 and 1997, the Southwest megapolitan cluster lost about a third of its farmland, though the loss was reduced to about 20 percent over the more recent period. Still, at this pace, the Southern California and Sun Corridor megapolitan areas could lose the rest of their farmland by mid-century. The Las Vegas megapolitan area lost proportionately the most farmland between 1987 and 1997, but the least between 1997 and 2007—a time of unprecedented development.

It might be argued that agriculture in the highly arid megapolitan areas of Las Vegas and the Sun Corridor should not be preserved over the long term. A principal reason is that the choice of crops tends to demand considerable amounts of water. Yet these areas also lead the nation in per capita consumption of public water (as opposed to water used for irrigation). An argument could therefore also be made that bringing water consumption down to just the national average could preserve farmland and all the collateral benefits it offers to those areas.

Table 13.18 shows water consumption trends over the period 1990–2005. We note that the Southern California megapolitan area has reduced water consumption substantially, at a rate 2.5 times faster than the nation as a whole. Water consumption in the Las Vegas megapolitan area reflects the demands placed on this area by the nation's largest tourism and convention operations, so calculating water consumption per capita is misleading. That its water consumption per capita has been reduced by nearly 10 percent, though still higher than the national average, is commendable, though much more can and is being done. The surprise is with the Sun Corridor megapolitan area, where per capita water consumption did

Table 13.17. Change in Farmland and Farmland Per 1,000 New Residents, 1987–2007, Southwest Megapolitan Cluster (acres of land)

Megapolitan Area	Farmland, 1987	Farmland, 1997	Percent Farmland Change, 1987–1997	Farmland Change Per 1,000 New Residents, 1987–1997	Farmland, 2007	Percent Farmland Change, 1997–2007	Farmland Change Per 1,000 New Residents, 1997–2007
Southern California	7,328,518	6,111,707	−16.6	(530)	4,716,644	−22.8	(650)
Las Vegas	2,523,193	1,316,581	−47.8	(1,598)	1,211,833	−8.0	(154)
Sun Corridor	8,903,240	5,697,326	−36.0	(2,525)	4,709,931	−17.3	(689)
Southwest cluster	18,754,951	13,125,614	−30.0	(1,304)	10,638,408	−18.9	(584)
National average				(425)			(342)

Source: Based on Woods & Poole Economics (2010)

Table 13.18. Change in Per Capita Water Consumption, 1990–2005, Southwest Megapolitan Cluster (gallons per day)

Megapolitan Area	Water Consumed Per Capita, 1990	Water Consumed Per Capita, 2005	Percent Change in Water Consumed Per Capita, 1990–2005
Southern California	235	194	−17.6
Las Vegas	359	324	−9.7
Sun Corridor	209	207	−1.0
Southwest cluster	237	205	−13.3
National average	184	171	−6.8

Source: Based on Woods & Poole Economics (2010)

not change over the 15-year period and is also among the nation's highest levels.

Table 13.19 shows the greenhouse gas emissions per capita from automobiles for the largest 100 metropolitan areas located in the Southwest megapolitan cluster. Except for the Los Angeles metropolitan area, all metropolitan areas in the Southern California megapolitan area exceed national averages, and usually by a considerable margin. Los Angeles, on the other hand, ranks 17th lowest in per capita emissions. Las Vegas actually does better, coming in at 15th lowest in per capita emissions, while the Phoenix and Tucson metropolitan areas in the Sun Corridor megapolitan area rank 22nd and 20th, respectively.

Challenges

Except for Southern California, the megapolitan areas of the Southwest megapolitan cluster are anomalies in growth. In 1950, the Phoenix metropolitan area had about 330,000 residents, while Las Vegas had just 50,000.

Although Phoenix was predicted to become a major metropolitan area that would rise to megalopolis status when combined with Tucson (see Chapters 1 and 3), Las Vegas was never thought by analysts to amount to much. Indeed, Las Vegas and Phoenix are the only two proximate major metropolitan areas not connected by a federal interstate highway.

Development in all the megapolitan areas of the Southwest megapolitan cluster is the most constrained of all the megapolitan areas nationally, a peculiarity in light of their historical and projected growth. As a result, the Southwest megapolitan areas are becoming the nation's most densely settled. The form of development, however, is not what one would associate with high densities. Instead, development patterns are and will continue to be characterized as low rise. Detached homes are constructed on very small lots with perhaps six feet or less of separation between structures. Along with this form of development is a lack of connectivity between land-use activities (see Lang and LeFurgy

Table 13.19. Greenhouse Gas Emissions Per Capita, Southwest Megapolitan Cluster MSAs, 2005 (in metric tons)

Metropolitan Area	Megaregion	Megapolitan Area	Auto Emissions	Percent Dispersion from Mean	Rank Among Top 100 Metros
Bakersfield, CA	Southwest	Southern California	1.303	29.8	86
San Diego–Carlsbad–San Marcos, CA	Southwest	Southern California	1.078	7.4	48
Oxnard–Thousand Oaks–Ventura, CA	Southwest	Southern California	1.116	11.2	54
Riverside–San Bernardino–Ontario, CA	Southwest	Southern California	1.289	28.4	83
Los Angeles–Long Beach–Santa Ana, CA	Southwest	Southern California	0.882	−12.2	17
Las Vegas–Paradise, NV	Southwest	Las Vegas	0.845	−15.8	12
Phoenix–Mesa–Scottsdale, AZ	Southwest	Sun Corridor	0.940	−6.4	22
Tucson, AZ	Southwest	Sun Corridor	0.924	−8.0	20
Mean transportation footprint for the 100 largest metropolitan areas			1.004		

Source: Adapted from Brown, Southworth, and Sarzynski (2008)

2007), so that, despite high densities, transit is difficult to support.

Whether this form of development can also be sustained over time is also questionable. For instance, with more than 7 million new residents projected for Southern California between 2010 and 2040, and with virtually no land left to urbanize, extensive infill and redevelopment will be needed. Indeed, at 0.57 acres of farmland lost per new resident, Southern California's growth could eliminate the agricultural economy by 2040. At its current pace, the Southern California megapolitan area could lose another 4 million acres of farmland, or nearly the size of New Jersey and virtually its entire supply existing in 2007 (see Chapter 9). The same fate could affect the Sun Corridor, where, at current trends (0.69 acres lost per new resident), nearly 2.5 million acres of farmland would be converted—nearly the land area of Connecticut, or more than half the Sun Corridor's farmland supply in 2007. Losses of this magnitude could well eliminate the critical mass of farmland needed to sustain the agricultural economy (see Nelson 1992; Daniels 2004). Although its rate of farmland lost per new resident is far lower in the Las Vegas megapolitan area, at 0.17 acres of farmland lost per new resident, it also has the smallest farmland base. At current trends, it could lose more than 300,000 acres of farmland, and that loss could also undermine the critical mass of farmland needed to sustain the agricultural economy.

Water supply will also be challenged. Although water consumption per capita in the Southern California megapolitan area is only about 10 percent higher than the national average, the region's growth—adding 7 million new residents between 2010 and 2040—simply cannot be accommodated, even with Draconian conservation. The region is exploring numerous options to develop new supplies. The Sun Corridor megapolitan area may actually have sufficient supply to meet development needs to mid-century, especially if it can reduce its per capita consumption by about one-third, to about the current national average. The Las Vegas megapolitan area, with the nation's highest domestic consumption per capita (a figure skewed by tens of millions of tourists visiting the area every year), is the most at risk of being unable to sustain growth. Explorations are already under way to transfer water from the Nevada-Utah Snake River Valley area and from Lake Powell in Utah, though these options may take decades and court challenges to perfect. Like the Mountain megapolitan cluster, the Southwest megapolitan cluster may be vulnerable to global climate change if it alters rainfall patterns and suppresses snowpacks.

Whether the individual megapolitan areas are up to the planning challenges is debatable. California's long, effective history of advance planning may bode well for its ability to address long-range planning challenges. We are not so optimistic about the ability of Arizona and Nevada to be similarly forward-looking, given their political cultures. For instance, in an area called "Superstition Vista" southeast of Phoenix, roughly between Phoenix and Tucson, the state of Arizona owns land many consider to be ideally suited to accommodate a million people, plus associated jobs. State law, however, prevents the state from planning for its use, so the private sector, substantially following its interests, is financing the planning.

On the other hand, light-rail construction with associated transit-oriented development master planning is under way in metropolitan Phoenix, with Las Vegas following into the 2010s.

Appendix 13.1. Counties in the Southwest Megapolitan Cluster			
County	Megapolitan Area	County	Megapolitan Area
Kern, CA	Southern California	Mohave, AZ	Las Vegas
Los Angeles, CA	Southern California	Clark, NV	Las Vegas
Orange, CA	Southern California	Nye, NV	Las Vegas
Riverside, CA	Southern California	Washington, UT	Las Vegas
San Bernardino, CA	Southern California	Maricopa, AZ	Sun Corridor
San Diego, CA	Southern California	Pima, AZ	Sun Corridor
Santa Barbara, CA	Southern California	Pinal, AZ	Sun Corridor
Ventura, CA	Southern California	Yavapai, AZ	Sun Corridor

14

MOUNTAIN MEGAPOLITAN CLUSTER

The Mountain megapolitan cluster is composed of two bands of metropolitan complexes, both extending along Rocky Mountain ranges (Figure 14.1). The Wasatch Range megapolitan area extends from the Logan, Utah, metropolitan area in the north to the Provo metropolitan area in the south, and includes development on both sides of the Wasatch Range. The Front Range megapolitan area extends from the Greeley-Loveland metropolitan area in northern Colorado south to the Colorado Springs metropolitan area. Appendix 14.1 lists the counties included in each metropolitan area. In this chapter, we profile the Mountain megapolitan cluster in terms of major demographic and housing trends, employment and development projections, the extent of economic dependency, and attractiveness characteristics. We conclude with our perceptions of major planning and development challenges.

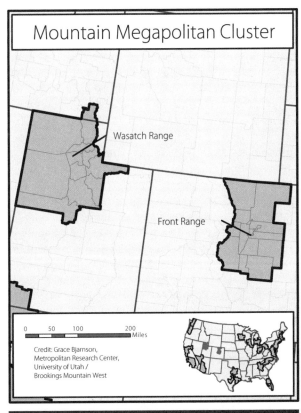

Figure 14.1. The Mountain megapolitan cluster, composed of the Wasatch Range and the Front Range megapolitan areas

Table 14.1. Mountain Megapolitan Cluster Rural-Megapolitan Continuum

Nelson-Lang Rural-Megapolitan Continuum Description	Counties	2010 Population (000s)
Counties in metropolitan areas of 1 million+ population	9	2,553
Counties in metropolitan areas of 250,000 to 1 million population	12	3,320
Counties in metropolitan areas of less than 250,000 population	3	389
Micropolitan area adjacent to a metropolitan area	2	73
Noncore counties adjacent to a metropolitan area	0	0
All other nonmetropolitan counties	0	0

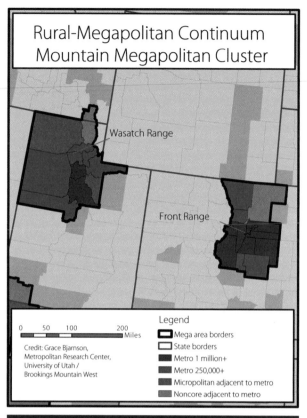

Rural-Megapolitan Continuum
Mountain Megapolitan Cluster

Wasatch Range

Front Range

0   50   100   200
Miles

Credit: Grace Bjarnson,
Metropolitan Research Center,
University of Utah /
Brookings Mountain West

Legend
☐ Mega area borders
☐ State borders
■ Metro 1 million+
■ Metro 250,000+
■ Micropolitan adjacent to metro
■ Noncore adjacent to metro

Figure 14.2. Nelson-Lang Rural-Megapolitan Continuum Codes applied to Mountain megapolitan cluster counties

Table 14.2. Mountain Megapolitan Cluster Land Area (in square miles)

Megapolitan Area	Total Land	Estimate of Privately Owned, Accessible Land
Wasatch Range	25,169	7,647
Front Range	18,379	7,546
Total	43,547	15,193

Major Demographic and Housing Trends

Essentially, all of the Mountain megapolitan cluster's population lives in metropolitan counties, with 95 percent living in metropolitan areas of more than 250,000 residents (Table 14.1 and Figure 14.2). In 2010, its nearly 6.6 million inhabitants occupied about 15,000 square miles of privately owned, reasonably accessible land (Table 14.2), at a density of about 760 people per square mile (Table 14.3). This is more than the population density of Great Britain. By 2040, the megapolitan cluster will grow to about 10 million people (Table 14.4), and its population density will approach that of the Netherlands.

Most of the growth in the Mountain megapolitan cluster during the period 2010–2040 will be attributable to minorities. In 2010, for example, minorities accounted for about 1.7 million of the 4.9 million people living in the cluster. Between then and 2040, the minority population will grow by about 2.5 million people, accounting for about 70 percent of the population change (Table 14.5), in contrast to the non-Hispanic white population, which will account for about 30 percent of the growth (Table 14.6). Hispanics will account for most of the change (Table 14.7), followed roughly equally by African Americans and Asians (Tables 14.8 and 14.9, respectively).

Compared to other megapolitan clusters (see, e.g., chapters on the Southwest, Great Lakes, Megalopolis, and Piedmont clusters), population change in the Mountain megapolitan cluster will not be dominated by growth in the population aged 65+. As shown in Table 14.10, seniors will account for only about square mile (Table 14.4). 14 percent of the change in population, making the Mountain megapolitan cluster the second most youthful of all megapolitan clusters (after the Texas Triangle).

Table 14.3. Mountain Megapolitan Cluster Density, 2010–2040

Megapolitan Area	Persons Per Square Mile, 2010	Comparable Developed Nation, 2010	Persons Per Square Mile, 2040	Comparable Developed Nation, 2040
Wasatch Range	535	>Italy	799	<Japan
Front Range	987	>Belgium	1,475	>The Netherlands
Mountain cluster total	759	>Great Britain	1,135	<The Netherlands

Note: The sign < means the megapolitan area density is about 50–200 fewer persons per square mile than in the comparable nation, while > means the density is about 50–200 more persons per square mile; no sign indicates the density is within about 50 persons per square mile. Figures compare developed nation population in 2010 to megapolitan cluster population in 2010 and 2040. All ranges are illustrative.

Table 14.4. Mountain Megapolitan Cluster Population, 2010–2040 (in thousands)

Megapolitan Area	Total Population, 2010	Total Population, 2025	Total Population, 2040	Total Change, 2010–2040	Percent Change, 2010–2040
Wasatch Range	2,479	3,212	3,962	1,484	59.9
Front Range	4,089	5,086	6,110	2,021	49.4
Mountain cluster	6,567	8,298	10,072	3,505	53.4

Source: Based on Woods & Poole Economics (2010)

Table 14.5. Mountain Megapolitan Cluster Minority Population, 2010–2040 (in thousands)

Megapolitan Area	Minority Population, 2010	Minority Population, 2025	Minority Population, 2040	Minority Population Change, 2010-2040	Minority Population Percent Change, 2010-2040	Minority Share of Population Change, 2010-2040
Wasatch Range	467	870	1,427	960	205.5	27.4
Front Range	1,210	1,884	2,715	1,505	124.5	43.0
Mountain cluster	1,677	2,754	4,142	2,465	147.0	70.3

Source: Based on Woods & Poole Economics (2010)

Table 14.6. Mountain Megapolitan Cluster White Non-Hispanic Population, 2010–2040 (in thousands)

Megapolitan Area	White Non-Hispanic Population, 2010	White Non-Hispanic Population, 2025	White Non-Hispanic Population, 2040	White Non-Hispanic Population Change, 2010–2040	White Non-Hispanic Population Percent Change, 2010–2040	White Non-Hispanic Share of Population Change, 2010–2040
Wasatch Range	2,011	2,343	2,535	524	26.0	14.9
Front Range	2,879	3,202	3,395	516	17.9	14.7
Mountain cluster	4,891	5,545	5,930	1,040	21.3	29.7

Source: Based on Woods & Poole Economics (2010)

Table 14.7. Mountain Megapolitan Cluster Hispanic Population, 2010–2040 (in thousands)

Megapolitan Area	Hispanic Population, 2010	Hispanic Population, 2025	Hispanic Population, 2040	Hispanic Population Change, 2010–2040	Hispanic Population Percent Change, 2010–2040	Hispanic Share of Population Change, 2010–2040
Wasatch Range	338	665	1,114	776	229.7	22.1
Front Range	843	1,385	2,058	1,215	144.2	34.7
Mountain cluster	1,181	2,050	3,172	1,991	168.6	56.8

Source: Based on Woods & Poole Economics (2010)

Table 14.8. Mountain Megapolitan Cluster African American Population, 2010–2040 (in thousands)

Megapolitan Area	African American Population, 2010	African American Population, 2025	African American Population, 2040	African American Population Change, 2010–2040	African American Population Percent Change, 2010–2040	African American Share of Population Change, 2010–2040
Wasatch Range	32	64	127	95	295.8	2.7
Front Range	196	246	305	108	55.3	3.1
Mountain cluster	228	310	431	203	89.1	5.8

Source: Based on Woods & Poole Economics (2010)

Table 14.9. Mountain Megapolitan Cluster Asian Population, 2010–2040 (in thousands)

Megapolitan Area	Asian Population, 2010	Asian Population, 2025	Asian Population, 2040	Asian Population Change, 2010–2040	Asian Population Percent Change, 2010–2040	Asian Share of Population Change, 2010–2040
Wasatch Range	80	121	169	89	111.5	2.5
Front Range	142	217	309	167	117.7	4.8
Mountain cluster	221	338	477	256	115.5	7.3

Source: Based on Woods & Poole Economics (2010)

Table 14.10. Mountain Megapolitan Cluster Population 65+, 2010–2040 (in thousands)

Megapolitan Area	Population 65+, 2010	Population 65+ as Share of Population, 2010	Population 65+, 2040	Population 65+ as Share of Population, 2040	Share of Population Change, 2010–2040
Wasatch Range	208	8.4	476	12.0	18.0
Front Range	404	9.9	950	15.5	27.0
Mountain cluster	613	9.3	1,426	14.2	23.2

Source: Based on Woods & Poole Economics Economics (2010)

Housing Development

The Mountain megapolitan cluster will add more than 1.3 million residential units to its inventory during the period 2010–2040 (Table 14.11). In addition, we estimate that about 320,000 housing units existing in 2010 will be rebuilt or replaced by 2040. In all, about 1.6 million residential units will be built or rebuilt between 2010 and 2040, equivalent to nearly two-thirds of all units existing in 2010.

Major Employment and Nonresidential Development Trends

The Mountain megapolitan cluster will enjoy impressive growth in jobs, both part- and full-time. Woods and Poole Economics data show the total number of jobs will grow from about 4.1 million in 2010 to about 6.4 million in 2040 (Table 14.12). Accounting for jobs in natural resources, construction, or other activities that do not require that workers occupy space, we estimate "land-use" jobs will increase by about 900,000 between 2010 and 2040 (Table 14.13).

The Mountain megapolitan cluster could support about 1.9 billion square feet of nonresidential space including industrial, commercial, and institutional uses, in 2010. By 2040, it will be able to support about 2.9 billion square feet of space, adding about 1.0 billion square feet over the period (Table 14.14). Counting space that will be replaced, sometimes twice, a total of 3.1 billion square feet is expected to be built. Growth-related and replaced space will be roughly equivalent to 1.6 times the nonresidential space existing in 2010.

Economic Dependency

According to the USDA, if more than 20 percent of a county's jobs or earnings were in one sector in 2010, it was deemed to be economically dependent on that sector. We apply the USDA's methodology to the Mountain megapolitan cluster, reporting economic dependency by megapolitan area in Table 14.15 and illustrate it by county in Figure 14.3. The population of counties classified as farming and manufacturing employment dependency

Table 14.11. Mountain Megapolitan Cluster Residential Development, 2010–2040 (in thousands)

Megapolitan Area	Units Supported, 2010	Increase in Inventory, 2010–2040	Units Recycled, 2010–2040	Total Units Constructed, 2010–2040	Percent of Units Supported, 2010
Wasatch Range	847	508	108	616	72.7
Front Range	1,662	811	211	1,022	61.5
Mountain cluster	2,510	1,319	319	1,638	65.3

Table 14.12. Mountain Megapolitan Cluster Total Employment, 2010–2040 (in thousands)

Megapolitan Area	Total Jobs, 2010	Total Jobs, 2040	Change, 2010–2040	Percent Change, 2010–2040
Wasatch Range	1,499	2,459	960	64.0
Front Range	2,582	3,906	1,324	51.3
Mountain cluster	4,081	6,365	2,284	56.0

Source: Based on Woods & Poole Economics (2010)

Table 14.13. Mountain Megapolitan Cluster Urban Land-Use Employment, 2010–2040 (in thousands)

Megapolitan Area	Total Land-Use Employment, 2010	Total Land-Use Employment, 2025	Total Land-Use Employment, 2040	Change in Land-Use Employment, 2010–2040	Percent Change in Land-Use Employment, 2010–2040
Wasatch Range	289	342	406	117	40.4
Front Range	406	453	506	101	24.8
Mountain cluster	695	795	912	217	31.3

Source: Based on Woods & Poole Economics (2010)

Table 14.14. Mountain Megapolitan Cluster Land-Use Employment Space Needs, 2010–2040 (millions of square feet)

Megapolitan Area	Total Land-Use Employment Space Supported, 2010	Total Land-Use Employment Space Supported, 2040	Increase in Land-Use Employment Space Inventory Supported, 2010–2040	Recycled Land-Use Employment Land-Use Space, 2010–2040	Total Land-Use Employment Space Constructed, 2010–2040	Land-Use Employment Space Constructed in 2010–2040 as Percent of Space in 2010
Wasatch Range	705	1,144	439	774	1,213	172.1
Front Range	1,192	1,794	601	1,309	1,910	160.2
Mountain cluster	1,897	2,938	1,040	2,082	3,123	164.6

Table 14.15. Mountain Megapolitan Cluster Economic Sector Dependence (in millions)

Megapolitan Area	Farming-Dependent Population, 2010	Mining-Dependent Population, 2010	Manufacturing-Dependent Population, 2010	Tourism and Entertainment–Dependent Population, 2010	Government-Dependent Population, 2010	Total Dependent Population, 2010	Total Population, 2010	Percent Dependent Population, 2010
Wasatch Range	13	0	170	0	370	614	2,479	24.8
Front Range	24	0	0	22	616	669	4,089	16.4
Mountain cluster	37	0	170	22	987	1,283	6,567	19.5

as a share of total jobs is very small, about 5 percent. Federal and state employment dependency affects the county population of about another 15 percent of the total megapolitan cluster population. However, the rate of economic-sector dependency is about half again as high in the Wasatch Range as in the Front Range. Because of its small rate of farming dependency and because federal and state government dependency is not in the kind of activities prone to large fluctuations (such as seen in areas dependent on defense contracting and military bases), we suspect that the Mountain megapolitan cluster is more resilient to national economic cycles than other megapolitan clusters. Indeed, its total level of population dependence is among the lowest.

Attractiveness to the Knowledge Class
The Mountain megapolitan cluster is the most attractive to the knowledge class, as summarized in Table 14.16 and illustrated in Figure 14.4. More than 80 percent of the megapolitan cluster's population lives in a knowledge class county—the highest rate in the nation. We also find that nearly all of the megapolitan cluster's population growth will occur in these counties. Figure 14.5 shows

the distribution of counties in the Mountain megapolitan cluster based on the quality of natural amenities.

Land, Water, and Air Resources
In this section we focus on the land, water, and air resource issues raised in Chapter 10. Farmland trends are shown in Table 14.17, including rate of change in farmland and change per 1,000 new residents, for the periods 1987–1997 and 1997–2007. While farmland is being lost in the Front Range megapolitan area at a pace less than the national average but still sizable, it is being lost in the Wasatch Range megapolitan area precipitously.

Indeed, well before mid-century, the farmland base in the Wasatch Range megapolitan area may be reduced by half, and will likely be gone by the end of the 21st century. However, this conversion may be a necessary trade-off. More so than any other megapolitan area, the Wasatch Range megapolitan area is constrained in accommodating growth. Mountain ranges, very large bodies of water, and federal and state land ownerships hem in development. Moreover, the farmland is of marginal quality.

Water consumption per capita is summarized in Table 14.18. Here we see that per capita consumption has been falling at considerably higher than the national rate. The Wasatch Range megapolitan area saw the largest reduction, more than 20 percent, in per capita consumption over the period 1990–2005, but it also had the highest level of consumption in 1990. Water consumption in the Front Range megapolitan area has fallen to nearly the national average.

Table 14.19 reports greenhouse gas production per capita from automobiles for the largest 100

metropolitan areas located in the Mountain megapolitan cluster. On a per capita basis, the Denver metropolitan area produces more greenhouse gases than either the national average or the other two large metropolitan areas in the Mountain megapolitan cluster. The Salt Lake City and Colorado Springs metropolitan areas produce less than the national average per capita, ranking 29th and 21st, respectively, among the 100 largest metropolitan areas.

Table 14.16. Mountain Megapolitan Cluster Knowledge Class Employment (in thousands)

Megapolitan Area	Knowledge Class Employment, 2010	Total Employment, 2010	Percent Knowledge Class Employment, 2010
Wasatch Range	1,961	2,479	79.1
Front Range	3,362	4,089	82.2
Mountain cluster	5,323	6,567	81.1

Source: Based on Woods & Poole Economics (2010)

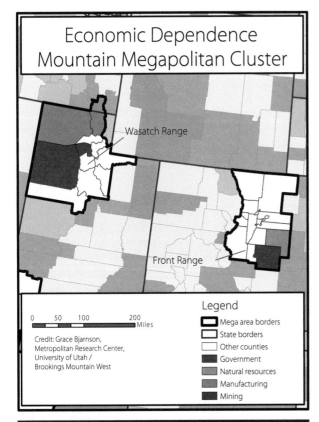

Figure 14.3. Mountain megapolitan cluster counties identified by the USDA as dependent on selected economic sectors

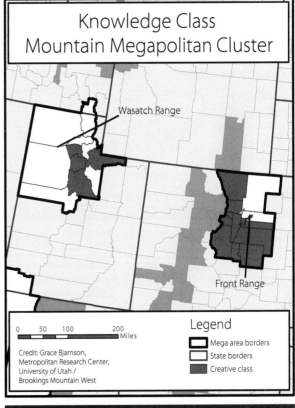

Figure 14.4. Distribution of knowledge class counties in the Mountain megapolitan cluster

Table 14.17. Change in Farmland and Farmland Per 1,000 New Residents, 1987–2007, Mountain Megapolitan Cluster (acres of land)

Megapolitan Area	Farmland, 1987	Farmland, 1997	Percent Farmland Change, 1987–1997	Farmland Change Per 1,000 New Residents, 1987–1997	Farmland, 2007	Percent Farmland Change, 1997–2007	Farmland Change Per 1,000 New Residents, 1997–2007
Wasatch Range	4,615,519	3,950,632	−14.4	(1,525)	3,700,516	−6.3	(481)
Front Range	6,587,405	6,263,429	−4.9	(391)	6,125,943	−2.2	(212)
Mountain cluster	11,202,924	10,214,061	−8.8	(782)	9,826,459	−3.8	(332)
National average				(425)			(342)

Source: Based on Woods & Poole Economics (2010)

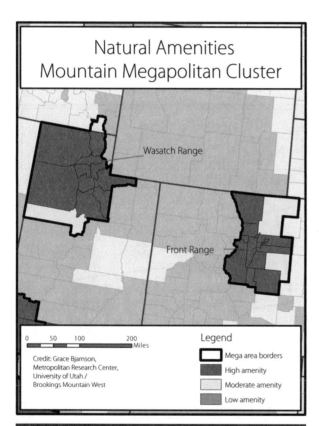

Natural Amenities
Mountain Megapolitan Cluster

Wasatch Range

Front Range

0   50   100   200
Miles

Credit: Grace Bjarnson,
Metropolitan Research Center,
University of Utah /
Brookings Mountain West

Legend

☐ Mega area borders

■ High amenity

☐ Moderate amenity

■ Low amenity

Figure 14.5. Distribution of counties based on natural amenities in the Mountain megapolitan cluster

Challenges

Development along both mountain ranges tends to be linear, enabling interesting corridor-based land-use planning and transportation options. This is especially the case with the Wasatch Range. We note that the actual population density of the Mountain megapolitan areas will be far higher than our estimates for the region as a whole because of extensive landscapes that are unlikely to be developed. For instance, the urbanized land population density of Salt Lake County was about 4,000 people per square mile in 2000, yet the county's population will double by 2040 on essentially the same land base. Already the nation's 15th most densely settled county, Salt Lake County will easily enter the top 10 within a generation. Utah County (Provo) will not be far behind. While development along the Front Range is not constrained eastward, water is difficult to access because of deep aquifers, so its counties are also much more densely settled than in other parts of the county.

Continued rapid growth combined with physical constraints make these megapolitan areas prime candidates for linear rail systems, which are already being constructed along the Wasatch Range. The major metropolitan areas of both megapolitan areas lead the nation in light rail construction, with plans for continued expansion through the next several decades. Transit-oriented development is capturing an ever increasing share of total development in both megapolitan areas as well.

The competition for land between farming and development is perhaps more intense in this megapolitan cluster than in any other. At 0.60 acres lost per new resident, the Wasatch Range ranks second only to the Sun Corridor in farmland reduction. At the current pace, the Wasatch Range will lose nearly one million acres of farmland by 2040, despite Utah's relatively high ranking on the

Table 14.18. Change in Per Capita Water Consumption, 1990–2005, Mountain Megapolitan Cluster (gallons per day)

Megapolitan Area	Water Consumed Per Capita, 1990	Water Consumed Per Capita, 2005	Percent Change in Water Consumed Per Capita, 1990–2005
Wasatch Range	300	237	−20.9
Front Range	206	183	−11.3
Mountain cluster	241	204	−15.6
National average	184	171	−6.8

Source: Based on Woods & Poole Economics (2010)

Table 14.19. Greenhouse Gas Emissions Per Capita, Mountain Megapolitan Cluster MSAs, 2005 (in metric tons)

Metropolitan Area	Megaregion	Megapolitan Area	Auto Emissions	Percent Dispersion from Mean	Rank Among Top 100 Metros
Salt Lake City, UT	Mountain	Wasatch Range	0.981	-2.3	29
Denver-Aurora, CO	Mountain	Front Range	1.116	11.2	55
Colorado Springs, CO	Mountain	Front Range	0.937	-6.7	21
Mean transportation footprint for the 100 largest metropolitan areas			1.004		

Source: Adapted from Brown, Southworth, and Sarzynski (2008)

Nelson-Lang Planning Index, at 9th place, largely because of mandated planning under state oversight. However, Utah's strong property rights orientation and inability to acquire open spaces through eminent domain likely facilitate this high loss rate. In contrast, while Colorado ranks 41st, its rate of farmland loss is far less; if current trends continue, it may lose about 300,000 acres of farmland between 2010 and 2040.

It is possible that continued demographic changes will reduce the pressure to convert farmland, but we do not see this as a strong deterrent because in many cases the only land reasonably available for urban development is nearby farmland. Still, with most growth attributable to minority populations who tend to earn less than whites, home ownership is likely to fall as the number and share of rental housing units increase. This will lead to higher demand for smaller units, more attached units, higher densities, and greater access to transit options in the future than in the past, which bodes well for planning efforts to preserve open spaces and advance urban infill and redevelopment.

Given the aridity of these lands, we are surprised by the volume of public water consumed for domestic purposes per capita. Indeed, the Mountain megapolitan cluster leads the nation. The reason is mostly lawn irrigation. If aggregate water consumption does not increase between now and 2040, there should be sufficient water to meet development needs.

Finally, the Mountain megapolitan cluster may be among the most susceptible to global climate change, if such change results in higher mean temperatures. The effect could be reduced snowpacks, which would affect the Wasatch Range especially, given its dependence on this source of water. Winter sports could also be affected adversely. This will be a new kind of planning challenge for this particular megapolitan cluster.

Appendix 14.1. Counties in the Mountain Megapolitan Cluster			
County, State	*Megapolitan Area*	*County, State*	*Megapolitan Area*
Franklin, ID	Wasatch Range	Boulder, CO	Front Range
Box Elder, UT	Wasatch Range	Broomfield, CO	Front Range
Cache, UT	Wasatch Range	Clear Creek, CO	Front Range
Davis, UT	Wasatch Range	Denver, CO	Front Range
Juab, UT	Wasatch Range	Douglas, CO	Front Range
Morgan, UT	Wasatch Range	Elbert, CO	Front Range
Salt Lake, UT	Wasatch Range	El Paso, CO	Front Range
Summit, UT	Wasatch Range	Gilpin, CO	Front Range
Tooele, UT	Wasatch Range	Jefferson, CO	Front Range
Utah, UT	Wasatch Range	Larimer, CO	Front Range
Wasatch, UT	Wasatch Range	Park, CO	Front Range
Weber, UT	Wasatch Range	Teller, CO	Front Range
Adams, CO	Front Range	Weld, CO	Front Range
Arapahoe, CO	Front Range		

15

TEXAS TRIANGLE MEGAPOLITAN CLUSTER

The Texas Triangle megapolitan cluster is comprised of three megapolitan areas: Dallas–Fort Worth; Central Texas, linking San Antonio and Austin; and Houston (Figure 15.1). Appendix 15.1 lists the counties included in each megapolitan area. We profile the Texas Triangle megapolitan cluster in the areas of major demographic and housing trends, employment and development projections, the extent of economic dependency, and attractiveness characteristics. We conclude with our perceptions of major planning and development challenges.

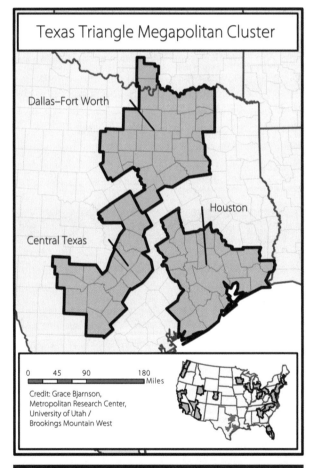

Texas Triangle Megapolitan Cluster

Dallas–Fort Worth

Houston

Central Texas

0   45   90   180
Miles

Credit: Grace Bjarnson,
Metropolitan Research Center,
University of Utah /
Brookings Mountain West

Figure 15.1. The Texas Triangle megapolitan cluster, composed of the Dallas–Fort Worth, Central Texas, and Houston megapolitan areas

Major Demographic and Housing Trends

At nearly 90 percent, the Texas Triangle megapolitan cluster has the nation's highest percentage of population living in counties of metropolitan areas of more than one million residents (Table 15.1 and Figure 15.2). Nearly all of its land area is privately owned and reasonably accessible to development (Table 15.2). Its 2010 population density of nearly 450 persons per square mile makes it about as densely settled as Switzerland. By 2040, the megapolitan cluster will have about 28 million residents (Table 15.3), and its density, at about 680 persons per square mile, will be about that of the United Kingdom in 2010 (Table 15.4).

Of the 9.7 million new residents added between 2010 and 2040 in the Texas Triangle megapolitan cluster, only about 1.4 million will be non-Hispanic whites (Table 15.5). About 85 percent of the population growth will be among minority populations (Table 15.6), dominated by Hispanics, who will double their number to about 12.1 million (Table 15.7). The Asian population will more than double (Table 15.8), but Asians will remain the third most populous ethnic minority. The African American population will grow by about a quarter (Table 15.9).

As Table 15.10 shows, the share of population change attributable to those aged 65+ will be only about 16 percent, the lowest among all the megapolitan clusters.

Housing Development

The Texas Triangle megapolitan cluster will add more than 4.3 million residential units to its inventory during the period 2010–2040 (Table 15.11). We also estimate that about 1.3 million units existing in 2010 will need to be rebuilt or replaced by 2040. In total, about 5.6 million residential units will be built or rebuilt between 2010

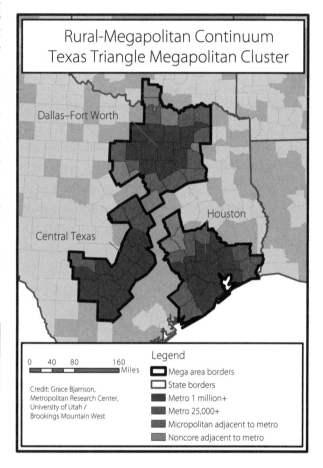

Rural-Megapolitan Continuum
Texas Triangle Megapolitan Cluster

Dallas–Fort Worth

Houston

Central Texas

0   40   80   160 Miles

Credit: Grace Bjarnson, Metropolitan Research Center, University of Utah / Brookings Mountain West

Legend
◻ Mega area borders
◻ State borders
■ Metro 1 million+
■ Metro 25,000+
■ Micropolitan adjacent to metro
■ Noncore adjacent to metro

Table 15.1. Texas Triangle Megapolitan Cluster Rural-Megapolitan Continuum

Nelson-Lang Rural-Megapolitan Continuum Description	Counties	2010 Population (000s)
Counties in metropolitan areas of 1 million+ population	35	16,288
Counties in metropolitan areas of 250,000 to 1 million population	6	771
Counties in metropolitan areas of less than 250,000 population	5	571
Micropolitan area adjacent to a metropolitan area	16	712
Noncore counties adjacent to a metropolitan area	2	86
All other nonmetropolitan counties	3	29

Table 15.2. Texas Triangle Megapolitan Cluster Land Area (in square miles)

Megapolitan Area	Total Land	Estimate of Privately Owned, Accessible Land
Dallas–Fort Worth	22,410	16,807
Central Texas	15,497	11,474
Houston	17,585	13,188
Total	55,492	41,471

and 2040, equivalent to more than 80 percent of all units existing in 2010.

Major Employment and Nonresidential Development Trends

The Texas Triangle will lead the nation in job growth, both part- and full-time. Woods and Poole Economics data show the total number of jobs will grow from about

10.9 million in 2010 to 17.1 million in 2040 (Table 15.12). Adjusting for jobs in natural resources, construction, or other activities that do not require that workers occupy space, we estimate "land-use" jobs will increase by about 6.2 million between 2010 and 2040 (Table 15.13).

In 2010, the Texas Triangle had sufficient employment to support about 5.4 billion square feet of nonresidential space, including industrial, commercial, and institutional

Table 15.3. Texas Triangle Megapolitan Cluster Population, 2010–2040 (in thousands)

Megapolitan Area	Total Population, 2010	Total Population, 2025	Total Population, 2040	Total Change, 2010–2040	Percent Change, 2010–2040
Dallas–Fort Worth	7,445	9,264	11,129	3,684	49.5
Central Texas	4,287	5,640	7,022	2,735	63.8
Houston	6,723	8,343	10,007	3,284	48.8
Texas Triangle cluster	18,456	23,247	28,158	9,702	52.6

Source: Based on Woods & Poole Economics (2010)

Table 15.4. Texas Triangle Megapolitan Cluster Density, 2010–2040

Megapolitan Area	Persons Per Square Mile, 2010	Comparable Developed Nation, 2010	Persons Per Square Mile, 2040	Comparable Developed Nation, 2040
Dallas–Fort Worth	443	<Switzerland	662	>Germany
Central Texas	374	>Denmark	612	Germany
Houston	510	Italy	759	<Japan
Texas Triangle cluster	445	Switzerland	679	United Kingdom

Note: The sign < means the megapolitan area density is about 50–200 fewer persons per square mile than in the comparable nation, while > means the density is about 50–200 more persons per square mile; no sign indicates the density is within about 50 persons per square mile. Figures compare developed nation population in 2010 to megapolitan cluster population in 2010 and 2040. All ranges are illustrative.

Table 15.5. Texas Triangle Megapolitan Cluster White Non-Hispanic Population, 2010–2040 (in thousands)

Megapolitan Area	White Non-Hispanic Population, 2010	White Non-Hispanic Population, 2025	White Non-Hispanic Population, 2040	White Non-Hispanic Population Change, 2010–2040	White Non-Hispanic Population Percent Change, 2010–2040	White Non-Hispanic Share of Population Change, 2010–2040
Dallas–Fort Worth	4,080	4,521	4,907	827	20.3	8.5
Central Texas	2,030	2,392	2,684	654	32.2	6.7
Houston	2,961	2,984	2,897	(64)	–2.2	–0.7
Texas Triangle cluster	9,071	9,897	10,488	1,417	15.6	14.6

Source: Based on Woods & Poole Economics (2010)

Table 15.6. Texas Triangle Megapolitan Cluster Minority Population, 2010–2040 (in thousands)

Megapolitan Area	Minority Population, 2010	Minority Population, 2025	Minority Population, 2040	Minority Population Change, 2010–2040	Minority Population Percent Change, 2010–2040	Minority Share of Population Change, 2010–2040
Dallas–Fort Worth	3,365	4,743	6,222	2,857	84.9	29.4
Central Texas	2,257	3,248	4,338	2,081	92.2	21.4
Houston	3,762	5,359	7,109	3,348	89.0	34.5
Texas Triangle cluster	9,385	13,350	17,670	8,286	88.3	85.4

Source: Based on Woods & Poole Economics (2010)

Table 15.7. Texas Triangle Megapolitan Hispanic Population, 2010–2040 (in thousands)

Megapolitan Area	Hispanic Population, 2010	Hispanic Population, 2025	Hispanic Population, 2040	Hispanic Population Change, 2010–2040	Hispanic Population Percent Change, 2010–2040	Hispanic Share of Population Change, 2010–2040
Dallas–Fort Worth	1,974	2,943	3,970	1,996	101.1	20.6
Central Texas	1,758	2,531	3,325	1,567	89.1	16.1
Houston	2,221	3,428	4,783	2,562	115.4	26.4
Texas Triangle cluster	5,954	8,902	12,079	6,125	102.9	63.1

Source: Based on Woods & Poole Economics (2010)

Table 15.8. Texas Triangle Megapolitan Cluster Asian Population, 2010–2040 (in thousands)

Megapolitan Area	Asian Population, 2010	Asian Population, 2025	Asian Population, 2040	Asian Population Change, 2010–2040	Asian Population Percent Change, 2010–2040	Asian Share of Population Change, 2010–2040
Dallas–Fort Worth	354	627	1,008	653	184.5	6.7
Central Texas	143	277	492	349	243.8	3.6
Houston	383	592	843	460	120.2	4.7
Texas Triangle cluster	880	1,496	2,343	1,463	166.2	15.1

Source: Based on Woods & Poole Economics (2010)

uses. By 2040, it will be able to support about 8.4 billion square feet of space, adding about 3.1 billion square feet over the period (Table 15.14). Counting space that will be replaced, a total of about 9.0 billion square feet is expected to be built. Growth-related and replaced space will be roughly equivalent to 1.7 times the nonresidential space existing in 2010.

Economic Dependency

Very little of the population in the Texas Triangle lives in counties that are classified as dependent on farming, mining, manufacturing, tourism, or federal and state government employment (Table 15.15 and Figure 15.3). Indeed, this megapolitan cluster is the least dependent on export-based economic sectors.

Table 15.9. Texas Triangle Megapolitan Cluster African American Population, 2010–2040 (in thousands)

Megapolitan Area	African American Population, 2010	African American Population, 2025	African American Population, 2040	African American Population Change, 2010–2040	African American Population Percent Change, 2010–2040	African American Share of Population Change, 2010–2040
Dallas–Fort Worth	990	1,118	1,187	198	20.0	2.0
Central Texas	337	420	503	166	49.4	1.7
Houston	1,136	1,313	1,452	317	27.9	3.3
Texas Triangle cluster	2,462	2,851	3,142	681	27.6	7.0

Source: Based on Woods & Poole Economics (2010)

Table 15.10. Texas Triangle Megapolitan Cluster Population 65+, 2010–2040 (in thousands)

Megapolitan Area/ Cluster	Population 65+, 2010	Population 65+ as Share of Population, 2010	Population 65+, 2040	Population 65+ as Share of Population, 2040	Share of Population Change, 2010–2040
Dallas–Fort Worth	710	9.5	1,805	16.2	29.7
Central Texas	419	9.8	1,161	16.5	27.1
Houston	612	9.1	1,610	16.1	30.4
Texas Triangle cluster	1,742	9.4	4,576	16.3	29.2

Source: Based on Woods & Poole Economics (2010)

Table 15.11. Texas Triangle Megapolitan Cluster Residential Development (in thousands)

Megapolitan Area	Units Supported, 2010	Increase in Inventory, 2010–2040	Units Recycled, 2010–2040	Total Units Constructed, 2010–2040	Percent of Units Supported, 2010
Dallas–Fort Worth	2,786	1,543	548	2,090	75.0
Central Texas	1,482	1,295	291	1,586	107.0
Houston	2,404	1,426	473	1,898	79.0
Texas Triangle cluster	6,673	4,263	1,312	5,575	83.5

Table 15.12. Texas Triangle Megapolitan Cluster Total Employment, 2010–2040 (in thousands)

Megapolitan Area	Total Jobs, 2010	Total Jobs, 2040	Change, 2010–2040	Percent Change, 2010–2040
Dallas–Fort Worth	4,484	6,735	2,250	50.2
Central Texas	2,472	4,192	1,720	69.6
Houston	3,942	6,207	2,265	57.5
Texas Triangle cluster	10,898	17,134	6,235	57.2

Source: Based on Woods & Poole Economics (2010)

Table 15.13. Texas Triangle Megapolitan Cluster Land-Use Employment, 2010–2040 (in thousands)

Megapolitan Area	Total Land-Use Employment, 2010	Total Land-Use Employment, 2025	Total Land-Use Employment, 2040	Change in Land-Use Employment, 2010–2040	Percent Change in Land-Use Employment, 2010–2040
Dallas–Fort Worth	4,369	5,380	6,613	2,244	51.4
Central Texas	2,422	3,163	4,136	1,714	70.8
Houston	3,792	4,776	6,033	2,241	59.1
Texas Triangle cluster	10,583	13,319	16,781	6,199	58.6

Source: Based on Woods & Poole Economics (2010)

Table 15.14. Texas Triangle Megapolitan Cluster Land-Use Employment Space Needs, 2010–2040 (millions of square feet)

Megapolitan Area	Total Land-Use Employment Space Supported, 2010	Total Land-Use Employment Space Supported, 2040	Increase in Land-Use Employment Space Inventory Supported, 2010–2040	Recycled Land-Use Employment Space, 2010–2040	Total Land-Use Employment Space Constructed, 2010–2040	Land-Use Employment Space Constructed in 2010–2040 as Percent of Space in 2010
Dallas–Fort Worth	2,233	3,331	1,098	2,451	3,549	158.9
Central Texas	1,217	2,073	856	1,336	2,192	180.1
Houston	1,912	3,027	1,114	2,099	3,213	168.0
Texas Triangle cluster	5,362	8,430	3,068	5,885	8,953	167.0

Table 15.15. Texas Triangle Megapolitan Cluster Economic Sector Dependence (in millions)

Megapolitan Area	Farming-Dependent Population, 2010	Mining-Dependent Population, 2010	Manufacturing-Dependent Population, 2010	Tourism and Entertainment–Dependent Population, 2010	Government-Dependent Population, 2010	Total Dependent Population, 2010	Total Population, 2010	Percent Dependent Population, 2010
Dallas–Fort Worth	104	0	238	65	9	352	7,445	4.7
Central Texas	42	0	0	0	367	409	4,287	9.5
Houston	59	0	179	0	571	809	6,723	12.0
Texas Triangle cluster	205	0	417	65	948	1,570	18,456	8.5

Attractiveness to the Knowledge Class

At about 72 percent (Table 15.16 and Figure 15.4), the Texas Triangle megapolitan cluster is about average in attractiveness to the knowledge class among all megapolitan clusters. But this representation is skewed. The figure is only 41 percent for the Texas Corridor megapolitan area (dominated by metropolitan San Antonio), whereas it is 83 percent for the Texas Gulf (dominated by the Houston metropolitan area). Figure 15.5 shows the Texas Triangle megapolitan cluster counties by their quality of natural amenities.

Table 15.16. Texas Triangle Megapolitan Cluster Knowledge Class Employment (in thousands)

Megapolitan Area	Knowledge Class Employment, 2010	Total Employment, 2010	Percent Knowledge Class Employment, 2010
Dallas–Fort Worth	5,827	7,445	78.3%
Central Texas	1,780	4,287	41.5%
Houston	5,593	6,723	83.2%
Texas Triangle cluster	13,200	18,456	71.5%

Source: Based on Woods & Poole Economics (2010)

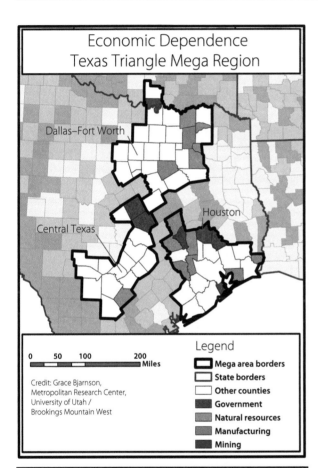

Figure 15.3. Texas Triangle megapolitan cluster counties identified by the USDA as dependent on selected economic sectors

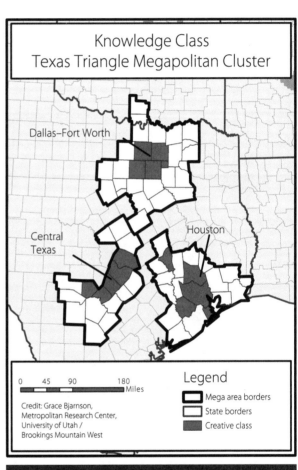

Figure 15.4. Distribution of knowledge class counties in the Texas Triangle megapolitan cluster

Land, Water, and Air Resources

Chapter 10 identified land, water, and air resources as key issues facing megapolitan clusters and areas. We explore them in more depth here for the Texas Triangle megapolitan cluster.

Total farmland, rate of change in farmland, and change per 1,000 new residents for the periods 1987–1997 and 1997–2007 are shown in Table 15.17. We find trends that are shared only by the Cascadia megapolitan cluster—in particular, the amount of farmland has

Table 15.17. Change in Farmland and Farmland Per 1,000 New Residents, 1987–2007, Texas Triangle Megapolitan Cluster (acres of land)

Megapolitan Area	Farmland, 1987	Farmland, 1997	Percent Farmland Change, 1987–1997	Farmland Change Per 1,000 New Residents, 1987–1997	Farmland, 2007	Percent Farmland Change, 1997–2007	Farmland Change Per 1,000 New Residents, 1997–2007
Dallas–Fort Worth	9,770,063	10,061,870	3.0	224	10,464,503	4.0	287
Central Texas	7,379,146	7,498,058	1.6	150	7,230,593	–3.6	(289)
Houston	6,595,180	6,565,430	-0.5	(29)	6,482,954	–1.3	(68)
Texas Triangle cluster	23,744,389	24,125,358	1.6	122	24,178,050	0.2	15
National average				(425)			(342)

Source: Based on Woods & Poole Economics (2010)

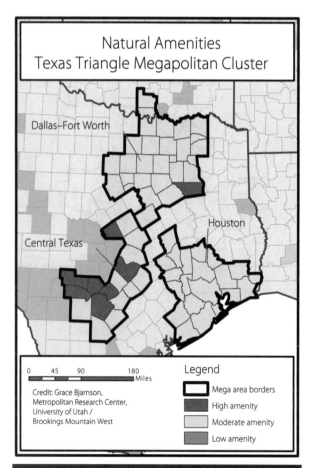

Figure 15.5. Distribution of counties based on natural amenities in the Texas Triangle megapolitan cluster

been increasing. While some of the individual megapolitan areas saw farmland losses, they were small. Most of the increase in farmland has occurred in the Dallas–Fort Worth megapolitan area. We surmise the reason for this trend is that much of the Texas countryside does not lend itself to septic systems, and groundwater access is problematic. Urban development is thus provided mostly by public systems, a factor that tends to rein in land-extensive suburban development patterns. Because less land is feasible for very low-density development, more of it is available for farming.

Oddly, water consumption in the Texas Triangle megapolitan cluster as a whole and in the Dallas–Fort Worth megapolitan area in particular increased over the period 1990–2005, though water consumption in the Central Texas megapolitan area fell at about the national rate (Table 15.18). Our review of precipitation records for 1990 and 2005 does not indicate anything that would suggest a climate-related reason for this difference. We surmise that water conservation is not an issue in this part of the country.

Greenhouse gas production per capita from automobiles for the largest 100 metropolitan areas located in the Texas Triangle megapolitan cluster is reported in Table 15.19. Except for the San Antonio metropolitan area, all metropolitan areas in this megapolitan cluster have somewhat higher (Houston at 2.6 percent) to moderately higher (Dallas–Fort Worth at 7.7 percent) than national average emissions per capita.

Table 15.18. Change in Per Capita Water Consumption, 1990–2005, Texas Triangle Megapolitan Cluster (gallons per day)

Megapolitan Area	Water Consumed Per Capita, 1990	Water Consumed Per Capita, 2005	Percent Change in Water Consumed Per Capita, 1990–2005
Dallas–Fort Worth	198	231	16.6
Central Texas	195	180	−7.3
Houston	166	159	−4.4
Texas Triangle cluster	185	193	4.1
National average	184	171	−6.8

Source: Based on Woods & Poole Economics (2010)

Table 15.19. Greenhouse Gas Emissions Per Capita, Texas Triangle Megapolitan Cluster MSAs, 2005 (in metric tons)

Metropolitan Area	Megaregion	Megapolitan Area	Auto Emissions	Percent Dispersion from Mean	Rank Among Top 100 Metros
Dallas–Fort Worth–Arlington, TX	Texas Triangle	Dallas–Fort Worth	1.081	7.7	49
San Antonio, TX	Texas Triangle	Texas Corridor	0.969	−3.5	27
Austin–Round Rock, TX	Texas Triangle	Texas Corridor	1.119	11.5	57
Houston–Sugar Land–Baytown, TX	Texas Triangle	Texas Gulf	1.030	2.6	41
Mean transportation footprint for the 100 largest metropolitan areas			1.004		17

Source: Adapted from Brown, Southworth, and Sarzynski (2008)

Challenges

The Texas Triangle megapolitan cluster has seen sustained growth for more than a century, with few downturns, the last major one occurring in the 1980s. The Texas state economy continues to diversify away from natural resources, including oil, into many other industries. Indeed, we find few major challenges facing sustained development in the Texas Triangle.

In terms of its land base, the Texas Triangle has been remarkable in witnessing virtually no reduction in farmland over the period 1997–2007, despite adding more than 3 million people. And its farmland base is considerable, exceeding 24 million acres. One reason is that urban development tends to be added incrementally adjacent to or relatively near existing urbanized areas. This pattern is due in large part to Texas's unique local improvement district laws, which facilitate the reasonably efficient formation and management of utility districts, but it also arises because in much of Texas, water is accessed either from small rivers or deep wells tapping aquifers. In addition, new suburban development tends to be of higher density than found elsewhere, especially in the Piedmont and Great Lakes megapolitan clusters.

Water does not appear to be a constraint, either. If domestic consumption is reduced to the national average, current water supplies would be sufficient to meet needs to 2040 and perhaps beyond.

An emerging area of challenge is meeting transportation needs. All three megapolitan areas face air quality issues that could affect future highway construction. In the 2000s, light-rail systems were initiated in the Greater Metroplex—the Dallas Area Rapid Transit (DART) and the Texas Gulf (Houston's METRO), and while DART continues to expand, METRO is on a decidedly slower pace. In the Texas Corridor, light-rail service is expected in Austin during the 2010s, but a system for San Antonio may not be operable until the 2020s.

Appendix 15.1. Counties in the Texas Triangle Megapolitan Cluster

County, State	Megapolitan Area	County, State	Megapolitan Area
Carter, OK	Dallas–Fort Worth	Caldwell, TX	Central Texas
Love, OK	Dallas–Fort Worth	Comal, TX	Central Texas
Collin, TX	Dallas–Fort Worth	Coryell, TX	Central Texas
Cooke, TX	Dallas–Fort Worth	Guadalupe, TX	Central Texas
Dallas, TX	Dallas–Fort Worth	Hays, TX	Central Texas
Delta, TX	Dallas–Fort Worth	Kendall, TX	Central Texas
Denton, TX	Dallas–Fort Worth	Kerr, TX	Central Texas
Ellis, TX	Dallas–Fort Worth	Lampasas, TX	Central Texas
Erath, TX	Dallas–Fort Worth	Medina, TX	Central Texas
Fannin, TX	Dallas–Fort Worth	Travis, TX	Central Texas
Grayson, TX	Dallas–Fort Worth	Williamson, TX	Central Texas
Henderson, TX	Dallas–Fort Worth	Wilson, TX	Central Texas
Hill, TX	Dallas–Fort Worth	Austin, TX	Houston
Hood, TX	Dallas–Fort Worth	Brazoria, TX	Houston
Hopkins, TX	Dallas–Fort Worth	Brazos, TX	Houston
Hunt, TX	Dallas–Fort Worth	Burleson, TX	Houston
Johnson, TX	Dallas–Fort Worth	Chambers, TX	Houston
Kaufman, TX	Dallas–Fort Worth	Fort Bend, TX	Houston
Lamar, TX	Dallas–Fort Worth	Galveston, TX	Houston
McLennan, TX	Dallas–Fort Worth	Grimes, TX	Houston
Navarro, TX	Dallas–Fort Worth	Hardin, TX	Houston
Palo Pinto, TX	Dallas–Fort Worth	Harris, TX	Houston
Parker, TX	Dallas–Fort Worth	Jefferson, TX	Houston
Rains, TX	Dallas–Fort Worth	Liberty, TX	Houston
Rockwall, TX	Dallas–Fort Worth	Matagorda, TX	Houston
Somervell, TX	Dallas–Fort Worth	Montgomery, TX	Houston
Tarrant, TX	Dallas–Fort Worth	Orange, TX	Houston
Van Zandt, TX	Dallas–Fort Worth	Robertson, TX	Houston
Wise, TX	Dallas–Fort Worth	San Jacinto, TX	Houston
Atascosa, TX	Central Texas	Walker, TX	Houston
Bandera, TX	Central Texas	Waller, TX	Houston
Bastrop, TX	Central Texas	Washington, TX	Houston
Bell, TX	Central Texas	Wharton, TX	Houston

16

TWIN CITIES MEGAPOLITAN AREA

The Twin Cities megapolitan area is comprised of the Minneapolis–St. Paul metropolitan area and extends to moderately sized metropolitan areas to the west, along the southern edge of Minnesota, and into Wisconsin (Figure 16.1). Appendix 16.1 lists the counties included in this megapolitan area. In this chapter we survey the Twin Cities megapolitan area in terms of major demographic and housing trends, employment and development projections, the extent of economic dependency, and attractiveness characteristics. We conclude with an assessment of major planning and development challenges.

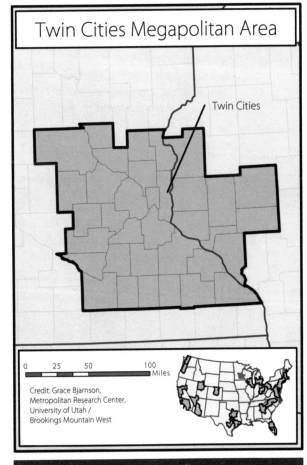

Figure 16.1. The Twin Cities megapolitan area

Major Demographic Trends

About three-quarters of the Twin Cities' residents live in counties in metropolitan areas of more than 1 million residents (Table 16.1). But this megapolitan area also has among the highest share of the population, one-quarter, living in small metropolitan, micropolitan, and rural counties. In 2010, its 4.4 million inhabitants occupied about 15,000 square miles of privately owned, reasonably accessible land (Table 16.2), at a density of about 300 people per square mile (Table 16.3)—the least densely settled of any megapolitan area and comparable to Portugal's population density. The Twin Cities megapolitan area is projected to have nearly 6 million people by 2040 (Table 16.4), gaining about 1.6 million people over the period. Its population density in 2040 will be comparable to that of Denmark's in 2010.

In the Twin Cities megapolitan area, growth in the population of non-Hispanic whites will account for the largest share of population change (Table 16.5), about 37 percent, compared to 63 percent for all minority populations combined (Table 16.6). And although the numbers of African Americans and Asians will double, and the number of Hispanics will triple, their share of population change will be about as evenly divided as in any megapolitan area (Tables 16.7, 16.8, and 16.9).

As seen in Table 16.10, the share of population age 65+ will increase from about 11 percent to about 19 percent—the third smallest shift among megapolitan areas, behind the Mountain and Texas Triangle megapolitan clusters.

Housing Development

Over the period 2010–2040, the Twin Cities megapolitan area will add about 0.8 million residential units to its inventory; it will also see the rebuilding or replacement of about 0.3 million units (Table 16.11). In all, about 1.1

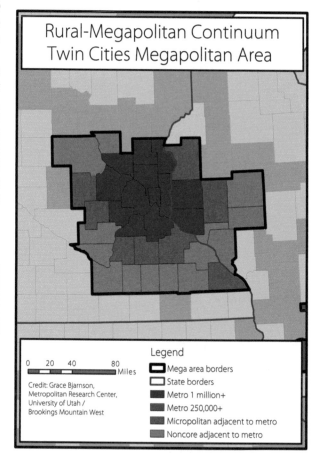

**Rural-Megapolitan Continuum
Twin Cities Megapolitan Area**

Legend

0   20   40   80 Miles

Credit: Grace Bjarnson,
Metropolitan Research Center,
University of Utah /
Brookings Mountain West

- Mega area borders
- State borders
- Metro 1 million+
- Metro 250,000+
- Micropolitan adjacent to metro
- Noncore adjacent to metro

Table 16.1. Twin Cities Megapolitan Area Rural-Megapolitan Continuum

Nelson-Lang Rural-Megapolitan Continuum Description	Counties	2010 Population (000s)
Counties in metropolitan areas of 1 million+ population	13	3,308
Counties in metropolitan areas of 250,000 to 1 million population	0	0
Counties in metropolitan areas of less than 250,000 population	7	544
Micropolitan area adjacent to a metropolitan area	8	338
Noncore counties adjacent to a metropolitan area	4	119
All other nonmetropolitan counties	3	36

Table 16.2. Twin Cities Megapolitan Area Land Area (in square miles)

Megapolitan Area	Total Land	Estimate of Privately Owned, Accessible Land
Twin Cities	19,847	14,885

Table 16.3. Twin Cities Megapolitan Area Density, 2010–2040

Megapolitan Area	Persons Per Square Mile, 2010	Comparable Developed Nation, 2010	Persons Per Square Mile, 2040	Comparable Developed Nation, 2040
Twin Cities	294	Portugal	402	>Denmark

Note: The sign < means the megapolitan area density is about 50–200 fewer persons per square mile than in the comparable nation, while > means the density is about 50–200 more persons per square mile; no sign indicates the density is within about 50 persons per square mile. Figures compare developed nation population in 2010 to megapolitan cluster population in 2010 and 2040. All ranges are illustrative.

Table 16.4. Twin Cities Megapolitan Area Population, 2010–2040 (in thousands)

Megapolitan Area	Total Population, 2010	Total Population, 2025	Total Population, 2040	Total Change, 2010–2040	Percent Change, 2010–2040
Twin Cities	4,377	5,166	5,982	1,605	36.7

Source: Based on Woods & Poole Economics (2010)

Table 16.5. Twin Cities Megapolitan Area White Non-Hispanic Population, 2010–2040 (in thousands)

Megapolitan Area	White Non-Hispanic Population, 2010	White Non-Hispanic Population, 2025	White Non-Hispanic Population, 2040	White Non-Hispanic Population Change, 2010–2040	White Non-Hispanic Population Percent Change, 2010–2040	White Non-Hispanic Share of Population Change, 2010–2040
Twin Cities	3,699	4,099	4,288	589	15.9	36.7

Source: Based on Woods & Poole Economics (2010)

Table 16.6. Twin Cities Megapolitan Area Minority Population, 2010–2040 (in thousands)

Megapolitan Area	Minority Population, 2010	Minority Population, 2025	Minority Population, 2040	Minority Population Change, 2010–2040	Minority Population Percent Change, 2010–2040	Minority Share of Population Change, 2010–2040
Twin Cities	678	1,067	1,694	1,016	149.8	63.3

Source: Based on Woods & Poole Economics (2010)

Table 16.7. Twin Cities Megapolitan Area Hispanic Population, 2010–2040 (in thousands)

Megapolitan Area	Hispanic Population, 2010	Hispanic Population, 2025	Hispanic Population, 2040	Hispanic Population Change, 2010–2040	Hispanic Population Percent Change, 2010–2040	Hispanic Share of Population Change, 2010–2040
Twin Cities	193	328	590	397	205.1	24.7

Source: Based on Woods & Poole Economics (2010)

Table 16.8. Twin Cities Megapolitan Area African American Population, 2010–2040 (in thousands)

Megapolitan Area	African American Population, 2010	African American Population, 2025	African American Population, 2040	African American Population Change, 2010–2040	African American Population Percent Change, 2010–2040	African American Share of Population Change, 2010–2040
Twin Cities	246	338	514	268	109.1	16.7

Source: Based on Woods & Poole Economics (2010)

Table 16.9. Twin Cities Megapolitan Area Asian Population, 2010–2040 (in thousands)

Megapolitan Area	Asian Population, 2010	Asian Population, 2025	Asian Population, 2040	Asian Population Change, 2010–2040	Asian Population Percent Change, 2010–2040	Asian Share of Population Change, 2010–2040
Twin Cities	208	369	561	354	170.3	22.0

Source: Based on Woods & Poole Economics (2010)

Table 16.10. Twin Cities Megapolitan Area Population 65+, 2010–2040 (in thousands)

Megapolitan Area	Population 65+, 2010	Population 65+ as Share of Population, 2010	Population 65+, 2040	Population 65+ as Share of Population, 2040	Share of Population Change, 2010–2040
Twin Cities	490	11.2	1,120	18.7	39.3

Source: Based on Woods & Poole Economics (2010)

Table 16.11. Twin Cities Megapolitan Area Residential Development, 2010–2040 (in thousands)

Megapolitan Area	Units Supported, 2010	Increase in Inventory, 2010–2040	Units Recycled, 2010–2040	Total Units Constructed, 2010–2040	Percent of Units Supported, 2010
Twin Cities	1,722	805	278	1,083	62.9

Table 16.12. Twin Cities Megapolitan Area Total Employment, 2010–2040 (in thousands)

Megapolitan Area	Total Jobs, 2010	Total Jobs, 2040	Change, 2010–2040	Percent Change, 2010–2040
Twin Cities	2,959	4,137	1,177	39.8

Source: Based on Woods & Poole Economics (2010)

million residential units will be built or rebuilt during this period, the equivalent of about two-thirds of all units existing in 2010.

Major Employment and Nonresidential Development Trends

The Twin Cities megapolitan area will see impressive job growth (both part- and full-time). Applying projections from Woods and Poole Economics data to the megapolitan cluster shows the total number of jobs will grow from about 3.0 million in 2010 to about 4.1 million in 2040 (Table 16.12). Some of those jobs will be in natural resources, construction, or other activities that do not require that workers occupy space. We estimate "land-use" jobs will increase by about 1.2 million between 2010 and 2040 (Table 16.13).

In 2010, the Twin Cities megapolitan area could support about 1.5 billion square feet of nonresidential space, including industrial, commercial, and institutional uses. By 2040, it will support about 2.1 billion square feet of space, adding about 0.6 billion square feet over the period (Table 16.14). Counting space that will be replaced, a total of about 2.3 billion square feet is expected to be built or rebuilt, about 1.5 times the nonresidential stock existing in 2010.

Economic Dependency

Table 16.15 shows and Figure 16.3 illustrates the extent of economic dependency in the Twin Cities megapolitan area. In all, about a quarter of the population lives in counties that are economically dependent, mostly on the manufacturing sector.

Attractiveness to the Knowledge Class

Figure 16.4 shows the knowledge class counties in the Twin Cities megapolitan area while Table 16.16 summarizes the population and share of population living in knowledge class counties for the megapolitan area. About 60 percent of the Twin Cities megapolitan area's population lives in a knowledge class county, which is also where about 90 percent of the megapolitan area's population growth will occur. Figure 16.5 shows the distribution of Twin Cities megapolitan area counties based on the quality of natural amenities.

Land, Water, and Air Resources

Here was expand on the land, water, and air resource issues raised in Chapter 10 as they relate to the Twin Cities megapolitan area.

Table 16.13. Twin Cities Megapolitan Area Land-Use Employment, 2010–2040 (in thousands)

Megapolitan Area	Total Land-Use Employment, 2010	Total Land-Use Employment, 2025	Total Land-Use Employment, 2040	Change in Land-Use Employment, 2010–2040	Percent Change in Land-Use Employment, 2010–2040
Twin Cities	2,902	3,448	4,076	1,173	40.4

Source: Based on Woods & Poole Economics (2010)

Table 16.14. Twin Cities Megapolitan Area Land-Use Employment Space Needs, 2010–2040 (millions of square feet)

Megapolitan Area	Total Land-Use Employment Space Supported, 2010	Total Land-Use Employment Space Supported, 2040	Increase in Land-Use Employment Space Inventory Supported, 2010–2040	Recycled Land-Use Employment Space, 2010–2040	Total Land-Use Employment Space Constructed, 2010-2040	Land-Use Employment Space Constructed in 2010–2040 as Percent of Space in 2010
Twin Cities	1,537	2,130	594	1,687	2,280	148.4

Table 16.15. Twin Cities Megapolitan Area Economic Sector Dependence (in millions)

Megapolitan Area	Farming-Dependent Population, 2010	Mining-Dependent Population, 2010	Manufacturing-Dependent Population, 2010	Tourism and Entertainment–Dependent Population, 2010	Government-Dependent Population, 2010	Total Dependent Population, 2010	Total Population, 2010	Percent Dependent Population, 2010
Twin Cities	36	0	913	0	41	990	4,377	22.6

Table 16.16. Twin Cities Megapolitan Area Knowledge Class Employment (in thousands)

Megapolitan Area	Knowledge Class Employment, 2010	Total Employment, 2010	Percent Knowledge Class Employment, 2010
Twin Cities	2,679	4,377	61.2

Source: Based on Woods & Poole Economics (2010)

Table 16.17 presents information on farmland, rate of change in farmland, and change per 1,000 new residents for the periods 1987–1997 and 1997–2007. We are astonished to find that for the past few decades, farmland has been lost in the Twin Cities megapolitan area at two to three times the national rate in terms of acres

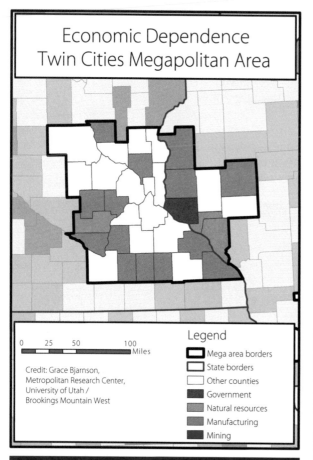

Figure 16.3. Twin Cities megapolitan area counties identified by the USDA as dependent on selected economic sectors

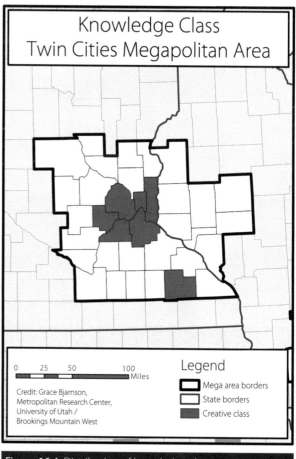

Figure 16.4. Distribution of knowledge class counties in the Twin Cities megapolitan area

Table 16.17. Change in Farmland and Farmland Per 1,000 New Residents, 1987–2007, Twin Cities Megapolitan Area (acres of land)

Megapolitan Area	Farmland, 1987	Farmland, 1997	Percent Farmland Change, 1987–1997	Farmland Change Per 1,000 New Residents, 1987–1997	Farmland, 2007	Percent Farmland Change, 1997–2007	Farmland Change Per 1,000 New Residents, 1997–2007
Twin Cities	8,849,698	8,359,938	−5.5	(939)	7,933,787	−5.1	(1,007)
National average				(425)			(342)

Source: Based on Woods & Poole Economics (2010)

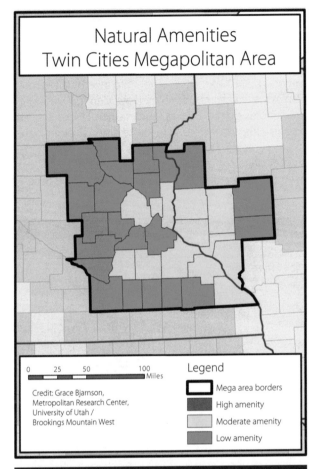

Natural Amenities
Twin Cities Megapolitan Area

Legend

☐ Mega area borders

■ High amenity

☐ Moderate amenity

■ Low amenity

0   25   50   100
Miles

Credit: Grace Bjarnson,
Metropolitan Research Center,
University of Utah /
Brookings Mountain West

Figure 16.5. Distribution of counties based on natural amenities in the Twin Cities megapolitan area

lost per 1,000 new residents. The moderating factor is that the megapolitan area is not growing very quickly. We know from our research and others' (see Ewing et al. 2003) that, despite a regional agency that has more control over regional planning for water, sewer, and transit systems than perhaps any other region in the nation, the Metro Council has no control over very low-density suburban fringe and exurban development beyond its jurisdictional boundaries.

Table 16.18 shows the change in water consumption per capita for the Twin Cities megapolitan area. Starting at slightly below the national average in 1990, water consumption per capita in this megapolitan area dropped by nearly 30 percent to become the second lowest in the nation, after the New York–Philadelphia megapolitan area.

Table 16.19 reports greenhouse gas production per capita from automobiles in the Twin Cities metropolitan area and ranks the area among the top 100 metropolitan areas nationally in terms of emissions from this source. At 50th, it ranks right in the middle.

Challenges

The Twin Cities megapolitan area appears to be growing substantially at the expense of the rural and micropolitan counties of the upper Midwest. Although it enjoys favorable airport and highway connections, its rail infrastructure is geared mostly to freight. We anticipate that the future of the Twin Cities megapolitan area will

Table 16.18. Change in Per Capita Water Consumption, 1990–2005, Twin Cities Megapolitan Area (gallons per day)

Megapolitan Area	Water Consumed Per Capita, 1990	Water Consumed Per Capita, 2005	Percent Change in Water Consumed Per Capita, 1990–2005
Twin Cities	177	126	−28.8
National average	184	171	−6.8

Source: Based on Woods & Poole Economics (2010)

Table 16.19. Greenhouse Gas Emissions Per Capita, Twin Cities Megapolitan Area MSA, 2005 (in metric tons)

Metropolitan Area	Megaregion	Megapolitan Area	Auto Emissions	Percent Dispersion from Mean	Rank Among Top 100 Metros
Minneapolis–St. Paul–Bloomington, MN–WI	Twin Cities	Twin Cities	1.090	8.6	50
Mean transportation footprint for the 100 largest metropolitan areas			1.004		

Source: Adapted from Brown, Southworth, and Sarzynski (2008)

depend on strengthening freight and passenger rail connections to Chicago, perhaps connecting through Madison, Wisconsin, along the way.

The Twin Cities area is also among the least densely settled megapolitan areas and will continue to remain such. This may not bode well for long-term economic development since efficient economic exchange requires higher densities than are seen in this area. On the other hand, the increasing value of farmland to meet global food and energy demands may dampen continued urban sprawl into productive farming regions.

The face of the Twin Cities is also going to change dramatically. Although non-Hispanic whites will continue to dominate the population, minority groups will account for about two-thirds of the megapolitan area's growth between 2010 and 2040. The shift in ethnicities may also signal shifts in housing markets. Generally, minority households do not earn as much as non-Hispanic white households, and they tend to rent housing at higher rates than whites do. The result may be a higher demand for smaller units, more attached units, higher densities, and access to transit options in the future than in the past.

Appendix 16.1. Counties in the Twin Cities Megapolitan Area

County	Megapolitan Area	County	Megapolitan Area
Anoka, MN	Twin Cities	Sherbourne, MN	Twin Cities
Benton, MN	Twin Cities	Sibly, MN	Twin Cities
Blue Earth, MN	Twin Cities	Stearns, MN	Twin Cities
Carver, MN	Twin Cities	Steele, MN	Twin Cities
Chisago, MN	Twin Cities	Wabasha, MN	Twin Cities
Dakota, MN	Twin Cities	Waseca, MN	Twin Cities
Dodge, MN	Twin Cities	Washington, MN	Twin Cities
Goodhue, MN	Twin Cities	Winona, MN	Twin Cities
Hennepin, MN	Twin Cities	Wright, MN	Twin Cities
Isanti, MN	Twin Cities	Buffalo, WI	Twin Cities
Le Sueur, MN	Twin Cities	Chippewa, WI	Twin Cities
McLeod, MN	Twin Cities	Dunn, WI	Twin Cities
Meeker, MN	Twin Cities	Eau Claire, WI	Twin Cities
Nicollet, MN	Twin Cities	Pepin, WI	Twin Cities
Olmstead, MN	Twin Cities	Pierce, WI	Twin Cities
Ramsey, MN	Twin Cities	Polk, WI	Twin Cities
Rice, MN	Twin Cities	St. Croix, WI	Twin Cities
Scott, MN	Twin Cities		

17

GREAT LAKES MEGAPOLITAN CLUSTER

The Great Lakes megapolitan cluster is composed of four megapolitan areas, the largest number of all megapolitan clusters. They include the megapolitan areas of the lakefront, which centers on Chicago, extending from Milwaukee, Wisconsin, south along Lake Michigan to beyond Gary, Indiana, and inland as far west as Madison, Wisconsin; the Michigan Corridor, which extends from Detroit and Toledo, Ohio, west across the middle of Michigan to Lake Michigan; the Ohio Valley, which is anchored by Cincinnati in the south, Columbus in the northeast, and Dayton in the north; and the Steel Corridor, which extends from Pittsburgh through Akron, Ohio, to Cleveland (Figure 17.1). Appendix 17.1 lists the counties included in each megapolitan area. In this chapter, we profile the Great Lakes megapolitan cluster in the areas of major demographic

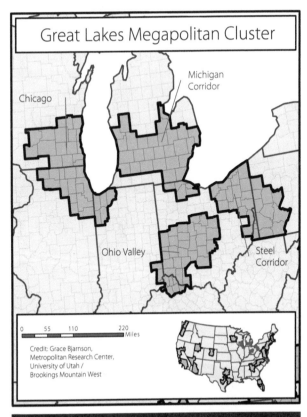

Figure 17.1. The Great Lakes megapolitan cluster, composed of the Chicago, Michigan Corridor, Ohio Valley, and Steel Corridor megapolitan areas

and housing trends, employment and development projections, the extent of economic dependency, and attractiveness characteristics. We conclude with our perceptions of major planning and development challenges.

Major Demographic and Housing Trends

About 70 percent of the residents in the Great Lakes megapolitan cluster live in a county of a metropolitan area of more than one million residents, and more than 95 percent live in a metropolitan area (Table 17.1 and Figure 17.2). Of the megapolitan cluster's nearly 70,000 square miles, about 52,000 square miles are privately owned and reasonably accessible to development (Table 17.2), making it the largest megapolitan cluster in terms of land area. Its 2010 population density of about 660 persons per square mile makes it about as densely settled as the United Kingdom. By 2040, the Great Lakes megapolitan cluster will have more than 40 million residents (Table 17. 3), and its population density, at about 770 persons per square mile, will make it just somewhat less densely settled than Japan in 2010 (Table 17.4).

However, there is considerable disparity in the pattern of growth. The Chicago megapolitan area, anchored by Chicago, will grow by about 2 million people, while the Michigan Corridor and Ohio Valley megapolitan areas will add about 1 million each. The Steel Corridor megapolitan area will barely grow, adding about 160,000 new residents (Table 17.3).

Over the period 2010–2040, the Great Lakes megapolitan cluster will add about 5.4 million people, but its non-Hispanic white population will fall (Table 17.5), while the minority population groups will increase by

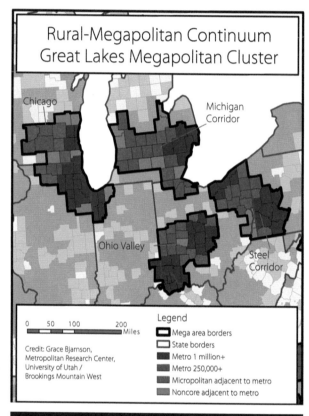

Figure 17.2. Nelson-Lang Rural-Megapolitan Continuum Codes applied to the Great Lakes megapolitan cluster counties

Table 17.1. Great Lakes Megapolitan Cluster Rural-Megapolitan Continuum

Nelson-Lang Rural-Megapolitan Continuum Description	Counties	2010 Population (000s)
Counties in metropolitan areas of 1 million+ population	59	24,148
Counties in metropolitan areas of 250,000 to 1 million population	31	6,451
Counties in metropolitan areas of less than 250,000 population	20	2,408
Micropolitan area adjacent to a metropolitan area	24	1,703
Noncore counties adjacent to a metropolitan area	0	0
All other nonmetropolitan counties	0	0

Table 17.2. Great Lakes Megapolitan Cluster Land Area (square miles)

Megapolitan Area	Total Land	Estimate of Privately Owned, Accessible Land
Chicago	20,320	15,240
Michigan Corridor	19,413	14,560
Ohio Valley	14,825	11,119
Steel Corridor	15,121	11,341
Total	69,679	52,259

Table 17.3. Great Lakes Megapolitan Cluster Population, 1970–2040 (in thousands)

Megapolitan Area	Total Population, 2010	Total Population, 2025	Total Population, 2040	Total Change, 2010–2040	Percent Change, 2010–2040
Chicago	13,452	14,990	16,607	3,155	23.5
Michigan Corridor	8,991	9,429	9,917	926	10.3
Ohio Valley	5,436	6,017	6,630	1,195	22.0
Steel Corridor	6,831	6,895	6,994	163	2.4
Great Lakes cluster	34,710	37,331	40,149	5,439	15.7

Source: Based on Woods & Poole Economics (2010)

Table 17.4. Great Lakes Megapolitan Cluster Density, 2010–2040

Megapolitan Area	Persons Per Square Mile, 2010	Comparable Developed Nation, 2010	Persons Per Square Mile, 2040	Comparable Developed Nation, 2040
Chicago	883	Belgium	1,090	<The Netherlands
Michigan Corridor	617	Germany	681	United Kingdom
Ohio Valley	489	Italy	596	Germany
Steel Corridor	602	Germany	617	Germany
Total	664	United Kingdom	768	<Japan

Note: The sign < means the megapolitan area density is about 50–200 fewer persons per square mile than in the comparable nation, while > means the density is about 50–200 more persons per square mile; no sign indicates the density is within about 50 persons per square mile. Figures compare developed nation population in 2010 to megapolitan cluster population in 2010 and 2040. All ranges are illustrative.

Table 17.5. Great Lakes Megapolitan Cluster White Non-Hispanic Population, 2010–2040 (in thousands)

Megapolitan Area	White Non-Hispanic Population, 2010	White Non-Hispanic Population, 2025	White Non-Hispanic Population, 2040	White Non-Hispanic Population Change, 2010–2040	White Non-Hispanic Population Percent Change, 2010–2040	White Non-Hispanic Share of Population Change, 2010–2040
Chicago	8,375	8,449	8,323	(52)	–0.6	–1.0
Michigan Corridor	6,765	6,695	6,513	(252)	–3.7	–4.6
Ohio Valley	4,466	4,644	4,642	176	3.9	3.2
Steel Corridor	5,719	5,512	5,281	(438)	–7.7	–8.0
Great Lakes cluster	25,325	25,300	24,759	(566)	–2.2	–10.4

Source: Based on Woods & Poole Economics (2010)

more than 60 percent (Table 17.6). The Hispanic population will gain the most, more than doubling its numbers and accounting for about two-thirds of the megapolitan cluster's population change (Table 17.7). The Asian population will also more than double (Table 17.8), while the African American population will increase by about a quarter (Table 17.9), becoming the second largest minority group, after Hispanics.

Table 17.6. Great Lakes Megapolitan Cluster Minority Population, 2010–2040 (in thousands)

Megapolitan Area	Minority Population, 2010	Minority Population, 2025	Minority Population, 2040	Minority Population Change, 2010–2040	Minority Population Percent Change, 2010–2040	Minority Share of Popula- tion Change, 2010–2040
Chicago	5,077	6,541	8,284	3,207	63.2	59.0
Michigan Corridor	2,226	2,734	3,404	1,178	52.9	21.7
Ohio Valley	969	1,373	1,988	1,019	105.1	18.7
Steel Corridor	1,112	1,383	1,713	601	54.0	11.0
Great Lakes cluster	9,385	12,031	15,389	6,005	64.0	110.4

Source: Based on Woods & Poole Economics (2010)

Table 17.7. Great Lakes Megapolitan Cluster Hispanic Population, 2010–2040 (in thousands)

Megapolitan Area	Hispanic Population, 2010	Hispanic Population, 2025	Hispanic Population, 2040	Hispanic Population Change, 2010–2040	Hispanic Population Percent Change, 2010–2040	Hispanic Share of Popula- tion Change, 2010–2040
Chicago	2,300	3,340	4,610	2,310	100.4	42.5
Michigan Corridor	433	655	941	508	117.2	9.3
Ohio Valley	133	296	602	469	352.1	8.6
Steel Corridor	166	292	436	270	163.0	5.0
Great Lakes cluster	3,033	4,583	6,590	3,557	117.3	65.4

Source: Based on Woods & Poole Economics (2010)

Table 17.8. Great Lakes Megapolitan Cluster Asian Population, 2010–2040 (in thousands)

Megapolitan Area	Asian Population, 2010	Asian Population, 2025	Asian Population, 2040	Asian Population Change, 2010–2040	Asian Population Percent Change, 2010–2040	Asian Share of Popula- tion Change, 2010–2040
Chicago	644	939	1,289	644	100.0	11.8
Michigan Corridor	264	441	703	439	166.5	8.1
Ohio Valley	126	219	359	233	184.1	4.3
Steel Corridor	109	170	252	143	131.3	2.6
Great Lakes cluster	1,143	1,769	2,602	1,459	127.6	26.8

Source: Based on Woods & Poole Economics (2010)

The Great Lakes megapolitan cluster is one of several whose share of population age 65+ will increase substantially, in this case from about 13 percent to more than 20 percent (Table 17.10). Indeed, those over 65 will account for about two-thirds of the megapolitan cluster's population change, the highest among megapolitan clusters.

Table 17.9. Great Lakes Megapolitan Cluster African American Population, 2010–2040 (in thousands)

Megapolitan Area	African American Population, 2010	African American Population, 2025	African American Population, 2040	African American Population Change, 2010–2040	African American Population Percent Change, 2010–2040	African American Share of Popula-tion Change, 2010–2040
Chicago	2,094	2,217	2,334	240	11.5	4.4
Michigan Corridor	1,487	1,592	1,713	225	15.2	4.1
Ohio Valley	694	841	1,009	315	45.4	5.8
Steel Corridor	823	905	1,008	185	22.5	3.4
Great Lakes cluster	5,098	5,555	6,064	966	18.9	17.8

Source: Based on Woods & Poole Economics (2010)

Table 17.10. Great Lakes Megapolitan Cluster Population 65+, 2010–2040 (in thousands)

Megapolitan Area	Population 65+, 2010	Population 65+ as Share of Population, 2010	Population 65+, 2040	Population 65+ as Share of Population, 2040	Share of Population Change, 2010–2040
Chicago	1,569	11.7	3,119	18.8	49.1
Michigan Corridor	1,137	12.6	2,101	21.2	104.1
Ohio Valley	665	12.2	1,179	17.8	43.0
Steel Corridor	1,089	15.9	1,792	25.6	430.6
Great Lakes cluster	4,460	12.8	8,192	20.4	68.6

Source: Based on Woods & Poole Economics (2010)

Table 17.11. Great Lakes Megapolitan Cluster Residential Development, 2010–2040 (in thousands)

Megapolitan Area	Units Supported, 2010	Increase in Inventory, 2010–2040	Units Recycled, 2010–2040	Total Units Constructed, 2010–2040	Percent of Units Supported, 2010
Chicago	5,054	1,395	816	2,211	43.7
Michigan Corridor	3,658	697	590	1,288	35.2
Ohio Valley	2,256	763	364	1,127	50.0
Steel Corridor	2,940	248	474	722	24.6
Great Lakes cluster	13,908	3,103	2,245	5,348	38.5

Source: Based on Woods & Poole Economics (2010)

Housing Development

The housing inventory of the Great Lakes megapolitan cluster will increase from about 13.49 million units in 2010 to about 17 million units in 2040, an increase of about 3.1 million homes (Table 17.11). We estimate that another 2.2 million units existing in 2010 will need to be rebuilt or replaced by 2040. Altogether, about 5.3 million residential units will need to be built or rebuilt between 2010 and 2040, equivalent to more than a third of all units existing in 2010.

Major Employment and Nonresidential Development Trends

Over the period 2010–2040, Woods & Poole Economics data indicate that the Great Lakes megapolitan cluster will add about 6.3 million part- and full-time jobs (Table 17.12). Adjusting for jobs in natural resources, construction, or other activities that do not require that workers occupy space, we estimate "land-use" jobs will increase by about 6.3 million between 2010 and 2040 (Table 17.13).

In 2010, there was sufficient employment in the Great Lakes megapolitan cluster to support about 10.4 billion square feet of nonresidential space, including industrial, commercial, and institutional uses. By 2040, it will be able to support about 13.5 billion square feet of space, adding about 3.1 billion square feet over the period 2010–2040 (Table 17.14). Counting space that will be replaced, a total of 11.4 billion square feet is expected to be built or rebuilt. Growth-related and replaced space will be roughly equivalent to 1.4 times the nonresidential space existing in 2010.

Table 17.12. Great Lakes Megapolitan Cluster Total Employment, 2010–2040 (in thousands)

Megapolitan Area	Total Jobs, 2010	Total Jobs, 2040	Change, 2010–2040	Percent Change, 2010–2040
Chicago	7,904	10,508	2,604	32.9
Michigan Corridor	4,720	6,087	1,367	29.0
Ohio Valley	3,282	4,471	1,189	36.2
Steel Corridor	4,016	5,141	1,124	28.0
Great Lakes cluster	19,923	26,207	6,284	31.5

Source Based on Woods & Poole Economics (2010)

Table 17.13. Great Lakes Megapolitan Cluster Land-Use Employment, 2010–2040 (in thousands)

Megapolitan Area	Total Land-Use Employment, 2010	Total Land-Use Employment, 2025	Total Land-Use Employment, 2040	Change in Land-Use Employment, 2010–2040	Percent Change in Land-Use Employment, 2010–2040
Chicago	7,844	9,072	10,443	2,599	33.1
Michigan Corridor	4,661	5,306	6,023	1,362	29.2
Ohio Valley	3,234	3,784	4,418	1,184	36.6
Steel Corridor	3,959	4,499	5,084	1,125	28.4
Great Lakes cluster	19,699	22,661	25,968	6,269	31.8

Source: Based on Woods & Poole Economics (2010)

Table 17.14. Great Lakes Megapolitan Cluster Land-Use Employment Space Needs, 2010–2040 (millions of square feet)

Megapolitan Area	Total Land-Use Employment Space Supported, 2010	Total Land-Use Employment Space Supported, 2040	Increase in Land-Use Employment Space Inventory Supported, 2010–2040	Recycled Land-Use Employment Space, 2010–2040	Total Land-Use Employment Space Constructed, 2010–2040	Land-Use Employment Space Constructed in 2010–2040 as Percent of Space in 2010
Chicago	4,134	5,405	1,271	4,537	5,808	140.5
Michigan Corridor	2,469	3,143	674	2,710	3,384	137.1
Ohio Valley	1,702	2,291	589	1,868	2,457	144.4
Steel Corridor	2,083	2,636	553	2,287	2,839	136.3
Great Lakes cluster	10,388	13,475	3,087	11,402	14,489	139.5

Economic Dependency

About a fifth of the population in the Great Lakes megapolitan cluster lives in counties that are classified as dependent on the manufacturing or federal and state government sectors, with a very small share dependent on mining and none dependent on farming (Table 17.15 and Figure 17.3). By far the greatest level of dependency is associated with manufacturing, which is to be expected, given the Great Lakes megapolitan cluster's long history as a global leader in manufacturing. However, total dependency, led by manufacturing dependency, is not as severe in the Chicago (18 percent), Ohio Valley (15 percent), or Steel Corridor (14 percent) megapolitan areas as it is in the Michigan Corridor (25 percent).

Attractiveness to the Knowledge Class

Figure 17.4 shows the knowledge class counties in the Great Lakes megapolitan cluster, while Table 17.16 summarizes the population and share of population living in knowledge class counties for the megapolitan cluster and its megapolitan areas. A bit more than half the population of the Great Lakes megapolitan cluster lives in a knowledge class county, but there are important variations among the megapolitan areas. Chicago, at 69 percent, is toward the high end of the attractiveness spectrum, while the Ohio Valley (65 percent) and Steel Corridor (52 percent) are in the middle and toward the lower end, respectively. Except for the Las Vegas megapolitan area, the Michigan Corridor at 35 percent has the lowest knowledge class score among megapolitan areas. Figure 17.5 shows the distribution of counties by quality of natural amenities in the Great Lakes megapolitan cluster.

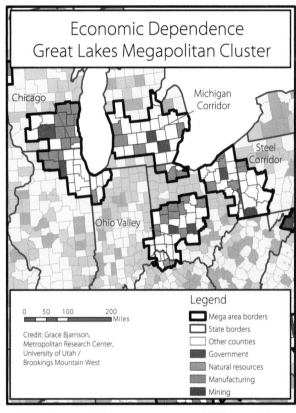

Figure 17.3. Great Lakes megapolitan cluster counties identified by the USDA as dependent on selected economic sectors

Table 17.15. Great Lakes Megapolitan Cluster Economic Sector Dependence (in millions)

Megapolitan Area	Farming-Dependent Population, 2010	Mining-Dependent Population, 2010	Manufacturing-Dependent Population, 2010	Tourism and Entertainment–Dependent Population, 2010	Government-Dependent Population, 2010	Total Dependent Population, 2010	Total Population, 2010	Percent Dependent Population, 2010
Chicago	0	0	1,783	62	608	2,452	13,452	18.2
Michigan Corridor	0	0	1,586	0	632	2,218	8,991	24.7
Ohio Valley	24	0	492	34	215	788	5,436	14.5
Steel Corridor	0	39	723	15	157	919	6,831	13.5
Great Lakes cluster	24	39	4,584	111	1,612	6,377	34,710	18.4

Table 17.16. Great Lakes Megapolitan Cluster Knowledge Class Employment (in thousands)

Megapolitan Area	Knowledge Class Employment, 2010	Total Employment, 2010	Percent Knowledge Class Employment, 2010
Chicago	9,257	13,452	68.8
Michigan Corridor	3,123	8,991	34.7
Ohio Valley	3,540	5,436	65.1
Steel Corridor	3,540	6,831	51.8
Great Lakes cluster	19,460	34,710	56.1

Source: Based on Woods & Poole Economics (2010)

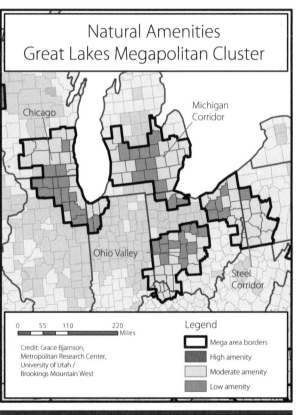

Figure 17.4. Distribution of knowledge class counties in the Great Lakes megapolitan cluster

Figure 17.5. Distribution of counties based on natural amenities in the Great Lakes megapolitan cluster

Land, Water, and Air Resources

We turn our focus now to issues related to land, water, and air resources raised initially in Chapter 10.

In Table 17.17, we report the farmland, rate of change in farmland, and change per 1,000 new residents for the periods 1987–1997 and 1997–2007. For the most part, there has been little change in the supply of farmland since 1997, in contrast to the previous decade, when the Great Lakes megapolitan cluster lost about 8 percent of its farmland base. The rise of ethanol combined with growing international markets for farm products produced in the megapolitan cluster may have stopped the trend.

Table 17.17. Change in Farmland and Farmland Per 1,000 New Residents, 1987–2007, Great Lakes Megapolitan Cluster (acres of land)

Megapolitan Area	Farmland, 1987	Farmland, 1997	Percent Farmland Change, 1987–1997	Farmland Change Per 1,000 New Residents, 1987–1997	Farmland, 2007	Percent Farmland Change, 1997–2007	Farmland Change Per 1,000 New Residents, 1997–2007
Chicago	8,513,314	7,756,100	−8.9	(637)	7,694,785	−0.8	(74)
Michigan Corridor	6,045,067	5,616,865	−7.1	(869)	5,609,762	−0.1	(76)
Ohio Valley	6,335,490	5,870,697	−7.3	(1,157)	5,782,347	−1.5	(246)
Steel Corridor	3,162,716	2,872,018	−9.2	(7,299)	3,019,416	5.1	na
Great Lakes cluster	24,056,587	22,115,680	−8.1	(914)	22,106,310	−0.0	(9)
National average				(425)			(342)

Source: Based on Woods & Poole Economics (2010)

Table 17.18 reviews changes in water consumption per capita for the Great Lakes megapolitan cluster between 1990 and 2005. The Chicago megapolitan area in particular saw its per capita water consumption drop by nearly a quarter, from more than the national average to substantially less. Nearly all other megapolitan areas also saw a reduction in per capita water consumption, though all the rest also started at below the national average. As a whole, the Great Lakes megapolitan cluster reduced water consumption at more than twice the rate of the nation.

Table 17.19 reports greenhouse gas production per capita from automobiles for the largest 100 metropolitan areas located in the Great Lakes megapolitan cluster. The range is considerable, from metropolitan areas with the 8th, 11th, and 19th lowest emissions per capita (respectively Chicago, Cleveland, and Pittsburgh) to a metropolitan area, Madison, with among the highest

emissions per capita, in 94th place (the case of Madison is interesting because it is a progressive university town that is also among the national leaders in bicycle use). While most of the population in these 100 largest metropolitan areas have fewer emissions per capita than the nation as a whole, most metropolitan areas per se have higher than the national average.

Challenges

In a very real sense, the Great Lakes megapolitan cluster is composed of three distinct kinds of megapolitan areas: one that is robust (Chicago), two that are stable (Ohio Valley and the Michigan Corridor), and one that is stagnant (the Steel Corridor).

The robust Chicago megapolitan area will add more than 3 million people and about 2.6 million full- and

Table 17.18. Change in Per Capita Water Consumption, 1990–2005, Great Lakes Megapolitan Cluster (gallons per day)

Megapolitan Area	Water Consumed Per Capita, 1990	Water Consumed Per Capita, 2005	Percent Change in Water Consumed Per Capita, 1990–2005
Chicago	193	145	−24.8
Michigan Corridor	181	158	−12.6
Ohio Valley	145	151	4.0
Steel Corridor	162	150	−7.9
Great Lakes cluster	176	150	−14.7
National average	184	171	-6.8

Source: Based on Woods & Poole Economics (2010)

part-time jobs requiring structures to work within. It will see 1.4 million new residential units constructed and a total of 2.2 million new and rebuilt units. It will add about 1.3 billion square feet to its nonresidential inventory but construct a total of 5.8 billion square feet, including rebuilt or replaced structures. Its economic base is diversified and, as a whole, one of the nation's most resilient. Indeed, the Chicago megapolitan area is poised to rank third among all megapolitan areas in terms of growth and development, after New York–Philadelphia and Southern California.

In addition, the Chicago metropolitan area has the nation's second largest network of public transit options (after New York City), including multiple rail options. New lines are being added and existing ones improved. About the only form of rail transportation it could be in need of would be high-speed rail (HSR) to connect it to the Twin Cities, Milwaukee, Indianapolis, and perhaps other destinations. HSR will become increasingly attractive as existing airports become more congested and unable to expand capacity.

The stable Ohio Valley and Michigan Corridor megapolitan areas will add about 1 million people each. Each area will see more than 1 million new and replaced homes built, and they will see about 1.9 billion square feet (Ohio Valley) and 2.7 billion square feet (Michigan Corridor) of new and replaced nonresidential space. Neither megapolitan area has rail transit serving any metropolitan areas, and it may be until the 2020s before envisioned systems are operating. Instead, existing and expanded highway systems will continue to depopulate urban areas. Suburban sprawl outside Detroit, Columbus, and Cincinnati, the largest metropolitan areas, has resulted in considerable excess construction of homes. For instance, while Ohio gained about 100,000 new residents between 2000 and 2008, about 300,000 new homes were built, well in excess of market demand. Michigan saw similar trends. The result is depressed housing values and an inventory not likely to be depleted until well into the 2010s.

Along with suburban sprawl, and despite slow growth rates, the Ohio Valley megapolitan area loses about 0.25 acres of farmland for each new resident. Over the period 2010–2040, a quarter million acres of farmland could be lost, although the base of farmland in 2007 was about 5.8 million.

The Steel Corridor is and will remain the nation's most stagnant in terms of growth. Between 1970 and 2010, it lost about 700,000 people, though it will add about 150,000 people between 2010 and 2040. Unfortunately, stagnant

Table 17.19. Greenhouse Gas Emissions Per Capita, Great Lakes Megapolitan Cluster MSAs, 2005 (in metric tons)

Metropolitan Area	Megaregion	Megapolitan Area	Auto Emissions	Percent Dispersion from Mean	Rank Among Top 100 Metros
Milwaukee–Waukesha–West Allis, WI	Great Lakes	Chicago	1.038	3.4	43
Madison, WI	Great Lakes	Chicago	1.353	34.8	94
Chicago–Naperville–Joliet, IL–IN–WI	Great Lakes	Chicago	0.820	–18.3	8
Grand Rapids–Wyoming, MI	Great Lakes	Michigan Corridor	1.197	19.2	69
Toledo, OH	Great Lakes	Michigan Corridor	1.190	18.5	68
Detroit–Warren–Livonia, MI	Great Lakes	Michigan Corridor	1.131	12.6	60
Lansing–East Lansing, MI	Great Lakes	Michigan Corridor	1.247	24.2	78
Dayton, OH	Great Lakes	Ohio Valley	0.898	–10.6	18
Columbus, OH	Great Lakes	Ohio Valley	1.176	17.1	67
Cincinnati–Middletown, OH–KY–IN	Great Lakes	Ohio Valley	1.140	13.5	61
Akron, OH	Great Lakes	Steel Corridor	1.023	1.9	39
Youngstown–Warren–Boardman, OH–PA	Great Lakes	Steel Corridor	1.015	1.1	38
Cleveland–Elyria–Mentor, OH	Great Lakes	Steel Corridor	0.842	–16.1	11
Pittsburgh, PA	Great Lakes	Steel Corridor	0.913	–9.1	19
Mean transportation footprint for the 100 largest metropolitan areas			1.004		

Source: Adapted from Brown, Southworth, and Sarzynski (2008)

growth can suppress recycling of existing structures. For instance, because of declining household size associated with a high share of aging population, this megapolitan area will need to build about 250,000 residential units to meet demand, and another 470,000 will need to be rebuilt or replaced. But under conditions of stagnant growth, where advantages of proximity to central locations are modest, it is possible that none of the units needing to be rebuilt or replaced would be, and instead all 700,000+ new and replaced units could go into suburban or exurban subdivisions. The same could happen as well with the nonresidential stock. While half a billion square feet of new space will be needed, about 2.3 billion existing square feet will need to be rebuilt or replaced—but much or all of that building could occur away from centers, further exacerbating efforts to facilitate economic development.

A major challenge, then, faces the Steel Corridor, as well as the Ohio Valley and the Michigan Corridor. If public policy, including planning, continues to allow development away from urban areas, though it may be less costly to the development community, agglomeration economies needed to sustain economic activity may be further eroded, thereby compromising opportunities for economic expansion.

Appendix 17.1. Counties in the Great Lakes Megapolitan Cluster

County, State	Megapolitan Area	County, State	Megapolitan Area
Boone, IL	Chicago	Ozaukee, WI	Chicago
Cook, IL	Chicago	Racine, WI	Chicago
DeKalb, IL	Chicago	Rock, WI	Chicago
DuPage, IL	Chicago	Sauk, WI	Chicago
Grundy, IL	Chicago	Sheboygan, WI	Chicago
Kane, IL	Chicago	Walworth, WI	Chicago
Kankakee, IL	Chicago	Washington, WI	Chicago
Kendall, IL	Chicago	Waukesha, WI	Chicago
Lake, IL	Chicago	Allegan, MI	Michigan Corridor
McHenry, IL	Chicago	Barry, MI	Michigan Corridor
Ogle, IL	Chicago	Bay, MI	Michigan Corridor
Stephenson, IL	Chicago	Calhoun, MI	Michigan Corridor
Will, IL	Chicago	Clinton, MI	Michigan Corridor
Winnebago, IL	Chicago	Eaton, MI	Michigan Corridor
Jasper, IN	Chicago	Genesee, MI	Michigan Corridor
Lake, IN	Chicago	Ingham, MI	Michigan Corridor
LaPorte, IN	Chicago	Ionia, MI	Michigan Corridor
Newton, IN	Chicago	Jackson, MI	Michigan Corridor
Porter, IN	Chicago	Kalamazoo, MI	Michigan Corridor
Columbia, WI	Chicago	Kent, MI	Michigan Corridor
Dane, WI	Chicago	Lapeer, MI	Michigan Corridor
Dodge, WI	Chicago	Lenawee, MI	Michigan Corridor
Fond du Lac, WI	Chicago	Livingston, MI	Michigan Corridor
Iowa, WI	Chicago	Macomb, MI	Michigan Corridor
Jefferson, WI	Chicago	Monroe, MI	Michigan Corridor
Kenosha, WI	Chicago	Muskegon, MI	Michigan Corridor
Milwaukee, WI	Chicago	Newaygo, MI	Michigan Corridor
Oakland, MI	Michigan Corridor	Marion, OH	Ohio Valley

(continued)

Appendix 17.1. Counties in the Great Lakes Megapolitan Cluster (*continued*)

County, State	Megapolitan Area	County, State	Megapolitan Area
Ottawa, MI	Michigan Corridor	Miami, OH	Ohio Valley
Saginaw, MI	Michigan Corridor	Montgomery, OH	Ohio Valley
St. Clair, MI	Michigan Corridor	Morrow, OH	Ohio Valley
Shiawassee, MI	Michigan Corridor	Pickaway, OH	Ohio Valley
Van Buren, MI	Michigan Corridor	Preble, OH	Ohio Valley
Washtenaw, Mi	Michigan Corridor	Ross, OH	Ohio Valley
Wayne, Mi	Michigan Corridor	Shelby, OH	Ohio Valley
Fulton, OH	Michigan Corridor	Union, OH	Ohio Valley
Lucas, OH	Michigan Corridor	Warren, OH	Ohio Valley
Ottawa, OH	Michigan Corridor	Ashtabula, OH	Steel Corridor
Sandusky, OH	Michigan Corridor	Belmont, OH	Steel Corridor
Wood, OH	Michigan Corridor	Carroll, OH	Steel Corridor
Dearborn, IN	Ohio Valley	Columbiana, OH	Steel Corridor
Franklin, IN	Ohio Valley	Cuyahoga, OH	Steel Corridor
Ohio, IN	Ohio Valley	Geauga, OH	Steel Corridor
Boone, KY	Ohio Valley	Jefferson, OH	Steel Corridor
Bracken, KY	Ohio Valley	Lake, OH	Steel Corridor
Campbell, KY	Ohio Valley	Lorain, OH	Steel Corridor
Gallatin, KY	Ohio Valley	Mahoning, OH	Steel Corridor
Grant, KY	Ohio Valley	Medina, OH	Steel Corridor
Kenton, KY	Ohio Valley	Portage, OH	Steel Corridor
Pendleton, KY	Ohio Valley	Stark, OH	Steel Corridor
Brown. OH	Ohio Valley	Summit, OH	Steel Corridor
Butler, OH	Ohio Valley	Trumbull, OH	Steel Corridor
Champaign, OH	Ohio Valley	Wayne, OH	Steel Corridor
Clark, OH	Ohio Valley	Allegheny, PA	Steel Corridor
Clermont, OH	Ohio Valley	Armstrong, PA	Steel Corridor
Clinton, OH	Ohio Valley	Beaver, PA	Steel Corridor
Darke, OH	Ohio Valley	Butler, PA	Steel Corridor
Delaware, OH	Ohio Valley	Fayette. PA	Steel Corridor
Fairfield, OH	Ohio Valley	Greene, PA	Steel Corridor
Fayette, OH	Ohio Valley	Lawrence, PA	Steel Corridor
Franklin, OH	Ohio Valley	Mercer, PA	Steel Corridor
Greene, OH	Ohio Valley	Washington, PA	Steel Corridor
Hamilton, OH	Ohio Valley	Westmoreland, PA	Steel Corridor
Knox, OH	Ohio Valley	Brooke, WV	Steel Corridor
Licking, OH	Ohio Valley	Hancock, WV	Steel Corridor
Logan, OH	Ohio Valley	Marshall, WV	Steel Corridor
Madison, OH	Ohio Valley	Ohio, WV	Steel Corridor

18

FLORIDA MEGAPOLITAN CLUSTER

There are two megapolitan areas in the Florida megapolitan cluster: the Florida Atlantic megapolitan area, extending from the Florida Keys north halfway up the Atlantic Coast to the Georgia border, and the Florida Corridor, extending across the middle of the state from Sarasota on the Gulf Coast through Orlando to Daytona Beach on the Atlantic Coast (Figure 18.1). Appendix 18.1 shows the counties included in each megapolitan area. In this chapter, we profile the Florida megapolitan cluster in the areas of major demographic and housing trends, employment and development projections, the extent of economic

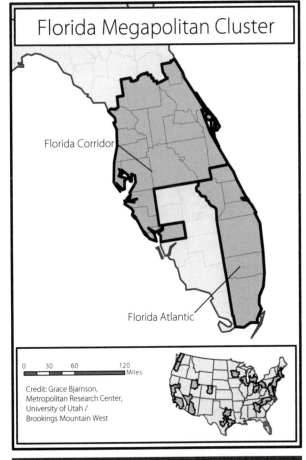

Figure 18.1. The Florida megapolitan cluster, composed of the Florida Corridor and Florida Atlantic megapolitan areas

dependency, and attractiveness characteristics. We conclude with our perceptions of major planning and development challenges.

Major Demographic and Housing Trends

More than 70 percent of the residents of the Florida megapolitan cluster live in a county with a metropolitan area of more than one million residents (Table 18.1 and Figure 18.2), and nearly all live in a metropolitan area. Of the megapolitan cluster's 22,000 square miles, about 15,700 square miles are privately owned and reasonably accessible to development (Table 18.2). Its 2010 population density of more than 900 persons per square mile makes it more densely settled than Japan or Belgium and the nation's second densest megapolitan cluster, just behind Megalopolis. By 2040, this megapolitan cluster will have about 21 million residents (Table 18.3), and its density, at about 1,350 persons per square mile, will make it more densely settled than South Korea was in 2010 (Table 18.4). Indeed, before 2025, the Florida megapolitan cluster will become the nation's most densely settled megapolitan cluster.

Between 2010 and 2040, more than 95 percent of the Florida megapolitan cluster's population change will be among minority populations (compare Tables 18.5 and 18.6). The Hispanic population will more than double, accounting for about 70 percent of the population change (Table 18.7). The African American population will increase by about half and remain the cluster's second largest minority group (Table 18.8), but the Asian population will be the fastest growing among all ethnic groups (Table 18.9).

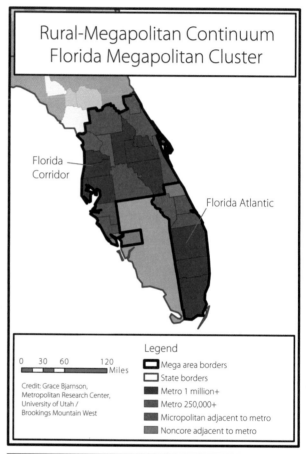

Figure 18.2. Nelson-Lang Rural-Megapolitan Continuum Codes applied to the Florida megapolitan cluster counties

Table 18.1. Florida Megapolitan Cluster Rural-Megapolitan Continuum

Nelson-Lang Rural-Megapolitan Continuum Description	Counties	2010 Population (000s)
Counties in metropolitan areas of 1 million+ population	11	10,513
Counties in metropolitan areas of 250,000 to 1 million population	8	3,132
Counties in metropolitan areas of less than 250,000 population	2	294
Micropolitan area adjacent to a metropolitan area	4	365
Noncore counties adjacent to a metropolitan area	0	0
All other nonmetropolitan counties	0	0

Table 18.2. Florida Megapolitan Cluster Land Area (square miles)

Megapolitan Area	Total Land	Estimate of Privately Owned, Accessible Land
Florida Atlantic	14,778	11,041
Florida Corridor	7,207	4,658
Total	21,985	15,699

Table 18.3. Florida Megapolitan Cluster Population, 2010–2040 (in thousands)

Megapolitan Area	Total Population, 2010	Total Population, 2025	Total Population, 2040	Total Change, 2010–2040	Percent Change, 2010–2040
Florida Corridor	8,130	10,078	12,081	3,952	48.6
Florida Atlantic	6,174	7,596	9,057	2,882	46.7
Florida cluster	14,304	17,673	21,138	6,834	47.8

Source: Based on Woods & Poole Economics (2010)

Table 18.4. Florida Megapolitan Cluster Population Density, 2010–2040

Megapolitan Area	Persons Per Square Mile, 2010	Comparable Developed Nation, 2010	Persons Per Square Mile, 2040	Comparable Developed Nation, 2040
Florida Corridor	1,326	South Korea	1,944	>Taiwan
Florida Atlantic	736	>United Kingdom	1,094	<The Netherlands
Total	911	Belgium	1,346	South Korea

Note: The sign < means the megapolitan area density is about 50–200 fewer persons per square mile than in the comparable nation, while > means the density is about 50–200 more persons per square mile; no sign indicates the density is within about 50 persons per square mile. Figures compare developed nation population in 2010 to megapolitan cluster population in 2010 and 2040. All ranges are illustrative.

Table 18.5. Florida Megapolitan Cluster White Non-Hispanic Population, 2010–2040 (in thousands)

Megapolitan Area	White Non-Hispanic Population, 2010	White Non-Hispanic Population, 2025	White Non-Hispanic Population, 2040	White Non-Hispanic Population Change, 2010–2040	White Non-Hispanic Population Percent Change, 2010–2040	White Non-Hispanic Share of Population Change, 2010–2040
Florida Corridor	5,617	5,948	5,982	365	6.5	5.3
Florida Atlantic	2,498	2,485	2,400	(98)	–3.9	–1.4
Florida cluster	8,115	8,433	8,382	267	3.3	3.9

Source: Based on Woods & Poole Economics (2010)

Table 18.6. Florida Megapolitan Cluster Minority Population, 2010–2040 (in thousands)

Megapolitan Area	Minority Population, 2010	Minority Population, 2025	Minority Population, 2040	Minority Population Change, 2010–2040	Minority Population Percent Change, 2010–2040	Minority Share of Population Change, 2010–2040
Florida Corridor	2,512	4,130	6,099	3,587	142.8	52.5
Florida Atlantic	3,677	5,110	6,657	2,980	81.0	43.6
Florida cluster	6,189	9,240	12,756	6,567	106.1	96.1

Source: Based on Woods & Poole Economics (2010)

Table 18.7. Florida Megapolitan Cluster Hispanic Population, 2010–2040 (in thousands)

Megapolitan Area	Hispanic Population, 2010	Hispanic Population, 2025	Hispanic Population, 2040	Hispanic Population Change, 2010–2040	Hispanic Population Percent Change, 2010–2040	Hispanic Share of Population Change, 2010–2040
Florida Corridor	1,316	2,490	4,037	2,722	206.9	39.8
Florida Atlantic	2,355	3,364	4,468	2,113	89.7	30.9
Florida cluster	3,671	5,854	8,506	4,835	131.7	70.8

Source: Based on Woods & Poole Economics (2010)

Table 18.8. Florida Megapolitan Cluster African American Population, 2010–2040 (in thousands)

Megapolitan Area	African American Population, 2010	African American Population, 2025	African American Population, 2040	African American Population Change, 2010–2040	African American Population Percent Change, 2010–2040	African American Share of Population Change, 2010–2040
Florida Corridor	948	1,221	1,446	498	52.5	7.3
Florida Atlantic	1,172	1,511	1,844	672	57.4	9.8
Florida cluster	2,120	2,732	3,290	1,170	55.2	17.1

Source: Based on Woods & Poole Economics (2010)

Table 18.9. Florida Megapolitan Cluster Asian Population, 2010–2040 (in thousands)

Megapolitan Area	Asian Population, 2010	Asian Population, 2025	Asian Population, 2040	Asian Population Change, 2010–2040	Asian Population Percent Change, 2010–2040	Asian Share of Population Change, 2010–2040
Florida Corridor	222	391	589	367	165.1	5.4
Florida Atlantic	137	220	328	191	139.5	2.8
Florida cluster	359	611	917	558	155.3	8.2

Source: Based on Woods & Poole Economics (2010)

The Florida megapolitan cluster has been viewed over the past several decades as a haven for retired people, and its share of population over 65 years will remain the highest of all megapolitan clusters (Table 18.10).

Housing Development

Between 2010 and 2040, the Florida megapolitan cluster will add more than 3.5 million residential units to its inventory (Table 18.11). We estimate that about 1.2 million units existing in 2010 will need to be rebuilt or replaced by 2040. In all, about 5.7 million residential units will be built or rebuilt between 2010 and 2040, equivalent to about three-quarters of all units existing in 2010.

Major Employment and Nonresidential Development Trends

Between 2010 and 2040, data from Woods and Poole Economics indicate that the Florida megapolitan cluster will add about 4.5 million part- and full-time jobs (Table 18.12). Allowing for jobs in natural resources, construction, or other activities that do not require that workers occupy space, we estimate "land-use" jobs will increase by about 4.5 million between 2010 and 2040 (Table 18.13).

The Florida megapolitan cluster had sufficient employment to support about 4.0 billion square feet of nonresidential space, including industrial, commercial,

Table 18.10. Florida Megapolitan Cluster Population 65+, 2010–2040 (in thousands)

Megapolitan Area	Population 65+, 2010	Population 65+ as Share of Population, 2010	Population 65+, 2040	Population 65+ as Share of Population, 2040	Share of Population Change, 2010–2040
Florida Corridor	1,513	18.6	3,039	25.2	38.6
Florida Atlantic	1,080	17.5	2,567	28.3	51.6
Florida cluster	2,593	18.1	5,607	31.7	44.1

Source: Based on Woods & Poole Economics (2010)

Table 18.11. Florida Megapolitan Cluster Residential Development, 2010–2040 (in thousands)

Megapolitan Area	Units Supported, 2010	Increase in Inventory, 2010–2040	Units Recycled, 2010–2040	Total Units Constructed, 2010–2040	Percent of Units Supported, 2010
Florida Corridor	3,690	2,207	725	2,932	79.5
Florida Atlantic	2,587	1,278	509	1,786	69.1
Florida cluster	6,277	3,485	1,234	4,719	75.2

Table 18.12. Florida Megapolitan Cluster Total Employment, 2010–2040 (in thousands)

Megapolitan Area	Total Jobs, 2010	Total Jobs, 2040	Change, 2010–2040	Percent Change, 2010–2040
Florida Corridor	4,414	7,009	2,595	58.8
Florida Atlantic	3,591	5,499	1,907	53.1
Florida cluster	8,005	12,508	4,503	56.2

Source: Based on Woods & Poole Economics (2010)

Table 18.13. Florida Megapolitan Cluster Land-Use Employment, 2010–2040 (in thousands)

Megapolitan Area	Total Land-Use Employment, 2010	Total Land-Use Employment, 2025	Total Land-Use Employment, 2040	Change in Land-Use Employment, 2010–2040	Percent Change in Land-Use Employment, 2010–2040
Florida Corridor	4,339	5,483	6,923	2,583	59.5
Florida Atlantic	3,544	4,409	5,443	1,900	53.6
Florida cluster	7,883	9,892	12,366	4,483	56.9

Source: Based on Woods & Poole Economics (2010)

and institutional uses, in 2010. By 2040, it will be able to support about 6.2 billion square feet of space, adding about 2.2 billion square feet over the period 2010–2040 (Table 18.14). Counting space that will be replaced, a total of 4.4 billion square feet is expected to be built. Growth-related and replaced space will be roughly equivalent to 1.7 times the nonresidential space existing in 2010.

Economic Dependency

Essentially none of the population in the Florida megapolitan cluster lives in counties that are classified as dependent on the farming, mining, manufacturing, or federal and state government sectors (Table 18.15 and Figure 18.3). About 20 percent of the population in the Florida Corridor megapolitan area lives in counties that are tourism dependent, however, second only to Las Vegas.

Table 18.14. Florida Megapolitan Cluster Land-Use Employment Space Needs, 2010–2040 (millions of square feet)

Megapolitan Area	Total Land-Use Employment Space Supported, 2010	Total Land-Use Employment Space Supported, 2040	Increase in Land-Use Employment Space Inventory Supported, 2010–2040	Recycled Land-Use Employment Space, 2010–2040	Total Land-Use Employment Space Constructed, 2010–2040	Land-Use Employment Space Constructed in 2010–2040 as Percent of Space in 2010
Florida Corridor	2,201	3,476	1,275	2,416	3,690	167.7
Florida Atlantic	1,798	2,748	950	1,974	2,924	162.6
Florida cluster	3,999	6,224	2,225	4,389	6,614	165.4

Table 18.15. Florida Megapolitan Cluster Economic Sector Dependence (in millions)

Megapolitan Area	Farming-Dependent Population, 2010	Mining-Dependent Population, 2010	Manufacturing-Dependent Population, 2010	Tourism and Entertainment–Dependent Population, 2010	Government-Dependent Population, 2010	Total Dependent Population, 2010	Total Population, 2010	Percent Dependent Population, 2010
Florida Corridor	0	0	0	1,225	97	1,489	8,130	18.3
Florida Atlantic	0	0	0	0	0	0	6,174	0.0
Florida cluster	0	0	0	1,225	97	1,489	14,304	10.4

Attractiveness to the Knowledge Class

Table 18.16 reports and Figure 18.4 illustrates the population and share of population living in knowledge class counties for the megapolitan cluster and its megapolitan areas. More than 70 percent of the Florida megapolitan cluster's population lives in a knowledge class county, but the difference between the megapolitan areas is striking. The figure is only 56 percent for the Florida Corridor megapolitan area (dominated by metropolitan Tampa and Orlando) but 93 percent for the Florida Atlantic (dominated by the Miami, Fort Lauderdale, and West Palm Beach metropolitan areas), the highest among all megapolitan areas. Figure 18.5 shows the distribution of Florida megapolitan cluster counties by the quality of natural amenities.

Land, Water, and Air Resources

Chapter 10 surveyed issues relating to land, water, and air resources. We expand on those issues here for the Florida megapolitan cluster.

Table 18.17 reviews the farmland, rate of change in farmland, and change per 1,000 new residents for the periods 1987–1997 and 1997–2007. We find interesting trends. During the first period, farmland losses were substantial, with the megapolitan areas losing more than 10 percent of their farmland base. Unlike in most other megapolitan areas, trends worsened during the period 1997–2007. We surmise that during the earlier period, the state's growth management laws were effective in at least reducing the rate of conversion. The later period, however, was marked by shifts in legislative and gubernatorial priorities that reduced the state's vigilance in preserving the farmland base (see Chapin et al. 2010). Based on recent trends, most of the state's existing farmland inventory will be gone by mid-century.

Table 18.18 shows changes in water consumption per capita for the Florida megapolitan cluster between 1990 and 2005. Basically, trends in reduced consumption paralleled the national average, though consumption per capita in both years was well below the national average.

Table 18.19 shows greenhouse gas production per capita from automobiles for the largest 100 metropolitan areas located in the Florida megapolitan cluster. All metropolitan areas have substantially higher emissions than the national average, while only the Miami metropolitan area has emissions that rank it below the national median (42nd). We note that Florida's metropolitan areas lag the nation in providing transit or in advancing modes of transportation other than vehicular.

Challenges

For the better part of a century, since the advent of air conditioning, the Florida megapolitan cluster has seen rapid growth. It has also been prone to peaks and troughs in its construction industry. It is almost as if Florida were

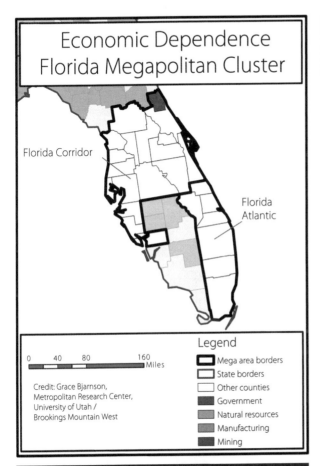

Figure 18.3. Florida megapolitan cluster counties identified by the USDA as dependent on selected economic sectors

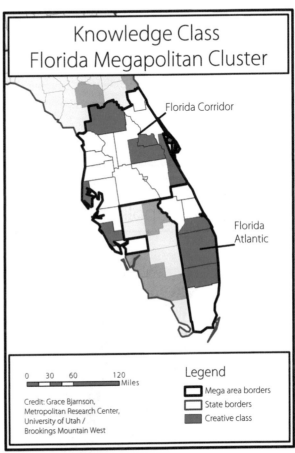

Figure 18.4. Distribution of knowledge class counties in the Florida megapolitan cluster

	Knowledge Class Employment Population, 2010	Total Employment, 2010	Percent Knowledge Class Employment, 2010
Megapolitan Area			
Florida Corridor	4,584	8,130	56.4
Florida Atlantic	5,716	6,174	92.6
Florida cluster	10,300	14,304	72.0

Table 18.16. Florida Megapolitan Cluster Knowledge Class Employment (in thousands)

Source: Based on Woods & Poole Economics (2010)

Table 18.17. Change in Farmland and Farmland Per 1,000 New Residents, 1987–2007, Florida Megapolitan Cluster (acres of land)

Megapolitan Area	Farmland, 1987	Farmland, 1997	Percent Farmland Change, 1987–1997	Farmland Change Per 1,000 New Residents, 1987–1997	Farmland, 2007	Percent Farmland Change, 1997–2007	Farmland Change Per 1,000 New Residents, 1997–2007
Florida Corridor	1,887,203	1,692,084	−10.3	(187)	1,379,875	−18.5	(460)
Florida Atlantic	4,216,552	3,755,137	−10.9	(377)	3,143,153	−16.3	(424)
Florida cluster	6,103,755	5,447,221	−10.8	(290)	4,523,028	−17.0	(436)
National average				(425)			(342)

Source: Based on Woods & Poole Economics (2010)

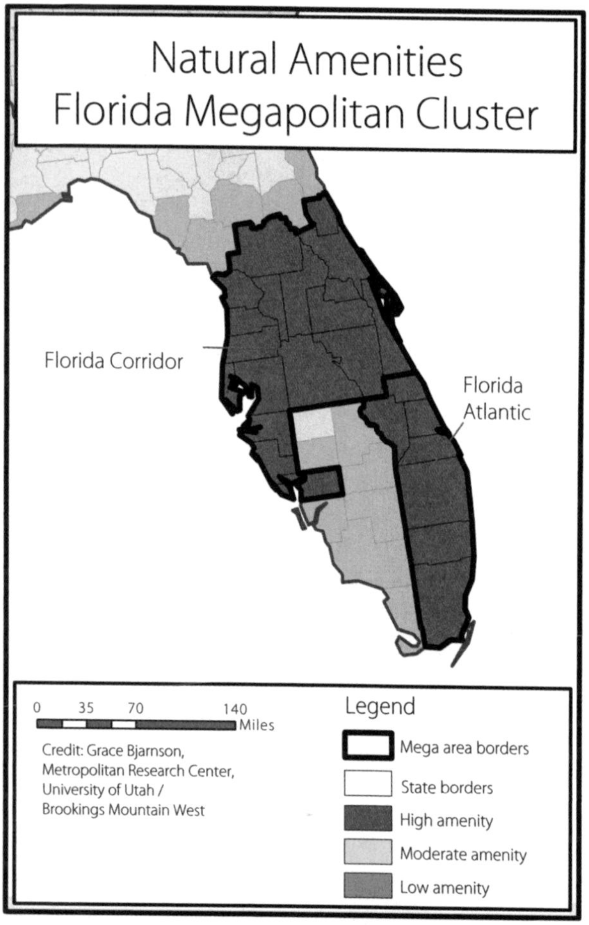

Figure 18.5. Distribution of counties based on natural amenities in the Florida megapolitan cluster

genetically programmed to never learn the overbuilding lessons of the past.

There are other factors working against Florida. The state's fiscal structure relies heavily on the sales tax and other taxes that have high incidences on tourists. As a consequence, when tourism is healthy, so are the state's finances, but when the national economy slacks, tourism is among the first casualties. Also, the state does not have an income tax, which makes it popular as a retirement location. Finally, local government's ability to adjust local taxes, especially property taxes, to meet growing needs seems to be constrained with each legislative session. The result is a growing reliance on fees for services and impact fees for infrastructure investment, and even these are seeing attempts at limitations.

At the same time, despite being the nation's most densely settled megapolitan cluster, with a population density expected to exceed the highest European population densities by 2025, the Florida megapolitan cluster is surprisingly underinvested in rail transportation options. This will change over time as the megapolitan areas become increasingly dense and congested with traffic. The Florida Atlantic megapolitan area is especially suitable for light-rail expansion because of its linear configuration, and it has a popular commuter-rail system. High-speed rail (HSR), which current state law mandates was to have been in place by 1995 connecting major metropolitan areas in both megapolitan areas, is not even in the design or right-of-way acquisition stage. Changing federal transportation priorities may lead to HSR service by the 2020s, however.

Florida has long been known as a major producer of agricultural products. At the current pace of farmland

Table 18.18. Change in Per Capita Water Consumption, 1990–2005, Florida Megapolitan Cluster (gallons per day)

Megapolitan Area	Water Consumed Per Capita, 1990	Water Consumed Per Capita, 2005	Percent Change in Water Consumed Per Capita, 1990–2005
Florida Corridor	157	143	–9.1
Florida Atlantic	183	170	–6.8
Florida cluster	166	155	–6.6
National average	184	171	–6.8

Source: Based on Woods & Poole Economics (2010)

Table 18.19. Greenhouse Gas Emissions Per Capita, Florida Megapolitan Cluster MSAs, 2005 (in metric tons)

Metropolitan Area	Megaregion	Megapolitan Area	Auto Emissions	Percent Dispersion from Mean	Rank Among Top 100 Metros
Orlando–Kissimmee, FL	Florida	Florida Corridor	1.277	27.2	81
Tampa–St. Petersburg–Clearwater, FL	Florida	Florida Corridor	1.212	20.7	71
Sarasota–Bradenton–Venice, FL	Florida	Florida Corridor	1.381	37.5	96
Palm Bay–Melbourne–Titusville, FL	Florida	Florida Corridor	1.295	29.0	85
Miami–Fort Lauderdale–Miami Beach, FL	Florida	Florida Atlantic	1.031	2.7	42
Mean transportation footprint for the 100 largest metropolitan areas			1.004		

Source: Adapted from Brown, Southworth, and Sarzynski (2008)

conversion, however, the Florida megapolitan cluster agricultural economy will be erased. At the current pace of conversion, with 0.40 acres lost per new resident, about 3 million of the 4.5 million acres of farmland existing in 2010 will be removed. It seems likely that the critical mass of farmland needed to sustain the megapolitan cluster's agricultural economy will disappear as well. This could further the state's dependence on tourism and retirement as principal sources of economic activity. The rate of farmland loss is especially surprising given state planning laws placing primacy on preserving farming and clearly separating urban and rural land uses. It is also surprising given it ranks 1st on the Nelson-Lang Planning Index based on the content of its planning laws, internal consistency, and state oversight. However, the level of state oversight has eroded since the late 1980s, the heyday of statewide planning, to the point where, at the beginning of the 2010s, the state

Department of Community Affairs was virtually powerless to challenge local land-use actions that would expand urban sprawl and lead to even more farmland losses.

There is one area where Florida has assumed planning leadership, and that is its acquisition of millions of acres of such open spaces as wetlands, floodplains, marshes, and other natural areas. Florida voters routinely approve extensions to its real estate transfer tax that help finance these acquisitions. By mid-century, the state may own a third of the state's land area.

Domestic water consumption in the Florida megapolitan cluster is about the national average, which may not be sustainable with 8 million more residents. On the other hand, modest increases in population density leading to fewer lawns to irrigate, as well as some conservation efforts, may be sufficient to ensure water capacity commensurate with growth.

Appendix 18.1. Counties in the Florida Megapolitan Cluster			
County, State	*Megapolitan Area*	*County, State*	*Megapolitan Area*
Brevard, FL	Florida Corridor	Polk, FL	Florida Corridor
Charlotte, FL	Florida Corridor	Sarasota, FL	Florida Corridor
Citrus, FL	Florida Corridor	Seminole, FL	Florida Corridor
Flagler, FL	Florida Corridor	Sumter, FL	Florida Corridor
Hernando, FL	Florida Corridor	Volusia, FL	Florida Corridor
Hillsborough, FL	Florida Corridor	Broward, FL	Florida Atlantic
Lake, FL	Florida Corridor	Indian River, FL	Florida Atlantic
Manatee, FL	Florida Corridor	Martin, FL	Florida Atlantic
Marion, FL	Florida Corridor	Miami–Dade, FL	Florida Atlantic
Orange, FL	Florida Corridor	Okeechobee, FL	Florida Atlantic
Osceola, FL	Florida Corridor	Palm Beach, FL	Florida Atlantic
Pasco, FL	Florida Corridor	St. Lucie, FL	Florida Atlantic
Pinellas, FL	Florida Corridor		

19

PIEDMONT MEGAPOLITAN CLUSTER

The Piedmont megapolitan cluster consists of the megapolitan areas of the Southern Piedmont and the Carolina Piedmont (Figure 19.1). The Southern Piedmont essentially extends about 100 miles around Atlanta, reaching into Alabama to the west and Tennessee and North Carolina to the north. The Carolina Piedmont extends among I-85 roughly 100 miles north and south from Charlotte. Appendix 19.1 notes the counties included in each. This chapter profiles the Piedmont megapolitan cluster in the areas of major demographic and housing trends, employment and development projections, the extent of economic dependency, and attractiveness

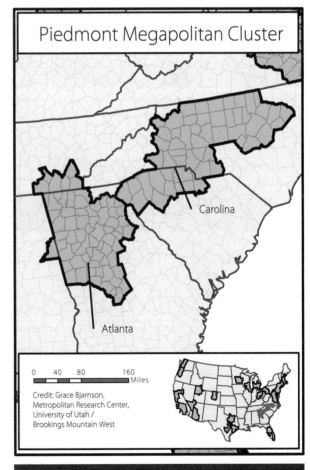

Figure 19.1. The Piedmont megapolitan cluster, composed of the Atlanta and Carolina megapolitan areas

characteristics. We conclude with our perceptions of major planning and development challenges.

Major Demographic and Housing Trends

About half the residents in the Piedmont megapolitan cluster live in a county with a metropolitan area of more than one million residents, and more than 85 percent live in a metropolitan area (Table 19.1 and Figure 19.2). Of the megapolitan cluster's nearly 49,000 square miles, we estimate that about 37,000 square miles are privately owned and reasonably accessible to development (Table 19.2). Its 2010 population density of about 390 persons per square mile makes it slightly more densely settled than Denmark. By 2040, the megapolitan cluster will have more than 21 million residents (Table 19.3) and its density, at nearly 570 persons per square mile, will make it about as densely settled as Germany in 2010 (Table 19.4).

Over the period 2010–2040, the non-Hispanic white population will account for about 20 percent of the Piedmont megapolitan cluster's growth (Table 19.5), while minorities will account for the remaining 80 percent (Table 19.6). The Hispanic and Asian populations will be the fastest-growing ethnic groups, tripling their numbers (Tables 19.7 and 19.8, respectively), while African Americans will remain the second largest ethnic group, though this population will grow about 40 percent (Table 19.9).

Growth of the Piedmont megapolitan cluster's population age 65+ will roughly parallel the national trend, increasing from about 11 percent of the population in 2010 to about 20 percent in 2040 (Table 19.10). This age group will account for only about 30 percent of the total change in population.

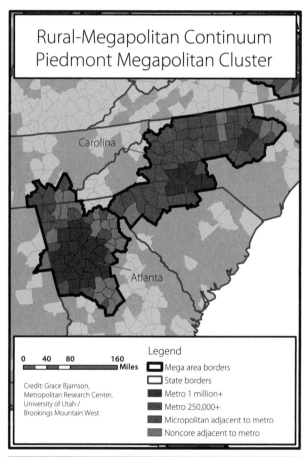

Figure 19.2. Nelson-Lang Rural-Megapolitan Continuum Codes applied to the Piedmont megapolitan cluster counties

Table 19.1. Piedmont Megapolitan Cluster Rural-Megapolitan Continuum

Nelson-Lang Rural-Megapolitan Continuum Description	Counties	2010 Population (000s)
Counties in metropolitan areas of 1 million+ population	34	7,328
Counties in metropolitan areas of 250,000 to 1 million population	28	4,647
Counties in metropolitan areas of less than 250,000 population	20	1,590
Micropolitan area adjacent to a metropolitan area	32	2,060
Noncore counties adjacent to a metropolitan area	1	26
All other nonmetropolitan counties	6	128

Table 19.2. Piedmont Megapolitan Cluster Land Area (square miles)

Megapolitan Area	Total Land	Estimate of Privately Owned, Accessible Land
Atlanta	21,755	16,317
Carolina	27,158	20,368
Total	48,913	36,685

Table 19.3. Piedmont Megapolitan Cluster Population, 2010–2040 (in thousands)

Megapolitan Area	Total Population, 2010	Total Population, 2025	Total Population, 2040	Total Change, 2010–2040	Percent Change, 2010–2040
Atlanta	7,807	9,621	11,486	3,679	47.1
Carolina	7,971	9,562	11,203	3,232	40.5
Piedmont cluster	15,778	19,183	22,689	6,911	43.8

Source: Based on Woods & Poole Economics (2010)

Table 19.4. Piedmont Megapolitan Cluster Population Density, 2010–2040

Megapolitan Area	Persons Per Square Mile, 2010	Comparable Developed Nation, 2010	Persons Per Square Mile, 2040	Comparable Developed Nation, 2040
Atlanta	498	Italy	740	>United Kingdom
Carolina	303	Denmark	445	Switzerland
Total	390	>Denmark	576	Germany

Note: The sign < means the megapolitan area density is about 50–200 fewer persons per square mile than in the comparable nation, while > means the density is about 50–200 more persons per square mile; no sign indicates the density is within about 50 persons per square mile. Figures compare developed nation population in 2010 to megapolitan cluster population in 2010 and 2040. All ranges are illustrative.

Table 19.5. Piedmont Megapolitan Cluster White Non-Hispanic Population, 2010–2040 (in thousands)

Megapolitan Area	White Non-Hispanic Population, 2010	White Non-Hispanic Population, 2025	White Non-Hispanic Population, 2040	White Non-Hispanic Population Change, 2010–2040	White Non-Hispanic Population Percent Change, 2010–2040	White Non-Hispanic Share of Population Change, 2010–2040
Atlanta	4,658	5,233	5,621	963	20.7	13.9
Carolina	5,464	5,915	5,887	424	7.8	6.1
Piedmont cluster	10,122	11,148	11,509	1,387	13.7	20.1

Source: Based on Woods & Poole Economics (2010)

Table 19.6. Piedmont Megapolitan Cluster Minority Population, 2010–2040 (in thousands)

Megapolitan Area	Minority Population, 2010	Minority Population, 2025	Minority Population, 2040	Minority Population Change, 2010–2040	Minority Population Percent Change, 2010–2040	Minority Share of Population Change, 2010–2040
Atlanta	3,149	4,388	5,865	2,716	86.2	39.3
Carolina	2,507	3,647	5,315	2,808	112.0	40.6
Piedmont cluster	5,657	8,035	11,180	5,524	97.7	79.9

Source: Based on Woods & Poole Economics (2010)

Table 19.7. Piedmont Megapolitan Cluster Hispanic Population, 2010–2040 (in thousands)

Megapolitan Area	Hispanic Population, 2010	Hispanic Population, 2025	Hispanic Population, 2040	Hispanic Population Change, 2010–2040	Hispanic Population Percent Change, 2010–2040	Hispanic Share of Population Change, 2010–2040
Atlanta	714	1,135	1,937	1,223	171.3	17.7
Carolina	627	1,171	2,291	1,664	265.4	24.1
Piedmont cluster	1,341	2,306	4,228	2,887	215.3	41.8

Source: Based on Woods & Poole Economics (2010)

Table 19.8. Piedmont Megapolitan Cluster Asian Population, 2010–2040 (in thousands)

Megapolitan Area	Asian Population, 2010	Asian Population, 2025	Asian Population, 2040	Asian Population Change, 2010–2040	Asian Population Percent Change, 2010–2040	Asian Share of Population Change, 2010–2040
Atlanta	293	588	968	675	230.0	9.8
Carolina	195	392	660	465	238.8	6.7
Piedmont cluster	488	980	1,628	1,140	233.5	16.5

Source: Based on Woods & Poole Economics (2010)

Table 19.9. Piedmont Megapolitan Cluster African American Population, 2010–2040 (in thousands)

Megapolitan Area	African American Population, 2010	African American Population, 2025	African American Population, 2040	African American Population Change, 2010–2040	African American Population Percent Change, 2010–2040	African American Share of Population Change, 2010–2040
Atlanta	2,119	2,639	2,931	812	38.3	11.7
Carolina	1,657	2,055	2,339	681	41.1	9.9
Piedmont cluster	3,777	4,694	5,270	1,493	39.5	21.6

Source: Based on Woods & Poole Economics (2010)

Table 19.10. Piedmont Megapolitan Cluster Population 65+, 2010–2040 (in thousands)

Megapolitan Area	Population 65+, 2010	Population 65+ as Share of Population, 2010	Population 65+, 2040	Population 65+ as Share of Population, 2040	Share of Population Change, 2010–2040
Atlanta	787	10.1	1,930	16.8	31.1
Carolina	960	12.0	1,917	17.1	29.6
Piedmont cluster	1,747	11.1	3,847	20.1	30.4

Source: Based on Woods & Poole Economics (2010)

Housing Development

From 2010 to 2040, the Piedmont megapolitan cluster will increase its housing inventory by about 3.2 million units (Table 19.11). We estimate that about 1.3 million units existing in 2010 will need to be rebuilt or replaced by 2040. All told, about 4.4 million residential units will need to be built or rebuilt between 2010 and 2040, equivalent to about two-thirds of all units existing in 2010.

Major Employment and Nonresidential Development Trends

Woods and Poole Economics data indicate that the Piedmont megapolitan cluster will add about 4.5 million part- and full-time jobs (Table 19.12). Reducing total jobs to account for jobs in natural resources, construction, or other activities that do not require that workers occupy space, we estimate "land-use" jobs will account for nearly all the increase in jobs between 2010 and 2040 (Table 19.13).

There was sufficient employment in the Piedmont megapolitan cluster to support about 4.6 billion square feet of nonresidential space, including industrial, commercial, and institutional uses, in 2010. By 2040, it will be able to support about 6.8 billion square feet of space,

adding about 2.2 billion square feet over the period 2010–2040 (Table 19.14). Counting space that will be replaced or rebuilt, a total of about 7.2 billion square feet is expected to be built. Growth-related and replaced space will be roughly equivalent to 1.6 times the nonresidential space existing in 2010.

Economic Dependency

About half the population in the Piedmont megapolitan cluster lives in counties that are classified as dependent on the manufacturing or federal and state government sectors, with a very small share dependent on farming (Table 19.15 and Figure 19.3). Federal and state government dependency is related to the large number of military bases throughout the megapolitan cluster, though the total population in counties dependent on this employment source is small. About two-thirds of the dependency is associated with manufacturing, which is attributable to

Table 19.11. Piedmont Megapolitan Cluster Residential Development (in thousands of units)

Megapolitan Area	Units Supported, 2010	Increase in Inventory, 2010–2040	Units Recycled, 2010–2040	Total Units Constructed, 2010–2040	Percent of Units Supported, 2010
Atlanta	3,010	1,575	592	2,167	72.0
Carolina	3,403	1,588	669	2,256	66.3
Piedmont cluster	6,412	3,163	1,260	4,424	69.0

Table 19.12. Piedmont Megapolitan Cluster Total Employment, 2010–2040 (in thousands)

Megapolitan Area	Total Jobs, 2010	Total Jobs, 2040	Change, 2010–2040	Percent Change, 2010–2040
Atlanta	4,357	6,596	2,239	51.4
Carolina	4,564	6,813	2,249	49.3
Piedmont cluster	8,922	13,409	4,488	50.3

Source: Based on Woods & Poole Economics (2010)

Table 19.13. Piedmont Megapolitan Cluster Land-Use Employment, 2010–2040 (in thousands)

Megapolitan Area	Total Land-Use Employment, 2010	Total Land-Use Employment, 2025	Total Land-Use Employment, 2040	Change in Land-Use Employment, 2010–2040	Percent Change in Land-Use Employment, 2010–2040
Atlanta	4,315	5,315	6,551	2,236	51.8
Carolina	4,502	5,488	6,748	2,246	49.9
Piedmont cluster	8,817	10,803	13,299	4,482	50.8

Source: Based on Woods & Poole Economics (2010)

Table 19.14. Piedmont Megapolitan Cluster Land-Use Employment Space Needs, 2010–2040 (millions of square feet)

Megapolitan Area	Total Land-Use Employment Space Supported, 2010	Total Land-Use Employment Space Supported, 2040	Increase in Land-Use Employment Space Inventory Supported, 2010–2040	Recycled Land-Use Employment Space, 2010–2040	Total Land-Use Employment Space Constructed, 2010–2040	Land-Use Employment Space Constructed in 2010–2040 as Percent of Space in 2010
Atlanta	2,219	3,328	1,109	2,436	3,545	159.7
Carolina	2,330	3,438	1,107	2,557	3,665	157.3
Piedmont cluster	4,550	6,766	2,216	4,993	7,209	158.5

Source: Based on Woods & Poole Economics (2010)

Table 19.15. Piedmont Megapolitan Cluster Economic Sector Dependence (in millions)

Megapolitan Area	Farming-Dependent Population, 2010	Mining-Dependent Population, 2010	Manufacturing-Dependent Population, 2010	Tourism and Entertainment–Dependent Population, 2010	Government-Dependent Population, 2010	Total Dependent Population, 2010	Total Population, 2010	Percent Dependent Population, 2010
Atlanta	14	0	1,273	0	566	1,735	7,807	22.2
Carolina	0	0	1,474	39	386	1,821	7,971	22.8
Piedmont cluster	14	0	2,747	39	952	3,556	15,778	22.5

Table 19.16. Piedmont Megapolitan Cluster Knowledge Class Employment (in thousands)

Megapolitan Area	Knowledge Population, 2010	Total Population, 2010	Percent Knowledge Population, 2010
Atlanta	4,016	7,807	51.4
Carolina	3,553	7,971	44.6
Piedmont cluster	7,569	15,778	48.0

Source: Based on Woods & Poole Economics (2010)

the large number of automobile assembly facilities located along the I-85 corridor between Atlanta and Charlotte and the growing automobile assembly operations in Alabama. For the most part, aside from the recession of 2007–2009, the manufacturing sector in the Piedmont megapolitan cluster is reasonably stable. The principal reason is its location, which is about the most efficient to serve the two-thirds of the nation's population that lives within a long day's truck drive or train to markets from the Texas Triangle to the Great Lakes to the Megalopolis and the Florida megapolitan clusters.

Attractiveness to the Knowledge Class

Figure 19.4 illustrates where the knowledge class counties are in the Piedmont megapolitan cluster while Table 19.16 summarizes the population and share of population living in knowledge class counties for the megapolitan cluster and its megapolitan areas. Less than half the population of the Piedmont megapolitan cluster lives in a knowledge class county, and there is little difference between the Atlanta (51 percent) and the Carolina (45 percent) megapolitan areas. The distribution of counties by quality of natural amenities is shown in Figure 19.5.

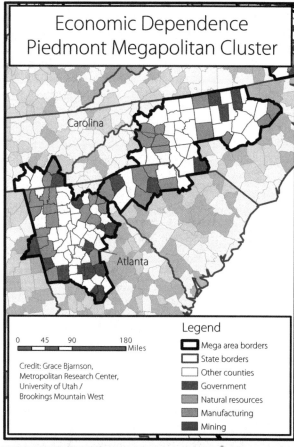

Economic Dependence
Piedmont Megapolitan Cluster

Carolina

Atlanta

| 0 | 45 | 90 | 180 |
Miles

Legend
- Mega area borders
- State borders
- Other counties
- Government
- Natural resources
- Manufacturing
- Mining

Credit: Grace Bjarnson,
Metropolitan Research Center,
University of Utah /
Brookings Mountain West

Figure 19.3. Piedmont megapolitan cluster counties identified by the USDA as dependent on selected economic sectors

Knowledge Class
Piedmont Megapolitan Cluster

Carolina

Atlanta

| 0 | 40 | 80 | 160 |
Miles

Legend
- Mega area borders
- State borders
- Creative class

Credit: Grace Bjarnson,
Metropolitan Research Center,
University of Utah /
Brookings Mountain West

Figure 19.4. Distribution of knowledge class counties in the Piedmont megapolitan cluster

Land, Water, and Air Resources

We now expand on the land, water, and air resource issues raised in Chapter 10 as they relate to the Piedmont megapolitan cluster.

Information about farmland, rate of change in farmland, and change per 1,000 new residents for the periods 1987–1997 and 1997–2007 is reported in Table 19.17. Following national trends, farmland inventory is falling steadily in the Piedment megapolitan cluster. However, the pace is less than half the national pace in terms of farmland lost per 1,000 new residents.

In Table 19.18, we review changes in water consumption per capita for the Piedmont megapolitan cluster. In both 1990 and 2005, per capita water consumption was less than the national average. The Atlanta megapolitan

area's consumption fell substantially, by about 15 percent, to become considerably less than the national average. It may be that state and local governments are attempting to conserve water to accommodate future growth and to hedge against potential U.S. decisions on the allocation of Chattahoochee River water among the states of Georgia, Alabama, and Florida.

Table 19.19 reports greenhouse gas production per capita from automobiles for the largest 100 metropolitan areas located in the Piedmont megapolitan cluster. Only the Greenville metropolitan area has per capita emissions that fall below the national average; all eight other metropolitan areas not only exceed national averages but do so by a wide margin.

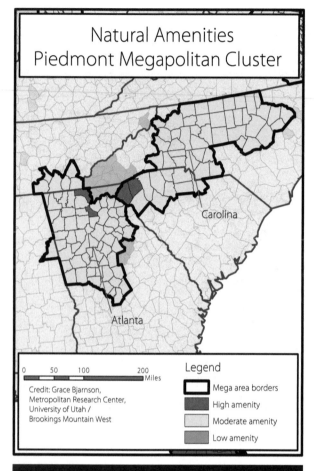

Natural Amenities
Piedmont Megapolitan Cluster

Carolina

Atlanta

0   50   100   200
                        Miles

Credit: Grace Bjarnson,
Metropolitan Research Center,
University of Utah /
Brookings Mountain West

Legend

☐ Mega area borders

■ High amenity

□ Moderate amenity

▨ Low amenity

Figure 19.5. Distribution of counties based on natural amenities in the Piedmont megapolitan cluster

Challenges

The Piedmont megapolitan cluster can be characterized as having steady growth, with few barriers to low-density development. Further, the soils are largely suitable for on-site sewerage treatment systems, and groundwater can be accessed in many places through wells of 100 feet or so in depth. This combination leads to some of the nation's most sprawling, low-density metropolitan areas, particularly Atlanta, Charlotte, Greenville, and the Research Triangle of North Carolina. In the Carolina Piedmont megapolitan area particularly, about 800,000 acres of farmland could be lost to low-density development, though the total farmland base will include about 4 million acres.

The developments that have emerged, and are likely to continue, do not lend themselves to supporting rail-based public transit. Metropolitan Atlanta's heavy-rail system, serving only two of its 20-some counties, is not likely to be expanded. Light rail there is also not likely until about the 2020s. Although Charlotte has a light-rail system, expansion connecting major suburban areas to downtown and to each other is not likely until the 2020s or beyond.

Commuter rail is also problematic. Unlike in other regions of the country, commuter rail in the Piedmont may depend largely on the willingness of railroads to grant access to their rails, which does not seem likely.

Water is a peculiar challenge as well, especially for metropolitan Atlanta. Although the region sees more than 50 inches of rain annually, one of the highest rates in the nation, water runs off the surface into rivers and the ocean or gulf. There is very little groundwater storage. Reservoirs are used to store surface water to meet water

Table 19.17. Change in Farmland and Farmland Per 1,000 New Residents, 1987–2007, Piedmont Megapolitan Cluster (acres of land)

Megapolitan Area	Farmland, 1987	Farmland, 1997	Percent Farmland Change, 1987–1997	Farmland Change Per 1,000 New Residents, 1987–1997	Farmland, 2007	Percent Farmland Change, 1997–2007	Farmland Change Per 1,000 New Residents, 1997–2007
Atlanta	3,121,937	2,919,592	−6.5	(136)	2,817,662	−3.5	(65)
Carolina	5,326,561	5,185,393	−2.7	(114)	4,830,745	−6.8	(274)
Piedmont cluster	8,448,498	8,104,985	−4.1	(126)	7,648,407	−5.6	(159)
National average				(425)			(342)

Source: Based on Woods & Poole Economics (2010)

Table 19.18. Change in Per Capita Water Consumption, 1990–2005, Piedmont Megapolitan Cluster (gallons per day)

Megapolitan Area	Water Consumed Per Capita, 1990	Water Consumed Per Capita, 2005	Percent Change in Water Consumed Per Capita, 1990–2005
Atlanta	180	153	−15.3
Carolina	173	169	−2.3
Piedmont cluster	177	161	−9.3
National average	184	171	−6.8

Source: Based on Woods & Poole Economics (2010)

Table 19.19. Greenhouse Gas Emissions Per Capita, Piedmont Megapolitan Cluster MSAs, 2005 (metric tons)

Metropolitan Area	Megaregion	Megapolitan Area	Auto Emissions	Percent Dispersion from Mean	Rank Among Top 100 Metros
Chattanooga, TN–GA	Piedmont	Atlanta	1.272	26.7	80
Atlanta–Sandy Springs–Marietta, GA	Piedmont	Atlanta	1.224	21.9	73
Augusta–Richmond County, GA–SC	Piedmont	Atlanta	1.226	22.1	74
Durham, NC	Piedmont	Carolina	1.119	11.5	56
Columbia, SC	Piedmont	Carolina	1.216	21.1	72
Raleigh–Cary, NC	Piedmont	Carolina	1.277	27.2	82
Greensboro–High Point, NC	Piedmont	Carolina	1.104	10.0	53
Greenville, SC	Piedmont	Carolina	0.874	−12.9	15
Charlotte–Gastonia–Concord, NC–SC	Piedmont	Carolina	1.256	25.1	79
Mean transportation footprint for the 100 largest metropolitan areas			1.004		

Source: Adapted from Brown, Southworth, and Sarzynski (2008)

needs. It is because of one reservoir in particular, creating Lake Lanier, that metropolitan Atlanta was able to more than double its population between 1970 and 2010, but this meant reducing downstream flow serving Alabama and Florida. Federal courts have intervened in ways that could effectively stop metropolitan Atlanta's growth, especially if Congress does not intervene.

Despite all these sprawl-inducing influences, demographic changes and changes in attitudes about urban form appear to be favoring higher densities, especially where transit does exist. Analysis by Levine and Frank

(2007), for example, indicates that half of suburbanites who want "walkable" communities do not have them. In addition, a large share of suburbanites would trade their large lot for a smaller one if that meant sidewalks, transit access, and the ability to walk to places. Other surveys seem to indicate that communities with these attributes are in demand by more than half the population, and the share seems to be growing (see Handy et al. 2008). The challenge will be for suburban communities especially to redesign their planning and zoning codes to facilitate changing market needs.

Appendix 19.1. Counties in the Piedmont Megapolitan Cluster

County, State	Megapolitan Area	County, State	Megapolitan Area
Cleburne, AL	Atlanta	Jones, GA	Atlanta
Banks, GA	Atlanta	Lamar, GA	Atlanta
Barrow, GA	Atlanta	Lumpkin, GA	Atlanta
Bartow, GA	Atlanta	Madison, GA	Atlanta
Bibb, GA	Atlanta	Meriwether, GA	Atlanta
Butts, GA	Atlanta	Monroe, GA	Atlanta
Carroll, GA	Atlanta	Morgan, GA	Atlanta
Catoosa, GA	Atlanta	Murray, GA	Atlanta
Chattooga, GA	Atlanta	Newton, GA	Atlanta
Cherokee, GA	Atlanta	Oconee, GA	Atlanta
Clarke, GA	Atlanta	Oglethorpe, GA	Atlanta
Clayton, GA	Atlanta	Paulding, GA	Atlanta
Cobb, GA	Atlanta	Peach, GA	Atlanta
Coweta, GA	Atlanta	Pickens, GA	Atlanta
Crawford, GA	Atlanta	Pike, GA	Atlanta
Dade, GA	Atlanta	Polk, GA	Atlanta
Dawson, GA	Atlanta	Rockdale, GA	Atlanta
DeKalb, GA	Atlanta	Spalding, GA	Atlanta
Douglas, GA	Atlanta	Stephens, GA	Atlanta
Fannin, GA	Atlanta	Troup, GA	Atlanta
Fayette, GA	Atlanta	Twiggs, GA	Atlanta
Floyd, GA	Atlanta	Upson, GA	Atlanta
Forsyth, GA	Atlanta	Walker, GA	Atlanta
Franklin, GA	Atlanta	Walton, GA	Atlanta
Fulton, GA	Atlanta	White, GA	Atlanta
Gilmer, GA	Atlanta	Whitfield, GA	Atlanta
Gordon, GA	Atlanta	Bradley, TN	Atlanta
Gwinnett, GA	Atlanta	Hamilton, TN	Atlanta
Habersham, GA	Atlanta	McMinn, TN	Atlanta
Hall, GA	Atlanta	Marion, TN	Atlanta
Haralson, GA	Atlanta	Polk, TN	Atlanta
Heard, GA	Atlanta	Sequatchie, TN	Atlanta
Henry, GA	Atlanta	Alamance, NC	Carolina
Houston, Ga	Atlanta	Alexander, NC	Carolina
Jackson, GA	Atlanta	Anson, NC	Carolina
Jasper, GA	Atlanta	Burke, NC	Carolina

Appendix 19.1. Counties in the Piedmont Megapolitan Cluster (*continued*)

County, State	Megapolitan Area	County, State	Megapolitan Area
Cabarrus, NC	Carolina	Rockingham, NC	Carolina
Caldwell, NC	Carolina	Rowan, NC	Carolina
Caswell, NC	Carolina	Rutherford, NC	Carolina
Catawba, NC	Carolina	Stanly, NC	Carolina
Chatham, NC	Carolina	Stokes, NC	Carolina
Cleveland, NC	Carolina	Surry, NC	Carolina
Davidson, NC	Carolina	Union, NC	Carolina
Davie, NC	Carolina	Vance, NC	Carolina
Durham, NC	Carolina	Wake, NC	Carolina
Edgecombe, NC	Carolina	Watauga, NC	Carolina
Forsyth, NC	Carolina	Wilkes, NC	Carolina
Franklin, NC	Carolina	Wilson, NC	Carolina
Gaston, NC	Carolina	Yadkin, NC	Carolina
Granville, NC	Carolina	Anderson, SC	Carolina
Guilford, NC	Carolina	Cherokee, SC	Carolina
Harnett, NC	Carolina	Chester, SC	Carolina
Iredell, NC	Carolina	Greenville, SC	Carolina
Johnston, NC	Carolina	Lancaster, SC	Carolina
Lee, NC	Carolina	Laurens, SC	Carolina
Lincoln, NC	Carolina	Oconee, SC	Carolina
Mecklenburg, NC	Carolina	Pickens, SC	Carolina
Nash, NC	Carolina	Spartanburg, SC	Carolina
Orange, NC	Carolina	Union, SC	Carolina
Person, NC	Carolina	York, SC	Carolina
Randolph, NC	Carolina		

20

MEGALOPOLIS MEGAPOLITAN CLUSTER

We end our profiles of megapolitan clusters and their megapolitan areas with where Jean Gottmann began: Megalopolis. Where Gottmann saw one continuous array of large, multiple metropolitan areas creating a whole, we decompose Megalopolis into three megapolitan parts: the Chesapeake megapolitan area, which extends from about Richmond, Virginia, northward through Washington, D.C., to Baltimore; the New York–Philadelphia megapolitan area; and the New England megapolitan area, which extends north from Hartford, Connecticut, through Boston to Portland, Maine (Figure 20.1). Appendix 20.1 lists the counties included

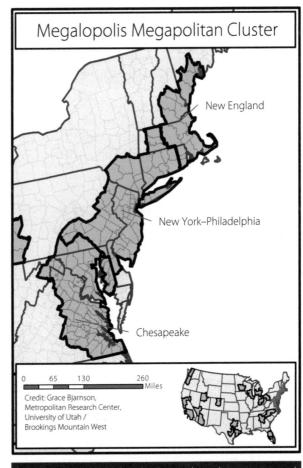

Figure 20.1. The Megalopolis megapolitan cluster composed of the Chesapeake, New York–Philadelphia, and New England megapolitan areas

in each megapolitan area. In this chapter, we profile the Megalopolis megapolitan cluster in the areas of major demographic and housing trends, employment and development projections, the extent of economic dependency, and attractiveness characteristics. We conclude with our perceptions of major planning and development challenges.

Major Demographic and Housing Trends

Megalopolis is the nation's largest megapolitan cluster. In 2010, about 80 percent of the residents in Megalopolis lived in a county of a metropolitan area of more than one million residents (Table 20.1 and Figure 20.2), and more than 95 percent lived in a metropolitan area. We estimate that Megalopolis contains about 50,000 square miles that are privately owned and reasonably accessible to development (Table 20.2). Its 2010 population density of about 1,100 persons per square mile makes it the nation's most densely settled megapolitan cluster (just ahead of the Florida megapolitan cluster), more densely populated than Japan and somewhat less densely populated than the Netherlands, Europe's most densely settled country. By 2040, Megalopolis will be home to more than 68 million people (Table 20.3) and will be more densely settled than the Netherlands in 2010 (Table 20.4).

The Megalopolis megapolitan cluster will see the biggest numerical change in ethnic composition of any megapolitan cluster. Between 2010 and 2040, its

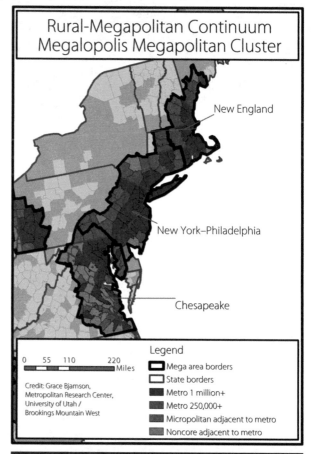

Figure 20.2. Nelson-Lang Rural-Megapolitan Continuum Codes applied to the Megalopolis megapolitan cluster counties

Table 20.1. Megalopolis Megapolitan Cluster Rural-Megapolitan Continuum

Nelson-Lang Rural-Megapolitan Continuum Description	Counties	2010 Population (000s)
Counties in metropolitan areas of 1 million+ population	104	43,658
Counties in metropolitan areas of 250,000 to 1 million population	25	8,489
Counties in metropolitan areas of less than 250,000 population	12	1,465
Micropolitan area adjacent to a metropolitan area	16	1,452
Noncore counties adjacent to a metropolitan area	1	18
All other nonmetropolitan counties	7	88

Table 20.2. Megalopolis Megapolitan Cluster Land Area (in square miles)

Megapolitan Area	Total Land	Estimate of Privately Owned, Accessible Land
Chesapeake	25,235	18,877
New York–Philadelphia	29,762	22,171
New England	11,778	8,833
Total	66,774	49,880

number of non-Hispanic whites will fall by about 2.7 million (Table 20.5), while the minority population will increase nearly 80 percent, adding nearly 16 million (Table 20.6). The Hispanic population will increase by nearly 9 million people, more than double its 2010 population, and accounting for two-thirds of the change in population (Table 20.7). The Asian population will be the fastest growing (Table 20.8), while the African American population will increase by a quarter and remain the second largest ethnic minority group (Table 20.9).

In addition, the Megalopolis megapolitan cluster will see an increase in the share of population age 65+ from 13 percent in 2010 to more than 21 percent in 2040. This group will nearly double its population, growing by more than 14 million and accounting for more than half the share in the change of population (Table 20.10).

Table 20.3. Megalopolis Megapolitan Cluster Population, 2010–2040 (in thousands)

Megapolitan Area	Total Population, 2010	Total Population, 2025	Total Population, 2040	Total Change, 2010–2040	Percent Change, 2010–2040
Chesapeake	12,541	15,240	18,020	5,478	43.7
New York–Philadelphia	33,901	36,830	39,954	6,053	17.9
New England	8,456	9,269	10,130	1,675	19.8
Megalopolis cluster	54,898	61,339	68,104	13,206	24.1

Source: Based on Woods & Poole Economics (2010)

Table 20.4. Megalopolis Megapolitan Cluster Population Density, 2010–2040

Megapolitan Area	Persons Per Square Mile, 2010	Comparable Developed Nation, 2010	Persons Per Square Mile, 2040	Comparable Developed Nation, 2040
Chesapeake	673	United Kingdom	968	>Belgium
New York–Philadelphia	1,529	>The Netherlands	1,802	Taiwan
New England	957	>Belgium	1,147	<The Netherlands
Total	1,104	<The Netherlands	1,370	The Netherlands

Note: The sign < means the megapolitan area density is about 50–200 fewer persons per square mile than in the comparable nation, while > means the density is about 50–200 more persons per square mile; no sign indicates the density is within about 50 persons per square mile. Figures compare developed nation population in 2010 to megapolitan cluster population in 2010 and 2040. All ranges are illustrative.

Table 20.5. Megalopolis Megapolitan Cluster White Non-Hispanic Population, 2010–2040 (in thousands)

Megapolitan Area	White Non-Hispanic Population, 2010	White Non-Hispanic Population, 2025	White Non-Hispanic Population, 2040	White Non-Hispanic Population Change, 2010–2040	White Non-Hispanic Population Percent Change, 2010–2040	White Non-Hispanic Share of Population Change, 2010–2040
Chesapeake	7,573	8,163	8,310	737	9.7	5.6
New York–Philadelphia	20,202	18,707	16,826	(3,376)	−16.7	−25.6
New England	6,926	6,988	6,894	(33)	−0.5	-0.2
Megalopolis cluster	34,702	33,859	32,030	(2,672)	−7.7	−20.2

Source: Based on Woods & Poole Economics (2010)

Table 20.6. Megalopolis Megapolitan Cluster Minority Population, 2010–2040 (in thousands)

Megapolitan Area	Minority Population, 2010	Minority Population, 2025	Minority Population, 2040	Minority Population Change, 2010–2040	Minority Population Percent Change, 2010–2040	Minority Share of Population Change, 2010–2040
Chesapeake	4,968	7,077	9,710	4,741	95.4	35.9
New York–Philadelphia	13,698	18,123	23,128	9,430	68.8	71.4
New England	1,529	2,281	3,237	1,707	111.6	12.9
Megalopolis cluster	20,196	27,480	36,074	15,878	78.6	120.2

Source: Based on Woods & Poole Economics (2010)

Table 20.7. Megalopolis Megapolitan Cluster Hispanic Population, 2010–2040 (in thousands)

Megapolitan Area	Hispanic Population, 2010	Hispanic Population, 2025	Hispanic Population, 2040	Hispanic Population Change, 2010–2040	Hispanic Population Percent Change, 2010–2040	Hispanic Share of Population Change, 2010–2040
Chesapeake	1,028	2,010	3,513	2,485	241.8	18.8
New York–Philadelphia	5,842	8,472	11,357	5,516	94.4	41.8
New England	662	1,024	1,465	802	121.1	6.1
Megalopolis cluster	7,531	11,506	16,334	8,803	116.9	66.7

Source: Based on Woods & Poole Economics (2010)

Table 20.8. Megalopolis Megapolitan Cluster Asian Population, 2010–2040 (in thousands)

Megapolitan Area	Asian Population, 2010	Asian Population, 2025	Asian Population, 2040	Asian Population Change, 2010–2040	Asian Population Percent Change, 2010–2040	Asian Share of Population Change, 2010–2040
Chesapeake	750	1,219	1,778	1,027	137.0	7.8
New York–Philadelphia	2,514	3,913	5,635	3,120	124.1	23.6
New England	398	645	979	581	146.1	4.4
Megalopolis cluster	3,662	5,776	8,391	4,729	129.1	35.8

Source: Based on Woods & Poole Economics (2010)

Housing Development

Between 2010 and 2040, the housing inventory of Megalopolis will grow from nearly 22 million units to nearly 29 million units, an increase of about 7.0 million homes (Table 20.11)—the most of any megapolitan cluster. We estimate that nearly another 3 million units existing in 2010 will need to be rebuilt or replaced by 2040. Altogether, nearly 10 million residential units will need to be built or rebuilt between 2010 and 2040, equivalent to 45 percent of all units existing in 2010.

Major Employment and Nonresidential Development Trends

Over the period 2010–2040, Woods and Poole Economics data indicate that Megalopolis will add about 11.7 million part- and full-time jobs (Table 20.12). Almost all the new jobs will be in "land-use" jobs (Table 20.13).

Table 20.9. Megalopolis Megapolitan Cluster African American Population, 2010–2040 (in thousands)

Megapolitan Area	African American Population, 2010	African American Population, 2025	African American Population, 2040	African American Population Change, 2010–2040	African American Population Percent Change, 2010–2040	African American Share of Population Change, 2010–2040
Chesapeake	3,302	3,991	4,594	1,293	39.1	9.8
New York–Philadelphia	5,259	5,635	6,011	753	14.3	5.7
New England	446	582	758	311	69.8	2.4
Megalopolis cluster	9,006	10,208	11,363	2,357	26.2	17.8

Source: Based on Woods & Poole Economics (2010)

Table 20.10. Megalopolis Megapolitan Cluster Population 65+, 2010–2040 (in thousands)

Megapolitan Area	Population 65+, 2010	Population 65+ as Share of Population, 2010	Population 65+, 2040	Population 65+ as Share of Population, 2040	Share of Population Change, 2010–2040
Chesapeake	1,500	12.0	3,518	19.5	36.8
New York–Philadelphia	4,554	13.4	8,473	21.2	64.8
New England	1,150	13.6	2,301	22.7	68.8
Megalopolis cluster	7,204	13.1	14,293	21.0	53.7

Source: Based on Woods & Poole Economics (2010)

Table 20.11. Megalopolis Megapolitan Cluster Residential Development (in thousands)

Megapolitan Area	Units Supported, 2010	Increase in Inventory, 2010–2040	Units Recycled, 2010–2040	Total Units Constructed, 2010–2040	Percent of Units Supported, 2010
Chesapeake	5,018	2,925	638	3,563	71.0
New York–Philadelphia	13,354	3,123	1,699	4,822	36.1
New England	3,505	1,045	446	1,491	42.6
Megalopolis cluster	21,876	7,093	2,783	9,876	45.1

In 2010, there was sufficient employment in the Megalopolis megapolitan cluster to support about 14.5 billion square feet of nonresidential space, including industrial, commercial, and institutional uses. By 2040, it will be able to support about 19.4 billion square feet of space, adding nearly 5 billion square feet over the period 2010–2040 (Table 20.14). Counting space that will be replaced or rebuilt, a total of 20.8 billion square feet is expected to be built.

Growth-related and replaced space will be roughly equivalent to 1.4 times the nonresidential space existing in 2010.

Economic Dependency

About a sixth of the population in the Megalopolis megapolitan cluster lives in counties that are classified as dependent, mostly on the manufacturing or federal and state government sectors (Table 20.15 and Figure 20.3).

Table 20.12. Megalopolis Megapolitan Cluster Total Employment, 2010–2040

Megapolitan Area	Total Jobs, 2010	Total Jobs, 2040	Change, 2010–12040	Percent Change, 2010–2040
Chesapeake	8,020	11,981	3,961	49.4
New York–Philadelphia	19,794	25,784	5,990	30.3
New England	5,356	7,134	1,778	33.2
Megalopolis cluster	33,170	44,899	11,729	35.4

Source: Based on Woods & Poole Economics (2010)

Table 20.13. Megalopolis Megapolitan Cluster Land-Use Employment, 2010–2040 (in thousands)

Megapolitan Area	Total Land-Use Employment, 2010	Total Land-Use Employment, 2025	Total Land-Use Employment, 2040	Change in Land-Use Employment, 2010–2040	Percent Change in Land-Use Employment, 2010–2040
Chesapeake	7,954	9,758	11,909	3,955	49.7
New York–Philadelphia	19,684	22,507	25,666	5,982	30.4
New England	5,324	6,158	7,097	1,773	33.3
Megalopolis cluster	32,962	38,424	44,673	11,711	35.5

Source: Based on Woods & Poole Economics (2010)

Table 20.14. Megalopolis Megapolitan Cluster Land-Use Employment Space Needs, 2010–2040 (millions of square feet)

Megapolitan Area	Total Land-Use Employment Space Supported, 2010	Total Land-Use Employment Space Supported, 2040	Increase in Land-Use Employment Space Inventory Supported, 2010–2040	Recycled Land-Use Employment Space, 2010–2040	Total Land-Use Employment Space Constructed, 2010–2040	Land-Use Employment Space Constructed in 2010–2040 as Percent of Space in 2010
Chesapeake	4,012	5,968	1,956	4,403	6,359	158.5
New York–Philadelphia	8,250	10,522	2,272	9,055	11,327	137.3
New England	2,245	2,912	667	2,464	3,131	139.5
Megalopolis cluster	14,507	19,402	4,895	15,922	20,817	143.5

Not surprisingly, about a third of the population in the Chesapeake megapolitan area, centered on Washington, D.C., lives in a county dependent on federal and state government jobs.

Attractiveness to the Knowledge Class

As seen in Table 20.16 and illustrated in Figure 20.4, about two-thirds of the Megalopolis megapolitan cluster population lives in knowledge class counties. The figure is nearly 80 percent for the New England megapolitan area and three-quarters for the Chesapeake megapolitan area, while it is less than 60 percent for the New York–Philadelphia megapolitan area. Figure 20.5 shows the distribution of Megalopolis megapolitan cluster counties by the quality of their natural amenities.

Land, Water, and Air Resources

Our final analytic discussion focuses on the land, water, and air resource issues we raised in Chapter 10.

In Table 20.17, we report the farmland, rate of change in farmland, and change per 1,000 new residents for the periods 1987–1997 and 1997–2007. Farmland loss rates were about one-third less than the national average over the whole period, with the New England megapolitan area actually seeing an increase in farmland per 1,000 new residents in the recent period—a distinct departure from the period 1987–1997, which saw the megapolitan cluster's largest reduction of 12 percent.

Table 20.18 reviews changes in water consumption per capita for the Megalopolis megapolitan cluster. This cluster has the lowest consumption of water per capita for both 1990 and 2005, and also saw one of the largest rates of reduction. The Megalopolis megapolitan area leads the nation, with just

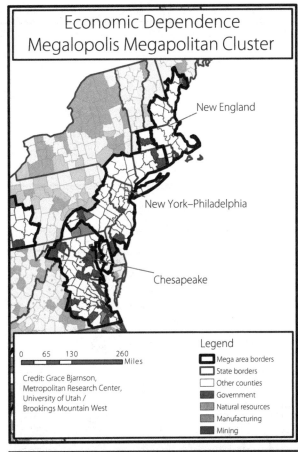

Figure 20.3. Megalopolis megapolitan cluster counties identified by the USDA as dependent on selected economic sectors

Table 20.15. Megalopolis Megapolitan Cluster Economic Sector Dependence (in millions)

Megapolitan Area	Farming-Dependent Population, 2010	Mining-Dependent Population, 2010	Manufacturing-Dependent Population, 2010	Tourism and Entertainment–Dependent Population, 2010	Government-Dependent Population, 2010	Total Dependent Population, 2010	Total Population, 2010	Percent Dependent Population, 2010
Chesapeake	10	0	755	29	4,551	5,186	12,541	41.4
New York–Philadelphia	0	0	131	418	1,523	2,261	33,901	6.7
New England	0	0	37	59	0	117	8,456	1.4
Megalopolis cluster	10	0	923	506	6,073	7,564	54,898	13.8

Table 20.16. Megalopolis Megapolitan Cluster Knowledge Class Employment (in thousands)

Megapolitan Area	Knowledge Population, 2010	Total Population, 2010	Percent Knowledge Population, 2010
Chesapeake	9,255	12,541	73.8
New York–Philadelphia	19,318	33,901	57.0
New England	6,689	8,456	79.1
Megalopolis cluster	35,262	54,898	64.2

Source: Based on Woods & Poole Economics (2010)

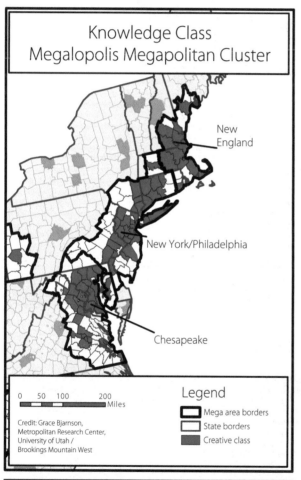

Figure 20.4. Distribution of knowledge class counties in the Megalopolis megapolitan cluster

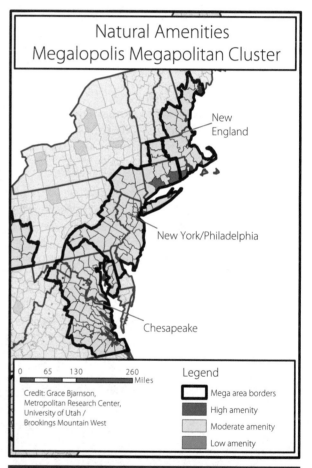

Figure 20.5. Distribution of counties based on natural amenities in the Megalopolis megapolitan cluster

126 gallons of daily water consumed per capita. On the other hand, there was a 5 percent increase in per capita water consumption for the New England megapolitan area.

Table 20.19 reports greenhouse gas production per capita from automobiles for the largest 100 metropolitan areas located in the Megalopolis megapolitan cluster. This megapolitan cluster has the largest number of such

Table 20.17. Change in Farmland and Farmland Per 1,000 New Residents, 1987–2007, Megalopolis Megapolitan Cluster (acres of land)

Megapolitan Area	Farmland, 1987	Farmland, 1997	Percent Farmland Change, 1987–1997	Farmland Change Per 1,000 New Residents, 1987–1997	Farmland, 2007	Farmland Change, 1997–2007	Farmland Change Per 1,000 New Residents, 1997–2007
Chesapeake	5,378,176	5,341,025	–0.7	(29)	4,984,509	–6.7	(261)
New York–Philadelphia	4,019,342	3,686,716	–8.3	(150)	3,663,995	–0.6	(15)
New England	801,056	705,206	–12.0	(181)	719,867	2.1	45
Megalopolis cluster	10,198,574	9,732,947	–4.6	(116)	9,368,371	–3.7	(113)
National average				(425)			(342)

Source: Based on Woods & Poole Economics (2010)

Table 20.18. Change in Per Capita Water Consumption, 1990–2005, Megalopolis Megapolitan Cluster (gallons per day)

Megapolitan Area	Water Consumed Per Capita, 1990	Water Consumed Per Capita, 2005	Change in Water Consumed Per Capita, 1990–2005
Chesapeake	164	145	–11.5
New York–Philadelphia	144	117	–19.1
New England	126	133	5.5
Megalopolis cluster	145	126	–13.7
National average	184	171	–6.8

Source: Based on Woods & Poole Economics (2010)

metropolitan areas—18. It also has the distinction of having the metropolitan area with the worst emissions per capita, Trenton, New Jersey, at 100, with emissions nearly 48 percent higher than the national average, and the best, New York, at 1, with emissions a third less than the national average.

Challenges

In many ways, the Megalopolis megapolitan cluster comes closest to having European-scale infrastructure systems as any, especially rail transportation. Of course, the megapolitan cluster industrialized largely around the same time Europe did, and such cities as Boston, New York, and Philadelphia installed subways at roughly the same time that London and Paris did.

As the nation's largest and oldest complex of metropolitan areas, Megalopolis is also the most in need

of rebuilding or replacing much of its built landscape. Of the 9.2 million homes to be built over the period 2010–2040—the most in the nation—3 million will be for replacement, also the most in the nation. Of the 19.1 billion square feet of nonresidential space to be constructed, 13.6 billion square feet will be rebuilt or replaced—also the most in the nation in both respects. In a very real sense, the Megalopolis megapolitan cluster has the chance to be rebuilt and even reshaped. It is already happening. For instance, in the Philadelphia metropolitan area, "Center City" and "University City" have seen the largest share of growth, even as many suburbs lost population. Manhattan, always among the nation's most glamorous places to live and certainly its most urbane, now has more children living in it than a generation ago. And, after decades of decline, the close-in areas of the Bronx and Brooklyn have seen a renaissance in redevelopment. Indeed, after decades

Table 20.19. Greenhouse Gas Emissions Per Capita, Megalopolis Megapolitan Cluster MSAs, 2005 (metric tons)

Metropolitan Area	Megaregion	Megapolitan Area	Auto Emissions	Percent Dispersion from Mean	Rank Among Top 100 Metros
Virginia Beach–Norfolk–Newport News, VA–NC	Megalopolis	Chesapeake	1.004	0.0	33
Baltimore–Towson, MD	Megalopolis	Chesapeake	1.044	4.0	44
Washington–Arlington–Alexandria, DC–VA–MD–WV	Megalopolis	Chesapeake	0.984	−2.0	30
Richmond, VA	Megalopolis	Chesapeake	1.335	33.0	92
Lancaster, PA	Megalopolis	New York–Philadelphia	0.767	−23.6	2
Harrisburg–Carlisle, PA	Megalopolis	New York–Philadelphia	1.320	31.5	89
Allentown–Bethlehem–Easton, PA–NJ	Megalopolis	New York–Philadelphia	0.964	−4.0	26
Bridgeport–Stamford–Norwalk, CT	Megalopolis	New York–Philadelphia	0.972	−3.2	28
Philadelphia–Camden–Wilmington, PA–NJ–DE–MD	Megalopolis	New York–Philadelphia	0.789	−21.4	5
Trenton–Ewing, NJ	Megalopolis	New York–Philadelphia	1.483	47.7	100
New York–Northern New Jersey–Long Island, NY–NJ–PA	Megalopolis	New York–Philadelphia	0.664	−33.9	1
Portland–South Portland–Biddeford, ME	Megalopolis	New England	1.097	9.3	51
Providence–New Bedford–Fall River, RI–MA	Megalopolis	New England	1.014	1.0	37
Boston–Cambridge–Quincy, MA–NH	Megalopolis	New England	0.872	−13.1	14
Springfield, MA	Megalopolis	New England	0.948	−5.6	23
New Haven–Milford, CT	Megalopolis	New England	0.876	−12.7	16
Hartford–West Hartford–East Hartford, CT	Megalopolis	New England	1.046	4.2	45
Worcester, MA	Megalopolis	New England	1.242	23.7	77
Mean transportation footprint for the 100 largest metropolitan areas			1.004		

Source: Adapted from Brown, Southworth, and Sarzynski (2008)

of trying to find ways to attract development, many neighborhoods now oppose it. Washington, D.C., for decades one of those blighted cities in America, has become a kind of European-style Mecca for those seeking low-rise, high-density, urban neighborhoods reminiscent of London and Paris, though not on the same scale or even density. As another 12.5 million people are added to the Megalopolis megapolitan cluster, many millions may want to live in or close to urban centers.

All the major metropolitan areas of Megalopolis have reasonably mature and expanding rail systems that include commuter and either light- or heavy-rail options. Megalopolis leads the nation in both the number and share of population currently and potentially served by rail systems (Reconnecting America 2004). Indeed, station-area rail capacity exists in all the major metropolitan areas—Baltimore, Boston, Philadelphia, New York, and Washington, D.C.—to accommodate virtually all 12.5 million people projected to be added to Megalopolis. Indeed, emerging literature suggests that as much as half the population wants to live near or with access to rail stations, which should provide Megalopolis with a competitive advantage relative to other megapolitan clusters.

Taking advantage of changing location preferences, and especially leveraging existing rail systems, will require advance planning and infrastructure investment to facilitate this. None of the states in the Megalopolis megapolitan cluster can be considered a true leader in planning, though Maryland comes closest, with a Nelson-Lang Planning Index of 12. Yet all have engaged in impressive transportation systems, especially commuter rail, in recent decades. Amtrak, the federal rail agency, operates the nation's only high-speed rail (HSR) service, connecting Boston to Washington, and the corridor is the only one generating profits for Amtrak. Because of this corridor's size and density, HSR transportation is seen as a more efficient way to connect urban centers than either air or highways. It is no accident that the most vibrant, value-enhanced areas of Megalopolis are those with reasonably convenient access to HSR.

Planning may be needed to address the inertia of continuing to construct low-density developments on farmland, especially given trends favoring infill and redevelopment. This is especially the case for the Chesapeake megapolitan area. At 0.17 acres of farmland lost for each new resident, the nearly 5 million new residents could reduce the inventory of farmland by about 800,000 acres.

Megalopolis and all its megapolitan areas consume by far the least amount of domestic water per capita than the rest of the nation—about one-quarter less. It appears that Megalopolis has sufficient water to meet future growth needs, especially if modest conservation occurs. If the rest of the nation had similar water consumption per capita, all megapolitan clusters could meet future development needs based on current supplies.

Jean Gottmann identified America's and perhaps the world's first complex of multiple metropolitan areas linked like beads on a chain, which he called Megalopolis. It is and will remain the largest megapolitan cluster. Despite rapid growth elsewhere, more homes will be built or rebuilt and more nonresidential space constructed in the Megalopolis megapolitan cluster than in any other.

Appendix 20.1. City, Counties, and Independent Cities in the Megalopolis Megapolitan Cluster

County/State	Megapolitan Area	County/State	Megapolitan Area
District of Columbia	Chesapeake	St. Mary's, MD	Chesapeake
Anne Arundel, MD	Chesapeake	Talbot, MD	Chesapeake
Baltimore, MD	Chesapeake	Washington, MD	Chesapeake
Calvert, MD	Chesapeake	Baltimore City, MD	Chesapeake
Caroline, MD	Chesapeake	Adams, PA	Chesapeake
Carroll, MD	Chesapeake	Franklin, PA	Chesapeake
Charles, MD	Chesapeake	York, PA	Chesapeake
Dorchester, MD	Chesapeake	Amelia, VA	Chesapeake
Frederick, MD	Chesapeake	Arlington, VA	Chesapeake
Harford, MD	Chesapeake	Caroline, VA	Chesapeake
Howard, MD	Chesapeake	Charles City, VA	Chesapeake
Kent, MD	Chesapeake	Chesterfield, VA	Chesapeake
Montgomery, MD	Chesapeake	Clarke, VA	Chesapeake
Prince George's, MD	Chesapeake	Culpeper, VA	Chesapeake
Queen Anne's, MD	Chesapeake	Cumberland, VA	Chesapeake

(continued)

Appendix 20.1. City, Counties, and Independent Cities in the Megalopolis Megapolitan Cluster (*continued*)

County/State	Megapolitan Area	County/State	Megapolitan Area
Essex, VA	Chesapeake	Hampton, VA	Chesapeake
Fauquier, VA	Chesapeake	Newport News, VA	Chesapeake
Gloucester, VA	Chesapeake	Norfolk, VA	Chesapeake
Goochland, VA	Chesapeake	Poquoson, VA	Chesapeake
Hanover, VA	Chesapeake	Portsmouth, VA	Chesapeake
Henrico, VA	Chesapeake	Richmond City, VA	Chesapeake
Isle of White, VA	Chesapeake	Suffolk, VA	Chesapeake
James City, VA	Chesapeake	Virginia Beach, VA	Chesapeake
King and Queen, VA	Chesapeake	Williamsburg, VA	Chesapeake
King George, VA	Chesapeake	Dinwiddie, Colonial Heights, Petersburg,* VA	Chesapeake
King William, VA	Chesapeake	Fairfax, Fairfax City, Falls Church,* VA	Chesapeake
Lancaster, VA	Chesapeake	Frederick Co., Winchester,* VA	Chesapeake
Loudoun, VA	Chesapeake	Prince George, Hopewell,* VA	Chesapeake
Louisa, VA	Chesapeake	Prince William, Manassas, Manassas Park,* VA	Chesapeake
Mathews, VA	Chesapeake	Spotsylvania, Fredericksburg,* VA	Chesapeake
Middlesex, VA	Chesapeake	Berkeley, WV	Chesapeake
New Kent, VA	Chesapeake	Hampshire, WV	Chesapeake
Northumberland, VA	Chesapeake	Jefferson, WV	Chesapeake
Nottaway, VA	Chesapeake	Morgan, WV	Chesapeake
Orange, VA	Chesapeake	Fairfield, CT	New York–Philadelphia
Powhatan, VA	Chesapeake	Hartford, CT	New York–Philadelphia
Rappahannock, VA	Chesapeake	Litchfield, CT	New York–Philadelphia
Richmond, VA	Chesapeake	Middlesex, CT	New York–Philadelphia
Southampton, VA	Chesapeake	New Haven, CT	New York–Philadelphia
Stafford, VA	Chesapeake	New London, CT	New York–Philadelphia
Surry, VA	Chesapeake	Tolland, CT	New York–Philadelphia
Warren, VA	Chesapeake	Windham, CT	New York–Philadelphia
Westmoreland, VA	Chesapeake	Kent, DE	New York–Philadelphia
York, VA	Chesapeake	New Castle, DE	New York–Philadelphia
Alexandria, VA	Chesapeake	Cecil, MD	New York–Philadelphia
Chesapeake, VA	Chesapeake	Franklin, MA	New York–Philadelphia
Fairfax City, VA	Chesapeake	Hampden, MA	New York–Philadelphia
Falls Church, VA	Chesapeake	Hampshire, MA	New York–Philadelphia
Franklin City, VA	Chesapeake	Atlantic, NJ	New York–Philadelphia

(*continued*)

Appendix 20.1. City, Counties, and Independent Cities in the Megalopolis Megapolitan Cluster (*continued*)

County/State	Megapolitan Area	County/State	Megapolitan Area
Bergen, NJ	New York–Philadelphia	Carbon, PA	New York–Philadelphia
Burlington, NJ	New York–Philadelphia	Chester, PA	New York–Philadelphia
Camden, NJ	New York–Philadelphia	Cumberland, PA	New York–Philadelphia
Cape May, NJ	New York–Philadelphia	Dauphin, PA	New York–Philadelphia
Cumberland, NJ	New York–Philadelphia	Delaware, PA	New York–Philadelphia
Essex, MJ	New York–Philadelphia	Lancaster, PA	New York–Philadelphia
Gloucester, NJ	New York–Philadelphia	Lebanon, PA	New York–Philadelphia
Hudson, NJ	New York–Philadelphia	Lehigh, PA	New York–Philadelphia
Hunterdon, NJ	New York–Philadelphia	Monroe, PA	New York–Philadelphia
Mercer, NJ	New York–Philadelphia	Montgomery, PA	New York–Philadelphia
Middlesex, NJ	New York–Philadelphia	Northampton, PA	New York–Philadelphia
Monmouth, NJ	New York–Philadelphia	Perry, PA	New York–Philadelphia
Morris, NJ	New York–Philadelphia	Philadelphia, PA	New York–Philadelphia
Ocean, NJ	New York–Philadelphia	Pike, PA	New York–Philadelphia
Passaic, NJ	New York–Philadelphia	Androscoggin, ME	New England
Salem, NJ	New York–Philadelphia	Cumberland, ME	New England
Somerset, NJ	New York–Philadelphia	Sagadahoc, ME	New England
Sussex, NJ	New York–Philadelphia	York, ME	New England
Union, NJ	New York–Philadelphia	Barnstable, MA	New England
Warren, NJ	New York–Philadelphia	Bristol, MA	New England
Bronx, NY	New York–Philadelphia	Essex, MA	New England
Dutchess, NY	New York–Philadelphia	Middlesex, MA	New England
Kings, NY	New York–Philadelphia	Norfolk, MA	New England
Nassau, NY	New York–Philadelphia	Plymouth, MA	New England
New York, NY	New York–Philadelphia	Suffolk, MA	New England
Orange, NY	New York–Philadelphia	Worcester, MA	New England
Putnam, NY	New York–Philadelphia	Belknap, NH	New England
Queens, NY	New York–Philadelphia	Hillsborough, NH	New England
Richmond, NY	New York–Philadelphia	Merrimack, NH	New England
Rockland, NY	New York–Philadelphia	Rockingham, NH	New England
Suffolk, NY	New York–Philadelphia	Strafford, NH	New England
Sullivan, NY	New York–Philadelphia	Bristol, RI	New England
Ulster, NY	New York–Philadelphia	Kent, RI	New England
Westchester, NY	New York–Philadelphia	Newport, RI	New England
Berks, PA	New York–Philadelphia	Providence, RI	New England
Bucks, PA	New York–Philadelphia	Washington, RI	New England

*Virginia independent cities included in surrounding county.

EPILOGUE
THE MEGAPOLITAN CENTURY

Given that the vast majority of the population growth in the United States is expected in megapolitan areas, the question emerges: Are we now in a "megapolitan century"? The likely answer is yes, but with some caveats. There is always a danger when making long-range projections that the world as we know it may be turned upside down and remade in ways that no linear forecast can capture. For example, in the mid-19th century it was predicted that New York City would be buried in several feet of horse manure a century later. That thought was based on estimated population growth, transportation demand, and equine fecal production. The invention of the internal combustion engine spared the city mountains of manure but in the process polluted its air and helped alter the world's climate. Exit one anticipated problem, enter another unpredictable one.

In a similar vein, estimating how many people will inhabit the United States in 100 years or where they will live is partly folly. Century-forward population predictions have been tried in the past, and most have been spectacularly off the mark.

Imagine trying to project the U.S. population today from the vantage point of 1910. The waves of immigrants entering the United States in the early 1900s and the sky-high birth rate at the time would have signaled robust growth over the next century, but a 1924 law severely limiting immigration and a big drop in fertility due to the Great Depression and war dampened these numbers.

Conversely, a post–World War II baby boom (1948–1964) and a 1965 law expanding immigration added millions to the nation and bumped the U.S. growth rate back up. In the end, the nation managed to more than triple its population, growing from about 92 million in 1909 to about 306 million in 2010. Most turn-of-the-20th-century estimates had the nation at 300 million by the middle of the 20th century, whereas that number was reached only in 2006.

Also unlikely would have been the prediction that so many people would live in the Sun Belt. A century ago, the Northeast and Midwest dominated the U.S. urban scene. There were some upstart cities along the West Coast, but virtually all major metro centers lay from Boston in the east to St Louis in the west. Today, only three of the largest U.S. cities are in the Northeast and Midwest, and these two regions rank number three and four among the census's four national geographic divisions. The South now ranks as the most populous division, followed by the West, which passed the Midwest in number of residents as of the 2010 Census. Will this pattern hold, as most demographers predict, or will we see a midwestern revival? The outcome depends on multiple variables, including global climate change.

Are there a half billion people in our future, or even a China-sized population? That depends on whom you ask. At the 2008 American Planning Association Conference in Las Vegas, one of us (Nelson) presented the case that we are on track to hit the census's high projection. He based his prediction in part on immediate past performance. Since 2000—the starting point for the Census Bureau's century-long projection—the United States has gained people on the high side of the range. He thought it could even reach 311 million residents by 2010, which was the upper benchmark for the decade (in fact, the 2010 population fell near the mark, at just under 309 million people).

As with the census's high estimate, Nelson assumes continued immigration and high fertility rates, but he also adds much longer life expectancy. He argues, too, that the United States can sustain many more people than it does now in part because Americans can build much denser urban environments than we have currently. Nelson even speculates that a sizable share of future population growth to 2100 can fit onto the nation's existing surface parking lots.

Writing in *Planning* magazine—for the "Centennial of *Planning*" issue—Lang, Alfonzo, and Dawkins (2009) projected that the United States could reach over half a billion residents by 2100. The estimate is based on several assumptions—first, that there will not be another world war or devastating global pandemic, and that the country does not face a depression like the Great Depression of the 1930s. Further, Lang assumes that, even without a "Mad Max" scenario, environmental stress and resource limits present enough of a technological challenge to at least slow world population growth. He also assumes that the United States remains attractive to immigrants but that the numbers decline in a few decades as world population growth slows. And, while some of us may want to live forever, humans will live only a bit longer throughout the 21st century. Finally, Lang predicts fertility will remain stable, and, perhaps more important, the high fertility rates among immigrants will drop substantially after one generation in the United States.

The Doomsters

The Census Bureau and we assume that the world's resources will be used in a way that adequately supports or even greatly expands America's population. The view has been described as "cornucopian" because its advocates assert that improving technology will allow humans to use natural resources in a way that does not limit population growth. It should be noted that so far, the cornucopian view has been correct.

Not everyone shares this rosy vision of the nation's future. An entire neo-Malthusian school has emerged that sees the nation shrinking back to its 19th-century population size. Critics call these folks the "doomsters." Perhaps the best-known doomster is James Howard Kunstler, familiar to many planners for his influential 1993 book, *The Geography of Nowhere*. In the book, Kunstler offers a harsh critique of suburbia, mostly in design terms (i.e., it is ugly and alienating). But in Kunstler's recent works, *The Long Emergency* (Kunstler 2005) and the fictional *World Made by Hand* (Kunstler 2008), a grimmer assessment of the suburban future emerges. Kunstler now argues that the suburbs—and America overall—are doomed because of resource depletion and global climate change.

This is not a new idea. Thomas Malthus proposed it at the start of the Industrial Revolution. The idea's best-known recent incarnation was the Club of Rome's report *The Limits to Growth* from the early 1970s, which argued that the world's population was about to overshoot the planet's carrying capacity (Meadows et al. 1972).

In the modern version of this view, the most important single force leading to America's inevitable population decline is "peak oil," the notion that we will now need to spend more to extract less petroleum and it is all downhill from here. While the idea that the world is nearing peak oil is an increasingly common view, it is Kunstler's interpretation of this event that makes him a doomster. He sees no possible substitution for oil. He argues that all alternative forms of carbon-based energy, such as coal, sand tar, and shale oil, are severely limited and impractical alternatives at best.

Kunstler also believes the United States is near peak natural gas, despite some recent breakthrough technology that has substantially increased U.S. gas reserves and production. As for other alternatives, including green technologies such as wind and solar energy, Kunstler says they can only help marginally, at best.

The bottom line for Kunstler and his fellow doomsters is that the planet now has far too many people and that lots of them will die premature deaths because their food supply and basic needs are heavily energy dependent, and we are running out of oil. There is even a term for this process—the "die-off" (not to mention a website, www.dieoff.org, and well over a million Google citations for the term).

How many will die off? Kunstler is a bit vague on the number, but he is certain that the sustainable population of the United States will be similar to that in the late 19th century, before oil became widely used. Thus, in his view, the United States could shrink to 75 or even 50 million by 2100. The world's population may fall to just a billion, and the most pessimistic doomsters—who see agriculture as a multimillennium failed experiment—caution that the world could be down to tens of millions.

The Politics and Unpredictability of Growth

A major factor in population growth is choice. As a nation, voters shape the public policy that can alter the course of how many people live in the United States and where they will live. For example, a dramatic shift in public opinion can produce a new politics of immigration. Recent anti-immigration legislation in Arizona (S.B. 1070) points to perhaps a more hostile mood toward newcomers. Immigrants and the children born to immigrants make up such a large share of the projected population growth that even slight changes to the numbers entering the United States over the next decade could dramatically alter the final estimate of how many people America will add over this century.

Predicting population growth is also like forecasting the weather—the further into the future one estimates, the less accurate the forecast. In predicting the weather, one can rely on a high statistical probability that the forecast will be accurate a few days out but that there will be a dramatic fall-off in predictability with each additional day. Population is much more stable than the weather, and the time horizon for prediction is longer. Days become years and decades; and in the end, both meteorology and demography often miss the mark.

Thus, population projections to the mid-21st century are more likely to be accurate than those extended out 100 years. Even so, adjustments to population projections are common. For example, when the U.S. population reached 300 million in 2006, the Census Bureau forecast that the nation would add another 100 million residents by 2043. In August 2008, however, the Census Bureau adjusted this estimate to reflect a faster than expected growth rate. Now the Census Bureau predicts the U.S. population will reach 400 million by 2039. With the 2010 Census showing growth slowing at the very end of the last decade, this benchmark could slide back into the 2040s. If we are now in a decade that produces sharply lower population growth, the United States may not reach 400 million until after 2050. Nevertheless, despite the small fluctuations in this projection, it is very likely that the U.S. population will be at 400 million by mid-century. After that point, the projections become fuzzier.

How Will the United States Stack Up?

Where does this put the United States in the global context? This nation is the only developed country that is on track to add substantial population. Other G-7 nations such as Germany and Japan will likely continue to contract, while the United Kingdom and France will grow slowly. If the United States jumps to 400 million by 2039, it will probably have added 100 million residents faster than all other nations except India and Pakistan, and will even outpace China.

Again, forces within our control will partly determine the rate of growth. If the United States lacks the will or the resources to substantially upgrade its crumbling infrastructure, its economic growth may slow, and that may diminish its attractiveness to immigrants. But if the United States remains open to immigration and its economy booms, we could see the next 100 million people at an even earlier date.

There are also external forces driving immigration, including such push factors as how attractive the United States is compared to other nations. Contrary to all the hype, the baby boomers can retire with some reasonable certainty that they will receive most of what they were promised from Social Security. Barring some breakthrough medical technology that cures old age, all it would take to secure these benefits is a year or two added to the Social Security minimum retirement age and a bit more income subject to payroll taxes (say, a jump from the $106,800 per year as of 2010 to $125,000, and then indexed to inflation thereafter).

Why the rosy forecast for Social Security? You can thank the 1965 immigration reform for that outlook. Just as the baby boom ended, the United States reopened to immigrants. The numbers were small at first, but in the last 20 years they equaled the immigrant boom of the late 19th and early 20th centuries. The result is that there will be more workers per retiree than anyone expected a generation ago, when Social Security taxes were raised substantially.

While the United States has legions of new workers who are rapidly moving into the American mainstream, Europe appears to be on a different track, with lots of retirees and few workers. Further, many immigrants in Europe remain unassimilated even after a multigeneration tenure in a European Union country.

We can envision a Europe that soon takes on the character of an enormous assisted living facility where the elderly are tended to by a resentful and alienated foreign-born workforce. Despite all of America's unsolved problems, one of the great forces adding to its population is that it remains an immigrant nation, whereas most of Europe retains too many sociocultural barriers to help foreign-born residents quickly assimilate.

Who Will Be White?

Many believe that by the mid-21st century, the U.S. population will have a majority of nonwhite residents. It is unlikely, however, that this will ever come to pass. It is more probable that current racial categories will be redefined, and in particular, that the definition of "white" will change.

Because the vast majority of Hispanics are already categorized as a subethnicity under "white," an overwhelmingly large proportion of the country is now "white." The term *minority majority* currently refers mostly to Hispanic whites. While it is true that Hispanic whites are the fastest growing ethnic group, many are intermarrying with non-Hispanic whites. In fact, both Hispanic whites and Asians, which are the fastest growing populations, now often intermarry with non-Hispanic whites.

When Hispanic whites are included, whites indeed form the majority of the U.S. population. By mid-century, it is more likely that the Hispanic ethnic barrier will fade. So, while whites in 2100 may not "look" like whites today, whites as defined by the census will still be the majority. A 2005 report on intermarriage put out by the Population Reference Bureau concluded that "most intermarriage still involves a white person married to a minority spouse. In this sense, intermarriage is 'whitening' U.S. minority populations" (Lee and Edmonston 2005: 33).

"Whiteness" has been redefined before. Early in the 20th century, there was a considerable social distance between Eastern and Southern Europeans (Italians, Russians, and Poles) and Americans descended from northwestern European immigrants who had arrived earlier. The newer groups were "hyphenated whites" or simply "white ethnics." Think of a solidly middle-class, old-stock European American living in 1900 and what that person's attitude might have been toward the "new immigrants" from Southern and Eastern Europe. We know the opinion was not high because in 1924, the older, established groups called for strict immigration laws to keep out other Europeans. People from one part of Europe fought to keep out immigrants from another part of Europe. In today's context that seems almost quaint. A century ago, it was difficult to imagine that northwestern Europeans would routinely intermarry with white ethnics and that their children and grandchildren would form a composite of pan-Europeanism that is now the non-Hispanic white population of the United States.

As a result of intermarriage and assimilation, neighborhoods that had previously been defined as Italian neighborhoods or Jewish neighborhoods came to be known solely as white neighborhoods. By the late 20th century, New York's Little Italy was more of a novelty, a remnant rather than an actual Italian neighborhood. Today, many Americans are products of pan-European marriages. This trend is likely to continue—or rather, accelerate.

The United States may emerge from pan-European to pan-Asian or, more likely, pan-world. President Obama personifies the racial evolution of the United States. In the end, while a residual black-white divide may still remain, the United States will never technically have a minority-majority population.

Where Will Americans Live?

At the turn of the 19th century, the United States was primarily a coastal country, with the majority of the U.S. population residing east of the Appalachian Mountains. But the 19th century was a time of western settlement. Until the 20th century, in fact, much of the nation's growth took the form of frontier expansion. By 1900 the United States had settled vast stretches of the continent, and the Census Bureau had declared the frontier "closed" in the preceding decades.

Every one of today's top 50 metropolitan areas was already established 100 years ago—the last one being Las Vegas in 1905. The subsequent 100 years of development, during the 20th and early 21st centuries, involved tremendous population growth within and extension of these urban areas, including the emergence of the megapolitan Sun Belt in the South and West.

A simple indicator—the center point population estimate—designed by Francis Walker of the Massachusetts Institute of Technology, the census director in 1870 and 1880, vividly showed western movement. This measure, which has been in use by the Census Bureau since 1870 (but projected back to 1790, the first census), is described as "the point at which an imaginary, flat, weightless, and rigid map of the United States would balance perfectly if weights of identical value were placed on it so that each weight represented the location of one person on the date of the census." (See Billings 1902.)

In 1790, this point was 23 miles east of Baltimore in Kent County, Maryland. By 1800 it had jumped the Chesapeake Bay to a spot west of Baltimore, and it has continued to head west ever since. From 1800 to 1940, the center moved pretty much due west from the Mid-Atlantic region, varying just a degree or two north or south every census.

Beginning in 1950, the center of population took a distinctly southern turn, and it has been headed in a southwestern direction since. The turn corresponds to the rise of the Sun Belt, where states such as California, Texas, and Florida emerged as major population centers that dragged the center southward. In 2000, the center stood in south-central Missouri, about 120 miles southwest of the symbolic Gateway Arch in St Louis. The 2010 Census located it just east of Springfield, Missouri.

If the current rate of growth and expansion in the West and the South continues, the center of population in the year 2100 is likely to be somewhere in Oklahoma, along the Turner Turnpike between Tulsa and Oklahoma City, perhaps in Lincoln County or Creek County. This projection is based on the number of decades that the mean center of population has been calculated, projected population growth, and current settlement patterns. It also assumes a relatively stable world climate that does not cause rising sea levels to flood major coastal cities of the South and does not dampen mountain snow packs and monsoonal flows in the West. These are, of course, real possibilities.

2100 and Beyond

Based on the census's middle scenario, by 2100 more than 500 million people will call America home. This is almost double the 2000 population. Our cities will expand to accommodate this additional growth, while the resource base fueling this expansion will become stressed but should not snap.

American ethnic identity will become more complex, and traditional racial and ethnic categories such as white and Hispanic will lose meaning. Intermarriage between whites and minorities will dramatically shift the social definition of racial and ethnic identities. Likewise, neighborhoods will also become more diverse, as ethnic and racial minorities move to suburbs in record numbers, black-white residential segregation continues to decline, and high-income households continue repopulating our cities.

Our plans and policies will shape this future. The ongoing debate over immigration reform may affect the pace and character of future immigration flows. The future of fair housing policy will affect the diversity of our cities and suburbs. Energy and environmental policies will determine the size of the future population's environmental footprint. And transportation policies will influence the economic and social interactions within and among metropolitan areas. Local plans will also continue to play an important role in altering the character and location of where new growth occurs.

Yet one prediction above all seems certain: Most of America's economy, people, and connections to the globe will continue to be megapolitan based. Which megapolitan area grows the fastest or where within megapolitans most people will reside remains unknown. But the rise of megapolitans as the dominant urban feature on the American urban landscape has already happened, and that position seems only likely to be strengthened in this century.

As settlement patterns have evolved, so also have approaches to defining them. Here we review the evolution of the U.S. Census Bureau's concepts of "urbanized area" and "metropolitan area." While the Census Bureau notes that despite its claim that such areas are defined solely for statistical purposes, many federal agency programs use the Census Bureau's definitions as the basis for implementing funding programs and determining qualification for participation in programs, including transportation programs, several health programs, urban and rural housing and development programs, economic assistance programs, and environmental protection programs. This appendix reviews the evolution of census definitions first for urban areas and then for metropolitan areas. In each section, we identify trends in census definitions that may recognize networks of multiple metropolitan areas creating what we call megapolitan areas.

Urban Areas

For more than a century, the Census Bureau has attempted to define what is meant by "urban," and, by default, what is also meant by "rural."[1] Before the 1950 Census, the Census Bureau defined as "urban" any incorporated place with a population of 2,500 or more. This simplistic approach required no calculation of population density or any special understanding of settlement patterns, nor did it account for densely settled areas outside incorporated places. The definition was considered adequate for much of the first half of the 20th century.

By mid-century, however, it had become clear that suburbanization outside the boundaries of cities had to be accounted for. This led to the adoption of the "urbanized area" concept used in the 1950 Census. Census Bureau geographers and demographers recognized that densely settled communities outside the boundaries of incorporated places were just as "urban" as areas inside incorporated places. Because of the technology available at the time for calculating and mapping population density, the delineation of urbanized areas was limited to cities of 50,000 or more population and their surrounding territory. The geographic units used to analyze settlement patterns were called "enumeration districts." To facilitate the mapping delineation process, if the overall population density of an enumeration district met the minimum threshold, it was included in its entirety in the urbanized area. "Urban" outside urbanized areas was still defined as any place (including unincorporated "Census Designated Places") with a population of at least 2,500.

Starting with the 1960 Census and continuing through the 1990 Census, the Census Bureau enhanced its methodology and criteria for identifying urbanized areas but never really changed its basic definition of an "urban" place, considered to be urbanized areas of 50,000 or more population defined on the basis of population density and urban places of 2,500 or more population located outside urbanized areas. Enhancements included:

1. Relaxing and eventually eliminating minimum population criteria for places that met the threshold criteria for delineating an urbanized area (urban areas with population over 50,000).

2. Identifying "extended cities" as incorporated places having substantial amounts of very low-density (less than 100 people per square mile) territory, which were then divided into urban and rural components.

3. Through the use of improved technology available for the 1990 Census, achieving greater flexibility in analyzing and defining urbanized areas, as opposed to using enumeration districts and other measurement units defined prior to improved data tabulation.

4. Changing the qualifying criterion for places to be included in an urbanized area to align with the existence of a densely populated "core" containing at least 50 percent of the place's population.

Two important changes were made to the Census Bureau's "urban" classification in the 2000 Census:

1. Urban clusters of at least 2,500 and less than 50,000 population were identified using the same residential population density–based criteria as applied to urbanized areas. As a result, the Census Bureau no longer identified "urban places located outside urbanized areas."

2. Incorporated place and census-designated place boundaries were ignored in defining urbanized areas and urban clusters. Implementing this change meant that low-density, mostly rural areas inside place boundaries (such as through annexation) would no longer be included in an urban area.

These changes created a consistent way in which to define urban areas. The earlier definitions had resulted in including low-density areas within urbanized areas when the place as a whole met minimum population density thresholds but excluding high-density areas when the place as a whole fell below those thresholds. In addition, because the previous definitions had lacked a density-based standard for defining urban areas of less than 50,000 people, urban areas were underbounded by excluding populations outside place boundaries. This was especially problematic in states where annexation lagged behind the expansion of densely settled areas, or where communities of 2,500–50,000 were not incorporated or were otherwise not defined as census-designated places.

We turn now to the evolution of definitions of a metropolitan area.

Metropolitan Areas

Perhaps more so than definitions of urban areas, definitions of metropolitan areas have undergone a dramatic evolution. While there are many ways in which to characterize agglomerations of cities and areas into metropolitan areas (MAs), or larger spaces, the federal government has assumed leadership to advance its interests. In particular, MAs are a federal statistical standard designed for the preparation, presentation, and comparison of data. Before the MA concept was introduced in 1949 with Standard Metropolitan Areas (SMAs) by the Bureau of the Budget, which is now the Office of Management and Budget (OMB), inconsistencies between statistical area boundaries and units made comparisons of data acquired by federal agencies difficult. MAs are thus defined according to specific, quantitative standards to help government agencies, researchers, and others achieve uniform use and comparability of data on a national scale. We review the evolution of the MA concept, the reasons leading to a major overhaul of the concept used in the 2000 Census, and the current application of the MA concept. In this section we rely almost exclusively on the Census Bureau's own language to describe concepts, historical perspectives, and current applications.[2]

Evolution of the Metropolitan Area Concept

As early as the first years of the 20th century, the federal government recognized the need to identify large cities and their surrounding areas as single geographic entities and to acquire data at that scale for social and economic analysis. Before the adoption of the MA concept in the late 1940s, several other kinds of related geographic areas were defined. These areas were based on different criteria and used by federal agencies for data-reporting purposes. Among these areas were the following:

Industrial Districts. Perhaps the first extensive attempt by the federal government to define areas based on a metropolitan concept was the identification of industrial districts for the 1905 Census of Manufactures. The Census Bureau published manufacturing and population data for 13 industrial districts composed of minor civil divisions (MCDs).

Metropolitan Districts. When adopted by the Census Bureau in 1910, each metropolitan district generally comprised a central city of at least 200,000 persons and all adjacent MCDs with population densities of at least 150 persons per square mile. Beginning in 1930, metropolitan districts were defined for all cities of at least 50,000 persons, with the additional requirement that each metropolitan district have a population of at least 100,000. Metropolitan districts were defined in terms of population density; measures of functional integration (such as commuting) were not used.

Industrial Areas. Industrial areas were introduced by the Census Bureau in the late 1920s for the Census of Manufactures to provide a coherent, integrated unit for reporting data related to industrial activity. Each industrial area comprised a county having an important manufacturing city and adjacent counties with significant concentrations of manufacturing industries. Each of these areas usually employed at least 40,000 factory wage earners. In 1931, there were 33 recognized industrial areas.

Labor Market Areas. Before 1950, labor market areas (LMAs) were defined by the Bureau of Employment Security and consisted of counties and MCDs. Since 1950, the Bureau of Labor Statistics (BLS) has been responsible for defining LMAs. Current LMA definitions use MAs as starting points and consist of aggregations of counties.

Lack of geographic comparability limited the use of data reported for these and other areas. In the mid-1940s, initial efforts to reconcile metropolitan districts and industrial areas failed, in part because of tensions between two groups, demographic data providers and economic data providers. The former wanted to continue using subcounty geographic building blocks to achieve greater precision and to maintain historical comparability with metropolitan districts. The latter had difficulty identifying the precise locations of establishments below the county level and also had concerns about the availability and confidentiality of subcounty data.

The Interagency Committee on Standard Metropolitan Areas decided in March 1948 that counties would form the building blocks of SMAs. The committee cited the greater availability of data for counties and concluded that use of a unit other than the county would restrict the amount of information available for SMAs and, consequently, would reduce the usefulness of the concept.

SMAs were first used for reporting data from the 1947 Census of Manufactures. The conceptual basis of the SMA was a community of nonagricultural workers who resided in and around a large city and were socially and economically linked with the central city as measured by commuting flows and telephone calls.

Changes to the standards since their adoption for the 1950 decennial census to 1990 are detailed in Table A.1. Few significant changes were made through the 1960s; those that were made affected the designation of central cities forming the cores of MAs. The standards became more complex in the 1970s and 1980s, in part to recognize the increasing variation in patterns of urban settlement. Requirements for central cities were adjusted for the 1980s, with the result that more cities were designated as central. Additional changes at that time meant MAs included fewer outlying counties, which needed to satisfy commuting requirements as well as a number of other criteria, including population growth rate, percent urban population, percent of population living inside an urban area, and overall population density. The 1990 (current) standards differ only modestly from those of the previous decade.

Since their adoption in the late 1940s, the MA standards have acknowledged that within states in New England, cities and towns are administratively more important than counties, and that a wide variety of data are compiled for these areas. For these reasons, cities and towns have been used as the building blocks of MAs in New England. The nonagricultural worker requirement that was present in the earlier standards was not applied in New England. Also, population density requirements differed between New England and elsewhere.

The standards for New England MAs remain different from the standards for the rest of the country. New England County Metropolitan Areas (NECMAs) as county-based alternatives to the city- and town-based MAs of that region were introduced in 1975 to facilitate comparisons between areas in New England and elsewhere.

In addition to MAs, other statistical area classifications currently are in use. These include:

Labor Market Areas. The BLS currently defines LMAs, which are used for a variety of purposes, including reporting local area unemployment statistics. LMAs follow county boundaries except in New England, where towns and cities are the geographic building blocks. The BLS defines major LMAs based on Metropolitan Statistical Areas (MSAs) and Primary Metropolitan Statistical Areas (PMSAs) as defined by the OMB. Outside of MAs, the BLS defines small LMAs by aggregating counties (or towns) on the basis of commuting. LMAs are nonoverlapping and geographically exhaustive.

Economic Areas. The Bureau of Economic Analysis (BEA) defines economic areas (EAs) for reporting geographically detailed economic data and for regional economic analysis. In delineating EAs, the BEA identifies economic nodes. These nodes consist of 310 MSAs and PMSAs (NECMAs in New England), plus 38 nonmetropolitan counties. Each county not included in these nodes is analyzed to determine the node with which it is most closely associated. Measures such as commuting patterns and regional newspaper circulation are used to aggregate counties into "component economic areas," which are then aggregated to form the final EAs. EAs are county-based, nonoverlapping, and geographically exhaustive.

The MA concept is part of a historical lineage of statistical geographic areas and is one of several current statistical geographic unit concepts used by federal agencies for reporting data.

Reasons for the Major Overhaul of Definitions for 2000

The MA standards, like other statistical standards, require review to ensure their continued usefulness. Previous reviews and revisions of the MA standards were completed in 1958, 1971, 1975, 1980, and 1990. During the 1990s, four widely held opinions regarding the existing MA standards argued for their revision:

1. Many users believed the existing standards were overly complex and burdened with ad hoc criteria. Simplifying the standards would improve the chances that the system and its associated data would be understood.

2. The MA concept had not changed significantly since 1950, yet population distribution and activity patterns in the United States had changed as a result of changes in transportation and other technologies, home/workplace relationships, and patterns of retail and other commercial location. Revised MA standards would better represent increasingly decentralized settlement and activity patterns.

3. Computer-related advances in data collection, storage, and analysis, especially in technologies related to data geocoding (data linked to their geographic location of occurrence), made it feasible to consider a subcounty unit as the basic geographic building block for constructing statistical areas to represent settlement.

4. MAs did not exhaustively classify the territory of the United States. As a result, social and economic linkages within the residual nonmetropolitan territory were not taken into account appropriately in statistical data series.

Current Core-Based Criteria Applied to the 2000 Census

Before the 2000 Census, the term "metropolitan area" (MA) was used and referred collectively to Metropolitan Statistical Areas (MSAs), Consolidated Metropolitan Statistical areas (CMSAs), and Primary Metropolitan Statistical Areas (PMSAs). The term "Core Based Statistical Area" (CBSA) became effective in 2000 and refers collectively to Metropolitan and Micropolitan Statistical Areas. The essential concept of a Metropolitan Statistical Area or a Micropolitan Statistical Area is that of an area containing a recognized population nucleus and adjacent communities with a high degree of integration with that nucleus.

The 2000 standards provide that each CBSA must contain at least one urban area of 10,000 or more population. Each Metropolitan Statistical Area must have at least one urbanized area of 50,000 or more inhabitants. Each Micropolitan Statistical Area must have at least one urban cluster of at least 10,000 but less than 50,000 residents.

Under the standards, the county (or counties) in which at least 50 percent of the population resides within urban areas of 10,000 or more population, or that contain at least 5,000 people residing within a single urban area of 10,000 or more population, is identified as a "central county" (counties). Additional "outlying counties" are included in the CBSA if they meet specified requirements of commuting to or from the central counties. Counties or equivalent entities form the geographic "building blocks" for Metropolitan and Micropolitan Statistical Areas throughout the United States and Puerto Rico.

If specified criteria are met, a metropolitan statistical area containing a single core with a population of 2.5 million or more may be subdivided to form smaller groupings of counties referred to as "metropolitan divisions." By the 2010 Census, there were 363 Metropolitan Statistical Areas and 577 Micropolitan Statistical Areas in the United States. (There were also eight Metropolitan Statistical Areas and five Micropolitan Statistical Areas in Puerto Rico.)

The largest city in each Metropolitan or Micropolitan Statistical Area is designated a "principal city." Additional cities qualify if specified requirements are met concerning population size and employment. The title (name) of each Metropolitan or Micropolitan Statistical Area consists of the names of up to three of its principal cities and the name of each state into which the Metropolitan or Micropolitan Statistical Area extends. Titles of metropolitan divisions also typically are based on principal city names but in certain cases consist of county names.

In view of the importance of cities and town in New England, the 2000 standards also provide for a set of geographic areas that are defined using cities and towns in the six New England states. The New England City and Town Areas (NECTAs) are defined using the same criteria as Metropolitan and Micropolitan Statistical Areas and are identified as either metropolitan or micropolitan based on the presence respectively of either an urbanized area of 50,000 or more population or an urban cluster of at least 10,000 but less than 50,000 population. If the specified criteria are met, a NECTA containing a single core with a population of at least 2.5 million may be subdivided to form smaller groupings of cities and towns, referred to as New England City and Town Area Divisions.

Changes since the 2000 Census

Very little changed in 2010 from the methodology used in the 2000 Census. At the recommendation of the Metropolitan and Micropolitan Statistical Area Standards Review Committee (or Review Committee), modifications have been made to the use of Combined Statistical Areas (CSAs). The Census Bureau also solicited comments on proposed changes to the urban and rural delineation methodology and on the elimination of the central place concept. (The comment period closed November 22, 2010.)

The Census Bureau adopted changes to the CSA concept at the recommendation of the Review Committee. The 2000 standards allowed the combination of areas with an "employment interchange measure" (or EIM) of between 15 and 25 to selectively choose to become a CSA, based on local opinion. Selective participation in CSAs led to ambiguous and incomplete statistics.

The 2010 standards eliminate the use of public opinion in CSAs with an EIM between 15 and 25. Consequently, participation in CSAs is no longer voluntary or experimental. CBSAs now qualify as a CSAs if they are "a geographic entity consisting of two or more adjacent Core Based Statistical Areas with employment interchange measure of at least 15." Further, the OMB eliminated the use of local opinion in titling CSAs. Each CSA is titled using the names of the two largest principal cities, as well as the name of the third largest principal city, if applicable.

The OMB adopted these changes to improve the comparability of CSAs. The enhancements give the federal statistical data community the credibility and consistency needed to use CSAs as a geographic tool in identifying and tracking urban trends. As such, CSAs are now firmly in place as part of the official U.S. metropolitan geography. Moreover, they are the best geographic tool for identifying the megapolitan formations of 2040.

In addition, for the 2010 Census the Census Bureau used the 2000 Census urban area delineation methodology for determining urban and rural areas. However, as with previous censuses, they sought comment on the specific criteria for addressing urban-rural classification. The Census Bureau anticipated the cumbersome nature of such large urban agglomerates to data users: "Use of this approach will result in some exceptionally large urban agglomeration of continuously developed territory. Although such areas do not reflect the reality of urbanization at one scale, the areas may be cumbersome and less satisfactory for more localized applications. For example, an area of virtually continuous urbanization exists from northeastern Maryland through the Philadelphia area, central New Jersey, the New York City area, and central Connecticut to beyond Springfield, MA. This area of near-continuous urbanization encompasses nine UAs defined for Census 2000" (*Federal Register*, August 24, 2010). For the first time the census combines New York and Philadelphia to create a region of 30 million people that sweeps over a dozen metropolitan areas. This geography mostly matches the megapolitan area definition for New York–Philadelphia used in this book.

The OMB adopted changes to outlying counties. A county qualifies as an outlying county of a CBSA if it meets one of the following commuting requirements: at least 25 percent of the workers living in the county work in the central county or counties of the CBSA, or at least 25 percent of the employment in the county is accounted for by workers who reside in the central county or counties of the CBSA. "Outlying counties of CBSAs that qualify after the first delineation (in 2013) will qualify on the basis of American Community Survey 5-year commuting estimates."

The Census Bureau proposed eliminating the identification of central places as part of the urban area delineation process. A "central place" is the most populous place within an urban area or any other place that meets specified population criteria. Since the 1990 Census, the identification of central places was no longer necessary for the process of delineating urban areas. In the 2000 Census, the urban delineation process moved away from a place-based definition of urban areas, which caused some central places to be split between urban and rural territory, in favor of identifying principal cities as part of the Metropolitan and Micropolitan Statistical Areas program. The identification and representation of central cities are similar to that for principal cities; therefore, the identification of central cities is no longer needed.

Table A.1 summarizes the evolution of the metropolitan concept into the 2010s.

Table A-1. Evolution of the "Metropolitan" Concept

Decade	Area Name	Central City and Central Core Criteria	Minimum Measures of Integration for Outlying County	Minimum Measures of Metropolitan Character for Outlying County
1950s	Standard Metropolitan Area	City of 50,000 or more population	• 15% or more commuting to central county, **OR** • 25% or more of the jobs in the county accounted for by commuting from central county, **OR** • at least four phone calls per subscriber per month to central county	• 10,000 or more nonagricultural workers, **OR** • 10% or more of the nonagricultural workers in MA, **OR** • 50% or more of population residing in MCDs with population density of at least 150 persons per square mile and contiguous to central city, • two-thirds or more of labor force must be nonagricultural
1960s	Standard Metropolitan Statistical Area	City of 50,000 or more population **OR** two contiguous cities with combined population of 50,000 or more	• 15% or more commuting to central county, **OR** • 25% or more of the jobs in the county accounted for by commuting from central county	• 75% or more of labor force must be nonagricultural, **AND** • 50% or more of population residing in contiguous MCDs with population density of at least 150 persons per square mile, **OR** • nonagricultural employment of the central county of at least 10,000, **OR** • number of nonagricultural workers residing in county is either at least 10% of nonagricultural workers residing in central county or at least 10,000

(continued)

Table A-1. Evolution of the "Metropolitan" Concept (continued)

Decade	Area Name	Central City and Central Core Criteria	Minimum Measures of Integration for Outlying County	Minimum Measures of Metropolitan Character for Outlying County
1970s	Standard Metropolitan Area	City of 50,000 or more population, **OR** city of at least 25,000 population together with contiguous places of population densities of at least 1,000 persons per square mile having a combined population of at least 50,000 in a county of at least 75,000 population	30% or more commuting to central county	• 75% or more of labor force must be nonagricultural, If less than 30% commute to central county, must meet two of the following: • 25% or more of population urban • 15% population growth rate • density of 50 or more persons per square mile and one of the following: 15% or more commuting to central county 15% or more commuting from central county 20% or more commuting exchange with central county
1980s	• Metropolitan Statistical Area (MSA) • Consolidated Metropolitan Statistical Area (CMSA) • Primary Metropolitan Statistical Area (PMSA) • New England County Metropolitan Area (NECMA)	• UA of at least 50,000 population • If largest city has less than 50,000 population, MSA/CMSA must have at least 100,000 population • Central cities include largest city in MSA and each city of at least 250,000 population or 100,000 workers **AND** each of at least 250,000 population or 100,000 workers **AND** each city of at least 25,000 population and 75 jobs per 100 workers and less than 60% out commuting **AND** each city of at least 15,000 population that is at least one-third the size of the largest central city and meets employment ratio and commuting percentage above	Commuting: 50% or more and → 40% or more and → 25% or more and → 15% or more and →	Character: 25 or more persons per square mile, **OR** 35 or more persons per square mile, **OR** 35 or more persons per square mile and one of the following: • 50 or more persons per square mile • 35% or more urban population • 10% or more of population, or at least 5,000 persons in UA, **OR** 50 or more persons per square mile and two of the following: • 60 or more persons per square mile • 35% or more urban population • population growth rate of at least 20% • 10% or more of population, or at least 5,000 persons in UA

(continued)

Table A-1. Evolution of the "Metropolitan" Concept (*continued*)

Decade	Area Name	Central City and Central Core Criteria	Minimum Measures of Integration for Outlying County	Minimum Measures of Metropolitan Character for Outlying County
1990s	Metropolitan Areas: • MSA • CMSA • PMSA • NECMA	• City of at least 50,000 population, **OR** • UA of at least 50,000 population in an MA of at least 100,000 population • Central cities include largest city of at least 250,000 population or at least 100,000 workers **AND** each city of at least 25,000 population and at least 75 jobs per 100 workers and less than 60% out commuting **AND** each city of at least 15,000 population that is at least 1/3 size of largest central city and meets employment ratio and commuting percentage above **AND** largest city of 15,000 population or more that meets employment ratio and commuting percentage above and is in a secondary noncontiguous UA **AND** each city in a secondary noncontiguous UA that is at least 1/3 size of largest central city of that UA and has at least 15,000 population and meets employment ratio and commuting percentage above.	Commuting: 50% or more and → 40% to 50% and → 25% to 40% and → 15% to 25% and → 15% to 25% and →	Character: 25 or more persons per square mile, or 10% or more of population, or at least 5,000 persons in UA , **OR** 35 or more persons per square mile, or 10% or more of population, or at least 5,000 persons in UA, **OR** 35 or more persons per square mile and one of the following: • 50 or more persons per square mile • 35% or more urban population • 10% or more of population or at least 5,000 persons in UA, **OR** 50 or more persons per square mile and two of the following: • 60 or more persons per square mile • 35% or more urban population • population growth rate of at least 20% • 10% or more of population, or at least 5,000 persons in UA Less than 50 persons per square mile and two of the following: • 35% or more urban population • population growth rate of at least 20% • 10% or more of population, or at least 5,000 persons in UA
2000s	Principal City, Core-Based Statistical Area (CBSA) Metropolitan Statistical Area (MetroSA), Micropolitan Statistical Area (MicroSA), Combined Statistical Area (CSA), New England City and Town Area (NECTA)	• Principal city is largest city in each MetroSA or MicroSA • CBSA contains population core, defined as MetroSA or MicroSA • MetroSA has a population of at least 50,000 • MicroSA has a population of at least 10,000 to 49,999 • CSAs have two or more adjacent CBSAs with employment interchange of at least 25%, adjacent CBSA with an employment interchange of 15 to 25% may be combined if local opinion in both areas favor combining	Commuting: 25% or more →	Character: workers living in the county work in the central county or counties, **OR** at least 25% of employment in the county accounted for by workers who reside in the central county or counties of the CBSA

(continued)

Table A-1. Evolution of the "Metropolitan" Concept (*continued*)

Decade	Area Name	Central City and Central Core Criteria	Minimum Measures of Integration for Outlying County	Minimum Measures of Metropolitan Character for Outlying County
2010s	Principal City, Metropolitan Statistical Area (MetroSA), Micropolitan Statistical Area (MicroSA), Combined Statistical Area (CSA), New England City and Town Area (NECTA)	• Proposed elimination of central city concept in favor of principal city concept • CBSA contains population core, defined as MetroSA or MicroSA • MetroSA has a population of at least 50,000 • MicroSA has a population of at least 10,000 to 49,999 • CSAs are two or more adjacent CBSAs with employment interchange of 15% regardless of local opinion	Commuting: 25% or more →	Character: workers living in the county work in the central county or counties, **OR** at least 25% of the employment in the county is accounted for by workers who reside in the central county or counties of the CBSA

NOTES

Prologue

1. According to Baigent (2004, 687), the term *megalopolis*, "meaning a large city, was in general press by the 1820s." The first scholarly use of "megalopolis" was by the English urban planner Patrick Geddes in 1927 (Thomas 2000). The word was originally a pejorative term for overgrown cities.

2. Gottmann used the term *megapolitan* as an adjectival form of megalopolis, as he does in the epigraph at the start of this section of the Prologue..

3. Even if the Census Bureau does not designate megapolitans in the short term, using existing census categories as basic building blocks creates a census-compatible geography that planning agencies could adopt.

4. The authors thank Robert Yaro, the current Regional Plan Association president, for suggesting a history of megapolitan thinking and providing guidance on the recent evolution of the idea.

5. Boris Pushkarev, the RPA's chief planner in 1967, was the principal author of "The Atlantic Urban Region."

6. It covered about a 150-county area that approximates the Megalopolis megapolitan cluster composed of the New England, New York–Philadelphia, and Chesapeake megapolitan areas that we develop in Chapter 3.

7. The RPA report significantly overestimated population growth in the Atlantic urban region as a result of using base years that included the peak of the baby boom. Yet despite there being fewer people than expected in the Northeast, the amount of current settled area looks similar to what the RPA predicted. This indicates that the Atlantic urban region has thinned out owing to fast growth at the low-density fringe.

8. The Dulles Corridor, sometimes referred to as the "Silicon Dominion," played a vital role in starting the Internet.

Chapter 2

1. See Innes, Booher, and Di Vittorio (2010) for a discussion of approaches to managing issues affecting multiple metropolitan areas.

Chapter 3

1. The long-term effect of the Internet, e-mail, and other social media on economic geography is difficult to predict. Moss and Townsend (2000) argue that the Internet is the backbone of the modern American metropolis, yet not in the way normally viewed. Conventional thinking holds that the Internet acts as a leveling technology among regions, but this has not been the case. While a high percentage of households across the nation and an even higher percentage of businesses use the Internet, economically lagging areas remain disconnected from the emerging American economy. Moss and Townsend worry that the Internet may actually aggravate economic disparity among regions, yet they pose no explanation.

It would also seem that telecommunications and the Internet might allow innovation to occur across the nation, yet this is also not the case. Lim (2003) demonstrates that the spatial distribution of population in the United States during the 1990s became more concentrated in clusters of metropolitan areas, not less. He concludes that the spatial distribution of innovation is highly concentrated in a relatively small number of metropolitan areas, including both coasts, the New England–Mid-Atlantic area, the Front Range, and emerging clusters in the South.

2. These include counties, boroughs, parishes, independent cities, and combinations thereof, as applied to Alaska, Colorado, Hawaii, New Mexico, and Virginia.

Chapter 4

1. This discussion is adapted substantially from "Measuring Rurality: Rural-Urban Continuum Codes," available at www.ers.usda.gov/briefing/rurality/ruralurbcon.

2. This coding scheme was originated in 1975 by David L. Brown, Fred K. Hines, and John M. Zimmer, then of the USDA's Economic Research Service, for the report *Social and Economic Characteristics of the Population in Metro and Nonmetro Counties: 1970*. It was updated after both the 1980 and 1990 Censuses, with more restrictive procedures use for determining metropolitan area adjacency.

3. This discussion is adapted substantially from "Measuring Rurality: Urban Influence Codes," available at www.ers.usda.gov/Briefing/Rurality/UrbanInf.

Chapter 5

1. For elaboration, see Scott and Marshall (2009). The core-periphery theory is also used in Marxist theory to help explain the world order of economic, political, and military power. Our focus here is on the regional economic application that helps explain how metropolitan areas grow, evolve, and advance while the nonmetropolitan periphery lags.

2. See www.ers.usda.gov/Briefing/Rurality/Typology/Methods.

Chapter 7

1. Data from www.census.gov/ipc/www/idb.

2. In particular, we use, with permission, Woods & Poole Economics, *The Complete Economic and Demographic Data Source* (2010).

3. See http.census.gov/Press-Release/www/releases/archives/population/012496.html.

4. To be sure, individual metropolitan areas, micropolitan areas, counties, and places outside megapolitan areas will certainly be majority minority, but the overall point is made about the potential geographically based ethnic divide that is looming.

5. The baby boom birth years are considered to be 1946 through 1964.

Chapter 8

1. Data from U.S. Bureau of the Census 1975 and U.S. Bureau of the Census 2008.

2. These estimates are based on the Commercial Buildings Energy Consumption Survey series for 1992, 1997, and 2002, published by the Energy Information Administration of the U.S. Department of Energy.

3. U.S. Census Bureau, Population Estimates Program, Report GCT-T9-R. "Housing Units." Available at http://factfinder.census.gov/servlet/GCTTable?_bm=y&-geo_id=01000US&-_box_head_nbr=GCT-T9-R&-ds_name=PEP_2007_EST&-redoLog=false&-format=US-9Sh&-mt_name=ACS_2006_EST_G00_GCT2501_US36&-CONTEXT=gct.

4. Comparable analyses were done using data from the Census Bureau's American Housing Survey for the period 1991–2001 and the Energy Information Administration's Residential Energy Consumption Survey.

5. Many states, in contrast, report only full-time-equivalent jobs, or only jobs associated with firms paying workers' compensation, thus excluding self-employed persons and part-time workers.

Chapter 9

1. As late as the mid-1990s, most of the road (U.S. 93) between Las Vegas and Phoenix remained a two-lane WPA-era highway. Its twisting roads and view-obstructing hills earned it the rubric of one of the most dangerous stretches of heavily traveled roads in the United States. The Arizona Department of Transportation took on the project of incrementally improving the road, and most of the highway today is four lanes wide. Yet U.S. 93 is still not an interstate because it lacks integration into both the Las Vegas and the Phoenix freeway networks, and there are no interstate-grade bridges and ramps to separate traffic.

2. New York to Washington ranked first, Philadelphia to Washington ranked second, Boston to New York ranked third, and Baltimore to New York ranked fourth.

3. The Acela line is an HSR in the Northeast megalopolis that runs from Boston to Washington, D.C. The train is capable of high-speed travel but is slowed by old alignments that run through the dense urban fabric of the Northeast. The train also makes numerous stops.

Chapter 10

1. See Table 350, Statistical Abstract of the United States, Census Bureau (2009).

2. See Nelson in Steinemann et al. 2004.

3. See www.agcensus.usda.gov/Publications/2007/Full_Report/Volume_1,_Chapter_1_US/usappxb.pdf.

4. See Nelson and Duncan (1995).

5. See http://water.usgs.gov/watuse.

6. Irrigation accounts for 65 percent of all water use in the United States. See http://pubs.usgs.gov/circ/2004/circ1268.

7. See Tri-State Water Rights Litigation, Case No. 3:07-md-01 (PAM/JRK), U.S. District Court, Middle District of Florida, July 17, 2009.

APPENDIX

1. See Mike Ratcliffe, "What Is Going On with Urbanized Area Boundaries?" Available at www.edthefed.com/uza/UA_Update.pdf.

2. Much of this discussion is adapted from documents made available by the U.S. Census Bureau: www.census.gov/population/www/metroareas/aboutmetro.html, http://www.census.gov/population/www/metroareas/files/00-32997.txt, www.census.gov/population/www/metroareas/files/98-33676.txt, and www.census.gov/population/www/metroareas/files/98-33676.pdf.

REFERENCES AND SELECTED BIBLIOGRAPHY

Abbott, Carl. 1993. *The Metropolitan Frontier: Cities in the Modern American West*. Tucson: University of Arizona Press.

Allmendinger, Philip. 2002. *Planning Theory*. Hampshire, U.K.: Palgrave.

Alonso, William. 1968. "Urban and Regional Imbalance in Economic Development." *Economic Development and Cultural Change* 17:1–14.

Altshuler, Alan. 1965. *The City Planning Process*. Ithaca, N.Y.: Cornell University Press.

Anderson, Margo J. 1988. *The American Census: A Social History*. New Haven, Conn.: Yale University Press.

Babbie, Earl R. 2001. *Practice of Social Research*. Belmont, Calif.: Wadsworth.

Baerwald, Thomas. 1982. "Land Use Change in Suburban Clusters and Corridors." *Transportation Research Record* 861:7–12.

Baigent, Elizabeth. 2004. "Patrick Geddes, Lewis Mumford and Jean Gottmann: Divisions Over Megalopolis." *Progress in Human Geography* 28 (6): 687–700.

Baldassare, Mark, Joshua Hassol, William Hoffman, and Abby Kanarek. 1996. "Possible Planning Roles for Regional Government." *JAPA* 62 (1): 17–26.

Bartik, T. J. 1990. "Market Failure Approach to Regional Economic Development." *Economic Development Quarterly* 4 (4): 361–70.

Berry, Brian, and Quentin Gillard. 1977. *The Changing Shape of Metropolitan America*. Cambridge, Mass.: Ballinger.

Berube, Alan, Bruce Katz, and Robert E. Lang, eds. 2006. *Redefining Cities and Suburbs: Evidence from Census 2000*, vols. 2 and 3. Washington, D.C.: Brookings Institution Press.

Berube, Alan, Audrey Singer, Jill Wilson, and William Frey. 2006. *Finding Exurbia: America's Fast-Growing Communities at the Metropolitan Fringe*. Brookings Institution Living Cities Census Series. Washington, D.C.: Brookings Institution.

Billings, John S. 1902. *Biographical Memoir of Francis Amasa Walker 1840–1897*. Washington, D.C.: National Academy Press.

Blanton, Whit. 2000. "Integrating Land Use and Transportation." *Planning Commissioners Journal* 40:9–13.

Bloom, Craig. 1986. "Strategic Planning in the Public Sector." *Journal of Planning Literature* 1 (2): 253–58.

Bluestone, Barry, and Bennett Harrison. 1982. *Deindustrialization of America*. New York: Basic Books.

Blumenfeld, Hans. 1986. "Metropolis Extended: Secular Changes in Settlement Patterns." *JAPA* 52 (3): 346–48.

Bolan, Richard. 1980. "The Practitioner as Theorist: The Phenomenology of the Professional Episode." *JAPA* 46 (3): 261–74.

Bolan, Richard, and Peng Xu. 2004. *Spatial Patterns of Information Workers in Six United States Metropolitan Areas*. Minneapolis: University of Minnesota, Humphrey Institute of Public Affairs.

Bolton, R. 1992. "Place Prosperity versus People Prosperity Revisited: An Old Issue with a New Angle." *Urban Studies* 29 (2): 185–203.

Bozeman, Barry. 1987. *All Organizations Are Public*. San Francisco: Jossey-Bass.

———. 2000. *Bureaucracy and Red Tape*. Upper Saddle River, N.J.: Prentice-Hall.

Brewer, Gary. 1973. *Politicians, Bureaucrats and the Consultant: A Critique of Urban Problem Solving*. New York: Basic Books.

Brooks, David. 2004. *On Paradise Drive: How We Live Now (and Always Have) in the Future Tense*. New York: Simon and Schuster.

Brooks, Michael. 2002. *Planning Theory for Practitioners*. Chicago: APA Planners Press.

Brown, David L., Fred K. Hines, and John M. Zimmer. 1970. *Social and Economic Characteristics of the Population in Metro and Nonmetro Counties*. Washington, D.C.: Economic Research Service, U.S. Department of Agriculture.

Brown, Marilyn, Frank Southworth, and Andrea Sarzynski. 2008. *Shrinking the Carbon Footprint of Metropolitan America*. Washington, D.C.: Brookings Institution.

Bruegmann, Robert. 2005. *Sprawl: A Compact History*. Chicago: University of Chicago Press.

Burgess, Ernest. 1925. "Growth of the City." In *The City*, ed. Robert Park, Ernest Burgess, and R. D. McKenzie. Chicago: University of Chicago Press.

Calhoun, Craig, Joseph Gerteis, James Moody, Steven Pfaff, Kathryn Schmidt, and Indermohan Virk, eds. 2002. *Classical Sociological Theory*. Malden, Mass.: Blackwell.

Calthorpe, Peter, and William Fulton. 2001. *Regional City: Planning for the End of Sprawl*. Washington, D.C.: Island Press.

Campbell, Scott, and Susan Fainstein, eds. 1996. *Readings in Planning Theory*. Malden, Mass.: Blackwell.

Carbonell, Armando, and Robert D. Yaro. 2005. "American Spatial Development and the New Megalopolis." *Land Lines* 17 (2): 1–4.

Cartwright, Timothy. 1973. "Problems, Solutions, and Strategies: A Contribution to the Theory and Practice of Planning." *JAIP* 39 (3): 179–87.

Castells, Manuel. 1996. *The Rise of Network Society*. London: Blackwell.

Cervero, Robert. 1998. *Transit Metropolis: A Global Inquiry*. Washington, D.C.: Island Press.

Champion, A. 2001. "A Changing Demographic Regime and Evolving Polycentric Urban Regions: Consequences for the Size, Composition, and Distribution of City Populations." *Urban Studies* 38 (4): 657–77.

Chapin, Timothy S., Charles E. Connerly, and Harrison T. Higgins. 2010. *Growth Management in Florida*. Aldershot, Hampshire, U.K.: Ashgate.

Chapple, Julian. 2004. "The Dilemma Posed by Japan's Population Decline." *Electronic Journal of Contemporary Japanese Studies*. Available at www.japanesestudies.org.uk/discussionpapers/Chapple.html.

Checkoway, Brian. 1980. "Large Builders, Federal Housing Programs, and Postwar Suburbanization." *International Journal of Urban and Regional Research* 4:21–45.

Chen, Don. 2001. *Americans Want Smarter Growth*. Washington, D.C.: Smart Growth America.

Christaller, Walter. 1966. *Central Places in Southern Germany*, trans. C. W. Baskin. London: Prentice Hall. Originally published as *Die zentralen Orte in Suddeutschland* (Jena, Germany: Fischer, 1933).

Chute, Charlton F. 1956. "Today's Urban Regions." *National Municipal Review* 45 (6–7): 274–80.

Coase, Ronald H. 1937. "Nature of the Firm." *Economica* 4 (November): 386–405.

Cohen, Mitchell, and Nicole Fermon, eds. 1996. *Princeton Readings in Political Thought: Essential Texts since Plato*. Princeton, N.J.: Princeton University Press.

Collins, George R. 1959. "The Ciudad Lineal of Madrid." *Journal of the Society of Architectural Historians* 18 (2): 38–53.

Cooke, P., and K. Morgan. 1993. "The Network Paradigm: New Departures in Corporate and Regional Development." *Environment and Planning D* 11:543–64.

Copeland, Larry. 2005. "Texas Is Set to Supersize Highways." *USA Today*, March 9, A3.

Creswell, John W. 1994. *Research Design: Qualitative & Quantitative Approaches*. Thousand Oaks, Calif.: Sage.

Cronon, William. 1991. *Nature's Metropolis: Chicago and the Great American West*. New York: W. W. Norton.

Daft, Richard. 1995. *Organization Theory and Design*. St. Paul, Minn.: West.

Dalton, Linda. 1986. "Why the Rational Paradigm Persists: The Resistance of Professional Education and Practice to Alternative Forms of Planning." *JPER* 5 (3): 147–53.

Daniels, Thomas L. 2004. "Measuring the Performance of Urban Growth Boundaries." Association of Collegiate Schools of Planning Conference, October 21, 2004, Portland, Oreg.

Daniels, Thomas L., and Katherine Daniels. 2003. *The Environmental Planning Handbook for Sustainable Communities and Regions*. Chicago: APA Planners Press.

Darwent, D. F. 1969. "Growth Poles and Growth Centers in Regional Planning: A Review." *Environment and Planning* 1 (1): 5–31.

Davis, Judy S., Arthur C. Nelson, and Kenneth J. Dueker. 1994. "The New 'Burbs.'" *JAPA* 60 (1): 45–60.

Dear, Michael, ed. 2002. *From Chicago to LA: Making Sense of Urban Theory*. Thousand Oaks, Calif.: Sage.

DeMers, Michael N. 2000. *Fundamentals of Geographic Information Systems*. New York: John Wiley and Sons.

Dewar, Margaret, and David Epstein. 2007. "Planning for 'Megaregions' in the United States." *Journal of Planning Literature* 22 (2): 108–24.

Downs, Anthony. 1992. *Stuck in Traffic: Coping with Peak Hour Traffic Congestion*. Washington, D.C.: Brookings Institution Press.

———. 1999. "Some Realities about Sprawl and Urban Decline." *Housing Policy Debate* 10 (4): 955–74.

Duany, Andres, Elizabeth Plater-Zyberk, and Jeff Speck. 2000. *Suburban Nation*. New York: North Point Press.

El Nasser, Haya, and Paul Overberg. 2001. "A Comprehensive Look at Sprawl in America." *USA Today*, February 22, A3.

Etzioni, Amitai. 1973. "Mixed Scanning: A Third Approach to Decision-making." *Public Administration Review* 27 (5): 385–92.

———. 1986. "Mixed Scanning Revisited." *Public Administration Review* 46 (1): 8–14.

Ewing, Reid. 1997. "Is Los Angeles–Style Sprawl Desirable?" *JAPA* 63 (1): 107–26.

———. 2005. "Can the Physical Environment Determine Physical Activity Levels?" *Exercise and Sport Sciences Review* 33 (2): 69–75.

Ewing, Reid, Keith Bartholomew, Steve Winkelman, Jerry Walters, and Don Chen. 2007. *Growing Cooler: The Evidence on Urban Development and Climate Change*. Washington, D.C.: Urban Land Institute.

Ewing, Reid, John Kostyack, Don Chen, Bruce Stein, and Michelle Ernst. 2005. *Endangered by Sprawl: How Runaway Development Threatens America's Wildlife*. Washington, D.C.: National Wildlife Federation and Smart Growth America.

Ewing, Reid, Rolf Pendall, and Don Chen. 2003. *Measuring Sprawl and Its Impact*. Washington, D.C.: Smart Growth America.

Faludi, Andreas, ed. 2002. *European Spatial Planning*. Cambridge, Mass.: Lincoln Institute of Land Policy.

Federal Highway Administration. 2003. "Vehicle Daily Averages by Metropolitan Area Interstates." Available at www.fhwa.dot.gov.

Federal Register. 1999. 64 FR 56628–44.

Findlay, John M. 1993. *Magic Lands: Western Cityscapes and American Culture after 1940*. Berkeley: University of California Press.

Fisher, Ronald C. 1996. *State and Local Public Finance*. Los Angeles: Irwin Times Mirror.

Fishman, Robert. 1987. *Bourgeois Utopias: The Rise and Fall of Suburbia*. New York: Basic Books.

———. 1990. "Megalopolis Unbound," *Wilson Quarterly*, Winter, 44–55.

———. 2000. "The American Planning Tradition." In *The American Planning Tradition: Culture and Policy*, ed. Robert Fishman, 1–29. Washington, D.C.: Woodrow Wilson Center Press.

Florida, Richard. 2002. *The Rise of the Creative Class*. New York: Basic Books.

Forester, John. 1989. *Planning in the Face of Power*. Berkeley: University of California Press.

———. 1993. *Critical Theory, Public Policy and Planning Practice: Toward a Critical Pragmatism*. Albany: State University of New York Press.

Frank, Lawrence. 1994. "Analysis of Relationships between Urban Form and Travel Behavior." PhD diss., University of Washington.

Frey, William. 2005. *Metropolitan America in the New Century: Metropolitan and Central City Demographic Shifts Since 2000*. Washington, D.C.: Brookings Institution Press.

Frey, William, Jill H. Wilson, Alan Berube, and Audrey Singer. 2006. "Tracking Metropolitan America into the 21st Century: A Field Guide to the New Metropolitan and Micropolitan Definitions." In *Redefining Cities and Suburbs: Evidence from Census 2000*, ed. Alan Berube, Bruce Katz, and Robert E. Lang, 3:191–234. Washington, D.C.: Brookings Institution Press.

Friedmann, John. 1968. "A Strategy of Deliberate Urbanization." *JAIP* 34:364–73.

———. 1971. "The Future of Comprehensive Planning." *Public Administration Review* 31 (May–June): 315–26.

———. 1987. *Planning in the Public Domain: From Knowledge to Action.* Princeton, N.J.: Princeton University Press.

Friedmann, John, and John Miller. 1965. "The Urban Field." *JAIP* 31:312–19.

Fulton, William, Rolf Pendall, Mai Ngyen, and Alicia Harrison. 2001. *Who Sprawls Most? How Growth Patterns Differ Across the U.S.* Brookings Institution Center on Urban and Metropolitan Policy Survey Series. Washington, D.C.: Brookings Institution.

Galster, George, Royce Hanson, Michael Radcliffe, Harold Wolman, Steven Coleman, and Jason Freihage. 2001. "Wrestling Sprawl to the Ground: Defining and Measuring an Elusive Concept." *Housing Policy Debate* 12 (4): 681–717.

Gammage, Grady, Jr., John Stuart Hall, Robert E. Lang, Rob Melnick, and Nancy Welch. 2008. *Megapolitan: The Arizona Sun Corridor.* Phoenix, Ariz.: Morrison Institute for Public Policy. May.

Gannett, Henry. 1882. "Settled Area and the Density of Our Population." *International Review* 12 (1): 70–77.

Garreau, Joel. 1981. *Nine Nations of North America.* New York: Avon Books.

———. 1991. *Edge City: Life on the New Frontier.* New York: Doubleday.

Gertz, Carsten. 2003. "Lessons from a Landmark US Policy for Transportation, Land Use and Air Quality, and Implications for Policy Changes in Other Countries." *International Social Science Journal* 55 (2): 176–89.

Gifford, Jonathan, Thomas Horan, and Louise White. 1994. "Dynamics of Policy Change: Reflections on 1991 Federal Transportation Legislation." *Transportation Research Record* 1466:19–24.

Giuliano, G. 1989. "New Directions for Understanding Transportation and Land Use." *Environment and Planning A* 21:145–59.

Glaeser, Edward L. 1994. "Cities, Information, and Economic Growth." *Cityscape: A Journal of Policy Development Research* 1 (1): 9–48.

Glaeser, Edward L., Joseph Gyourko, and Raven E. Saks. 2005. "Urban Growth and Housing Supply." Discussion Paper No. 2062. Cambridge, Mass.: Harvard Institute of Economic Research.

Gomez-Ibanez, William Tye, and Clifford Winston, eds. 1999. *Essays in Transportation Economics and Policy.* Washington, D.C.: Brookings Institution Press.

Gonick, Larry, and Woollcott Smith. 1993. *Cartoon Guide to Statistics.* New York: HarperCollins.

Goodman, Robert. 1979. *The Last Entrepreneurs: America's Regional Wars for Jobs and Dollars.* New York: Simon and Schuster.

Gordon, Peter, Harry W. Richardson, and Yeol Choi. 1992. "Tests of the Standard Urban Model: Micro (Trade-off) Alternative." *Review of Urban and Regional Development Studies* 4 (1): 50–66.

Gottmann, Jean. 1961. *Megalopolis: The Urbanized Northeastern Seaboard of the United States.* New York: Twentieth Century Fund.

———. 1987. *Megalopolis Revisited: 25 Years Later.* College Park: University of Maryland, Institute for Urban Studies.

Gottmann, Jean, and Robert A. Harper. 1990. *Since Megalopolis: The Urban Writings of Jean Gottmann.* Baltimore: Johns Hopkins University Press.

Grimm, Lawrence G., and Paul R. Yarnold, eds. 1998. *Reading and Understanding Multivariate Statistics.* Washington, D.C.: American Psychological Association.

Guthrie, Dwayne Pierce. 2007. *Understanding Urban, Metropolitan and Megaregion Development to Improve Transportation Governance.* Blacksburg, Va.: Virginia Tech.

Hackworth, Jason. 2005. "Emergent Urban Forms, or Emergent Post-Modernisms? A Comparison of Large U.S. Metropolitan Areas." *Urban Geography* 26 (6): 484–519.

Hagler, Yoav, and Petra Todorovich. 2009. "Where High-Speed Rail Works Best." Regional Plan Association's America 2050 Initiative. Available at www.america2050.org/infrastructure.html.

Hall, P., and K. Pain. 2006. *The Polycentric Metropolis: Learning from Mega-City Regions in Europe.* London: Earthscan.

Hamilton, David K., and Patricia S. Atkins, eds. 2008. *Urban and Regional Policies for Metropolitan Livability.* Armonk, N.Y.: M. E. Sharpe.

Handy, S., J. Sallis, D. Weber, E. Maibach, and M. Hollander. 2008. "Is Support for Traditionally Designed Communities Growing? Evidence from Two National Surveys." *JAPA* 74 (2): 209–21.

Hanlon, B., T. J. Vicino, and J. R. Short. 2006. "The New Metropolitan Reality: Rethinking the Traditional Model in the US." *Urban Studies* 43 (12): 2129–43.

Harris, Chauncy D., and Edward L. Ullman. 1945. "The Nature of Cities." *Annals of the American Academy of Political and Social Science* 242:7–17.

Hart, Chris. 1998. *Doing a Literature Review*. London: Sage.

Harvey, David. 1985. *The Urbanization of Capital: Studies in the History and Theory of Capitalist Urbanization*. Baltimore: Johns Hopkins University Press.

Hayden, Dolores. 2004. *Building Suburbia: Green Fields and Urban Growth, 1820–2000*. New York: Vintage Books.

Healey, Joseph F. 1999. *Statistics: A Tool for Social Research*. Belmont, Calif.: Wadsworth.

Henderson, J. V. 1974. "The Sizes and Types of Cities." *American Economic Review* 64:640–56.

———. 1996. "Ways to Think about Urban Concentration: Neoclassical Urban Systems versus the New Economic Geography." *International Regional Science Review* 19 (1–2): 31–36.

Hendler, Sue. 1995. *Planning Ethics: A Reader in Planning Theory, Practice and Education*. New Brunswick, N.J.: Rutgers University, Center for Urban Policy Research.

Higgins, Benjamin, and Donald J. Savoie. 1995. *Regional Development Theories and Their Application*, Part 1. New Brunswick, N.J.: Transaction.

Hillier, Bill. 1996. "Non-discursive Technique." In *Space Is the Machine*, 88–145. Cambridge: Cambridge University Press.

———. 1999. "Centrality as a Process: Accounting for Attraction Inequalities in Deformed Grids." *Urban Design International* 4:107–27.

Hirschman, A. O. 1958. *Strategy of Economic Development*. New Haven, Conn.: Yale University Press.

Hoch, Charles. 1984. "Doing Good and Being Right: The Pragmatic Connection in Planning Theory." *JAPA* 50 (3): 335–45.

———. 1984. "Pragmatism, Planning and Power." *JPER* 4 (2): 86–95.

Hotelling, Harold. 1929. "Stability in Competition." *Economic Journal* 39 (March): 41–57.

Hoyt, Homer. 1939. *The Structure and Growth of Residential Neighborhoods in American Cities*. Washington, D.C.: Federal Housing Administration, U.S. Government Printing Office.

Ingram, Gregory, Armando Carbonell, Yu-Hung Hong, and Anthony Flint, eds. 2009. *Smart Growth Policies: An Evaluation of Programs and Outcomes*. Cambridge, Mass.: Lincoln Institute of Land Policy.

Innes, Judith. 1995. "Planning Theory's Emerging Paradigm: Communicative Action and Interactive Practice." *JPER* 14 (3): 183–89.

Innes, Judith E., David E. Booher, and Sarah Di Vittorio. 2010. "Strategies for Megaregion Governance: Collaborative Dialogue, Networks, and Self-Organization." *JAPA* 77 (1): 55–67.

Isard, Walter, Iwan J. Azis, Matthew P. Drennan, Ronald E. Miller, Sidney Saltzman, and Erik Thorbecke. 1998. *Methods of Interregional and Regional Analysis*. Brookfield, Vt.: Ashgate.

Jackson, Kenneth. 1985. *Crabgrass Frontier: The Suburbanization of the United States*. New York: Oxford University Press.

Jones, David. 1985. *Urban Transit Policy: An Economic and Political History*. Englewood Cliffs, N.J.: Prentice-Hall.

Kaldor, N. 1970. "The Case for Regional Policies." *Scottish Journal of Political Economy* 17 (3): 337–48.

Kartez, Jack. 1989. "Rational Arguments and Irrational Audiences." *JAPA* 55 (4): 445–56.

Katz, Bruce, ed. 2000. *Reflections on Regionalism*. Washington, D.C.: Brookings Institution.

Katz, Bruce, and Robert E. Lang, eds. 2003. *Redefining Cities and Suburbs: Evidence from Census 2000*, vol. 1. Washington, D.C.: Brookings Institution Press.

Kenworthy, Jeffrey, and Peter Newman. 1990. "Cities and Transportation Energy: Lessons from a Global Survey." *Ekistics* 344–45:258–68.

Klosterman, Richard. 1994. "An Introduction to the Literature on Large-Scale Urban Models." *JAPA* 60 (1): 41–43.

Kunstler, James Howard. 1993. *The Geography of Nowhere: The Rise and Decline of America's Man-Made Landscape*. New York: Free Press.

———. 2005. *The Long Emergency: Surviving the Converging Catastrophes of the Twenty-first Century*. New York: Grove/Atlantic.

———. 2008. *World Made by Hand*. New York: Grove/Atlantic.

Lake, Robert. 1995. "Spatial Fix 2: The Sequel." *Urban Geography* 16:189–91.

Lang, Robert E. 2002. "Open Spaces, Bounded Places: Does the American West's Arid Landscape Yield Dense Metropolitan Growth?" *Housing Policy Debate* 13 (4): 755–78.

———. 2003. *Edgeless Cities: Exploring the Elusive Metropolis*. Washington, D.C.: Brookings Institution Press.

Lang, Robert E., Mariela Alfonzo, and Casey Dawkins. 2009. "American Demographics—Circa 2109." *Planning* 75(5): 10–15.

Lang, Robert E., Edward J. Blakely, and Meghan Gough. 2005. "Keys to the New Metropolis: America's Big, Fast-Growing Suburban Counties." *JAPA* 71 (4): 381–91.

Lang, Robert E., and Dawn Dhavale. 2004. "Micropolitan America: A Brand New Geography." *Census Note* 04:01. Alexandria, Va.: Metropolitan Institute at Virginia Tech.

———. 2005. "America's Megapolitan Areas." *Land Lines* 17 (3):1–5.

———. 2006. "Micropolitan America: A Brand New Geography." In *Redefining Cities and Suburbs: Evidence from Census 2000,* ed. A. Berube, B. Katz, and R. E. Lang, 3:237–58. Washington, D.C.: Brookings Institution Press.

Lang, Robert E., Dawn Dhavale, and Kristin Haworth. 2004. "Micro Politics: The 2004 Presidential Vote in Small-Town America." *Census Note* 04:03. Alexandria, Va.: Metropolitan Institute at Virginia Tech.

Lang, Robert E., and Meghan Gough. 2005. *Growth Counties: Home to America's New Suburban Metropolis.* Brookings Institution Center on Urban and Metropolitan Policy Survey Series. Washington, D.C.: Brookings Institution.

Lang, Robert E., and John S. Hall. 2007. *The Sun Corridor: Planning Arizona's Megapolitan Area.* Tempe, Ariz.: Morrison Institute for Public Policy.

Lang, Robert E., and Paul K. Knox. 2007. "The New Metropolis: Rethinking Megalopolis." *Regional Studies* 43 (6): 789–802.

Lang, Robert E., and Jennifer LeFurgy. 2007. *Boomburbs: The Rise of America's Accidental Cities.* Washington, D.C.: Brookings Institution Press.

Lang, Robert E., and Arthur C. Nelson. 2006. "Beyond the Metroplex: Examining Commuter Patterns at the 'Megapolitan' Scale." Cambridge, Mass.: Lincoln Institute of Land Policy.

———. 2007. "America 2040: The Rise of the Megapolitans." *Planning* 73 (1): 7–12.

Lang, Robert E., Deborah Epstein Popper, and Frank J. Popper. 1995. "Progress of the Nation: The Settlement History of the Enduring American Frontier." *Western Historical Quarterly* 23 (3): 289–307.

———. 1997. "Is There Still a Frontier? The 1890 Census and the Modern West." *Journal of Rural Studies* 13 (4): 377–86.

Lang. Robert E., Andrea Sarzynski, and Mark Muro. 2008. *Mountain Megas: America's Newest Metropolitan Places and a Federal Partnership to Help Them Prosper.* Washington, D.C.: Brookings Institution. Available at www.brookings.edu/reports/2008/0720_mountainmegas_sarzynski.aspx.

Lee, Sharon M., and Barry Edmonston. 2005. "New Marriages, New Families: U.S. Racial and Hispanic Intermarriage." *Population Bulletin* 60, no. 2. Washington, D.C.: Population Reference Bureau.

Leinberger, Christopher. 1995. "The Changing Location of Development and Investment Opportunities." *Urban Land* 45 (5): 31–36.

———. 2007. *Footloose and Fancy Free: A Field Survey of Walkable Urban Places in the Top 30 U.S. Metropolitan Areas.* Washington, D.C.: Brookings Institution.

Levine, Jonathan, and Lawrence Frank. 2007. "Transportation and Land-Use Preferences and Residents' Neighborhood Choices: The Sufficiency of Compact Development on the Atlanta Region." *Transportation* 34 (2): 255–74.

Lewis, Peirce F. 1983. "The Galactic Metropolis." In *Beyond the Urban Fringe,* ed. R. H. Pratt and G. Macinko. Minneapolis: University of Minnesota Press.

———. 1995. "The Urban Invasion of Rural America: The Emergence of the Galactic City." In *The Changing American Countryside: Rural People and Places*, ed. Emery N. Castle, 39–62. Lawrence: University Press of Kansas.

Lim, Up. 2003. "The Spatial Distribution of Innovative Activity in U.S. Metropolitan Areas: Evidence from Patent Data." *Journal of Regional Analysis and Policy* 33 (2): 97–126.

Lösch, August. 1940. *The Spatial Organization of the Economy.* New Haven, Conn.: Yale University Press.

———. 1954. *The Economics of Location.* New Haven, Conn.: Yale University Press.

Lubowski, Ruben N., Shawn Bucholtz, Roger Claassen, Michael J. Roberts, Joseph C. Cooper, Anna Gueorguieva, and Robert Johansson. 2006. *Environmental Effects of Agricultural Land-Use Change: The Role of Economics and Policy.* Economic Research Report No. 25. Washington, D.C.: U.S. Department of Agriculture, Economic Research Service.

Lynch, Thomas. 1998. *High Speed Rail in the U.S.* Amsterdam: Gordon and Breach.

Lyons, William. 1994. "FTA-FHWA Metropolitan Planning Organization Reviews: Planning Practice under Intermodal Surface Transportation Efficiency Act and Clean Air Act Amendments." *Transportation Research Record* 1466:23–30.

Markusen, Ann. 1987. *Regions: The Economics and Politics of Territory.* Totowa, N.J.: Rowman and Littlefield.

Markusen, Ann R., Yong-Sook Lee, and Sean DiGiovanna, eds. 1999. *Second Tier Cities: Rapid Growth Beyond the Metropolis.* Minneapolis: University of Minnesota Press.

Martin, R., and P. Sunley. 1998. "Slow Convergence: The New Endogenous Growth Theory and Regional Development." *Economic Geography* 74 (3): 201–27.

Mason, Robert J. 2008. *Collaborative Land Use Management: The Quieter Revolution in Place-Based Planning*. Plymouth, U.K.: Rowman and Littlefield.

McCarthy, Linda, and Paul L. Knox. 2005. *Urbanization*. Englewood Cliffs, N.J.: Prentice Hall.

McCarthy, Patrick. 2001. *Transportation Economics*. Malden, Mass.: Blackwell.

McGranahan, David. 1999. *Natural Amenities Drive Rural Population Change*. Agriculture Economic Report No. 781. Washington, D.C.: U.S. Department of Agriculture, Economic Research Service.

———. 2007. "The Importance of Natural Amenities." Annex 6 in *Handbook on Rural Households' Livelihood and Well-Being: Statistics on Rural Development and Agriculture Household Income*. New York: United Nations.

McGranahan, D. A., and T. R. Wojan. 2007. "The Creative Class: A Key to Rural Growth." *Amber Waves* 5 (2): 16–21.

———. 2009. "Recasting the Creative Class to Examine Growth Processes in Rural and Urban Counties." *Regional Studies* 41:197–216.

McGuigan, James, R. Charles Moyer, and Frederick Harris. 2002. *Managerial Economics: Applications, Strategy and Tactics*. Cincinnati: South-Western/Thomson Learning.

McKenzie, R. D. 1933. *The Metropolitan Community*. New York: McGraw-Hill.

McLean, Mary L., and Kenneth P. Voytek. 1992. *Understanding Your Economy*. Chicago: APA Planners Press.

McShane, Clay. 1994. *Down the Asphalt Path: The Automobile and the American City*. New York: Columbia University Press.

Meadows, Donella H., Dennis L. Meadows, et al. 1972. *The Limits to Growth: A Report for the Club of Rome's Project on the Predicament of Mankind*. New York: Universe Books.

Meck, Stuart. 2002. *Growing Smart Legislative Guidebook*. Chicago: APA Planners Press.

Meinig, D. W. 2004. *The Shaping of America: A Geographical Perspective on 500 Years of History*. Volume 4, *Global America, 1915–2000*. New Haven, Conn.: Yale University Press.

Metropolitan Institute at Virginia Tech. 2005. "America's East and West Coast Main Streets: Comparing Growth along I-95 and I-5." Available at http://mivt.blogspot.com.

Meyer, Michael, and Eric Miller. 2001. *Urban Transportation Planning*. New York: McGraw-Hill.

Meyerson, Martin. 1956. "Building the Middle-Range Bridge for Comprehensive Planning." *JAIP* 22:2.

Mills, Edwin S. 1970. "Urban Density Functions." *Urban Studies* 7:5–20.

———. 1972. *Studies in the Structure of the Urban Economy*. Baltimore: Johns Hopkins Press for Resources for the Future.

Mills, Edwin, and M. R. Lav. 1964. "A Model of Market Areas with Free Entry." *Journal of Political Economy,* June, 278–88.

Mineta, Norman Y. 2005. "Starving Amtrak to Save It." *New York Times*, February 23, A19.

Molotch, Harvey. 1976. "The City as Growth Machine: Toward a Political Economy of Place." *American Journal of Sociology* 82:309–32.

Moore, Terry, and Thorsnes, Paul. 1994. *The Transportation/Land Use Connection*. Chicago: American Planning Association.

Moore, Terry, Paul Thorsnes, and Bruce Appleyard. 2007. *The Transportation/Land Use Connection*, new ed. PAS Report 546/547. Chicago: American Planning Association.

Morrill, Robert, John Cromartie, and George Hart. 1999. "Metropolitan, Urban and Rural Commuting Areas: Toward a Better Depiction of the United States Settlement System." *Urban Studies* 20:727–48.

Moss, Mitchell L., and Anthony M. Townsend. 2000. "The Internet Backbone and the American Metropolis." *Information Society* 16:35–47.

Muller, Peter. 1976. "The Outer City: Geographical Consequences of the Urbanization of the Suburbs." Resource paper. Washington, D.C.: Association of American Geographers.

Muro, Mark. 2010. "Self Organizing Sun Corridor." *New Republic*, February 19.

Muth, R. 1961. "Economic Change and Rural-Urban Land Conversions." *Econometrica* 29 (1): 1–23.

Myers, Dowell, ed. 1990. *Housing Demography: Linking Demographic Structure and Housing Markets*. Madison: University of Wisconsin Press.

———. 1992. *Analysis with Local Census Data*. Boston: Academic Press.

Myrdal, Gunnar. 1957. *Economic Theory and Underdeveloped Regions*. London: Duckworth.

National Agricultural Statistics Service. 1999. *1997 Census of Agriculture*. Washington, D.C.: USDA.

———. 2009. 2007 *Census of Agriculture*. Washington, D.C.: USDA

National Association of Counties. 2005. Facts About Counties. Available at www.naco.org/Template .cfm?Section=About_Counties.

Naughton, Keith. 2006. "The Long and Grinding Road." *Newsweek*, May 1, 41–44.

Neary, J. P. 2001. "Of Hype and Hyperbolas: Introducing the New Economic Geography." *Journal of Economic Literature* 39 (2): 536–61.

Nelson, A[rthur]. C. 1992. "Characterizing Exurbia." *Journal of Planning Literature* 6 (4): 350–68.

———. 2000. "New Kid in Town: The Georgia Regional Transportation Authority and Its Role in Managing Growth in Metropolitan Georgia." *Wake Forest Law Review* 35 (3): 625–44.

———. 2004. *Toward a New Metropolis: The Opportunity to Rebuild America*. Brookings Institution Metropolitan Policy Program Survey Series. Washington, D.C.: Brookings Institution.

———. 2005. "The Next 40 Trillion." Speech before the American Institute of Architects, Washington, D.C. April 9. Available at www.mi.vt.edu.

———. 2006. "Longer View: Leadership in a New Era." *JAPA* 72 (4): 493–506.

———. 2008. "Urban Enthusiasm." *Units* 32 (10): 30–41.

Nelson, A. C., C. J. Dawkins, and T. W. Sanchez. 2007. *The Social Impacts of Urban Containment*. London: Ashgate.

Nelson, Arthur C., with William J. Drummond and D. S. Sawicki. 1995. "Exurban Industrialization." *Economic Development Quarterly* 9 (2): 119–33.

Nelson, Arthur C., and Kenneth J. Dueker. 1990. "The Exurbanization of America." *Journal of Planning Education and Research* 9 (2): 91–100.

Nelson, Arthur C., and James B. Duncan. 1995. *Growth Management Principles and Practice*. Chicago: APA Planners Press.

Nelson, Arthur C., and Robert E. Lang. 2009. *The New Politics of Planning*. Washington, D.C.: Urban Land Institute.

Nelson, Arthur C., and Thomas W. Sanchez. 1997. "Exurban and Suburban Households: A Departure from Traditional Location Theory?" *Journal of Housing Research* 8 (2): 249–76.

———. 1999. "Debunking the Exurban Myth." *Housing Policy Debate* 10 (3): 689–709.

Nijkamp, Peter, and Jacques Poot. 1998. "Spatial Perspectives on New Theories of Economic Growth." *Annals of Regional Science* 32:7–37.

North, D. C. 1955. "Location Theory and Regional Economic Growth." *Journal of Political Economy* 63 (3): 243–58.

———. 1956. "Exports and Regional Economic Growth: A Reply." *Journal of Political Economy* 64 (2): 165–68.

Norusis, Marija J. 2002. *SPSS 11.0 Guide to Data Analysis*. Upper Saddle River, N.J.: Prentice Hall.

Noyelle, Thierry J. 1983. "The Rise of Advanced Services: Some Implications for Economic Development in U.S. Cities." *JAPA* 49 (3): 280–90.

Noyelle, Thierry J., and Thomas M. Stanbeck Jr. 1983. *The Economic Transformation of American Cities*. Totowa, N.J.: Rowman and Allenheld.

Oates, W. E., and R. W. Schwab. 1988. "Economic Competition among Jurisdictions: Efficiency Enhancing or Distortion Inducing?" *Journal of Public Economics* 35 (3): 333–54.

Office of Management and Budget. 2003. OMB Bulletin No. 03-04, June 6. Washington, D.C.: Office of Management and Budget.

Orfield, Myron. 2002. *American Metropolitics: The New Suburban Reality*. Washington, D.C.: Brookings Institution Press.

O'Sullivan, Arthur. 2007. *Urban Economics*. New York: McGraw-Hill.

Park, Robert, Ernest W. Burgess, and Roderick D. McKenzie. 1925. *The City*. Chicago: University of Chicago Press.

Patton, Carl V., and David S. Sawicki. 1993. *Basic Methods of Policy Analysis and Planning*. Upper Saddle River, N.J.: Prentice Hall.

Peet, Richard, and Elaine Hardwick. 2009. *Theories of Development*, 2nd ed. New York: Guildford Press.

Perloff, H. S., E. S. Dunn Jr., E. E. Lampard, and R. F. Muth. 1960. *Regions, Resources, and Economic Growth*. Baltimore: Johns Hopkins University Press.

Perroux, F. 1950. "Economic Space: Theory and Application." *Quarterly Journal of Economics* 64:89–104.

Perry, David, and Alfred Watkins, eds. 1977. *Rise of the Sunbelt Cities*. Beverly Hills, Calif.: Sage.

Pickard, Jerome P. 1962. "Urban Regions of the United States." *Urban Land*, April, 61–66.

———. 1966. "Urban Regions of the U.S." *Urban Land*, April, 3–10.

———. 1970. "Is Megalopolis Inevitable?" *Futurist*, October, 151–55.

Pierce, Neal, Curtis Johnson, and John Stuart Hall. 1993. *Citistates: How Urban America Can Prosper in a Competitive World*. Washington, D.C.: Seven Locks Press.

Pivo, Gary. 1990. "The Net of Mixed Beads: Suburban Office Development in Six Regions." *JAPA* 56 (4): 457–69.

Popper, Deborah, Robert Lang, and Frank Popper. 1997. "Is There Still a Frontier? The 1890 U.S. Census and the Modern American West." *Journal of Rural Studies* 13(4): 377–86.

———. 2001. "From Maps to Myth: The Census, Turner, and the Idea of the Frontier." *Journal of American and Comparative Popular Cultures* 23 (1): 91–102.

Popper, Deborah E., and Frank J. Popper. 1996. "The Storytellers." *Planning*, October, 7–10.

Population Reference Bureau. 2000. "Goodbye 'Metropolitan?'" *PRB On-Line*, April–June. Available at www.prb.org.

Pressman, Neil. 1985. "Forces for Spatial Change." In *The Future of Urban Form: The Impact of New Technology*, ed. John Brotchie. London: Croom Helm.

Pucher, John, and Christian Lefevre. 1996. *The Urban Transportation Crisis*. London: Macmillan.

Puentes, Robert, and Adie Tomer. 2009. *Expect Delays: An Analysis of Air Travel Trends in the United States*. Metropolitan Policy Program, October. Washington, D.C.: Brookings Institution.

Rainey, Hal. 1997. *Understanding & Managing Public Organizations*. San Francisco: Jossey-Bass.

Reconnecting America. 2004. *Hidden In Plain Sight: Capturing the Demand for Housing Near Transit*. Center for Transit-Oriented Development, Reconnecting America, for the Federal Transit Administration. Available at www.reconnectingamerica.org/pdfs/Ctod_report.pdf.

Regional Plan Association. 1960. *Plan for Greater New York*. New York: Regional Plan Association.

———. 1967. *The Region's Growth: A Report of the Second Regional Plan*. New York: Regional Plan Association.

Richardson, H. W. 1973. *Regional Growth Theory*. London: Macmillan.

Robbins, Stephens. 2000. *Essentials of Organizational Behavior*. Upper Saddle River, N.J.: Prentice-Hall.

Robinson, Ira. 1965. "Beyond the Middle-range Planning Bridge." *JAIP* 31 (November): 4.

Rondinelli, Dennis. 1973. "Urban Planning as Policy Analysis," *JAIP* 39 (1): 3–22.

Rosen, Harvey S. 1999. *Public Finance*. Boston: Irwin McGraw-Hill.

Ross, Catherine L. 2009. *Megaregions: Planning for Global Competitiveness*. New York: Island Press.

Ross, Catherine, and Anne Dunning. 1997. *Land Use Transportation Interaction: An Examination of the 1995 NPTS Data*. Atlanta: Georgia Institute of Technology.

Rostow, Walt W. 1956. "The Take-Off into Self-Sustained Growth." *Economic Journal* 66 (261): 25–48.

Salamon, Lester, ed. 2002. *Tools of Government: A Guide to the New Governance*. New York: Oxford University Press.

Samuelson, Paul A. 1953. "Prices of Factors and Goods in General Equilibrium." *Review of Economic Studies* 21 (October): 1–20.

———. 2009. "A Rail Boondoggle, Moving at High Speed." *Washington Post*, August 24, A18.

Sanchez, Thomas W., and Arthur C. Nelson. 1997. "Exurban and Suburban Residents: A Departure from Traditional Location Theory?" *Journal of Housing Research* 8 (2): 249–76.

Sassen, Saskia. 1988. *Mobility of Labor and Capital: A Study in International Investment and Labor Flow*. Cambridge: Cambridge University Press.

Saxenian, A. L. 1994. *Regional Advantage: Culture and Competition in Silicon Valley and Route 128*. Cambridge, Mass.: Harvard University Press.

Schon, K. P. 2002. Map in *European Spatial Planning*, ed. Andreas Faludi, 28. Cambridge, Mass.: Lincoln Institute of Land Policy.

Scott, John, and Gordon Marshall. 2009. *A Dictionary of Sociology*. New York: Oxford University Press.

Scott, P., and P. Auerbach. 1995. "Cumulative Causation and the 'New' Theories of Economic Growth." *Journal of Post Keynesian Economics* 17 (3): 381–402.

Siksna, Arnis. 1997. "The Effects of Block Size and Form in North American and Australian City Centres." *Urban Morphology* 1:19–33.

Sklar, Debbie L. 2003. "The Next Capital of Cool." *Irvine World News*, February 20.

Solof, Mark. 1998. *History of Metropolitan Planning Organizations*. Newark: North Jersey Transportation Planning Authority.

Southworth, Michael, and Peter Owens. 1993. "The Evolving Metropolis: Studies of Community, Neighborhood and Street Form at the Urban Edge." *JAPA* 54 (3): 271–87.

Spectorsky, Auguste. 1955. *The Exurbanites*. Philadelphia: Lippincott.

Starner, Ron. 2005. "Top Micropolitans." *Site Selection Magazine*, March.

Steinemann, Ann, William C. Apgar, and H. James Brown. 2004. *Microeconomics for Public Decisions*. Mason, Ohio: South-Western Publishing.

Sternlieb, George, and James W. Hughes. 1988. "The Suburban Growth Corridor." In *America's New Market Geography*, ed. George Sternlieb. New Brunswick, N.J.: Rutgers University, Center for Urban Policy Research.

Sudjic, Deyan. 1992. *100 Mile City*. San Diego: Harcourt Brace.

Surface Transportation Policy Project and Center for Neighborhood Technology. 2000. *Driven to Spend*. Washington, D.C.: Surface Transportation Policy Project.

Taylor, Peter J. 2004. *World City Network: A Global Urban Analysis*. New York: Routledge.

Taylor, Peter J., and David Evans. 2005. "Summary Report: Quantitative Analysis of Service Business Connections." Loughborough, U.K.: Department of Geography, Loughborough University.

Taylor, Peter J., and Robert E. Lang. 2005. *US Cities in the World City Network*. Brookings Institution Center on Urban and Metropolitan Policy Survey Series, February. Washington, D.C.: Brookings Institution.

Thomas, John L. 2000. "Holding the Middle Ground." In *The American Planning Tradition: Culture and Policy*, ed. Robert Fishman, 33–63. Washington, D.C.: Woodrow Wilson Center Press.

Thompson, Wilbur R. 1975. "The National System of Cities as an Object of Public Policy." In *Regional Policy: Readings in Theory and Applications*, ed. John Friedmann and William Alonso. Cambridge, Mass.: MIT Press.

Tiebout, C. M. 1956a. "Exports and Regional Economic Growth." *Journal of Political Economy* 64 (2): 160–64.

———. 1956b. "Exports and Regional Economic Growth: Rejoinder." *Journal of Political Economy* 64 (2): 169.

Todorovich, Petra, and Yoav Hagler. 2009. *New Strategies for Regional Economic Development*. Cambridge, Mass.: Lincoln Institute of Land Policy.

———. 2011. "High Speed Rail in America." Regional Plan Association's America 2050 Initiative. Available at www.america2050.org/infrastructure.html.

Tomer, Adie, and Robert Puentes. 2009. "Expect Delays: An Analysis of Air Travel Trends in the United States." Washington, D.C.: Brookings Institution.

Toossi, Mitra. 2002. "A Century of Change: U.S. Labor Force, 1950–2050." *Monthly Labor Review*. Washington, D.C.: Bureau of Labor Statistics.

Transportation Research Board, National Research Council. 1994. *Curbing Gridlock: Peak-Period Fees to Relieve Traffic Congestion*. Transportation Research Board Special Report 242. Washington, D.C.: National Academy Press.

———. 2001. *Making Transit Work*. Transportation Research Board Special Report 257. Washington, D.C.: National Academy Press.

———. 2006. *Third National Report on Commuting Patterns and Trends*. Transportation Research Board Special Report 550. Washington, D.C.: National Academy Press.

Turner, Jonathan. 2003. *Structure of Sociological Theory*. Belmont, Calif.: Wadsworth/Thompson Learning.

U.S. Bureau of the Census. 1975. *American Housing Survey of the United States for 1973*. Washington, D.C.: U.S. Department of Commerce.

———. 2001. Census 2000 Summary File One. Available at http://factfinder.census.gov/servlet/BasicFactsServlet.

———. 2002. "Census 2000 PHC-T-40: Estimated Daytime Population and Employment-Residence Ratios: 2000." Washington, D.C.: U.S. Department of Commerce.

———. 2003. Estimates and Projections Area Documentation Subcounty Total Population Estimates. Available at http://eire.census.gov/popest/topics/methodology/citymeth.php.

———. 2004. Table SUB-EST2002-03—City and Town Population Estimates: April 1, 2000 to July 1, 2003. Population Division, July 10. Available at www.census.gov/popest/archives/2000s/vintage_2002/SUB-EST2002-03.html.

———. 2005. Census 2000 Summary File 1 (SF 1) 100-Percent Data. Available at http://factfinder.census.gov.

———. 2008. *American Housing Survey of the United States for 2007*. Washington, D.C.: U.S. Department of Commerce.

———. 2009. *Statistical Abstract of the United States*. Washington, D.C.: U.S. Department of Commerce.

———. 2010. Population Estimates Program, Report GCT-T9-R. "Housing Units." Available at http://factfinder.census.gov/servlet/GCTTable?_bm=y&-geo_id=01000US&-_box_head_nbr=GCT-T9-R&-ds_name=PEP_2007_EST&-redoLog=false&-format=US-9Sh&-mt_name=ACS_2006_EST_G00_GCT2501_US36&-CONTEXT=gct.

U.S. Department of Agriculture (USDA), Economic Research Service. 2003. *Measuring Rurality*. Washington, D.C.: USDA; available at www.ers.usda.gov/briefing/rurality.

———. 2004a. "Economic Type of All Counties, 1998–2000," in *Measuring Rurality: 2004 County Typology Codes*. Available at www.ers.usda.gov/briefing/rurality/typology/Maps/Econtype.htm.

———. 2004b. U.S. Department of Agriculture. "Housing Stress Counties," in *Measuring Rurality: 2004 County Typology Codes*. Available at www.ers.usda.gov/briefing/rurality/typology/maps/Housing.htm.

U.S. Department of Energy, Energy Information Administration. Commercial Buildings Energy Consumption Survey series for 1992, 1997, and 2002. Washington, D.C.: U.S. Department of Energy.

U.S. Geological Survey. Water Use in the United States series. Washington, D.C.: U.S. Department of the Interior. Available at http://water.usgs.gov/watuse.

Vance, James. 1986. *Capturing the Horizon: Historical Geography of Transportation*. New York: Harper and Row.

Vance, James E., Jr. 1964. *Geography and Urban Evolution in the San Francisco Bay Area*. Berkeley: University of California, Institute of Government.

———. 1977. *This Scene of Man: The Role and Structure of the City in the Geography of Western Civilization*. New York: Harper's College Press.

Vicino, Thomas, Bernadette Hanlon, and John Short. 2007. "Megalopolis 50 Years On: The Transformation of a City Region." *International Journal of Urban and Regional Research* 31 (2): 344–67.

Volpe National Transportation Systems Center. 2003. *Journey-To-Work Trends in the United States and Major Metropolitan Areas 1960–1990*. Cambridge, Mass.: U.S. Department of Transportation.

Vuchic, Vukan. 2000. *Transportation for Livable Cities*. New Brunswick, N.J.: Rutgers University, Center for Urban Policy Research.

Wachter, Susan, Leo Penne, and Arthur Nelson, eds. 2000. *Bridging the Divide Proceedings*. Washington, D.C.: U.S. Department of Housing and Urban Development.

Wallerstein, I. 1988. *The Modern World System*, vol. 3. New York: Academic Press.

Warner, Sam Bass. 1962. *Streetcar Suburbs: The Process of Growth in Boston, 1870–1900*. Cambridge, Mass.: Harvard University Press.

Warner, Sam Bass, Jr. 1995. *The Urban Wilderness: A History of the American City*. Berkeley: University of California Press.

Weinstein, Bernard L., Harold T. Gross, and John Rees. 1985. *Regional Growth and Decline in the United States*. New York: Praeger.

Whebell, C. F. J. 1969. "Corridors: A Theory of Urban Systems." *Annals of the Association of American Geographers* 59 (1): 1–26.

Williamson, Oliver E. 1985. *The Economic Institutions of Capitalism*. New York: Free Press.

Wojan, T. R., D. M. Lambert, and D. A. McGranahan. 2007. "The Emergence of Artistic Havens: A First Look." *Agricultural and Resource Economics Review* 36 (1): 53–70.

Wojan, T. R., and D. A. McGranahan. 2007. "Ambient Returns: Creative Capital's Contribution to Local Manufacturing Competitiveness." *Agricultural and Resource Economics Review* 36 (1): 133–48.

Woods & Poole Economics. 2010. *The Complete Economic and Demographic Data Source*. Washington, D.C.: Woods & Poole Economics.

Yaro, Robert D., and Armando Carbonell. 2004. *Toward an American Spatial Development Perspective*. Policy Roundtable Report. Cambridge, Mass.: Lincoln Institute of Land Policy and the Regional Plan Association.

Yaro, Robert D., Armando Carbonell, and Jonathan Barnett. 2004. *Planning for America in a Global Economy*. City Planning Studio Report. Philadelphia: University of Pennsylvania School of Design.

Zelinsky, Wilbur. 1973. *The Cultural Geography of the United States*. Englewood Cliffs, N.J.: Prentice-Hall.

INDEX

ABOUT THE AUTHORS

Arthur C. Nelson, FAICP, is Presidential Professor of City and Metropolitan Planning at the University of Utah, where he is also the founding director of the Metropolitan Research Center, adjunct professor of finance in the David Eccles School of Business, and the founding codirector of the Master's of Real Estate Development program.

Previously, Nelson served as the founding director of the Urban Affairs and Planning Program at Virginia Tech's Alexandria Center, where he was also founding director of the Planning Academy at Virginia Tech and codirector of the Metropolitan Institute. He also served on the planning faculty at Georgia Tech, where he was founding coordinator of the certificate programs in land development and urban policy.

Nelson has conducted pioneering research in smart growth, public facility finance, economic development, and metropolitan development patterns. He has written more than 20 books and more than 300 other works. Among his planning books are *Growth Management Principles and Practices* (with James B. Duncan), noted as one of the 25 most important planning books in the first quarter century of the American Planning Association, *Urban Containment in the United States* (with Casey J. Dawkins), and *Planner's Estimating Guide*.

Numerous organizations have sponsored Nelson's research, including the National Science Foundation; National Academy of Sciences; U.S. departments of Housing and Urban Development, Commerce, and Transportation; Environmental Protection Agency; Lincoln Institute of Land Policy (including a fellowship); Fannie Mae; American Planning Association; National Association of Realtors; Urban Land Institute; and the Brookings Institution, among many others.

Nelson serves in various editorial capacities for the *Journal of the American Planning Association*, *Journal of Urban Affairs*, *Journal of Planning Education and Research*, *Housing Policy Debate*, and the *Journal of Planning Literature*.

Nelson's work has been featured in *USA Today*, the *Wall Street Journal*, the *New York Times*, the *Washington Post*, the *Los Angeles Times*, the *Chicago Tribune*, and the *Boston Globe*, among others. *CBS Evening News* has also featured his work, while *Time* declared his suburban redevelopment projections to be among the most important trends to watch in the next decade.

Nelson's doctorate is from Portland State University. His current work focuses on how demographic economic forces, along with shifts in housing preference, will reshape America's metropolitan areas for the rest of this century.

Robert E. Lang is a professor of sociology and the director of Brookings Mountain West at the University of Nevada–Las Vegas. He is also the director of the Lincy Institute at UNLV. In addition, Lang is currently a nonresident senior fellow at the Brookings Institution and a fellow of the Urban Land Institute, both in Washington, D.C. In 2008, Lang was a Fulbright fellow at the École Normale Supérieure in Paris. In 2006, he was a visiting distinguished professor at Arizona State University. Lang was also recently a planning and development fellow of the Lincoln Institute of Land Policy in Cambridge, Massachusetts, and a distinguished visiting fellow of the University of California–Riverside.

Prior to joining UNLV, Lang was a professor and director of the Urban Affairs and Planning program at Virginia Tech in Alexandria, Virginia, and served as the founding director of the Metropolitan Institute. Previously, he was director of urban and metropolitan research at Fannie Mae in Washington, D.C. Lang has also served as an editor on several academic journals, including *Housing Policy Debate* and the *Journal of the American Planning Association*.

Lang received a PhD in sociology from Rutgers University, where he also taught urban studies. His research specialties include suburban studies, real estate, demographic and spatial analysis, economic development, and metropolitan governance. He has authored more than 150 academic and professional publications on a wide range of topics and has developed many new urban planning concepts such as "Boomburbs," "Edgeless Cities," and "Megapolitan Areas." Lang has managed more than $14 million in research and foundation grants since 1996. He has also given more than 250 professional and academic talks since then. Lang's research has been featured in *USA Today*, the *New York Times*, the *Washington Post*, the *Wall Street Journal*, and *US News and World Report* and reported on by NPR, CNN, MSNBC, FOX News, and *ABC World News Tonight*.

Lang's work includes the books *Edgeless Cities: Exploring the Elusive Metropolis* (2003) and *Boomburbs: The Rise of America's Accidental Cities* (2007). He is also coauthor of three edited volumes on the census titled *Redefining Urban and Suburban America: Evidence from Census 2000*. Lang's most recent book is *The New Politics of Planning* (2009).